"America's leading source of self-help legal information." ★★★★
—Yahoo!

W9-CAJ-586

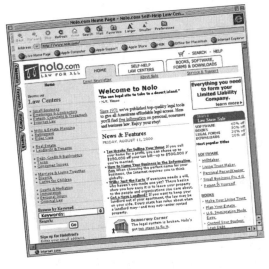

LEGAL INFORMATION ONLINE ANYTIME
24 hours a day

www.nolo.com

AT THE NOLO.COM SELF-HELP LAW CENTER, YOU'LL FIND

- **Nolo's comprehensive Legal Encyclopedia filled with plain-English information on a variety of legal topics**
- **Nolo's Law Dictionary—legal terms <u>without</u> the legalese**
- **Auntie Nolo—if you've got questions, Auntie's got answers**
- **The Law Store—over 200 self-help legal products including Downloadable Software, Books, Form Kits and eGuides**
- **Legal and product updates**
- **Frequently Asked Questions**
- **NoloBriefs, our free monthly email newsletter**
- **Legal Research Center, for access to state and federal statutes**
- **Our ever-popular lawyer jokes**

Quality LAW BOOKS & SOFTWARE FOR EVERYONE

Nolo's user-friendly products are consistently first-rate. Here's why:

- A dozen in-house legal editors, working with highly skilled authors, ensure that our products are accurate, up-to-date and easy to use
- We continually update every book and software program to keep up with changes in the law
- Our commitment to a more democratic legal system informs all of our work
- We appreciate & listen to your feedback. Please fill out and return the card at the back of this book.

OUR "NO-HASSLE" GUARANTEE

Return anything you buy directly from Nolo for any reason and we'll cheerfully refund your purchase price. No ifs, ands or buts.

Read This First

The information in this book is as up to date and accurate as we can make it. But it's important to realize that the law changes frequently, as do fees, forms and procedures. If you handle your own legal matters, it's up to you to be sure that all information you use—including the information in this book—is accurate. Here are some suggestions to help you:

First, make sure you've got the most recent edition of this book. To learn whether a later edition is available, check the edition number on the book's spine and then go to Nolo's online Law Store at www.nolo.com or call Nolo's Customer Service Department at 800-728-3555.

Next, even if you have a current edition, you need to be sure it's fully up to date. The law can change overnight. At www.nolo.com, we post notices of major legal and practical changes that affect the latest edition of a book. To check for updates, find your book in the Law Store on Nolo's website (you can use the "A to Z Product List" and click the book's title). If you see an "Updates" link on the left side of the page, click it. If you don't see a link, that means we haven't posted any updates. (But check back regularly.)

Finally, we believe accurate and current legal information should help you solve many of your own legal problems on a cost-efficient basis. But this text is not a substitute for personalized advice from a knowledgeable lawyer. If you want the help of a trained professional, consult an attorney licensed to practice in your state.

3rd edition

Form Your Own
Limited
Liability
Company

by Attorney Anthony Mancuso
edited by Attorney Beth Laurence

THIRD EDITION	
THIRD PRINTING	SEPTEMBER 2003
EDITORS	RALPH WARNER, BETH LAURENCE, ILONA BRAY AND PEG HEALY
BOOK DESIGN	JACKIE MANCUSO
PRODUCTION	SARAH HINMAN
INDEX	THÉRÈSE SHERE
ILLUSTRATOR	MARI STEIN
COVER DESIGN	TONI IHARA
PROOFREADERS	KRISTIN BARENDSEN AND KATHERINE L. KAISER
PRINTING	ARVATO SERVICES, INC.

Mancuso, Anthony.
    Form your own limited liability company / by Anthony Mancuso. -- 3rd ed.
        p. cm.
    Includes index.
    ISBN 0-87337-797-4
    1. Limited partnership—United States—Popular works. 2. Private companies--United
States--Popular works.   I. Title.

    KF1380.Z9 M36 2000
    346.73'0668 21--dc21   99-040306

Acknowledgments

The author thanks Lisa Goldoftas for a superb job of editing and organizing the material for the first edition, Beth Laurence for ongoing editing, Jake Warner for being backup editor and providing his usual keen insight in making this a better book, Steve Elias for his helpful suggestions on intellectual property law issues, Stan Jacobsen for his research help, and all the other hard-working people at Nolo.

About the Author

Tony Mancuso is a California attorney and the author of Nolo's best-selling corporate law series, including *Incorporate Your Business: A 50-State Legal Guide to Forming a Corporation* and *How to Form Your Own California Corporation*. Tony authored Nolo's *The Corporate Minutes Book* and *Your Limited Liability Company: An Operating Manual*, national titles on holding meetings, preparing and maintaining corporate and LLC records and taking care of important ongoing corporate and LLC legal and tax business. He is also the author of *How to Form a Nonprofit Corporation*, a national title that provides forms and instructions for forming a nonprofit corporation in each state and line-by-line instructions for obtaining tax-exempt 501(c)(3) status with the IRS. He is the programmer and author of Nolo's *LLC Maker* program, an interpretive Windows software product that produces the forms to organize a limited liability company in each state. Tony is a jazz guitarist and a licensed helicopter pilot.

TABLE OF CONTENTS

Introduction

CHAPTER 1
Overview of the LLC

CHAPTER 2
Basic LLC Legalities

Introduction

This book shows you how to form one of the newest and most exciting kinds of business entities available in the U.S.: the limited liability company (LLC). LLCs give business owners two main benefits. First, owners receive the tax advantages and capital flexibility of a partnership. Second, owners enjoy the limited liability protection previously unique to the corporation—that is, personal protection from business debts and claims.

The unique tax and legal benefits of this emerging business form, which is legal in all U.S. states plus the District of Columbia, makes it essential that every small business person gain at least a passing familiarity with LLCs. A large number of small business owners currently operating as sole proprietorships or partnerships will conclude that they absolutely must form or convert to an LLC. In fact, the legal protection an LLC offers almost always makes it preferable to a partnership.

Are there any disadvantages to forming an LLC? Not many. True, LLCs are a relatively new legal entity and, as a result, you might run into some minor hassles with some state and local bureaucracies and commercial institutions. Fortunately, the passage of LLC-enabling legislation has received reams of favorable publicity, so by and large you shouldn't expect any major red tape. In a later chapter, we'll show you how to assure outside institutions and businesses that yours is a validly formed legal entity, operating under an established set of rules. For now, read on to gain an appreciation of this fledgling business entity that promises to change the face of small business throughout the U.S.

An existing partnership may use this book to convert to an LLC. If you and your business associates are already doing business as a general or limited partnership, you can use this book to convert your partnership to an LLC. In some states, you may need to perform one or two additional simple tasks—for example, you may need to file a special form of LLC articles of organization to convert a partnership to an LLC. The procedures are, however, essentially the same as those followed by a start-up LLC. (We discuss the special steps that may be necessary to convert an existing partnership to an LLC in Chapter 7, Section A2.)

A. Who May Form an LLC?

The typical candidates for forming an LLC are business associates, friends or family members who decide to pool energies and resources to own and operate a business.

Keep the following two basic LLC formation rules in mind:

*   *Rule 1: In all states, you can form an LLC with just one person.*

*   *Rule 2: LLCs work best for smaller businesses.* Generally LLCs are suitable for businesses with no more than 35 or so owners and investors (this is our ballpark figure—not a hard and fast legal rule).

    With few exceptions, LLCs may be formed for all types of businesses. You may even form one LLC to engage in several businesses—for example, furniture sales, trucking and redecorating all under one legal, if not physical, roof.

BUSINESSES THAT MAY NOT FORM REGULAR LLCs

Depending on state law, certain kinds of businesses may either be restricted or prohibited from setting up an LLC. State laws often have special restrictions for:

*   businesses formed to engage in banking, trust or insurance transactions—these normally can't do business as an LLC, and

*   businesses formed to practice a licensed profession such as medicine, law or accounting. In some states, these professions cannot form LLCs, although they may be able to obtain some of the benefits that LLCs enjoy by forming a special type of entity called a professional limited liability company or a limited liability partnership. (We discuss how to form this kind of professional practice in Chapter 4, Section D2.)

Recent Tax Rules Make LLCs More Flexible: This book contains the recent federal "check the box" business entity tax rules, which allow LLCs to choose how they wish to be treated for tax purposes by the IRS. We'll have more to say about these rules in Chapter 3, but for now just know that LLCs now are automatically treated as partnerships for tax purposes by the IRS (or sole proprietorships if the LLC has one member)—this is the tax treatment most LLCs will want. If an LLC wishes to be taxed as a corporation, it can elect corporate tax treatment by filing IRS Form 8832, *Entity Classification Election.*

ANNOUNCING LLC MAKER™—NOLO'S NATIONAL LLC SOFTWARE

Nolo produces *LLC Maker*, an interactive software program for Windows® that prepares the articles of organization, operating agreement, and other essential legal forms for you. Just fill in the information for your LLC according to the state-specific instructions on the screen, and LLC Maker will assemble the forms required in your state. It contains online legal and program help, plus tables of state-by-state LLC rules and information for your reference. Cut through the legal red tape and form your LLC in minutes with this new software program! LLC Maker is available for download from http://www.nolo.com.

B. How to Use This Book

This book gives basic background legal and tax information that applies to LLCs. It covers all the information you need to make an informed choice on whether to form an LLC. It also provides helpful information and forms for existing LLCs, such as information on ongoing legal formalities and instructions for preparing minutes of LLC meetings.

If you decide to set up your business as an LLC, either from scratch or by converting an existing partnership, this book will also give you the step-by-step information you need to form an LLC in your state. Specifically, you'll find out:

- which state administrative offices to contact
- how to prepare standard organizational and operational documents to get your LLC started, including LLC articles of organization and an LLC operating agreement, and
- how to comply with legal rules for your state. The state sheets in Appendix A will help you follow your state's particular legal requirements.

In general, we recommend checking with a small business tax or legal advisor before taking the plunge and filing your papers with the state.

Consultations of this sort are invaluable to make sure that an LLC is your best choice, that you have up-to-date state-specific information and that you have considered all legal and tax angles that apply to your particular business. Although you'll have to pay for an initial consultation with a tax or legal advisor, you'll save quite a bit by not handing over all your paperwork to a professional. We believe it is well worth the price in terms of the peace of mind you'll get knowing you've reached the right business conclusions. In Chapter 8, we discuss how to find a legal "coach"—a helpful legal professional who will work with you, review your papers and augment (not redo) your self-help legal efforts in organizing and operating your LLC.

We are confident that a careful reading of this book can help make you an informed LLC organizer, manager and member. We wish you all the best on the road to forming and running a successful LLC.

NOTES AND ICONS

Throughout this book, we have included special notations and icons to help organize the material and underscore particular points:

 A legal or commonsense tip to help you understand or comply with legal requirements.

 A caution to slow down and consider potential problems.

 A suggestion to seek the advice of a professional.

 An indication that you may be able to skip some material.

 A cross-reference to another section of this book, or a suggestion to consult another book or resource.

Forms CD-ROM

Included at the back of this book is a CD-ROM containing files with word processing (rich text format) versions of the tear-out forms included in Appendix D. For specific instructions for using the forms on the CD, see Appendix C.

Macintosh Users: This CD-ROM should work on a Macintosh. Please note, however, that Nolo cannot provide technical support for non-Windows users. Please see Appendix C for instructions on how to use this CD.

Overview of the LLC

In this chapter, we briefly trace the history of the limited liability company (LLC), discuss its legal and tax characteristics and compare it to the traditional ways of organizing and doing business in the U.S. We'll delve more into the specific legal and tax characteristics of LLCs in the next two chapters.

If you are familiar with LLCs. If you have followed the development of the LLC over the last few years and know its general legal and tax characteristics (or you simply want to look at the specifics of forming an LLC right now), you can skip the introductory material in this and the following two chapters. Move right ahead to Chapter 4, where you'll learn how to prepare LLC articles of organization.

A. Development of the LLC

The LLC is a relatively recent version of a type of business organization that has existed for years in other countries. It resembles the German *GmbH*, the French *SARL* and the South American *Limitada* forms of doing business, all of which allow small groups of individuals to enjoy limited personal liability while operating under partnership-type rules (rather than the complex rigmarole that applies to corporate-type structures).

The Wyoming legislature enacted the first state LLC legislation in 1977, eventually followed by Florida in 1982. In those early days, this new type of business entity was a risky proposition, because no one knew whether the IRS would tax an LLC as a corporation or a partnership. Because the idea behind forming an LLC—to enjoy the tax status of a partnership without the legal liabilities—seemed almost too good to be true, few business people were brave enough to avail themselves of this new

business model without clarification from the IRS. Similarly, other states were unwilling to jump in with LLC legislation of their own.

The first big break in the LLC stalemate came in 1988, when the IRS ruled on the tax treatment of Wyoming LLCs in Revenue Ruling 88-76. (A copy of this ruling is in Appendix B.) To the surprise of many tax practitioners, the IRS agreed that an LLC formed under the Wyoming statute was eligible for partnership tax status. The IRS's nod of approval created huge amounts of enthusiasm for LLCs, ultimately resulting in all states plus the District of Columbia passing LLC legislation.

The second big break came on January 1, 1997 when the IRS threw out its old, and unnecessarily complicated, business entity tax classification regulations and agreed that LLCs should be taxed as partnerships (or sole proprietorships if they have one owner) without jumping through a number of technical hoops. Moreover, the IRS now lets an LLC elect corporate tax treatment if it wants it (by filing IRS Form 8832—see Chapter 3).

B. LLCs at a Glance: The Best Thing Since Sliced Bread?

In the U.S., the LLC stands as a unique alternative to five traditional legal and tax ways of doing business: sole proprietorships, general partnerships, limited partnerships, C (regular) corporations and S corporations. The business press has heralded the arrival of the LLC with enthusiasm and hyperbole. Finally, you can establish a business entity with the limited liability of a corporation while retaining a level of tax simplicity that resembles a partnership. Is this fanfare justified? In large part, we think so, at least for smaller startup businesses and existing partnerships. It doesn't often happen that a new business form comes along, particularly one that is blessed by the IRS with the favorable tax ruling bestowed upon the LLC.

THERE'S NEVER LIMITED LIABILITY FOR PERSONALLY GUARANTEED DEBTS

No matter how a small business is organized (LLC, corporation, partnership or sole proprietorship), its owners must normally co-sign business loans made by banks—at least until the business establishes its own positive credit history.

When you co-sign a loan, you promise to voluntarily assume personal liability if your business fails to pay back the loan. In some cases, the bank may ask you to pledge all your personal assets as security for repayment of the guaranteed loan; in others, it may require you to pledge specific personal assets—for example, the equity in your home—to secure repayment of the loan.

Example: A married couple owns and operates Books & Bagels, a coffee shop *cum* bookstore. In need of funds (dough, really) to expand into a larger location, the owners go to the bank to get a small loan for their corporation. The bank grants the loan on the condition that the two owners personally pledge their equity in their house as security for the loan. Because the owners personally guaranteed the loan, the bank can seek repayment from the owners personally by foreclosing on their home if Books & Bagels defaults. No form of business ownership can insulate them from the personal liability they agreed to.

If you want more information about pledging personal assets to secure business loans, see *The Legal Guide for Starting and Running a Small Business*, by Fred Steingold (Nolo).

1. Limited Liability Status

The legal characteristic most interesting to the business world is undoubtedly the limited liability status of LLC owners. With the exception of corporate entities, the LLC is the only form of legal entity that lets *all* of its owners off the hook for business debts and other legal liabilities, such as court judgments and legal settlements obtained against the business. Another way of saying this is that an investor in an LLC normally has at risk only his or her share of capital paid into the business.

2. Business Profits and Losses Taxed at Individuals' Income Tax Rates

The LLC is recognized by the IRS as a "pass-through" type of tax entity. That is, the profits or losses of the LLC pass through the business and are reflected and taxed on the individual tax returns of the owners, rather than being reported and taxed at a separate business level. (Other pass-through entities include general and limited partnerships, sole proprietorships and S corporations—those that have elected S corporation tax status with the IRS. A detailed discussion of pass-through taxation is in Section D, below.)

3. Flexible Management Structure

LLC owners are referred to as members. A member may be an individual or, generally, a separate legal entity, such as a partnership or corporation. Members invest in the LLC and receive a percentage ownership interest in return. This ownership interest is used to divide up the assets of the LLC when it is sold or liquidated, and is typically used for other purposes as well—for example, to split up profits and losses of the LLC or to divide up its voting rights.

LLCs are run by their members unless they elect management by a management group, which may consist of some members and/or nonmembers. Small LLCs are normally member-managed—after all, most small business owners want and need to have an active hand in the management of the business. However, this isn't always true. Especially with a growing business or one that makes fairly passive investments, such as in real estate, investors may not want a day-to-day role. Fortunately, an LLC can easily adopt a management-run structure in situations such as these:

- the members want the LLC to be managed by some, but not all, members
- the members decide to employ outside management help, or
- the members choose to cater to an outsider who wishes to invest in or loan capital to the LLC on condition that he or she be given a vote in management.

UNIFORM LLC LAWS

For many years, legal scholars and state legislators have worked hard to have all states adopt the same (or very similar) laws affecting key areas of American business and life. A bit belatedly, efforts are being made to adopt a national model LLC act that can be used by individual state legislatures to pass future LLC legislation. One model is the Prototype Limited Liability Company Act, sponsored by the American Bar Association's Section of Business Law. Another is the Uniform Limited Liability Company Act, developed by the National Conference of Commissioners on Uniform State Laws.

Both of these acts are still in development, and there is justified skepticism as to whether states will replace current LLC laws with either model act. More likely, states probably will adopt portions of the model acts to supplement their current LLC statutes. In short, while LLC laws are fairly similar (they generally try to conform to IRS regulations and to LLC statutory schemes in other states), state-by-state differences are likely to remain.

---

4. Flexible Distribution of Profits and Losses

Business owners may want flexibility in how they split their profits and losses. An LLC allows you to decide what share of the LLC profits and losses each owner will receive. Rather than being restricted to dividing up profits proportionate to the members' capital contributions (this is the standard legal rule for corporations), you may split up LLC profits and losses any way you wish (this flexibility is afforded partnerships as well).

Example: Steve and Frankie form an educational seminar business. Steve puts up all the cash necessary to purchase a computer with graphics and multimedia presentation capabilities, rent out initial seminar sites, send out mass mailings and purchase advertising. As the traveling lecturer, cash-poor Frankie will contribute services to the LLC. Although the two owners could agree to split profits and losses equally, they decide that Steve will get 65% for the first three years as a way of paying him back for taking the risk of putting up cash.

By contrast, rules governing the distribution of corporate profits and losses are fairly restrictive. A regular (C) corporation cannot allocate profits and losses to shareholders at all—shareholders get a financial return from the corporation by receiving corporate dividends or a share of the corporation's assets when it is sold or liquidated. In an S corporation (a corporation that has made a special tax election with the IRS, covered in Section D5, below), profits and losses pass through to the owners and profits and losses generally must follow shareholdings. For example, an S corporation shareholder holding 10% of the shares ordinarily must be allocated a 10% share of yearly profits and losses.

There are a few wrinkles in the flexibility afforded to LLCs. Because LLCs are treated like partnerships for tax purposes, LLCs must comply with technical partnership tax rules:

- *Special (disproportionate) allocations of LLC profits or losses are subject to rules that require such allocations to have "substantial economic effect."* Generally, they must reflect some economic reality of the business—for example, the member with the greater share of profits should also be at risk for a greater share of losses. Rather than squabble with the IRS on this issue, LLCs that make special allocations usually have their tax advisor add technical provisions to their operating agreement to make sure their allocations will be respected by the IRS. (See the discussion in Chapter 3, Section D2.)

- *Members contributing future services to the LLC may be subject to income taxes on the value of their services.* A member promising to contribute services to the LLC may face personal income tax liability on the value of those services—although there are some ways around this. (We'll have more to say about the tax problems associated with a member's contribution of services in Chapter 3, Section D1.)

C. Which Businesses Would Benefit as LLCs?

Here is an overview of the types of persons and businesses for which the LLC form makes the most and least sense. Bear in mind that this discussion is not meant to be set in stone—certainly you may find that your business breaks the mold.

1. Businesses That Benefit From the LLC Structure

LLCs generally work best for:

- *Actively run businesses with a limited number of owners.* Owners numbering between one and about 35 keep the logistics of making collective business decisions manageable. With the LLC form, all owners of the business enjoy limited liability and the flexibility of pass-through (partnership) tax treatment.

- *Small startup companies.* New businesses generally wish to pass possible early-year losses along to owners to deduct against their other income (usually salary earned working for another company or income earned from investments).

- *Anyone thinking of forming an S corporation.* An S corporation is a corporation formed under state law, which files a special IRS tax election to have corporate profits pass through the business and be taxed only at the shareholder level (similar to the tax treatment of LLCs, but less flexible, as discussed below). Like LLCs, S corporations also provide limited liability protection to all owners. The S corporation tax election comes at a fairly heavy price: S corporations must limit the number and types of shareholders. They are restricted as to how they allocate profits and losses among owners, the types of losses they can pass along to owners to ease their income tax burden, and the kinds of stock they can issue to investors. Even if a business meets the S corporation tax requirements, it can inadvertently lose its eligibility—

for example, when a disqualified shareholder inherits or buys the stock—resulting in a big tax bill. (For more on S corporations, see Section D5, below.)

- *Existing partnerships.* Only the LLC provides pass-through tax treatment of business income while insulating *all* owners (not just limited partners as in the case of a limited partnership) from personal liability for business debts.

- *Businesses planning to hold property that will appreciate, such as real property.* Regular corporations (also called C corporations) and their shareholders are subject to a double tax on this appreciation when assets are sold or liquidated—in other words, taxation occurs at both the corporate and individual level. S corporations that were organized as C corporations prior to making an S corporation tax election also may be subject to a double tax on "built-in gains" from asset appreciation, as well as a penalty tax if their passive income (money from rents, royalties, interest, dividends) gets too high. Because the LLC is a true pass-through tax entity, it allows a business that will hold appreciating assets to avoid double taxation. When the business is sold, generally just the owners, not the entity itself, pay taxes on the profits from the sale.

2. Businesses That Should Normally Not Form an LLC Using This Book

The LLC is not normally suitable for:

- *Existing S or C (regular) corporations.* The tax cost of converting a corporation to an LLC, as well as security law uncertainties, are problematic. It may be possible to convert an existing corporation to an LLC without hefty tax or legal costs, but you'll need the help of a lawyer and a tax advisor to make sure you don't get stung.

- *Highly profitable LLCs in certain states.* In states with a graduated LLC license fee schedule, the more profitable the LLC, the higher the tax. In California, for example, LLCs with reportable income over $5 million must pay an annual fee of $8,000 or more. Such a stiff tax is unusual; check your state sheet in Appendix A or ask your tax advisor to be sure you understand whether you face the unpleasant prospect of paying excessive state LLC fees. Of course, in states with a high LLC fee or tax, chances are good that the state also has enacted fees that apply to other pass-through tax entities (limited partnerships and S corporations). In these states, you may decide that forming a general partnership, which isn't taxed separately, is the least expensive way to go—but you won't qualify for limited liability for business debts.

D. Comparison of LLCs and Other Business Forms

Anyone considering an LLC will want to compare this business form to the three traditional ways of doing business:

- sole proprietorships
- partnerships, and
- C (regular) corporations.

In addition, to fully understand the pros and cons of LLC status, you'll need to compare the LLC to two variants on these traditional business forms that come closest to resembling the legal and tax characteristics of the LLC:

- limited partnerships, and
- S corporations.

This section provides general information on the characteristics of each type of legal entity, focusing on the main reasons why business people adopt one form over another. Our aim is to explain most of the information you'll need to make an informed decision as to whether the LLC is right for you. However, please realize that we can't cover every nuance of tax and business organization law as it applies to your business, especially if yours involves a number of owners with different and complicated personal tax situations. Furthermore, the area of pass-through taxation is no piece of cake, even to tax specialists. You will need to check with a tax advisor to make sure the LLC makes sense to you from a tax standpoint, and to learn about any of the special tax areas that may have special relevance to your business (some of which are covered in Chapter 3).

> ### OTHER WAYS OF DOING BUSINESS: MORE INFORMATION FROM NOLO
>
> For a more complete examination of the legal and tax characteristics of the various ways of doing business, see the following Nolo titles:
> * *Legal Guide for Starting & Running a Small Business*, by Fred S. Steingold. This book provides a thorough summary of the legal and tax characteristics of sole proprietorships, partnerships, corporations and LLCs.
> * *The Partnership Book*, by Denis Clifford and Ralph Warner. This book discusses general partnerships and shows you step-by-step how to prepare a general partnership agreement.
> * *How to Form Your Own California Corporation* and *Incorporate Your Business* (a national state-by-state title), by Anthony Mancuso. These books provide an in-depth treatment of the corporate structure and show you how to incorporate in each state. Incorporation forms are included as tear-outs and on CD-ROM.

1. Sole Proprietorship

The simplest way of being in business for yourself is as a sole proprietor. This is just a fancy way of saying that you are the owner of a one-person business. There's little red tape and cost—other than the usual business licenses, sales tax permits and local and state regulations that any business must face. As a practical matter, most one-person businesses start out as sole proprietorships just to keep things simple.

a. Sole Proprietorship Is Limited to One Person

If your sole proprietorship grows, you'll need to move to a more complicated type of business structure. Once you decide to own and split profits with another person (other than your spouse), by definition, you have at least a partnership on your hands.

b. Sole Proprietor Is Personally Liable for Business Debts

Unfortunately, although a sole proprietorship is simple, it can also be a dangerous way to operate, especially if your business may result in debts or liabilities from lawsuits. The sole proprietor is personally liable for all debts and claims against a business. For example, if someone slips and falls in a sole proprietor's business and sues, the owner is on the line for paying any court award (if commercial liability insurance doesn't cover it). The owner's personal assets, such as a home, car and bank accounts, are fair game for the repayment of these uncovered amounts. Similarly, if the business fails to pay suppliers, banks or other businesses' bills, the owner is personally liable for the unpaid debts.

c. Sole Proprietor's Taxes

Sole proprietors report business profits or losses on an *IRS Schedule C, Profit and Loss From Business (Sole Proprietorship)*, included with a *1040* individual federal tax return. Profits are taxed at the owner's individual income tax rates.

Because the owner is self-employed, he or she must pay an increased amount of self-employment (FICA) tax based upon these profits—about twice as much as an incorporated business or corporate employee would personally pay. This increased FICA tax doesn't necessarily mean that sole proprietorships are more expensive tax-wise than other business forms. In fact, if you are both a corporate shareholder and employee, as is the case

for the owner/employees of most small corporations, you end up paying close to the same total FICA taxes.

d. Sole Proprietorships Compared to LLCs

The LLC requires more paperwork to get started and is more complicated than a sole proprietorship from a legal and tax perspective. Although LLC owners, like sole proprietors, report business profits on their individual tax returns, the LLC itself is treated as a partnership and must prepare its own annual informational tax return. The payoff of the LLC for this added complexity is that owners are not personally liable for business claims or debts (unless personally guaranteed, as with a personally guaranteed bank loan).

2. General Partnerships

A partnership is a business in which two or more owners agree to share profits. If you go into business with at least one other person and you don't file formal papers with the state to set up an LLC, corporation or limited partnership, the law says you have formed a general partnership. A general partnership can be started with a handshake (a simple verbal agreement or understanding) or a formal partnership agreement.

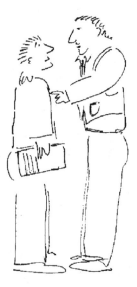

Partners should always create a written partnership agreement. Without an agreement, the default rules of each state's general partnership law apply to the business. These provisions usually say that profits and losses of the business should be split up equally among the partners, regardless of the amount of capital contributed to the business by each partner. Rather than relying on state laws, general partners should prepare an agreement that covers issues such as the division of profits and losses, the payment of salaries and draws to partners and the procedure for selling partnership interests back to the partnership or to outsiders.

a. Number of Partners in a General Partnership

General partnerships may be formed by two or more people; there is no such thing as a one-person partnership. Legally, there is no upper limit on the number of partners who may be admitted into a partnership, but general partnerships with many owners may have problems reaching a consensus on business decisions and may be subject to divisive disputes between contending management factions.

b. General Partnership Liability

Each owner of a general partnership is individually liable for the debts and claims of the business. In other words, if the partnership owes money, a creditor may go after any member of the partnership for the entire debt, regardless of his or her ownership percentage (although one partner can sue other partners to force them to repay their shares of the debt).

Legally, each partner may bind the partnership to contracts or enter a business deal that binds the partnership, as long as the contract or deal is generally within the scope of business undertaken by the partnership. In legal jargon, this authority is expressed by saying that each partner is an agent of the partnership. If the partnership can't fulfill a contract or other business deal, each partner may be held personally liable for the amount owed. This personal liability for partnership debts, coupled with the agency authority of each partner, makes the general partnership riskier than limited liability businesses (corporations, LLCs and limited partnerships).

c. General Partnership Taxes

A general partnership is not a separate taxable entity. Profits (and losses) pass through the business to the partners, who pay taxes on profits at their individual tax rates. Although the partnership does not pay its own taxes, it must file an information return each year, IRS Form 1065, *U.S. Partnership Return of Income*. The partnership must give each partner a filled-in IRS Schedule K-1 (1065), *Partner's Share of Income, Credits, Deductions*, which shows the proportionate share of profits or losses each person carries over to his or her individual 1040 tax return at the end of the year.

d. General Partnerships Compared to LLCs

General partnerships are less costly to start than LLCs because most states do not require a state filing (and fees) to form general partnerships. The major downside to running a general partnership over an LLC is the exposure to personal liability by each of the general partners. Although a general business insurance package (possibly supplemented by more specialized coverage for unusual risks) can mitigate possible effects, each partner is still personally responsible for any liabilities and debts not picked up by the business's insurance policy. LLC owners, on the other hand, avoid this personal liability problem altogether.

General partnerships and LLCs come out about even on a couple of important issues:

- *Partnership agreement or operating agreement.* Even a small general partnership should start off with a good written general partnership agreement. This, of course, takes time and, if you don't do the work yourself, is likely to cost $1,000 to $5,000 in legal fees, depending on the complexity of your partnership and the thickness of your lawyer's rug. You'll also need to draw up an operating agreement if you form an LLC; this agreement is similar in scope to a partnership agreement. (We take you through the steps involved in preparing an operating agreement in Chapters 5 and 6 of this book.)
- *Taxes.* General partnerships and LLCs can count on about the same amount of tax complexity, preparation time and paperwork. Even though you'll probably turn over most year-end tax work to a tax advisor to prepare a partnership return, understanding and following basic partnership tax procedures takes a fair amount of time and effort.

3. C (Regular) Corporations

To establish a C (regular) corporation, you prepare and file formal articles of incorporation papers with a state agency (usually the secretary of state) and pay corporate filing fees and initial taxes. A corporation assumes an independent legal and tax life separate from its owners, with the result that it pays taxes at its own corporate tax rates and files its own income tax returns each year (IRS Form 1120). LLCs can elect corporate tax treatment by filing IRS Form 8832—see Chapter 3.

Corporations are owned by shareholders and managed by a board of directors. Most management decisions are left to the directors, although a few must be ratified by the shareholders as well, such as the amendment of corporate articles of incorporation, sale of substantially all of the corporation's assets or the merger or dissolution of the corporation. Corporate officers are normally appointed by the board of directors to handle the day-to-day supervision of corporate business, and usually consist of a corporate president, vice president, secretary and treasurer.

A "C" corporation is nothing more than a regular corporation. The letter "C" simply distinguishes the regular corporation (one taxed under normal corporate income tax rules) from a more specialized type of corporation regulated under Subchapter "S" of the Internal Revenue Code. The latter type of corporation, the S corporation, makes a special tax election and is treated differently under the Internal Revenue Code. (We compare the LLC to the S corporation in Section D5, below.)

a. Number of Corporate Shareholders and Directors

In most states, one or more persons can form and operate a corporation. In a few states, the number of persons necessary to manage a multi-owner corporation (that is, the number of directors) is proportionate to the number of shareholders. For example, if there are two shareholders, two or more directors must be named; if three shareholders, then three or more directors are necessary.

b. Corporate Limited Liability

As we have mentioned, a corporation provides all its owners (shareholders) with the benefits of limited liability—traditionally, a major reason why many businesses have organized as corporations. The LLC is the latest arrival on the legal and business scene that also gives all business owners this significant legal advantage.

LIMITED LIABILITY FOR THE MASSES: THE TREND CONTINUES

Historically, it was the development of the corporation and the concept of limited liability that made it possible to capitalize large corporations and create modern capitalism. This same sort of revolution has taken place on a small scale among successful small business people. Surely, the great majority of America's 50,000 most successful smaller businesses are incorporated. Extending the concept of limited liability to the small business world has produced amazing results, and we're sure the momentum of the LLC as an emerging business vehicle is bound to continue this trend.

---

c. Corporation's Separate Legal and Tax Existence

The corporation has a legal and tax existence separate from its owners. This leads to the following corporate characteristics (note that since the LLC can now elect corporate tax treatment, it can take on the corporate tax characteristics discussed below):

- *Separate taxes.* A corporation files its own income tax return and pays its own income taxes. LLCs (like partnerships) file an informational return only and do not pay their own income taxes (unless the LLC elects to be taxed as a corporation).
- *Tax benefits of employee fringe benefits.* Even small corporations have the opportunity to offer their employees unique fringe benefits. The corporate form allows owner-employees (shareholders who also work in the business) to deduct a number of corporate fringes paid to them as employees from corporate income,

such as the 100% deductibility of health insurance premiums. Other corporate fringes include the direct reimbursement of medical expenses and stock bonus and stock option plans. There is not much difference between corporate and noncorporate pension and profit sharing plans, but corporate defined benefit plans usually afford better retirement options and benefits than those available under a noncorporate (Keogh) plan.

- *Legal formalities.* Because a corporation has a separate legal existence, you must pay more attention to its legal care and feeding. This means you must don directors' and shareholders' hats and hold and document annual meetings required under state law. You must keep minutes of meetings, prepare other formal documentation of important decisions made during the life of the corporation and keep a paper trail of all financial dealings between the corporation and its shareholders. You also need to tend to other formalities, such as appointing officers required under corporate statutes. A corporation should issue stock to its shareholders and keep adequate capitalization on hand to handle foreseeable business debts and liabilities.

Problems with shoddy corporate procedures. There are dangers if you set up a thinly capitalized corporation, treat corporate coffers as an incorporated pocketbook for your personal finances, fail to issue stock, neglect to hold meetings or overlook other formalities required under your state's corporation code. If you do (or don't do) these things, a court or the IRS may "pierce the corporate veil" (a metaphor carried over from a long line of court cases) and decide that the corporation is simply an "alter ego" of the shareholders of a small corporation. If this happens, the business owners (shareholders) can be held personally liable for any money awarded by a court against the corporation.

Help with corporate forms and formalities. For those who wish to explore more fully the formalities (holding annual and special meetings) and ins and outs of doing business as a corporation (approving contracts, leases, promissory notes and numerous other important legal, tax and business decisions), see *The Corporate Minutes Book*, by Anthony Mancuso (Nolo).

d.   Corporations Compared to LLCs

Corporations are similar to LLCs in the types of paperwork and fees necessary to get them started with the state. Both must prepare and file organizational papers with the secretary of state and pay filing fees. Both should adopt a set of operating rules that set out the basic legal requirements for operating the business under state law—corporations adopt Bylaws; LLCs adopt operating agreements.

What sets the corporate form apart from LLCs is how they are taxed. Corporations are taxed separately from their owners at corporate income tax rates. LLCs are not, and start out being treated as partnerships (if they have two or more owners) or sole proprietorships (if they have one owner) by the IRS. But this corporate tax distinction can be eliminated if the LLC members wish. That is, they can elect to have their LLC taxed as a corporation by filing IRS Form 8832 (and checking the "corporation" box). If an LLC makes this filing, it must file separate corporate income tax returns, and pay corporate income taxes on money left in the LLC (not paid out to members as salaries or in other forms deductible by the business).

Corporate tax treatment can result in tax savings if money is left in a business for expansion or for other business needs. This advantage stems from the fact that the initial tax rates applied to corporate income are lower than the individual tax rates of business owners.

Example: Justine and Janine own and operate Just Jams & Jellies, a specialty store selling gourmet canned preserves. Business has boomed and their net taxable income, split equally by the partners, has reached a level where it is taxed at an individual tax rate of over 30%. If the owners incorporate, or if they form an LLC and elect corporate tax treatment, they can keep money in their business, which is taxed at the lower corporate tax rates of 15% and 25%, saving overall tax dollars on business income.

WHAT ABOUT THE DOUBLE TAXATION OF CORPORATE PROFITS?

We're sure you've read about the awful consequence of double taxation when a corporation makes money. Specifically, the tax law says that corporate profits are first taxed at the corporate level, then any profits paid out as dividends to shareholders are taxed at each shareholder's individual income tax rate. Doesn't this result in a big comparative benefit to LLC businesses taxed as partnerships (and other pass-through entities such as partnerships and sole proprietorships), where the owners just pay taxes once on business income at their personal rates?

For small, actively run corporations, we say no. Here's why. To avoid the penalty of double taxation, smaller corporations rarely pay dividends to the owners. Instead, the owner-employees are paid salaries and fringe benefits that are tax deductible to the corporation. As a result, only employee-shareholders pay income taxes on this business income.

So cast a critical eye on any article decrying the double taxation of corporate profits. Unless you are forming a corporation with passive investors who expect to receive regular dividends as a return on their investment in your corporation, double taxation will generally not be a big deal.

Exception: When a successful corporation is sold, both the corporation and its owners may have to pay income taxes on profits from the sale. If you are thinking of incorporating, it's important to plan for this possibility of double taxation of sales proceeds.

Even though an LLC may now elect corporate tax treatment, there may be other reasons to favor the corporate form over the LLC. Some are the increased deductibility of corporate-employee fringes, and generally better retirement benefits or options under a corporate retirement plan. The increased respectability of doing business as a corporation may seem overrated, but a number of people—perhaps including persons you may wish to hire as key employees and reward with stock option and stock bonus incentives—associate the corporate form with an added degree of formality and solidity. And, of course, the ability to go public (make a public offering of corporate shares) is a traditional feature of the corporate form that more successful small businesses may be able to capitalize on. (Forget about going public with an LLC; the legal and practical restrictions on transferring membership interests rule out this possibility.)

There are several downsides to corporate life. We've already mentioned the complexity of complying with state law corporate procedures by preparing annual and special director and shareholder meetings. (Some states have tried to lessen the impact of these state-mandated formalities with the creation of the close corporation form—see the sidebar on the following page, "A Look at Close Corporations.")

4. Limited Partnerships

To get this special type of partnership started, you must file papers (Certificate of Limited Partnership) with the state and pay an initial filing fee. Legally, a limited partnership is similar to a general partnership (discussed in Section D2, above), except that instead of only being comprised of general partners, it has two types:

- *Limited partners.* One or more partners contribute capital to the business. Limited partners neither participate in its day-to-day operations nor have personal liability for business debts and claims.
- *General partners.* One or more partners manage business operations and have personal liability for business debts and claims.

a. Number of Partners

Limited partnerships must be formed by two or more people, with:
- at least one person acting as the general partner, who has management authority and personal liability, and
- at least one person in the role of limited partner.

b. Limited Liability Only for Limited Partners

Limited partners enjoy the same kind of limited liability for the debts and liabilities of the business as do the shareholders of a corporation and the members of an LLC. General partners of limited partnerships, on the other hand, have the same personal liability described above for general partnerships. (See Section D2.)

c. Limited Partnership Taxes

For tax purposes, limited partnerships normally are treated like general partnerships, with all owners having to report and pay taxes personally on their share of the profits each year. The limited partnership files an informational tax return only, and is not subject to an entity level federal income tax.

A LOOK AT CLOSE CORPORATIONS

Several states have enacted special corporate statutes that allow corporations to dispense with normal operating rules. These corporations, called "close" or "statutory close" corporations, generally must meet a number of legal requirements:

- The corporation must have a limited number of shareholders, usually no more than 35.
- Shares of stock must not be sold or transferred to outsiders unless approved by all shareholders.
- The corporation must elect close corporation status in its formation documents or an amendment to these papers.
- The corporation must operate under partnership-type rules specified in a shareholders' agreement. (The drafting of this agreement is time-consuming and can involve fairly high attorney fees.)

Ten to 15 years ago, legislators in corporately active states, including California, Delaware, Illinois and Texas, expected business organizers to line up to form close corporations under recently enacted state laws, but few were formed. The close corporation's failure to spark the interest of business organizers was caused by reasons such as the following:

- Few corporations want to forego the customary formality of appointing a board of directors, electing officers and assuming the other traditional accoutrements of corporate life.
- Management of a corporation by its shareholders is normally seen as novel and potentially chaotic.
- Preparation and adoption of a custom-tailored shareholders' agreement is a time-consuming incorporation step most organizers want to avoid.
- Shareholders do not want restrictions on their right to sell or transfer shares, which are mandatory under typical close corporation statutes.

In many ways, the close corporation resembles the LLC by giving owners the protection of limited liability while allowing them to operate under partnership-type legal rules. The big difference is that unlike LLCs, the IRS never bestowed the general mantle of pass-through tax treatment on close corporations. Had close corporations successfully obtained pass-through tax treatment with the IRS and been able to operate informally without having to prepare a special shareholders' agreement, perhaps they would be vying today for the popular attention currently enjoyed by LLCs.

d. Limited Partnerships Compared to LLCs

There are two major differences between limited partnerships and LLCs. First, a limited partnership must have at least one general partner, who is personally liable for the debts and other liabilities of the business. This differs from LLCs, where all members are covered by the cloak of limited liability.

Second, limited partners are generally prohibited from managing the business. If a limited partner is active in the business of the limited partnership, he or she typically loses the limited partner status with its attendant limited liability protection. (There are exceptions to this ban under the newer Revised Uniform Limited Partnership Act, which has made the rounds through state legislatures and has been adopted, at least in part, in most states.) In contrast, LLC members are given a free hand in managing and running the business, either by themselves or in conjunction with outside managers.

This second restriction of the limited partnership makes it more of a gamble for investors, who must turn over management of the business to a general partner. Such an arrangement may work well for outsiders who want to invest a little cash or property in a business run by others, but it won't work well for businesses that are funded and run primarily by their owners. Investors in actively run businesses who want limited liability status for all owners generally benefit by forming an LLC or corporation; both of these entities permit investors to help run the business while enjoying the personal protection of limited liability.

5. S Corporations

Now we come to our last comparison, and the one with the nicest (that is, most picayune) technical distinctions: the S corporation versus the LLC. Below, we address the main similarities and differences, but you may need to ask your tax person for further particulars if you want to understand the ins and outs of comparing these two business forms.

For starters, an S corporation follows the same state incorporation formalities as a C (regular) corporation. Typically, this means filing Articles of Incorporation and paying a state filing fee. An S corporation also must make a special one-page tax election under Subchapter S of the Internal Revenue Code to have the corporation taxed as a partnership (by filing IRS Form 2553, the *S Corporation Tax Election* form, with the IRS).

a. Number of S Corporation Owners

Generally, an S corporation may have no more than 75 shareholders (who must be individuals or certain types of trusts or estates). But spouses who own shares in an S corporation are counted as one shareholder.

b. Limited Liability of S Corporation Shareholders

All S corporation shareholders are granted personal protection from the debts and other liabilities of the business, just like regular C corporation shareholders and LLC members.

c. Tax Election of S Corporation

Once a corporation makes a Subchapter S tax election, its profits and losses pass through the corporation and are reported on the individual tax returns of the S corporation's shareholders. This is the same basic pass-through treatment afforded partnerships and LLCs. The S corporation's profits and losses are generally not taxed at the business entity level (as is the case for a regular C corporation).

d. S Corporations Compared to LLCs

Like any other type of corporation, an S corporation requires some care and feeding—more than typically needed for an LLC. Regular and special meetings of directors and shareholders should be held and recorded to transact important corporate business or decide key legal or tax formalities. And although profits and losses of an S corporation are passed along to its shareholders, the S corporation must prepare and file an S corporation annual income tax return each year (IRS Form 1120S). This requirement is similar, from a time and energy standpoint, to the task of a co-owned LLC's preparing its own partnership informational tax return each year.

The main difference between S corporations and LLCs has to do with the requirements for electing S corporation tax treatment and some of the unique tax effects that result from this election. To be eligible to make an S corporation tax election with the IRS, the corporation and its shareholders must meet a number of special requirements. Here are a few of the S corporation tax requirements that can present a problem:

* *Individual shareholders of an S corporation must be U.S. citizens or have U.S. residency status.* If shares are sold, passed to (by will, divorce or other means), or otherwise fall into the hands of a foreign national, the corporation loses its S corporation tax status.

- *Shareholders must be individuals or certain types of qualified trusts or estates.* S corporations can't have partnerships or other corporations as shareholders. Under typical state statutes, LLCs may have both natural (individual) and artificial (corporate, partnership, trust and estate) members.

- *There can be no more than 75 shareholders in an S corporation.*

- *S corporations must have only one class of stock.* Different voting rights are permitted, meaning that S corporations may have one class of voting shares and another consisting of nonvoting shares. But all shares must have the same rights to participate in dividends and the assets of the corporation when the business is sold or liquidated. Having only one class of stock limits the usefulness of the S corporation as an investment vehicle. Investors typically like to receive special classes of shares that have preferences regarding corporate dividends and participation in the liquidation assets of the corporation when it is sold or dissolved.

- *An S corporation that loses its status cannot reelect it for five years.* An S corporation can lose its tax status—perhaps inadvertently, for example, if some shares fall into the hands of a disqualified shareholder. Even if the corporation again becomes qualified, it must wait until five years have elapsed from the year of the disqualification.

Two special tax effects not suffered by other pass-through tax entities, such as LLCs and limited partnerships, often present problems for S corporation shareholders:

1. S corporation shareholders can't receive special allocations of profits and losses. Corporate profits and losses must be split up proportionately to the percentage of shares owned by each shareholder. This point may sound technical or theoretical, but even for smaller businesses it has practical—and sometimes negative—significance.
   Example: Ted and Natalie want to go into business designing solar-powered hot tubs. Ted is the

"money" person and agrees to pitch in 80% of the first-year funds necessary to get the business going. Natalie is the hot tub and solar specialist and will contribute her skills as a solar systems and hot tub designer in overseeing the design and manufacture of the tubs. Ted and Natalie want a portion of her first-year salary to go toward paying for her initial shares in the enterprise. They also want Ted to get a disproportionate number of shares in recognition of the extra risk associated with putting cash into the business up front. Instead of getting two shares for every one of Natalie's shares, which reflects the ratio of Ted's cash to the value of Natalie's services, they want him to receive four shares for every share that she gets. Unfortunately, while this disproportionate doling out of shares may make a lot of practical sense, it is not permitted under S corporation rules.

2. *S corporation entity-level debt can't be passed along to shareholders.* An S corporation generally can't pass the potential tax benefits of borrowing money along to its shareholders. Here's a short rundown of this issue. In other pass-through entities, such as partnerships and LLCs, business debt (money borrowed by the business) increases the tax basis of the owners (we're simplifying here, but this is the effect of these special rules). This is good for a couple of reasons. First, the owners can deduct more losses from the business on their tax returns. Second, the higher the basis, the less gain—and the lower the taxes due—when owners sell their interests or the business itself is sold. This technical tax point is illustrated in the following example.
   Example: Mitch's Barbecue Pit Corp., organized as an S corporation, is a promising business in search of outside capital for expansion. A special blend of seasonings in Mitch's secret rib sauce consistently brings in overflow crowds to his two downtown locations. A number of people have expressed interest in investing in Mitch's expansion into other cities. It's expected that the venture will generate business losses in its first years immediately following the capital infusion. Mitch's will borrow funds

from banks to supplement cash reserves and working capital. At first, interested investors plan to simply use the early S corporation losses to offset other income on their personal tax returns. However, the investors' tax advisors warn that because S corporation debt cannot be used to increase the tax basis of the shares held by the investors (as it could in a partnership or LLC) investors won't get to write off all the expected business losses on their individual tax returns. This technical tax disadvantage of the S corporation ultimately results in Mitch having difficulty finding investors to fund his planned business expansion.

We won't go into this technical point further. Just realize that an S corporation has less flexibility than other pass-through entities to use borrowed money of the business to increase the tax deductions of the owners on their annual individual tax returns and lower the tax bite when the business or their interests in it are ultimately sold. These technical considerations can have important real-world effects. Your tax advisor can fill you in on the details if you want more information.

To summarize, even if S corporation status makes sense to gain the benefits of limited liability for the owners but keep the pass-through tax status for business income and losses (and maybe save on self-employment taxes as mentioned in the sidebar), it is often inconvenient or uncertain because of the requirements for adopting and keeping S corporation tax eligibility. By comparison, the tax status of an LLC is sustained and certain throughout the life of the business. Further, the above technical tax considerations make the S corporation less attractive to investors seeking to maximize the deductions and losses they can pass through the business and claim on their individual tax returns.

E. Business Entity Comparison Tables

In the tables below, we highlight and compare general and specific legal and tax traits of each type of business entity. We include a few technical issues in our chart (partially covered in Section D, above) to tweak your interest. Should any of the additional points of comparison seem relevant to your particular business operation, we encourage you to talk them over with a legal or tax professional.

BUSINESS ENTITY COMPARISON CHART—LEGAL CHARACTERISTICS

	Sole Proprietorship	General Partnership	Limited Partnership	C Corporation	S Corporation	LLC
Who owns business?	sole proprietor	general partners	general and limited partners	shareholders	same as C corporation	members
Personal liability for business debts	sole proprietor personally liable	general partners personally liable	only general partner(s) personally liable	no personal liability of shareholders	same as C corporation	no personal liability of members
Restrictions on kind of business	may engage in any lawful business	may engage in any lawful business	same as general partnership	some states prohibit formation of banking, insurance and other special businesses	same as C corporation —but excessive passive income (such as from rents, royalties, interest) can jeopardize tax status	same as C corporation, and some states may prohibit the performance of professional services
Restrictions on number of owners	only one sole proprietor	minimum two general partners	minimum one general partner and one limited partner	most states allow one-person corporations; some require two or more shareholders	same as C corporation, but no more than 75 shareholders permitted	One member allowed in all states
Who makes management decisions?	sole proprietor	general partners	general partner(s) only (not limited partners)	board of directors	same as C corporation	ordinarily members; or managers if manager-managed LLC
Who may legally obligate business?	sole proprietor	any general partner	any general partner (not limited partners)	directors and officers	same as C corporation	ordinarily any member; or any manager if manager-managed LLC
Effect on business if an owner dies or departs	dissolves automatically	dissolves automatically unless otherwise stated in partnership agreement	same as general partnership	no effect, unless corporation is solely owned	same as C corporation	in some states, dissolves unless remaining members vote to continue business

	Sole Proprietorship	General Partnership	Limited Partnership	C Corporation	S Corporation	LLC
Limits on transfer of ownership interests	free transferability	consent of all general partners usually required under partnership agreement	same as general partnership	transfer of stock may be limited under securities laws or restrictions in Articles of Incorporation or Bylaws	same as C corporation—but transfers limited to persons and entities that qualify as S corporation shareholders	unanimous consent of nontransferring members may be required under state law or operating agreement
Amount of organizational paperwork and ongoing legal formalities	minimal	minimal; partnership agreement recommended	startup filing required; partnership agreement recommended	startup filing required; Bylaws recommended; annual meetings of shareholders required	same as C corporation	startup filing required; operating agreement recommended; meetings not normally required
Source of startup funds	sole proprietor	general partners	general and limited partners	initial shareholders (in some states, cannot invest with promise to perform services or contribute cash in the future)	same as C corporation—but cannot issue different classes of stock with different financial provisions	members (may usually invest with promise to perform services or contribute cash in the future)
How business usually obtains capital, if needed	sole proprietor's contributions; working capital loans backed by personal assets of sole proprietor	capital contributions from general partners; business loans from banks backed by partnership and personal assets	investment capital from limited partners; bank loans backed by general partners' personal assets	flexible; outside investors may buy various classes of shares; bank loans backed by shareholders' personal assets (if corporation has insufficient credit history); may go public if needs substantial infusion of cash	generally same as C corporation—but can't have foreign, partnership or corporate shareholders; must limit number of shareholders to 75; can't offer different classes of stock to shares without voting rights	capital contributions from members; bank loans backed by members' personal assets (if LLC has insufficient credit history) investors except for

	Sole Proprietorship	General Partnership	Limited Partnership	C Corporation	S Corporation	LLC
Ease of conversion to another business form	may change form at will; legal paperwork involved	may change to limited partnership, corporation or LLC; legal paperwork involved	may change to corporation or LLC; legal paperwork involved	may change to S corporation by filing simple tax election; change to LLC can involve tax cost and legal complexity	generally same as C corporation—may terminate S tax status to become C corporation but cannot reelect S status for five years after	may change to general or limited partnership or corporation; legal paperwork involved
Is establishment or sale of ownership interests subject to federal and state securities laws?	generally not	generally not	yes, issuance or sale of limited partnership interests must qualify for securities laws exemptions, otherwise must register with federal and state securities laws offices	yes, issuance or transfer of stock subject to state and federal securities laws or must qualify for securities laws exemptions	same as C corporation	probably not, if all members are active in business
Who generally finds this the best way to do business?	owner who wants legal and managerial autonomy and minimal organizational red tape	joint owners who are not concerned with personal liability for business debts	joint owners who want partnership tax treatment and some nonmanaging investors; general partners must be willing to assume personal liability for business debts	owners who want limited liability and ability to split income between themselves and a separately taxed business	owners who want limited liability and individual tax rates to apply to business income; must be willing to meet initial and ongoing S corporation requirements	generally, owners who want limited liability and either pass-through or corporate taxation (see below); particularly beneficial for smaller, privately held businesses

BUSINESS ENTITY COMPARISON CHART—TAX CHARACTERISTICS

	Sole Proprietorship	General Partnership	Limited Partnership	C Corporation	S Corporation	LLC
How business profits are taxed	individual tax rates of sole proprietor	individual tax rates of general partners, unless business elects corporate treatment	individual tax rates of general and limited partners, unless business elects corporate tax treatment	split up and taxed at corporate rates and individual tax rates of shareholders	individual tax rates of shareholders	individual tax rates of members, unless LLC files IRS Form 8832 and elects corporate taxation
Tax-deductible fringe benefits available to owners who work in business	sole proprietor may set up IRA or Keogh retirement plan; may deduct a portion of medical insurance premiums	general partners and other employees may set up IRA or Keogh plans; may deduct a portion of medical insurance premiums	same as general partnership	tax-deductible fringe benefits for employee-shareholders; may fully deduct medical insurance premiums and reimburse employees' medical expenses	same as general partnership, but employee-shareholders owning 2% or more of stock are restricted from receiving corporate fringe benefits	owners get benefits associated with sole proprietorship (one-member LLCs) or partnership (multi-member LLCs)
Automatic tax status	yes	yes	yes, upon filing certificate of limited partnership with state corporate filing office	yes, upon filing Articles of Incorporation with state corporate filing office	no; must meet requirements and file tax election form with IRS (and sometimes state); revoked or terminated tax status cannot be re-elected for five years	yes, with IRS; unless LLC wishes to elect corporate tax treatment (by filing IRS Form 8832); most states treat LLC same as IRS for state income tax purposes
Are taxes due when business is formed?	generally tax-free to set up	generally tax-free to set up; individual income taxes may be due if a general partner contributes services as capital contribution	usually same as general partnership	generally not taxable unless existing business is incorporated and new owners are brought into the business who own more than 20% of the initial shares	same as C corporation	generally tax-free to set up; individual income taxes may be due if a member contributes services as capital contribution

	Sole Proprietorship	General Partnership	Limited Partnership	C Corporation	S Corporation	LLC
Deductibility of business losses	owner may use losses to deduct against other income on individual tax returns (subject to active-passive loss rules that apply to all businesses)	partners may use losses to deduct other income on individual tax returns if "at risk" for loss or debt and subject to active-passive loss rules	same as general partnership, but limited partners may only deduct "nonrecourse debts" (for which general partners are not specifically liable)	corporation may deduct business losses (shareholders may not deduct losses)	shareholders may deduct share of corporate losses on individual tax returns, but must comply with active-passive loss limitations; shareholders normally do not get the tax benefit of entity-level debt	follows sole proprietorship, partnership or corporate loss rules depending on tax status of LLC
Tax level when business is sold	personal tax level of owner	personal tax level of individual general partners	personal tax level of individual general and limited partners	two levels: shareholders and corporation may be taxed on sale of business	normally taxed at personal tax levels of individual shareholders, but corporate level tax sometimes due if S corporation was formerly a C corporation	follows sole proprietorship, partnership or corporate tax rules depending on tax status of LLC

Basic LLC Legalities

This chapter examines legal issues and procedures involved in setting up and running an LLC. Here you'll find chunks of information not presented elsewhere on a number of important LLC legal issues. If a particular legal area provokes special questions or concerns that you think apply to your LLC, you may wisely choose to do additional reading. (Check with a legal coach or tax advisor.)

A. Number of Members

You can have as many LLC members as you want (although we think that more than 35 is unwieldy). You can have only one member if you want. You indicate the ownership percentages of each member in your operating agreement, discussed in Chapters 5 and 6.

B. Paperwork Required to Set Up an LLC

Let's look at the basic legal documents and procedures involved with starting your own LLC. Fortunately, it's a simple process, meaning that it should take you relatively little time to turn your idea of forming an LLC into a legal reality.

One person may prepare and file the paperwork. Generally, one person may prepare, sign and file the basic documents to set up an LLC. This person need not be a member of the LLC, but must turn the reins of management over to LLC members or a management team after the LLC is formed. Of course, what the legislatures have in mind is that a lawyer can do the filing for you—which is fine if that's what you want. Normally, you can just as well prepare the paperwork yourself and drop it in the nearest mailbox.

1. LLC Articles of Organization

The only formal legal step normally required to create an LLC is to prepare and file LLC Articles of Organization with your state's LLC filing office. A few states require an additional step: the publication in a local newspaper of a simple notice of intention to form an LLC prior to filing your Articles. (See your state sheet in Appendix A for particulars.)

The LLC filing office is usually the same one that handles your state's corporate filings, typically the Department or Secretary of State's office, located in each state's capital city. Larger states usually have branch filing offices in secondary cities as well.

LLC Articles of Organization don't have to be lengthy or complex. In fact, you can usually prepare your own in just a few minutes by filling in the blanks and checking the boxes on a relatively simple form provided by your state's LLC filing office. Typically, you need only specify a few basic details about your LLC, such as its name, principal office address, agent and office for receiving legal papers, and the names of its initial members (or managers, if you're designating a special management team to run the LLC).

Instructions for completing Articles of Organization. We provide a sample LLC Articles of Organization form with instructions, and show you how to get your state's form to fill in and file in Chapter 4.

2. LLC Operating Agreement

An LLC should always create a written operating agreement to define the basic rights and responsibilities of LLC members (and managers, if you decide to form a manager-run LLC—more on this option later).

Although not advisable, an LLC that is registered with your state may be operated on a handshake without a formal operating agreement among the owners. No matter how busy you are, we believe it's a big mistake to delay preparing an operating agreement. Without a written agreement to refer to, you may get stuck in a crisis trying to answer such questions as:
- When members are faced with an important management decision, does each get one vote, or do they vote according to their percentage interests in the LLC?
- Are owners expected to make additional capital contributions (the money invested in the business) if the LLC needs additional operating capital?
- Are owners entitled to periodic draws from the profits of the business?
- Will interest be paid to the owners on their capital contributions?
- May members leave the LLC any time they wish and expect an immediate payout of their capital contributions?
- How much should an owner be paid when he or she decides to leave the business?
- Is a departing owner allowed to sell an interest to an outsider?

Please believe us when we say that these kinds of unanswered questions can, and frequently do, come back to haunt small businesses. They are far better addressed in a written operating agreement, signed around the time your new LLC entity is created.

Instructions for completing LLC operating agreements. Chapters 5 and 6 provide instructions for completing two different types of operating agreements included in Appendix D.

C. Responsibility for Managing an LLC

At least one person needs to be responsible for overall management of a business, and the LLC is no exception. Under most states' default legal rules, all members (owners) are automatically responsible for managing the business (this arrangement is called "member-management"), unless they specifically appoint one or more members and/or nonmembers to manage the LLC (this option is called "manager-management").

1. Member-Managed or Manager-Managed LLC?

Most LLC owners will choose member-management, not manager-management. The reason is that most smaller LLCs won't want an extra (management) level of bureaucracy; they'll want to let the LLC members run the business they own without oversight by or interference from a separate management team. So, don't get too distracted by manager-management possibilities. Unless you are planning to bring in outside investors who want a management role in your business, which might be appropriate if you own an interest in a sideline business that you prefer be operated by others, it's likely that you'll naturally decide to let all your members run your LLC.

Tax Consequence: But take note of the fact that LLC members who work 500 hours or less in the business may be able to avoid payment of self-employment taxes on their share of LLC profits if the LLC is *manager-managed* and the member is not selected as one of its managers. If you set up a member-managed LLC, it appears that federal regulations require even nonvoting members of a member-managed

LLC to pay self-employment taxes (see Chapter 3, Section C and ask your tax advisor).

Securities Law Consequence: We cover the securities law implications of LLC management choices in Section E below. For now, just realize if one or more of your members does not participate in management—that is, if you choose a manager-management structure for your LLC—membership interests in your LLC may be considered "securities," and you may need to comply with extra federal and state securities procedures when setting up your LLC.

NONVOTING VS. NONMANAGING MEMBERS

Members are given special voting rights under state law, which include voting to amend the articles or operating agreement of the LLC, to merge or dissolve the LLC, to approve the admission of new members, and to approve the transfer of an LLC membership by an existing member to an outsider. Further, in manager-managed LLCs, members have a right to vote to elect or reelect the managers (even though some members may also be managers and can vote to reelect themselves). Many of these voting rights can be eliminated or restricted in LLC articles or an operating agreement by giving the member no voting power in the LLC operating agreement. Even here, though, some states require the vote, and sometimes approval, of all or a majority of members to certain major structural changes to the LLC, such as amending the articles or operating agreement or dissolving the LLC, no matter what your operating agreement says. This issue of membership voting power leads to the following question: Is eliminating the voting power of a member the same thing as making the member a nonmanaging member? The answer, in our view, is no. State LLC statutes, for the most part, treat members' voting rights as separate from members' management responsibilities, and make all LLC members of a member-managed LLC responsible for managing the LLC without reference to specific voting rights of the member. For example, state law typically says that all members of a member-managed LLC are charged with managing it

in good faith, and can act as "agents" of the LLC by binding it to a contract or business deal with outsiders.

Another way to look at this issue is to think of members as you would the shareholders (owners) of a corporation. We all know that shareholders can be given voting or nonvoting shares in a corporation, but the people responsible for management of a corporation are the board of directors, regardless of the types of shares (voting or nonvoting) held by the owners. Unless you select a separate management team for your LLC—by choosing a manager-management structure—state law pretty much treats your members as the "board of directors" of your LLC, each of whom is responsible for its management (without considering whether these LLC members also have specific voting rights under state law or your operating agreement). In fact, in some states like North Dakota, this corporate analogy is embodied in the state LLC law, with the managers of the LLC (whether the LLC is member- or manager-managed) called the "Board of Governors." Finally, one of the primary voting rights of a member in a manager-managed LLC is the right to vote for the election or reelection of the managers—clearly, state law intends to make membership voting rights separate from management power, just as in the corporate context where voting shareholders get to vote for the election of the board of directors.

LLC LACKING OPERATING AGREEMENT IS CONTROLLED BY STATE LLC STATUTES

If you run your LLC without an operating agreement, your state's LLC statute will control basic elements of how your LLC is run and terminated. Your state's LLC statutes may not reflect the choices you want to make for your LLC. For example, typical state statutes specify that an LLC is managed by the members (owners). In addition, most states establish that profits and losses are to be divided up among the members equally, regardless of each member's capital contribution.

Example: Yvonne and Joe form an LLC with Yvonne contributing 30% of the capital to get started and Joe contributing 70%. Under their state's default rule, Yvonne and Joe each would be entitled to receive one-half the profits of the LLC each year, even though they pay disproportionate amounts to get the LLC up and running. If Yvonne and Joe prepare their own operating agreement, however, they can divide profits in a way they consider more equitable.

2. Selection and Removal of Members and Managers

Initial members or managers of the LLC are usually named in the Articles of Organization filed with the state LLC filing office. As a default rule in most states, which operates unless your operating agreement says something else, new members can only be admitted by the vote of all members of the LLC. If your LLC has chosen manager-management, the default rule is that anyone selected to replace an initial manager must be voted in by a majority of the members. But you can vary this latter rule to let the managers (by a majority or greater vote), rather than the members, vote to fill a manager vacancy.

State law is usually silent on the issue of how and why members or managers of an LLC may be removed. Under typical provisions found in LLC operating agreements, members cannot be removed from the LLC member roster except for specific reasons, such as bankruptcy, incapacity or another listed reason, and then only with the vote of all other members.

Manager removal is usually easier under most operating agreements, and often is allowed "without cause" (for any or no particular reason) upon a vote of the membership. Managers are also typically elected by the members to specific terms of office—in other words, they can be voted out of office at the expiration of their management term if the members elect someone else in their place.

MANAGER-MANAGED LLC OPTIONS

If you wish to elect a special management team for your LLC (instead of staying with the default structure of management by all members—called member-management), a group of managers must be selected. These are the options when selecting managers in such a manager-managed LLC:

- *You can select members as managers.* Some larger LLCs—for example, those with passive investors who will not work in the business—may decide to delegate management to the active members only, naming them as managers of the manager-managed LLC.

- *Select only nonmembers.* Some LLCs decide that management should consist exclusively of nonmembers with particular expertise in the business of the LLC (by hiring an outside consultant or an LLC officer as manager).

- *Select some or all LLC members, plus nonmembers as managers.* Still other LLCs may settle for a combination of members, investors and nonmember managers.

3. Legal Authority of LLC Members and Managers

Generally, the members (if your LLC is member-managed) or managers (if the LLC is manager-managed), or other duly appointed representative (such as an officer) of the LLC can legally bind the LLC to a contract, business transaction or course of action, as long as the transaction is within the LLC's normal scope of business. In other words, one member, manager or officer has the unfettered right to commit the LLC to a loan, debt or other obligation. A common legal exception states that a contract with an outsider who knows, or should have known, that the LLC agent does not have specific authority for a transaction is not binding on the LLC. Unfortunately, this type of knowledge is hard to prove.

Example: Gary is a member and VP of Fish and Fritters Fast Foods, LLC ("4F")—a member-managed LLC. He orders $500 in stationery from Joe's Stationery Supply Company, a local merchant, consisting of $400 of LLC stationery and $100 of personal letterhead. When he places the order, he does so on behalf of his LLC, and charges the bill to his LLC's account. Joe gets a check from 4F for $400, with a note from the LLC accounts payable officer advising Joe to collect the $100 balance from Gary because the order for personal letterhead was not approved by the LLC. Would a small claims court let Joe recover the $100 balance from the LLC itself? Probably. Joe would normally be justified in believing that an officer of the LLC had authority to place the full order on behalf of the LLC, unless Gary specifically told Joe that the extra stationery should be billed to him alone.

Generally, it's safest to assume that any contract or transaction signed on behalf of your LLC by anyone in management will be legally binding. This legal authority should not present a problem if you make sure you choose the right people to be members or managers of your LLC.

If you're uncomfortable with the idea that others could obligate your business, an LLC is probably not the right form of business for you. You may want to stick to a sole proprietorship, where you have the only say, or to a limited partnership, where you can get full management authority if you become the only general partner.

4. Member and Manager Voting Rules

The default laws of most states (those that apply unless your operating agreement says otherwise) specify that members' voting rights are allocated according to the capital contributions made by each member (some states use members' interests in LLC profits, which may be different from capital interests, as the default measure of member voting rights). In other words, a member contributing 50% of the capital to the LLC usually gets 50% of the voting power of the LLC. But in some states, the default voting right rule is that members are given voting rights on a per capita basis (one vote per member) if the LLC operating agreement doesn't set a different standard.

Under state default rules, most LLC matters brought to a vote of the members must be approved by at least a majority of the LLC's voting power—that is, by more than 50% of the full voting interests of the members.

Example: Sit-u-ational Awareness, LLC, a three-member computer furniture ergonomics consulting firm, has parceled out its voting interests to the three owners as follows: Kathlyn—30%, Evan—25% and Alyson—45%. The vote of at least two of the three members is necessary to obtain a majority and decide an issue brought to the membership for resolution.

If the LLC is manager-managed, states typically give managers one vote each, with a majority-manager vote required to approve a decision.

Example: Dollars to Donuts, LLC, an emerging franchiser and promoter of the one-buck-per-dozen-donut discount offer on every tenth purchase, is owned by four entrepreneurs, but managed by a team of five persons consisting of the four members and a nonmember pastry chef, Pierre (who brings the recipe for a delectable French twist pastry—the hallmark of the enterprise—to the business, plus his formidable baking skills). When an important management vote needs to be made, each manager gets one vote, and the vote of at least three of the five managers is required to resolve the matter. Pierre doesn't function as a fifth wheel on the management team—he becomes the all-important deadlock-breaking vote whenever the four owners don't see eye-to-eye and split their votes two-to-two.

Remember, as with most state law rules mentioned in this chapter, these are default member and manager voting rules. You can override them by defining voting rights any way you wish in your operating agreement.

Special voting rules for certain important LLC matters. State LLC statutes contain special voting rules concerning the membership vote required to admit members into the LLC who have been transferred an LLC membership interest from a former member, and the vote necessary to continue the LLC after a member dies, resigns or is expelled. These rules are carryovers from the days when the IRS required LLCs to establish special voting procedures to qualify for pass-through tax status. Nonetheless, until the states repeal these (now unnecessary) voting rules, your operating agreement must conform to these special provisions. We show you how to do this in Chapters 5 and 6.

Nonvoting Members: You can have one or more nonvoting members—just specify in your operating agreement that the nonvoting member has zero votes. Just realize that even if you give a member

zero votes, the nonvoting member may be given some voting power in special situations under your state's LLC statute. For example, it is common for state law to require the votes, if not approval, of all LLC members to amendments to the LLC Articles of Organization or operating agreement, in a decision to dissolve the LLC, or in other significant legal matters involving changes to the structure of the LLC.

5. Membership and Management Meetings

Most states do not give mandatory rules for when and how membership meetings should take place. It's ordinarily up to you to come up with your own rules for the frequency, notification procedures and conduct of membership meetings.

Regular LLC meetings are not required using the forms in this book (although you can require meetings if you're so inclined), because we believe most smaller LLCs are better off spending their time taking care of business and making money, rather than filling up their records books with page upon page of formal LLC meetings. Ordinarily, you should need to meet for formal LLC meetings (which are recorded in written minutes) only in situations such as these:

- An important legal or tax formality needs to be approved and recorded (the LLC is undertaking a legal or tax election that should be documented in your LLC records, such as approving the buy-back of a departing member's interest in the LLC).
- You need to meet face-to-face with your full membership and formally approve an out-of-the-ordinary or disputed business decision (sell important LLC assets or dissolve the LLC contrary to the wishes of some of the members).
- You have elected a management team (set up a manager-managed LLC) and need to reelect them to another term (more on this just below).

Membership meeting to elect managers if your LLC is manager-managed. States typically say that members must elect the managers at a membership meeting, without specifying terms of office for managers or how often members should meet to elect or reelect managers. Some states do limit the term for managers to one year unless you override it in your operating agreement. If your LLC is manager-managed and you adopt a one-year term for your managers, you will want to hold annual membership meetings to reelect your managers. Generally, the appointment of managers is a routine task for most LLCs unless a manager is withdrawing or is not performing satisfactorily.

For forms and instructions, plus state-by-state legal requirements, for holding LLC meetings and taking care of ongoing LLC business, see *Your Limited Liability Company: An Operating Manual,* by Anthony Mancuso (Nolo).

D. Member and Manager Liability to Insiders and Outsiders

One of the nicest parts of forming an LLC is the general immunity from personal liability the members and managers enjoy. But it's important to realize that this immunity has its limits; there are some situations in which a person acting as an LLC member or manager may end up liable to the LLC, other members or managers, or even outsiders. We discuss these exceptions below.

1. LLC Members and Managers Must Act in Good Faith Towards Each Other

Members of a member-managed LLC and managers of a manager-managed LLC have a legal obligation in managing the LLC to act in good faith, in the best interests of the LLC and its members. In legal jargon, this duty is known as their "duty of care." It is similar to the obligation corporate directors have to a corporation.

Courts have interpreted this duty in the corporate context by promulgating the "business judgment rule." This says that in making management decisions, honest business mistakes will not subject managers and members to personal liability. Another way of saying this is that, under this rule, decisions that have some rational basis—based upon facts known to managers and members or presented to them in a report from someone else with superior knowledge—should not give rise to personal liability if they turn out to be wrongheaded and result in financial loss to other members or to the LLC.

Example: Robert and Juliet are two of three owners of the Lucky Lock Company LLC—a member-managed LLC. They vote at a management meeting to use one-quarter of the company's accumulated earnings to market and sell Bob's Big-Lock, a unique, three-by-five-foot lock plate with a neon clock display that Bob invented. Greg, the third owner at the meeting, is against the idea of committing company funds to promote a device with such an uncertain future. The uncertainty of the profitability of Bob's Big-Lock is fully discussed at the membership meeting, but Greg is outvoted two-to-one by his co-owners. The clock-lock idea catches on slowly, and the project loses money big time. Can Greg sue the other owners personally for their bad business judgment? As long as Bob and Juliet made a bad business decision without underhandedness, concealment or misrepresentation of facts, or other fraud or illegality, the answer should be "no" under the business judgment rule. But let's say Bob and Juliet knew that certain features of the purported master-timepiece would be difficult to produce, yet kept this knowledge from Greg when they pitched Bob's Big-Lock idea. Greg may be able to recover some or all of the clock-loss money personally from Bob and Juliet for failing to disclose all material facts at the management meeting.

The above example points out a basic LLC legal rule: Full and fair disclosure of facts is part and parcel of an LLC member/manager's duty to the LLC—a duty that isn't mitigated or otherwise lessened by the business judgment rule.

2. Liability to Other Members for Unjustifiable Loss

Most states have provisions in their LLC act that permit members to sue other members or managers on behalf of (in the name of) the LLC. Often called "derivative actions" in legal lingo, these can occur if a member feels that other members or managers caused unjustifiable financial loss to the LLC.

Example: Let's use the same Lucky Lock Company LLC described above. But this time, members Bob and Juliet siphon off some of the funds for themselves, personally, rather than using them to prototype and sell Bob's Big-Lock. Bob and Juliet can expect to be sued by and be held personally liable to the LLC and/or to Greg for the amount of the diverted funds.

Many states have indemnification provisions in their LLC laws. This fancy legal word means that the LLC will pay the legal expenses, settlements, court judgment awards, fines, fees and other liabilities personally assessed or awarded against an LLC member or manager for ill-advised management decisions or other liability-causing events. Generally, state rules say that the person to be indemnified must have acted in good faith, in the best interests of the LLC, before he or she can be reimbursed or advanced legal expenses or receive other indemnification. And, as you might guess, intentional misconduct, fraud and illegal acts normally can't be covered under these statutes. Indemnification provisions vary and are technical, so check with an LLC legal coach or take a closer look at your state's LLC indemnification statute if this area of LLC law interests you.

3. Member and Manager Liability to Outsiders

No matter how an LLC is managed—whether by LLC members or a management team—one basic limited liability rule applies. LLC members and managers are not normally personally responsible to outsiders for any mistakes in management that they make.

Example: A customer of Jen & Len's Computers LLC sues the company, as well as each owner personally, for not fixing a problem with his two-gigabyte hard drive, resulting in 40 hours of extra work for her to get the data back on line. Are Jen and Len personally liable to the customer? No. Limited liability should protect them.

But what about torts? (Here we're talking about the legal, not edible, kind.) Basically, a tort is a negligent act that harms another person and causes monetary loss—for example, running a red light, which causes an accident and damages another automobile. Members of an LLC, like corporate directors, partners and all other business managers, can be personally liable for financial loss caused by their tortious behavior. Whether working for an LLC as an employee or acting in the capacity of a member, if a member does something negligently, and the action causes harm to another person or that person's property, the member can be held personally liable for the damage.

Example: Otto, one of the two employee/members of Otto's Oughto Order Auto Parts Supply LLC, gets in his Mazda Miata to pick up a throwout bearing for a customer's Mercedes station wagon. On the way, he *negligently sideswipes a slow-moving Geo, a stunt that results in a $5,000 repair bill to the Geo owner and a $25,000 medical claim for whiplash to George, the Geo driver. Otto can be held personally liable for $30,000.*

Of course, insurance—commercial, automotive, workers' compensation or even the employee's individual homeowner policy—may cover some or all damage caused by LLC manager or worker torts. Check LLC and personal insurance policies to see what protection may be available to you in the event of an accident.

LLCs SHOULD HAVE LIABILITY INSURANCE COVERAGE

Our advice is to get reliable liability insurance to cover potential personal and business liabilities arising from the LLC's operations. Typically, a commercial general liability insurance policy will cover:

• tort liability (bodily injury and property damage, so-called "slip-and-fall" coverage) caused by business owners and employees in the course of business or on the business premises, and

• fire, theft, catastrophe and the like.

Most smaller LLCs, at least to begin with, rely primarily on their commercial liability insurance to protect them in the event of lawsuits brought by outsiders. They may go beyond this basic coverage later if they can afford to supplement it with personal liability policies for members or other managers. Such policies can protect members and managers from personal liability for torts to outsiders as well as inside liability to the LLC for losses caused by members' or managers' faulty decisions.

Make sure you look for newer policies that recognize the legal status of your LLC and its members. Because LLCs are relatively new, insurance companies may need to adapt their current corporate director and officer errors and omissions policies for use by LLC members and managers.

E. Are LLC Membership Interests Considered Securities?

When someone buys into or invests in an LLC, they are being sold an interest in the business. Is this sale of an LLC interest the sale of a "security" within the meaning of state or federal law? If it is, it must either be registered at the federal level—with the Securities and Exchange Commission—and with the state securities office, or it must be eligible for an exemption from these federal and state securities registration requirements.

The question of whether and under what circumstances LLC memberships may be a security interest is too new to provide a black-and-white analysis, but we'll mention a few basic expectations of the securities law treatment of LLCs. A helpful generalization is that when the owner of an interest in a business relies on his or her own efforts to make a profit, the interest normally is not a security interest under federal and state law. Conversely, if a person invests in a business with the expectation of making money from others' efforts, federal and state statutes as well as the courts usually treat the interest purchased with the investment as a security.

1. Member-Managed LLCs and Securities Laws

If you and your co-owners plan to set up a member-managed LLC— where, by definition, all members are legally responsible for its management—it is likely that your membership interests will not be treated as securities. Why? Because all members plan to make a profit in the business from their own efforts, not the efforts of others. California is one state that has enacted legislation that says that membership interests in an LLC where *all* members actively participate in management are not securities under state law. Other states are starting to follow this trend, but it is too soon to tell if the majority of states will jump on the "member-management" bandwagon.

2. Manager-Managed LLCs and Securities Laws

If you set up a manager-managed LLC, it is likely that the interests of at least the nonmanaging members will be treated as securities under state and federal law. It's even possible that the feds and the state will treat all membership interests as securities (securities agencies have been known to take an "all-or-none" position—either all LLC memberships are exempted from the definition of securities or none are).

Don't give up even if you decide to form a manager-managed LLC or your LLC membership interests fall within the definition of "securities." There are other exemptions from securities that your LLC may qualify for if it is a one-state operation or it has a limited membership. Below is a summary of the most commonly relied upon federal securities law exemptions that may apply to your LLC. Many states either defer to or adopt one or more of these federal exemptions in their securities statutes and regulations. Note that the first two exemptions do not require the filing of any paperwork—you informally rely on them without notification to any securities agency.

- *Private placements.* Under federal statutes and case (court-developed) law, the selling of securities privately—without advertising or promotion—to a limited number of people may be eligible for the private placement exemption contained in Section 4(2) of the federal Securities Act of 1933. You stand a better chance of getting this exemption if transfers of the securities—memberships—are restricted (for example, language restricting transfer of the stock is placed on all membership certificates and a conspicuous notation is made in the LLC membership book that memberships are non-transferable) and if persons buying memberships are doing so for themselves (that is, not for resale to other investors). Many smaller LLCs will neatly fit within this traditional securities law exemption because memberships are issued to a limited number of people (the number 35 is often used, but not written into this section of law), memberships are a personal investment and transfer of memberships to outsiders is restricted to satisfy tax requirements (for more on this point, see Chapter 3, Section B4).

- *One-state sales.* Another federal exemption, the intrastate offering exemption contained in Section 3(a)(11) of the Securities Act, exempts from registration the offer and sale of securities made within one state only. If you privately offer and sell memberships within one state to residents of that state only, you may qualify for this exemption from federal registration of your memberships.

- *Regulation D.* Regulation D is a formal process. It requires that you follow specific requirements contained in the Regulation D statutes and file a Form D with the Securities and Exchange Commission (SEC). When using Regulation D, you can seek an exemption under one of three rules: Rules 504, 505 or 506. We won't cover the requirements of each rule, but offer the following gloss: You stand a good chance of qualifying under one of the Regulation D rules if you privately offer and sell a small (measured in dollar value; the limits vary from $1 million to $5 million, although Rule 506 does not have a monetary limit) amount of memberships to 35 or fewer people, each of whom is a close personal friend, family member or business associate or has the capability to protect his or her own interests (because of past investment history or current and anticipated net worth and income earning capacity). In addition, you must place restrictions on the transfer of your LLC memberships (language on membership certificates and in LLC membership records that limits transfers), as explained in the discussion above of the Section 4(2) private placement exemption.

Again, state law securities exemptions tend to parallel one or more of the federal exemptions. For example, a state may exempt from registration the private sale of securities solely within the state or to a limited number of persons, such as 10 or 35. In some states, you may need to file an exemption form, sometimes along with a filing fee.

3. How Should You Handle Securities Law Issues?

Securities laws are meant to protect investors from unscrupulous operators, not active business owners from the results of their own business decisions. Your decision on how to approach securities law issues will be a personal decision, based upon the particular facts of your LLC formation and your own personal comfort level in this unsettled area of law. For example, if you're setting up a small LLC with your spouse and you plan to actively run the business yourself (say a car repair service, retail outlet or consulting business), you will very likely decide that you are exempt from securities laws and need not file paperwork. Similarly, if you are setting up your LLCs with a handful of owners who know one another and have worked together in the past and who will actively run the LLC, you may likely conclude that you are also on safe legal ground if you do not treat your memberships as securities.

If, however, you bring in outside LLC members who are not active in the day-to-day business of the LLC, or if you bring in outside managers, we strongly recommend making sure your LLC qualifies from exemptions from both federal and state securities laws. You can do your own research in this area, but the securities laws are murky, and the newness of the LLC throws a little extra mud in the water.

The LLC securities law area is an evolving one. The best way to find out the latest LLC securities laws rules in your state is to call the State Securities Board (or similar agency) and ask for a copy of state laws and regulations dealing with the issuance and sale of LLC membership interests. If you don't want to deal with this admittedly complex analysis, *call a small business lawyer.* Brainstorming with an LLC legal coach to learn the latest legal rules and come up with a safe securities law approach should be well worth the estimated one to three hours' worth of legal fees necessary to put this technical issue to rest. (See Chapter 8, Section B, for guidelines to follow when searching for an LLC legal coach.)

THE MOST IMPORTANT SECURITIES LAW RULE OF ALL: DISCLOSE, DISCLOSE, DISCLOSE!

One important securities law rule always applies to any business venture: Always fully disclose all pertinent facts to potential investors. Let everyone know all known and foreseeable risks of investing in your enterprise, and make all financial records available to prospective purchasers. If you go out of your way to disclose all possible risks of investment, you'll stand a much better chance of fending off securities law problems later if a member or investor starts feeling surly about lower-than-expected profits or returns from the LLC.

CHAPTER 3

Tax Aspects of Forming an LLC

This chapter covers the tax treatment of LLCs. The good news is that the IRS now lets LLC owners decide for themselves whether their LLC will be taxed as a pass-through tax entity (like a partnership or sole proprietorship) or as a corporation.

A. Most LLC Owners Prefer Pass-Through Tax Status (or Sole Proprietorship Status for a Sole Proprietor)

Pass-through tax status allows you to enjoy the tax advantages of a partnership. Business income is taxed just once when it is distributed as profits to the members of the LLC, or allocated to each member's LLC account. The LLC members pay individual income taxes on these profits. There is no worry about paying separate taxes on business income at the business entity level as a corporation does, and then having business profits taxed a second time when distributed to the owners as profits (as is the case when a corporation pays a dividend to shareholders). For these reasons,. LLC owners usually decide that pass-through tax treatment is the best way to go. If this is your choice, there is no need to file any "electing tax entity" tax papers with the IRS.

LLCs Can Elect Corporate Tax Treatment: If your LLC members decide that being taxed like a corporation is what they want—with separate corporate tax rates applied to net income left in the business (not paid out as salaries and other deductible expenses)—you can obtain this result by filing IRS Form 8832 as explained in the sidebar. But remember—this is a "tax status," not a "legal status," election—even if you elect corporate tax status, your limited liability company will still be treated as an LLC under state law even after you elect corporate income tax treatment for your LLC.

NEW IRS CHECK-THE-BOX TAX CLASSIFICATION SCHEME FOR LLCs WISHING TO BE TAXED AS CORPORATIONS

The IRS has acknowledged that the traditional tax rules for distinguishing between corporations and pass-through tax entities (partnerships and LLCs) do not serve any useful purpose. Accordingly, it now agrees that LLCs will be treated as pass-through tax entities (like partnerships for multi-member LLCs; like sole proprietorships for one-member LLCs) unless they file IRS Form 8832 electing to be taxed like a corporation. If you wish to make this election, you will find a tear-out copy of this form, with instructions, in Appendix D. We include the text of the IRS tax classification regulations, upon which this form is based, in Appendix B.

State laws are still catching up with IRS rules. The IRS "check-the-box" tax system for business entities eliminates a lot of technical tax hurdles and makes it automatic for LLC organizers to be taxed as a pass-through entity. But some state LLC laws have not caught up—they still contain the technical requirements the IRS used to insist on before LLC members could qualify for pass-through tax status. What this means is you still may be required, under your state's LLC law, to include special provisions in your LLC operating agreement. In a few years, these rules will undoubtedly be swept away in every state. In the meantime, don't worry—we clearly explain how your LLC can easily comply with any of these "leftover" state laws.

B. How LLCs Report and Pay Federal Income Taxes

We have established the broad proposition that tax treatment of an LLC depends on whether the business entity wishes to be taxed as a pass-through entity (partnership for multi-member LLCs or sole proprietorship for one-member LLCs) or a corporation. In this section, we look at what, if anything, your LLC needs to do to qualify for the type of tax status it prefers.

1. *If an LLC wants pass-through tax status:* If an LLC has more than one owner (member), and does not elect to be taxed as a corporation by filing IRS Form 8832, it is automatically treated as a partnership for federal tax purposes (we discuss state income tax treatment of LLCs in Section D, below). In short, no election form needs to be filed with the IRS to achieve this result. Each tax year, your LLC must prepare and file the same tax forms used by a partnership—IRS Form 1065, *U.S. Partnership Return of Income,* which includes a Schedule K showing the allocation of profits, losses, credits and deductions passed through to your members. Your LLC also must prepare and distribute to each member a Schedule K-1 form, which shows each member's allocation of LLC profits, losses, credits and deductions. The members, in turn, use this Schedule K-1 information to complete in their annual 1040 income tax returns.

   If an LLC has one member (as permitted in most states—see Chapter 2, Section A), and it has not elected to be taxed as a corporation using IRS Form 8832, the IRS treats the LLC as a sole proprietorship. This means business profits (and losses, credits and deductions) are reported on the Schedule C, "Profit or Loss From a Business," of the sole member's individual income tax return.

2. *If an LLC wants corporate tax status:* If an LLC, whether owned by one or more members, wants corporate tax treatment, it must check the "corporation" box on IRS Form 8832 (the line next to this box reads: "A domestic eligible entity electing to be classified as an association taxable as a corporation"). The election takes effect on the date you specify on the form, but this date cannot be more than 75 days before or more than 12 months after the date the form is filed. In other words, for a new LLC that wishes to start out being taxed as a corporation, this election should be filed within 75 days of the date its articles of organization are filed with the state LLC filing office. An election to be taxed as a corporation cannot normally be changed for 60 months, but there are exceptions to this 5-year rule—for example, the LLC can ask to change its tax status within the 5 years of its election if there has been a fifty percent or greater change in LLC ownership.

An LLC that has elected to be taxed as a corporation must file a corporate tax return, IRS Form 1120, for each year the corporate tax election is in effect. The LLC pays income taxes on profits left in the business at corporate income tax rates, which range from 15% to 25% of net taxable incomes roughly below $75,000. Profits above this threshold are taxed at rates of up to 34% on taxable incomes up to $10 million (with a 39% rate "bubble" on taxable incomes between $100,001—$335,000, which eliminates the benefit of the lower 15% and 25% tax rates). Higher corporate tax rates of 35% and 38% apply to net taxable incomes of $10 million or more. Because of the low corporate tax rates on relatively low taxable incomes, and because some LLCs want to keep profits in the business anyway—for example, for expansion purposes or because it is tied up in inventory—electing corporate tax treatment may result in a net tax savings. This savings results from the fact that the 15% and 25% rates applied to profits left in a LLC that elects corporate tax treatment are almost surely lower than the individual tax rates of the LLC members, which would apply to all LLC profits if the LLC does not elect to be taxed as a corporation (most individuals pay income taxes at rates of 25% to 33% and higher; the top individual rate is 35%).

> *Example: Sally and Randolph run their own lumber supply LLC (S & R Wood, LLC), and have elected corporate tax treatment for their LLC knowing that they will need to keep profits in the business to buy new equipment and increase inventory. Sales for the year are $1.2 million, and after payment of business expenses including salaries and bonuses to the working members of the LLC, the LLC shows a $70,000 net taxable profit. This is taxed at the corporate rates of 15% on the first $50,000 and 25% on the next $20,000. If Sally and Randy had not elected corporate tax treatment for their LLC, these profits would be passed along to them and taxed at their undoubtedly higher individual income tax rates.*

A FLAT CORPORATE TAX RATE APPLIES TO CERTAIN PROFESSIONAL SERVICE LLCs THAT ELECT CORPORATE TAX TREATMENT

If your LLC elects corporate tax treatment and it provides professional services in the fields of health, law, engineering, architecture, accounting, actuarial science, performing arts or consulting, a flat federal corporate income tax rate of 35% applies to all its net taxable income. Or, put another way, if these particular professional service LLCs choose to be taxed as corporations, they are not eligible for the lower graduated corporate income tax rates of 15% and 25% that apply to most corporations.

C. LLCs and Self-Employment Taxes

The issue of the payment of federal self-employment taxes on LLC members' profits is a contentious and changing one. Basically, the rule (with some exceptions—see below) is that all income a member of an LLC receives is subject to self-employment tax. This is a major issue for some LLC organizers who feel that the current self-employment tax rate of 15.3% is far too high. In fact, some disgruntled business organizers choose to form an S corporation instead of an LLC because S corporation shareholders are only required to pay self-employment taxes on money paid to them as compensation for services, not on profits that automatically pass through the S corporation to them (see Chapter 1, Section D5).

Specifically, the most recent federal tax regulations on this point (Proposed Treasury Regulation Section 1.402(a)-2(h)(2) and following) say you, as an LLC member, must pay self-employment taxes (currently 15.3%) on your entire share of LLC profits if *any one* of the following four conditions apply.

1. You participate in the trade or business for more than 500 hours during the LLC's tax year. In short, if you work 501 hours or more for the LLC, you will have to pay self-employment taxes under current IRS rules.

2. You work in your LLC (even if you work less than 501 hours) and it renders professional services in the fields of health, law, engineering, architecture, accounting, actuarial science, or consulting.

3. You have personal liability for the debts of or claims against the LLC by reason of being a member. Since, by definition, your LLC protects you from personal liability for business debts, you should be able to avoid this condition.

4. You have authority to execute contracts on behalf of your LLC. Under the law of most states, all members of a member-managed LLC have this type of "agency" authority, but non-

managing members in a manager-managed LLC do not. In other words, if you can avoid the three conditions listed above, it may make sense for you to set up a manager-managed LLC. By so doing, members not appointed as managers should avoid this condition and not have to pay self-employment taxes on their share of LLC profits.

These tax rules may change: Lots of people have pointed to the absurdity of these LLC tax rules (especially in light of the fact that the S corporation rules are different), which should mean, logically, that they will be changed (but, of course, there are lots of other absurd tax laws, so logic doesn't always prevail). If this area of tax law is of concern to you, check to see if new rules are in place.

D. State Law and the Tax Treatment of LLCs

As you know, LLCs are regulated by state law. This means you must organize and operate your LLC under the provisions of your state's LLC Act in addition to following the federal tax rules. The main sources of state regulation that impact an LLCs tax treatment can be found in the state's LLC Act and in its tax statutes and regulations.

1. State LLC Act Provisions Related to an LLC's Tax Status

In past years, many states included provisions in their LLC Acts designed to help you achieve favorable tax status with the IRS (the IRS used to require that LLCs be organized substantially different than

corporations). This may sound good, but these state laws are no longer necessary—as we've explained, the IRS now lets you choose how your LLC will be taxed—as a pass-through entity or as a corporation. The result is that existing state statutes that require your LLC to be set up and operated a certain way no longer serve a useful purpose, and have become a nuisance. We are not going to make a big deal of these rules, except to summarize them below, because: 1) all states that haven't already done so are expected to quickly repeal these outdated tax-related provisions, and 2) in Chapters 5 and 6, we show you how to deal with them in a way that meets the most stringent of old-fashioned rules without compromising the efficient operation of your LLC.

To help you understand what is involved if you bump into any of these outdated requirements in your state, here are two types of laws you may encounter:

1. *Limited duration of the LLC:* Some states ask you to limit the legal life of your LLC in your articles of organization to a specific date in the future, or to a set number of years from the date your Articles are filed. The articles of organization section of your state sheet in Appendix A alerts you to any duration requirements still in effect in your state, and shows you how to fill in this item if required in your state's Articles. But here's why this isn't a big worry: Even if you must follow your state's requirement to limit the duration of your LLC in your Articles now, when your state deletes this requirement, you can file amended Articles with your secretary of state which do not limit your LLC's duration. Or in the unlikely event that this requirement is still in effect when the duration of your LLC is up (thirty or more years from now), you can then simply file amended Articles with your state to extend the duration of your LLC for another thirty or more years.

2. *Membership voting rules when a member sells or loses a membership interest.* Many states still have LLC laws on the books that require the approval of all or a majority of members in two circumstances: 1) when an existing member wishes to transfer his membership to a new person (a nonmember); and 2) when a member is dissociated—when she loses her membership interest due to withdrawal from the LLC, death, incapacity, expulsion, or for another reason—the remaining members must unanimously, or by a majority, vote to continue the business of the LLC. Even if these approvals are required under your state's law (we tell you if they are in the "Default Transfer Rule" and "Default Continuation Rule" paragraphs, respectively, of the Operating Rules section of your state sheet in Appendix A), all you need to do is have the nontransferring or remaining members agree to the sale of membership or to the continuance of LLC business when these issues arise. In Chapters 5 and 6, we show you how to adopt provisions in your operating agreement to establish membership voting procedures that comply with these state requirements.

2. State Tax Statutes and Regulations

Don't confuse the old-fashioned state LLC Act organizational requirements just discussed with how your state classifies your LLC for state income tax purposes (assuming your state has an income tax). The above state rules were enacted to help you get favorable tax treatment with the IRS at a time when the IRS was fussy about qualifying LLCs for tax treatment as pass-through entities.

So how will your state classify your LLC for state income tax purposes? Probably, exactly the same as the IRS. Rather than get bogged down in all of this technical material, just call your state tax department (listed in your state sheet), and ask if your state follows the current federal tax classification system for business entities. One easy way to ask is: "If my LLC is classified as a partnership, sole proprietorship or corporation under the IRS rules, will the state tax department do the same?" If they say "No—not yet," have your tax advisor check your LLC papers before you file your Articles or Certificate of Organization. He should be able to do any necessary tweaking of your documents to make sure you apply for and get the proper tax classification under your state's special tax classification rules. Most likely he will agree that the Membership Transfer Provisions and Dissolution Provisions in our tear-out operating agreements entitle you to pass-through tax treatment even under an old-fashioned state tax classification scheme.

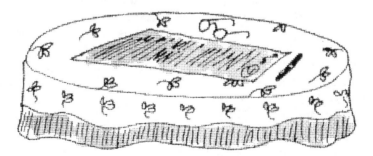

See your state treatment sheet to get started. We list the expected tax treatment of your LLC by your state in the Tax Status section of your state sheet. This treatment may change to keep step with the latest federal tax classification regulations, so you will want to call the state tax office (or ask your tax advisor) as explained above to double-check our information on this important issue.

E. Other LLC Formation Tax Considerations

Now that we've warmed you up to thinking about tax technicalities, let's turn to two other tax issues that may arise when you're forming your LLC:

- tax liability for members who are interested in contributing services or property to start the LLC, and
- the division of LLC profits and losses among LLC members.

Specifically, we will focus on questions that are likely to arise as you fill in your LLC operating agreement (as part of Chapters 5 or 6).

Consult your tax advisor for help. Don't get too slowed down by this material. If any point is confusing or raises a red flag as far as organizing your LLC is concerned, ask your tax advisor for more information. There may be alternate ways you can accomplish your objectives without paying higher taxes or causing extra complications with the IRS. The types of questions raised here relate to partnership tax law (the LLC inherits the complexities and benefits of this branch of tax law). This field is a specialty all to itself, so if your questions are important enough, it makes sense to buy yourself some specialized tax advice to find an answer. (See Chapter 8, and think about asking your regular LLC legal or tax advisor for a referral to a partnership tax specialist.)

1. Capital Contributions of Services or Property

Let's start with some background on how start-up LLCs are usually funded. The initial members, like partners in a partnership, ordinarily make financial contributions to the business. In return, each member normally gets a percentage (capital) interest in the LLC. This capital interest reflects how much of the assets a member is entitled to when the business is sold, and establishes a value for the membership interest when it is sold prior to a sale of the LLC itself. For example, a member having a 50% capital interest in an LLC receives $25,000 when the business (which has no bills to pay) sells for $50,000 (an oversimplified example, but one that makes our basic point).

In addition to receiving a stake in the LLC's assets upon distribution—a so-called capital interest—LLC members are also entitled to share in its profits and losses. Typically, divisions of profits and losses parallel LLC members' capital interests, although they may be distributed disproportionately. Disproportionate splitting of profits and losses is called "special allocations" under the tax law and is subject to special rules discussed below in Section E2.

Example 1: Tony and Lisa set up Elk-n-Stuff LLC. Both members contribute equal amounts of start-up capital. In their operating agreement, Tony and Lisa agree that each member has a 50% capital interest and will receive 50% of the business's profits (or losses, if antler-shaped back scratchers, wapiti-musk potpourri, coyote-call whoopee cushions and other mountain-state miscellany merchandised by the LLC don't sell as well as they expect).

Example 2: Tony and Lisa set up the same Elk-n-Stuff LLC, but this time Tony puts up the cash, while Lisa signs a promissory note to contribute cash in installments over the first two years of LLC life. They agree that Tony will have a 50% capital interest and will receive 75% of the business's profits (or losses) for the first two years. Lisa will have a 50% capital interest and will get 25% of the business's profits (or losses) during the business's initial two years—after that, both members will split LLC profits and losses 50-50.

Under most state statutes, members may make capital contributions of cash, property or services—or the promise to provide any of these in the future. As we discuss in the remainder of this section, any member who contributes property or services should take into account several important tax considerations. Your state sheet in Appendix A alerts you to any special contribution rules or restrictions in your state. For example, a few states prohibit or restrict capitalizing an LLC with (issuing memberships in return for) a promise to pay cash, property or services later, after the LLC is set up. If your state has such a rule, we list it under the item "Special Statutory Rules" in the "Operating Rules" section of your state sheet.

If all LLC members will contribute cash. When all members contribute cash, or a promise to contribute cash in the future (usually in the form of a promissory note—but check your state sheet in Appendix A to make sure your state does not prohibit or restrict the use of promissory notes to fund an LLC), there are no special tax consequences. Skip below to Section E2 to read about special profit and loss rules that may affect your LLC.

a. Contribution of Services

If a person is given a capital interest in an LLC in return for the performance of services, the IRS views the transaction as payment for personal services rendered. This means the member has to pay income taxes on the value of the membership, just as any other worker would upon receiving payment for services performed. In other words, the moment LLC members create and sign an operating agreement allocating capital contributions in exchange for a member's (generally future, unpaid) services, the member agrees to be hit with

a personal income tax bill for the value of the services.

Example: Five Austin computer programmers start Future Tex LLC. Four put up $20,000 each as their 20% capital contributions. Cash-strapped Sharon is allotted her 20% membership in exchange for a promise to work for the company for six months without pay. The IRS considers this $20,000 allocation as Sharon's personal income. She will be liable for personal income taxes on the entire $20,000 (estimated and paid by her during the year).

Reporting and paying personal service income on the value of the capital interest in an LLC is normally doubly painful to the service-member, who generally has to wait to receive income from the LLC before he or she can afford to pay the taxes that result from joining the LLC. Fortunately, there are several ways around this income tax liability problem:

*   *Member may be given a profits interest only.* If a member who's contributing services is given only an interest in the profits of the LLC, but not a capital (percentage) interest in LLC assets, income taxes normally are not due until profits are actually paid to the member. This may be easier for the member, who should at least receive some cash closer to the time when taxes must be paid.

    Example: Hubert Allis Overalls, Ltd. Co., a supplier of denim fabric to clothes manufacturers, brings Hank Allis (son of founding member Hubert) to help run the LLC. Business is busting at the rivets, with HAO supplying fabric to all leading domestic brand-name jeans manufacturers. In return for signing a ten-year employment contract, Hank is given a 25% stake in LLC profits, plus a guaranteed annual salary. Because Hank does not receive a capital interest in the LLC, he will not be taxed up front on his promise to perform services for HAO.

*   *Member may get a loan from the LLC, another member or an outside source to buy a capital interest for cash.* To help define and secure repayment of the loan, the member may be

asked by the lender to sign a promissory note specifying repayment terms, including interest. He or she may also be required to pledge property as security for repayment.

Example: Bella and Xavier form Happy Hoofs Equestrian Academy and Stables LLC, with the idea of operating a horse-riding and boarding facility in the rolling foothills of California. Bella can contribute $50,000 in cash and property as her stake in the new business—enough to finance a down-payment on a well-situated, if weather-worn, barn with surrounding acreage that can be converted to a stable with riding trails. Xavier is low on funds, but champing at the bit with energy that he'll use to fix up and convert the farm. Bella agrees to loan Xavier the money to become a cash member of the LLC at the start. Xavier will receive a capital interest without having to pay taxes on the value of the future services he promises to perform for the LLC. Instead, as Xavier gets paid for his services, he can pay Bella back (of course, he'll also pay individual income taxes on the salary the LLC pays him).

- *Member may buy into membership later.* Yet another approach is for a member wannabe to hold off joining the LLC until he or she has the cash to buy in. For example, a person can enter the LLC ranks as an employee, and buy a capital interest in the LLC (assuming the members agree) with savings the employee socks away out of earned LLC salary.

Example: Let's return to the Happy Hoofs Equestrian Academy and Stables LLC. Bella and her husband, Clyde, form the LLC as the two initial members. Xavier bides his time to buy into the LLC. He does not become a member right away, but simply works for the ranch as a regular employee and saves his money. When Xavier has sufficient cash, he buys out Clyde's capital interest in the LLC.

If you want to bring in members who will contribute services in return for a capital and/or profits interest in the LLC. One of the flexibilities granted LLCs is their ability to admit members who have worked or will work for the LLC. However, as highlighted above, there are tax issues to resolve first. Again,

ask your tax advisor about the best way to handle each service member in your LLC.

b. Capital Contribution of Property to an LLC

Tax technicalities also arise when a member wants to contribute property to the LLC that has appreciated (increased in value) since the time he or she purchased, inherited or otherwise received title to the property. Ordinarily, this will involve real property—an interest in land or a building—although this discussion applies to any appreciated personal property (collectibles, airplanes, and so on). Below, we quickly look at a few of the tax issues involved with this kind of transaction and alert you to check the tax ramifications with a tax advisor before you set up your LLC with contributions of property.

First the good news. Contributions of property to an LLC are generally tax-free at the time they occur. The tax consequences are generally realized later when the LLC or a member's interest in it is sold. (By the way, this is one benefit of forming a pass-through tax business such as an LLC or partnership. Corporations are not so kindly treated; transfers of property to a corporation must pass muster under technical "control tests" required by Internal Revenue Code (IRC) Section 351 to be tax-free.)

The not-so-good news is that taxes on the appreciation (increase in value) that occurred prior to the property's transfer to the LLC must eventually be paid. The transferring member will be liable for taxes when the LLC is sold or when the member sells his or her LLC interest. This is accomplished by having the property owner's income tax basis (known simply as "basis") in the property carry over to his or her basis in the LLC. Only when the membership interest is sold will the basis of the membership be used to determine how much tax the owner must pay. The result is that taxes due from appreciation on the property transferred to the LLC are paid later by the member when he or she sells an LLC membership, not when it is contributed to the LLC. The following example illustrates how this works.

Example: Jim owns a building he bought for $20,000. It is worth $120,000 when he transfers it to his newly formed LLC (it has appreciated $100,000). For the transfer of this property, he receives a $120,000 capital stake in his LLC. Jim's "basis" in the property is $20,000 (his cost—we are being very simplistic and assuming there have been no adjustments to basis; in real life, basis increases with capital improvements and decreases as depreciation is taken on property). Jim pays no taxes at the time of transfer, but his basis in his LLC membership becomes $20,000 (again, his basis in the real property at the time of transfer).

Assuming no further adjustments to Jim's basis in his LLC (another unrealistic but convenient assumption), when the LLC is liquidated or sold, or when Jim sells his interest in the LLC to another person, his amount of gain—the amount he will have to pay taxes on—will equal the amount he receives for the sale of his LLC interest minus the amount of his basis in the interest. In other words, if Jim decides to retire from his LLC and sell his interest back to the other members for $120,000 (assuming his interest is worth the same amount when he sells as when he bought it), then he will have to report a gain of $100,000 and pay taxes on that amount at the time of sale. As you can see, Jim doesn't avoid taxes by selling his building to the LLC; he simply transfers his basis in the appreciated property to his LLC interest, and pays taxes on this appreciation later when his LLC interest is sold.

Be sure you understand the tax consequences before transferring real property to an LLC. There are additional complexities when real property is contributed to an LLC. For example, separate tax issues arise when real property is encumbered (subject to a mortgage or other debt), as it usually is. Not only does this liability need to be reflected as a liability on the LLC books, it also has bearing on gains or losses realized by LLC members when

the business or membership interests are later sold. The bottom line: Before transferring property to your LLC, ask your tax advisor about any immediate and deferred tax consequences.

2. Special Allocations of LLC Profits and Losses

Like partnerships, LLCs are subject to special IRS rules if members decide not to follow the standard practice of splitting up profits and losses proportionately with each member's capital contribution. The disproportionate splitting of profits and losses is known as a "special allocation." For example, a special allocation would take place if an LLC allocates a member who contributes 10% of the initial LLC cash or assets a 20% share of profits and losses.

Although special allocations are perfectly legal, the IRS has pages upon pages of regulations designed to handle them. Basically, these regulations say that for special allocations of profits and losses to be valid (recognized and accepted by the IRS), they must have "substantial economic effect." This jargon refers to the fact that the IRS wants you to divide up profits and losses to reflect some economic reality of the enterprise. In other words, special allocations should not be made simply to lessen the tax burden of the owners. For instance, the IRS might balk if, without further justification, an LLC allocated all its losses to a member with significant income from non-LLC sources, simply so that member can fully deduct these losses and scale down on his or her personal income taxes.

Example: Up Up and Away Ventures, LLC, is a passive investment company that puts investors' money into business operations run by others. Its prime money-makers are multi-tiered car parking garages located in inner city business districts, plus a widely dispersed network of vending machines installed at suburban shopping malls. Joe and Kenneth have invested equally, and each holds a 50% capital interest in the business. Joe wants the parking lot income each year and Kenneth wants the vending machine profits (let's just say Joe likes cars and Ken has a yen for vending machines, or more likely, their accountants see this as the best way for each to maximize personal income and minimize taxes on their individual tax returns). Will the IRS object? Probably, unless there are additional facts we don't know about—or the LLC follows special IRS rules, discussed just below. Because neither Joe nor Kenneth is involved with either operation personally, and neither is specifically on the hook (at risk) for losses involved with a particular side of the business, there seems to be no reasonable business reason—no substantial economic reason or effect—associated with this allocation.

a. IRS Regulations Permit Special Allocations

Now that we've told you how the IRS rules are supposed to operate, we are going to turn the tables again and explain that you can allocate profits and losses any way you want and the IRS will still say that your allocations have substantial economic effect. How is this possible, you reasonably ask? Again, the simple answer is that complicated tax rules have been designed to be broken (by lawyers and accountants who charge handsomely to show you how).

Here's how this major loophole works. If your operating agreement recites special language taken from the 75 or so pages of special IRS regulations adopted under Section 704(b) of the Internal Revenue Code (these are the special allocations regulations), then all of your special allocations will have "substantial economic effect" under the Internal Revenue Code (even if they don't in real life) and will not be challenged by the IRS.

Example: Cuneiform Widgets Works Ltd. Liability Co. is founded by Sol Shimmaker. The business makes

wedge-shaped objects of all descriptions, including a unique form-fitting door stopper named the Toe-Hold 2000. Expanding orders spur Sol on to seek additional capital to retool and expand CWW's fabrication facilities. Arnie and Lillian have the bucks, and agree to contribute an amount of cash equal to one-half of the existing capital of the enterprise. They insist, however, on receiving a five-year 65% profits interest in the Toe-Hold 2000, plus a 50% share of net profits derived from other CWW product sales. Is there any substantial economic reason for this special splitting of profits to the new investors? Let's assume there isn't. The LLC protects itself from IRS challenge to these special allocations of profits by asking its tax advisor to prepare and add the special Internal Revenue Code Section 704(b) language to its operating agreement.

b. Other Special Allocations Considerations

There are some real financial and tax consequences associated with adopting Internal Revenue Code Section 704(b) special allocation regulations in your LLC operating agreement. Generally, the lengthy series of provisions that you must adopt in your operating agreement to satisfy the IRS safe-harbor special allocations rules come down to three basic points:

1. The business's capital accounts must be carried and handled on the financial books under special rules based upon Section 704(b) of the Internal Revenue Code. These rules do not follow generally accepted accounting practices (known as "GAAP" in the trade) This is not a particular problem, just a quirk that must be taken into consideration by your tax person.

2. Distributions of cash or property to owners upon liquidation of the business must be made in accordance with capital accounts maintained under Internal Revenue Code Section 704(b), as mentioned just above.

3. When an owner leaves or the business is sold or liquidated, any partners or members with a negative capital account balance (capital accounts go negative if members are allocated losses in excess of their capital account balance) must restore the account to a zero balance. They do this by contributing cash or property equal to their negative capital account balance before their interest or the LLC itself is sold or liquidated.

If you want to make special (disproportionate) allocations of profits or losses in your LLC, do what a big business would—hand your operating agreement over to a partnership tax specialist to insert the various technical provisions you'll need in order to rely on the IRS safe-harbor rules for special allocations. These rules are lengthy and subject to periodic change. For all these reasons, plus the fact that most smaller LLC owners will not wish to make special allocations of profits and losses, we don't include them in the operating agreements provided in this book.

●

CHAPTER 4

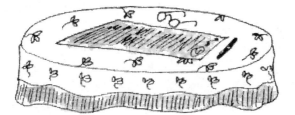

How to Prepare LLC Articles of Organization

In this chapter, we explain how to prepare articles of organization for your LLC and file them with your state LLC filing office. Once you perform this important task, your LLC will be a legal entity recognized by your state, as well as other states.

**LLC MAKER™—
NOLO'S NATIONAL LLC SOFTWARE**

Nolo produces *LLC Maker*, an interactive software program for Windows® that prepares the articles of organization, operating agreement, and other essential legal forms for you. Just fill in the information for your LLC according to the state specific instructions on the screen, and LLC Maker will assemble the forms required in your state. It contains online legal and program help, plus tables of state-by-state LLC rules and information for your reference. Cut through the legal red tape and form your LLC in minutes with this software program!

Don't be concerned if your state uses different LLC terminology. Different states use different legalese in their LLC statutes, regulations and bureaucracies. We have tried to use the most common terms to describe LLC documents and offices, but your state may use other language. For example, although we refer to the charter document used to form an LLC as the articles of organization, some states use a different name—for example, Delaware, Mississippi, New Hampshire, New Jersey and Washington refer to this document as a certificate of formation. Massachusetts and Pennsylvania call the document a "certificate of organization."

A. Read State Sheets and Order LLC Materials

Each state has its own requirements for preparing and filing LLC articles of organization. Make sure you follow the steps below to learn about your state's LLC rules. As you'll see, an important part of this process involves contacting your state's LLC filing office to obtain forms and state-specific information (usually by simply going online to your state's LLC website).

Get forms quickly over the Internet. All Secretary of State offices have a Web page. From most sites, you can download the latest version of the state's LLC articles form. We list Internet addresses in the state sheets.

MATERIALS AVAILABLE FROM LLC FILING OFFICES

Each state's LLC filing office and website operate a little differently, but most states are likely to supply a number of helpful materials, including:

- fill-in-the-blank or sample LLC articles of organization with instructions

- a fee schedule showing current charges for filing, copying and certifying various LLC documents

- forms and instructions to check LLC name availability and reserve an LLC name for your use

- forms and instructions for post-formation procedures—these may include materials to amend LLC articles, change the LLC's registered office or registered agent, or register an assumed or fictitious LLC name (one that is different from the official LLC name shown in the articles of organization), and

- a summary or complete collection of the state's LLC statutes (sometimes available for a small fee). Some states don't supply the statutes, but tell you how to obtain them from a commercial publisher. This material is usually worth having on hand to answer any LLC formation or operation questions that may arise (and eliminate the time necessary to go to the law library or the expense of asking a lawyer each time you need LLC statutory information). The statutes will also help you prepare your own LLC articles if your state doesn't provide a form.

1. First Read Your State Sheet

Your first step is to locate and carefully read your state sheet in Appendix A. Among other valuable information, your state sheet provides the title, web address, physical address and phone number of your state's LLC filing office. Most state LLC filing offices are part of the Secretary of State's Division of Corporations office located at the state capitol, but some are a division of the Department of State or a different state office. Many of the more populous states maintain LLC filing branch offices in several cities.

Most states provide their own fill-in-the-blank LLC articles of organization form. Some states give a sample form that is completed for a fictional or sample company; you retype the form and provide information that applies to your LLC. State forms are updated regularly, and their accompanying instructions contain the latest information on state filing procedures and fees.

We don't include copies of each state's articles of organization form. If your state provides fill-in-the-blank forms, you are better off getting the latest version from your state's LLC filing office or its website when you decide to form an LLC. If your state does not provide its own form, we give information about how to use the sample articles of organization form in Appendix C to meet the requirements in your state.

2. Order LLC Materials

Going to your state's website is the quickest way to get available LLC information. If you can't find what you need there, call your state's LLC filing office. Your state's LLC filing office phone number is listed on your state sheet in Appendix A. Ask for the LLC materials we list in the sample LLC contact letter shown below.

Sometimes a letter can be used as a last resort (if you don't use a computer). In Appendix C, we provide a tear-out LLC contact letter you can use to request specific information on forming an LLC in your state. A sample letter with instructions follows.

The LLC Contact letter is included on the CD-ROM at the back of this book.

SAMPLE LLC CONTACT LETTER

date
_____

name and address of your state's LLC filing office
_____

LLC Filings Office:

I am in the process of forming a domestic limited liability company (LLC). Please note: ❶

☐ I am _or_ ☐ I am not converting an existing __**if applicable, specify "general" or "limited"**__ partnership to an LLC.

☐ I am _or_ ☐ I am not forming an LLC to perform the professional services of _____**if applicable, specify name of profession**_____, which are licensed by the state.

Please send me the following forms, material and other information:

1. printed, sample or specimen LLC articles of organization, with instructions. If your office reviews articles of organization for correctness prior to filing, please advise me of the procedure I should follow to obtain this pre-filing review;

2. the telephone number or address I can contact to determine if a proposed limited liability company name is available for my use, plus any forms necessary to reserve an LLC name;

3. a current schedule of fees for LLC filings;

4. other LLC forms and publications provided by your office (or a list of these) for forming, operating and dissolving an LLC in this state; and

5. the name and price of a publication that contains the limited liability company statutes of this state. Please indicate whether it may be ordered from your office or, if applicable, another office or supplier.

If there is a fee for any of the above materials, please advise. Enclosed is a self-addressed, stamped envelope for your reply.

Thank you for your assistance,

your signature ❷
_____

your name, address and phone number
_____

_____

Enclosure: self-addressed, stamped envelope

❶ In the first paragraph, you'll need to check the appropriate boxes to indicate whether or not you are converting an existing partnership to an LLC and whether or not your LLC is being set up to perform state-licensed professional services. The state office will use this information to supply you with the proper form for articles of organization. Some states have a special form for forming an LLC that is converting from a general or limited partnership form; some have a separate form for forming a professional LLC.

Here's how to complete the blanks:

- If converting a partnership, insert whether you are converting a "general" or "limited" partnership in the first blank.
- If forming an LLC to practice a state licensed profession, insert the name of the profession in the blank in the second sentence, such as "law," "accounting," "medicine," "engineering" or "architecture."

❷ Sign the letter and fill in your name, address and telephone number in the space provided at the bottom. Enclose a self-addressed, stamped envelope and mail the letter to your LLC filing office, keeping a copy for your own files.

B. Review and Organize Your State's LLC Information

Once your state LLC materials are in hand or available for viewing on your computer, take a little time to check them over.

If you prefer to print out the material, do so. Then, get an accordion file or large file folder (or if you are an extra tidy sort, a number of folders) and place all forms, statutes and other legal material you received or downloaded from the filing office in it. You may want to organize this material with index tabs or dividers, separating out forms for articles of organization, name reservation, fee information and the like.

In any case, make sure to save the forms and instructions in a safe folder on your computer. Or, if you print the material, keep it in an accessible file folder. You will need to refer to this information throughout your LLC formation process and don't want to lose any of it. (We show you how to obtain and set up a formal LLC records book, including one available from Nolo, in Chapter 7, Section C4.)

C. Choose a Name for Your LLC

When you prepare your LLC articles of organization, you'll need to supply the name of your LLC. If your proposed LLC name, or one similar to it, is already in use by another LLC on file with the LLC filing office, your articles of organization will be returned unfiled to you. It pays, therefore, to plan ahead and check the availability of your proposed LLC name before you complete your Articles. Take a little time to read through the material in this section and to choose a good name for your LLC.

1. Important Legal Issues When Choosing an LLC Name

Our primary task is to show you how to choose a name that is acceptable to your state's LLC office when you file your articles.

a. Name Cannot Resemble Another Business's Name

Make sure your proposed name is not very similar to any famous business name (McDonald's, Procter & Gamble, The Quaker Oats Company, Honda and the like). If so, you shouldn't use the name, even if it is available for use by an LLC in your state. Companies with famous names and marks are fanatical about protecting them.

b. Name Cannot Infringe on Trademarks or Service Marks

If your LLC name will be used to identify and market goods and services sold by your LLC, and if this name is the same or similar to one already registered by another business (LLC or otherwise) as a federal or state trademark or service mark, the other business may be able to sue you for trademark or service mark infringement. The infringed business may also stop you from continuing to use your name to market your goods and services, and seek money damages from your LLC.

WHAT ARE TRADEMARKS AND SERVICE MARKS?

A trademark generally consists of a distinctive word, phrase, logo or graphic symbol that is used to identify a product and distinguish it from anyone else's. Well-known trademarks include Ford cars and trucks, IBM computers and Kellogg's cereal.

A service mark promotes services in the same way that a trademark promotes products. Some common service marks are Blue Cross (sells health insurance) and Greyhound (transports people by bus).

If you will use your LLC name to market goods and services, we show you several things you can do to help satisfy yourself that your proposed LLC name is not in use by others as a federal trademark or service mark in Section C4.

How to learn more about trademark law. Our recommendation is to get a copy of *Trademark: Legal Care for Your Business & Product Name*, by Stephen Elias (Nolo), which you can find at the library or purchase using the order form at the back of this book. In addition to educating you about trademark law,

the book will help you choose a strong marketing name, search for possibly conflicting trademarks and service marks, and, if the circumstances warrant, register your LLC name as a mark with state and federal trademark agencies. For a general overview of trademark law and other intellectual property law, you may be interested in *Patent, Copyright and Trademark: An Intellectual Property Desk Reference*, by Stephen Elias (Nolo).

c. Other Considerations If Your LLC Name Will Identify Products or Services

Businesses often market goods or services using a name that is different from their company name—for example, Bausch & Lomb manufactures Renu® contact lens cleaner. Companies do, however, frequently use (and register) their business names as trademarks or service marks: The Rug Doctor (company) puts out The Rug Doctor® Steam Cleaner (product) and McDonald's Corp. uses "McDonald's" as a service mark. And of course, many companies use their business name together with additional words and symbols to make up trademarks and service marks for their products and services—for example, Apple Computer Corporation uses the name Apple® Macintosh for its personal computer line.

If your LLC decides to use its business name as, or as part of, a trademark or service mark to identify products or services, you will face a number of issues:

- *Does the name do a good job of marketing your goods or services?* A strong mark will be unique, memorable or suggestive of your LLC's products or services.
- *Is the name identical or similar to any trademark or service mark being used on goods or services that are similar or related enough to yours to likely cause marketplace confusion?* To answer this you will need to conduct what's called a trademark search.

- *Assuming your name doesn't conflict with an existing mark, do the circumstances justify the time and expense involved in placing the name on the federal trademark register and/or your state's trademark register?* If you do the work yourself, you can easily keep costs to a minimum.

Don't overlook these important additional legal chores now, before you choose an LLC name, if you anticipate marketing goods or services later under your proposed LLC name. If you hastily choose a name for your LLC and later use it to promote products sales in a competitive market, you may face a legal conflict just when business is humming and your LLC and its product or service names are beginning to become known. (Again, for a discussion of these and other trademark related questions, as well as step-by-step instructions for searching existing marks and registering a mark, see Nolo's *Trademark: Legal Care for Your Business & Product Name*, by Stephen Elias.)

2. State LLC Name Requirements

Your LLC name must conform to your state's legal requirements. Your state sheet in Appendix A summarizes these LLC name requirements, but it's a good idea to double-check this information against the materials you receive from your state LLC office before selecting a name. Most states' LLC name requirements usually incorporate the basic rules that follow.

a. LLC Designator Is Required in LLC Name

Your LLC name must normally include an LLC designator, such as "Limited Liability Company" or "Limited Company." Capitalization is normally not specified under state statutes—upper or lower case may generally be used for these words.

You must, however, follow your state's specific rules for abbreviations. Some states allow both "LLC" and "L.L.C." as acceptable abbreviations; others stick with one of these two forms. Further, the words "limited" and "company" can usually be abbreviated as "Ltd." and "Co., " but you normally can't abbreviate the word "liability"—for example, "Liab." is normally not a valid abbreviated form. The result is usually that the words "Limited Liability Company" can be abbreviated in most states to "Ltd. Liability Co."

Finally, realize that in a minority of states, you may be required to place the LLC designator—the words "Limited Liability Company" or one of the other approved LLC designators—at the end of your LLC name. For example, you'd have to settle on "Maladroit Ventures LLC," not Maladroit LLC Ventures." So be on the lookout for this requirement as you peruse your state sheet and state materials.

Example: Valid names for the ABC limited liability company would typically include one or more of the following:

- *ABC Limited Liability Company*
- *ABC Limited Liability Co.*
- *ABC Ltd. Liability Co.*
- *ABC Limited Company*
- *ABC Ltd. Co.*
- *ABC L.C.*
- *ABC L.L.C., or*
- *ABC LLC.*

Easy way to pick a required LLC designator. Ending your LLC name with the words "Limited Liability Company" will meet the name requirements of all states except Florida and Iowa—in these two states, "Limited Company" or "L.C." is required.

b. Certain Words Are Prohibited or Restricted in LLC Name

An LLC name usually cannot include words reserved for use by special businesses. In many states, prohibited words include references to banking, insurance, trust companies or similar financial service businesses.

Many states either prohibit regular (non-professional) LLCs from practicing certain state-licensed professions, or require that they set up professional LLCs and operate under special rules. Hence, words related to professions ordinarily cannot be included in a regular (non-professional

practice) LLC's name, such as "law," "accounting," "medical," "engineering," "architecture," "real estate" and similar professional practice terms. Of course, if you want to organize an LLC for a licensed professional practice, you very well may want to use words that denote the profession.

What if you are forming an LLC that serves the needs of a licensed profession, but doesn't provide licensed services itself—such as a legal copying center, a medical supplies company, or a computer programming business for accountants—can you use the words "medical," "legal" or "accounting" in your name? We don't have a ready-made answer that applies in all states. If you want to use these words in an LLC name, call and ask the name section of the state LLC filing office if you will be allowed to do so. If you can't get a satisfactory answer over the phone, you can try reserving your name or filing articles of organization—the worst that can happen is that your paperwork will be returned unfiled if these words are not allowed in your LLC's name.

c. LLC Name Must Not Conflict With a Name Already On File

Another state LLC name requirement is that your LLC name must not be the same as, or too closely similar to, the name of an LLC already on file with the state LLC filing office. Names on file that are not available for your LLC may include the names of:

- domestic LLCs (those formed in the state)
- foreign LLCs (registered out-of-state LLCs that have qualified to do business in the state), and
- names on reserve for LLCs in the process of formation (names being held for 30 to 120 days by businesses planning to form or qualify LLCs in the state soon; see Section C5, below, for more on reserving names).

Some states also check proposed LLC names against names of other business structures. Some state LLC filing offices check proposed LLC names against names used in the state for corporations and limited partnerships, both of which must also file formation papers with the Department or Secretary of State. If your proposed LLC name is the same or similar to one in use by a corporation or limited partnership in these states, you will not be able to use it.

If your proposed LLC name is similar to another name already on file with the state LLC office, some states allow you to use it anyway if you can get the other business's written approval to use your similar name. But there are problems with this approach. For starters, the other business is likely to refuse to let you use the similar name unless you carefully limit or distinguish it in some way from its own name. Even if the other business does agree, it probably will ask you to pay big bucks to use any version of the name. In addition, it's messy to use a name already in use by others—even if you get their permission.

So, if you find that your proposed LLC name resembles one already on file with your state LLC office, or generally conflicts with a name discovered in your search efforts explained in Section C4, below, we recommend you come up with another name. We know that finding just the right sounding name for your business can be a chore, and that you may feel a little put out by having to select another name. With patience, however, and the usual amount of serendipity, you'll find that you can come up with two or three alternative names that suit your taste and your LLC business.

IMPORTANT BUSINESS NAME FACTS

There's a lot of misinformation and confusion about choosing names for LLCs and other businesses. Here are a few points of clarification:

- *Filing your LLC name with the LLC filing office does not guarantee your right to use it.* We've said this already, but it bears repeating: Another business may be able to prevent you from using the name if the other business is already using your LLC name (or one close to it) in a trademark or service mark to identify goods or services.

- *You are allowed to use a name that's different from the official name shown in your articles of organization.* If you do, this alternate name is known as an assumed or fictitious business name, and you may need to register it at the state and/or county level. (See Chapter 7, Section D3.)

- *You can change your official LLC name later by amending your articles.* You may later decide to change the name of your LLC to a new name (again, which must be available for your use with the LLC filing office) by amending your articles of organization. Naturally, most LLC owners choose not to change their LLC name after they have been in business for a while, but this option is available if absolutely necessary.

3. Check Availability of LLC Name With the State

Let's say you've come up with a name or two that you'd like to use for your LLC. How can you find out if it is available for your use? Simple. Just call your state LLC filing office at the telephone number listed in your state sheet in Appendix A, and ask. The state LLC office will normally tell you over the phone, at no charge, whether one or two proposed names are available for your use. A few offices will ask you to send a written name availability request. If this happens, we suggest you use a written letter to request that your proposed LLC name be reserved for your use if it is available. (We show you how to reserve a proposed LLC name in Section C5, below.) Also note that many state filing offices let you check business name availability online from the state LLC filing office website.

Don't count on using a name that you haven't reserved or filed. An online telephone or written name check is just a preliminary indication of the availability of your proposed LLC name. Unless you formally reserve your name (as explained in Section C5, below), you do not secure your right to use your name with the state LLC office until you file your articles of organization. So don't order your business stationery, cards, signs or anything else until your name has been secured for your use (after your articles have been filed with the LLC filing office, or after reserving your name if you are absolutely certain that you will file your articles within the reservation period).

4. Consider Performing Your Own Name Search

There are a few simple business name searching procedures you can use, in addition to checking the availability of your name with the state LLC office, to get a sense of whether your proposed LLC name is in use by other businesses. Why is this important to know? For one thing, most business owners would like their names to be as unique as possible.

Another reason, mentioned earlier, is that you'd like to stay as clear as possible from names already being used by other businesses to market their goods and services. This not only helps you avoid names that others will lay legal claim to as trademarks and service marks, but can help you if you wish to use your LLC name yourself as a registered state or federal trademark or service mark (to identify and market your LLC's goods and services).

Below are several self-help search techniques you can employ to see if others are using a name similar to your proposed LLC name. If you are interested in performing any of these steps, it makes sense to do so before filing your LLC articles—to avoid having to amend your articles to change your name if you find your proposed name is already in use by another business.

- *Check state and county assumed business name files.* Your state LLC materials should indicate whether assumed (or fictitious) business names are registered with your Secretary of State's office, at the county level, or both. If they are registered at the state level, call the assumed or fictitious business name section of the Secretary of State's office and ask if your proposed LLC name is the same or similar to a registered assumed or fictitious name. Also call your local county clerk's office to ask how you can check assumed business name filings; in most states, assumed or fictitious business name statements, or "doing business as" (dba) statements, are filed with the county clerk's office. Generally, you must go in and check the assumed business name files in person—it takes just a few minutes to do this.
- *Check business directories.* Check such sources as major metropolitan phone book listings, business directories and trade directories to see if

another company or group is using a name similar to your proposed LLC name. Larger public libraries keep phone directories for many major cities throughout the country, as well as trade directories. A local business branch of a public library may have a special collection of business research materials—check these first for listings of local and national trade and business groups.

- *Check state trademarks and service marks.* Call the trademark section of your Secretary of State's office and ask if your proposed LLC name is the same or similar to trademarks and service marks registered with the state. Some offices may ask for a written request and a small fee before performing this search.

- *Check the federal Trademark Register.* Another logical step is to check federal trademarks and service marks. The federal *Trademark Register* consists of a listing of trademark and service mark names broken into categories of goods and services. The Register is available for free searching from the federal Patent and Trademark Office's website. Go to http://www.uspto.gov for information. If you wish to search the Register in printed form, go to a large public library or special business and government library in your area that carries the Register.

5. Reserve Your LLC Name

Let's say you have decided on an LLC name and checked that it is available by checking online or calling your LLC filing office as explained in Section C3, above. Most states allow you to reserve available LLC names. During the reservation period, only you—the person who reserved a

name—may file articles of organization using this name. The reservation period and the fees vary, but generally an available LLC name can be reserved for 30 to 120 days for $10 to $50. In many states, you can reserve the same name more than once if you don't get around to filing your articles of organization during the first reservation period. We show your state's LLC name reservation rules in your state sheet in Appendix A.

It makes sense to reserve your name if you will not be filing your articles of organization immediately. Start by checking your state website or the materials downloaded or mailed from your state LLC filing office. A sample or fill-in-the-blanks reservation of LLC name form may be included, or you may find instructions for preparing one from scratch. A fee schedule in your materials should show how much you must pay for a name reservation, as well as indicate the period of reservation.

If this material is not available, call your state LLC filing office and ask the clerk to send you instructions and a form to reserve your proposed LLC name. If the state LLC filing office requires a written name reservation, but does not provide a form, you can use the tear-out reservation of LLC name letter included in Appendix C. Following is a sample with instructions.

The LLC Reservation of Name letter is included on the CD-ROM at the back of this book.

SAMPLE RESERVATION OF LLC NAME LETTER

date _____

name and address of your state's LLC filing office _____

LLC Filings Office:

Please reserve the following proposed limited liability company name for my use for the allowable period specified under state law:

insert your proposed LLC name; make sure it conforms to your state's _____

name requirements as shown in your state sheet in Appendix A _____

☐ If the above name is not available, please reserve the first available name from the following list of alternative names: ❶

Second Choice: _____

Third Choice: _____

I enclose a check in payment of the reservation fee. ❷ Please send a certificate, receipt for payment, or other acknowledgment or approval of my reservation request to me at my address shown below.

Thank you for your assistance,

your signature ❸ _____

your name, address and phone number _____

_____

Enclosures: check for reservation fee; stamped, self-addressed envelope

---

SPECIAL INSTRUCTIONS

❶ You may wish to include alternative names in case your first choice is not available. In that case, check the box and fill in the names in the blanks below.

❷ Include a check or money order for fees. Note that a few states only accept payment in the form of money orders or cashier's checks.

❸ Make sure that the person signing this letter will be available to sign articles of organization on behalf of your LLC. The LLC name is reserved for this person's use only. (Although inconvenient, there may be a way around this problem. If the requesting person drops out of the LLC, some states will allow him or her to file a transfer of reservation of name form.)

D. Check Your State's Procedures for Filing Articles

We cover the general procedures and rules below for preparing and filing articles of organization for LLCs. Again, make sure you check your state sheet in Appendix A for important rules or procedures that may apply in your state.

1. Some States Have Additional Filing Procedures

The laws and regulations of some states include special requirements prior to or when filing LLC articles of organization. Most common are:

- *Supplemental forms.* An additional legal or tax form may be required to be filed with your articles. For example, a separate designation of registered agent and office, a standard industry code form that you check to show the LLC's primary business, or a state tax form may be included in your LLC materials to be completed and submitted with your articles. These extra forms may be available for downloading from your state website.
- *Publication of notice.* Some states require a pre- or post-filing publication in a legal newspaper of your intention to do business as a limited liability company. A local legal newspaper can handle any required publication and filings associated with this formality.

Your state sheet in Appendix A will alert you to extra formalities that apply when filing articles of organization in your state. The instructions for any additional forms and special procedures should be provided online at your state's website.

2. Special Requirements for Licensed Professionals

In some states, licensed professionals can form LLCs as long as they comply with additional requirements or filing formalities. For example, some states allow licensed professionals to form an LLC as long as they file a special form of articles of organization for a Professional LLC and the LLC name ends with the words "Professional Limited Liability Company" or the abbreviations "PLLC" or P.L.L.C."

Your state sheet and state materials should alert you to special requirements, but double-check with your profession's state licensing board to be doubly sure. Our LLC contact letter in Section A2, above, specifically asks the LLC filing office if the state has a special form for use by professional service LLCs. This is simply another way to find out if you can go ahead in your state and form a professional LLC.

The special state rules that apply to professional LLCs typically limit LLC membership to licensed professionals only (and, generally, to the particular licensed profession only). Other rules may apply as well—for example, minimum malpractice insurance coverage or bonding may be required for each member who practices in the LLC.

Typically, lawyers, doctors, accountants, engineers and health care professionals must abide by these extra rules, but other licensed professions may be exempt. To find out whether any special professional LLC rules apply to your licensed profession, call the state board or agency that regulates your profession and ask ("May I form a limited liability company in this state to render licensed professional services of [your field] ?"). If the answer is yes, ask whether any special requirements apply to operating your professional LLC in the state. If so, ask to be sent a copy of these special rules.

E. Prepare LLC Articles of Organization

The articles of organization form is your primary formation document: your LLC comes into existence on the date you successfully file the articles with your state LLC filing office. Here's how to go about preparing it.

1. Locate Articles in Your State LLC Materials

Most state LLC filing offices websites provide LLC articles of organization forms that meet the state's basic statutory requirements. Unless you plan to organize an LLC with a complicated organizational structure (with the help of a lawyer, accountant or other specialist), the basic state form will work fine. So, before you do anything else, check your state's LLC office website and download LLC articles and instructions. If the website does not provide a downloadable form, call your state office to have it mailed to you.

2. If Your State Does Not Provide Forms: Check the State Sheets

If your state does not provide a fill-in-the-blanks form or sample articles or certificate of organization, look at the "Special Instructions and Filing Requirements" portion of the Articles/Certificate of Organization section of your state sheet in Appendix A. It lists the required contents of articles or a certificate of organization if your state does not provide a ready-to-use form, and gives you specific wording to use for any tricky items. If you read this information, and draft your articles or certificate according to our instructions in Section E5, below, we're sure you'll do fine.

If you are drafting your own articles or certificate of organization, you may want to make sure the statutory requirements listed for your state in the state sheet are current. To do this, you'll need to look up the section of your state's LLC Act titled "Articles (or "Certificate") of Organization." The best way to check your state's LLC act is to look for a link to your state's LLC act on the state LLC filing office website or go to the Nolo state law web page at http://www.nolo.com. If you can't find a link that leads you to your LLC act, call your state filing office and ask for a copy of the state LLC act—many Secretaries of State will provide a copy for free or for a small fee. Note: your state sheet in Appendix A tells you how to use a state-provided link to find your state's LLC act online. In most cases, the link should still be valid when you use it—you won't need to call the state or go to a law library to read your state's LLC law. Chances are, the requirements for this document have not changed from the information provided in the state sheets, but it does happen from time to time—for example, a state may delete the requirement that your articles specify the duration of your LLC.

3. How to Complete Articles of Organization

The basic clauses required in most states' LLC articles of organization are similar. Below, we provide sample language and explanations for provisions you are likely to find in the articles provided by your LLC filing office and required under your state's LLC statutes. You'll find a tear-out form containing all the provisions discussed here in Appendix C.

By following the material below and referring to the specific instructions for preparing articles of organization provided by your LLC office (or the statute that lists the required contents of LLC articles in your state), you should be able to prepare your own articles without difficulty. Here are some hints to make this job easier:

- *Scan our sample articles of organization.* Glancing through the language of our sample articles below, before you begin filling in your own articles, will help you get a general idea of the types of provisions included in standard LLC articles of organization. This overview will help you understand the form and instructions provided by your LLC office, or evaluate how each provision can be used to satisfy your state's statutory requirements if you are drafting your own form.

- *Prepare a draft first.* If your state LLC office provides a fill-in-the-blanks form, print and photocopy it, and prepare a draft. If your state provides a sample form that must be retyped, first word process, type or write out a draft copy.

- *Use instructions as guidance.* If you get stuck with a particular article or provision in a state-provided form, refer to our instructions below for a similar item in our sample form.

- *Use the state sheets and state LLC office materials.* To locate any special LLC formation requirements in your state, see your state materials and your state sheet in Appendix A. For example, your state may require you to specify in your articles whether members of your LLC can vote to continue the legal existence of your LLC after the dissociation (the loss of membership rights) of a member; we show each state's statutory requirements for this "default continuation rule" in the state sheets.

- *Use sample articles if you are preparing your articles from scratch.* If you are crafting your own articles of organization based upon the requirements listed in your state's LLC Act, you will use one or more of the sample provisions below to prepare your articles. We show how to use our sample article provisions to create articles of organization for the state of Texas in Section E5.

The sample LLC articles of organization is included on the CD-ROM at the back of this book.

We'll start at the top of the articles, and discuss each part of the form separately. Each provision is shown, followed by explanatory text. The bold information contains instructions for filling in blanks in a given provision.

Pay attention to state format requirements. Most state LLC filing offices expect articles of organization to be typed or printed on one side of a page only, with letter-size (8½" x 11") now being the customary page size (though many will still accept 8½" x 14" legal-sized paper). Whatever type of typewriter or printer you use—for example, dot-matrix, laser or ink jet—make sure the printed text is legible and of good contrast.

a.   Heading of Articles

ARTICLES OF ORGANIZATION
OF
NAME OF LLC

State law does not normally specify any format for the heading of the articles, but it's common practice to give the title of the document, usually "Articles of Organization," followed by the proposed name of the LLC. Some states use a different title for this document—for example, Delaware and a few other states call this document the "Certificate of Formation." If a name other than "Articles of Organization" is used for this form, it will be shown on your state sheet and in your state's articles or articles instructions.

In the blank, fill in the correct, full name of your LLC. Make sure the name you list is exactly want you want your LLC to be named. As discussed in Sections C3 and C5, we suggest you check the availability of your proposed name and, if appropriate, reserve it prior to filing your articles. By reserving your name, you avoid having your articles returned unfiled because another LLC is already using your proposed name (or a similar one) as the name of its LLC listed with the state LLC office.

b.   Statement of Statutory Authority

The undersigned natural person(s), of the age of eighteen years or more, acting as organizer(s) of a limited liability company under the State of _____**name of state**_____ Limited Liability Company Act, adopt(s) the following articles of organization _____**or other title for form, such as "Certificate of Formation"**_____ for such limited liability company.

Although not required, it is traditional in many states to include a preliminary statement of statutory authority after the heading to the articles of organization and before the first article. You will normally see language of this sort on state-provided forms.

c. Name of Limited Liability Company

Article 1. Name of Limited Liability Company. The name of this limited liability company is ___**name of LLC**___.

Insert the proposed name of your LLC in the blank. This should be identical to the name listed in the heading.

Numbering or lettering of articles of organization. State law does not normally specify any particular numbering or lettering scheme for articles. We employ Arabic numerals, but other number or letter sequences are permissible—such as "Article One," "Article I" or "Article A."

d. Name and Address of Initial Registered Office and Agent

Article 2. Registered Office and Registered Agent. The initial registered office of this limited liability company and the name of its initial registered agent at this address are: ___**name and address of LLC initial registered agent and office**___.

Most states require that articles of organization include both of the following:
- *The name of the LLC's initial registered agent.* The agent is sometimes called the "agent for service of process." He or she is authorized to receive legal papers on behalf of the LLC. Typically, the agent must be a resident of the state and at least 18 years of age.

- *The address of the initial registered office.* The registered office is the address where the agent maintains a place of business—where papers may be mailed, and where service of process can be personally performed on the agent. The registered office address must be located in the state.

Although the registered office may be different from the principal office of the LLC (the actual office or business location of the LLC) in many states, most LLCs keep things simple and appoint one of the members as the initial agent, showing the principal address of the LLC as the registered office address (where the agent can be contacted personally and receive mail). A street address, not a post office box, is normally required as the address of the registered office.

Some states supply a separate Designation of Registered Agent form (or one with a similar title) to be filed with the articles, which the agent signs to show his or her consent to act as registered agent for the LLC. In other states, a simple statement at the end of the articles, signed by the initial agent, is needed—such as, "The undersigned hereby accepts appointment as registered agent for the above named limited liability company."

Don't needlessly hire a registered agent company. Most states allow you to designate another business as a registered agent, and, indeed, some companies specialize in acting as registered agents for LLCs and corporations for an annual fee. Because acting as a registered agent simply involves being available to receive mail (and personal service), most readers will handle this task themselves and not bother to hire an outside firm.

Some states also require an LLC to designate the Secretary of State or another state official as the person who is entitled to receive legal notices on behalf of the LLC in case the registered agent resigns, cannot be located or is otherwise unable or unavailable to act as agent for the LLC in the future. In some states, this designation of state official as alternate agent happens automatically as a matter of law; in other states, specific language to this effect must be inserted in the articles. The ready-to-use or sample articles provided by your state should include any required language.

Example: Here is the alternate-agent language used in articles of organization for Utah LLCs (which is included in the state's sample articles of organization form): "Appointment of the Director of the Division of Corporations and Commercial Code of the Utah Department of Commerce as Agent for Service of Process. The Director of the Division of Corporations and Commercial Code of the Utah Department of Commerce is hereby appointed the agent of the limited liability company for service of process if the registered agent has resigned, the registered agent's authority has been revoked, or the registered agent cannot be found or served with the exercise of reasonable diligence."

e.   Statement of Purposes

Article 3. Statement of Purposes. The purposes for which this limited liability company is organized are:

list purposes of the LLC business, for example, "to operate a computer repair and retail store, and to engage in any other lawful business for which limited liability companies may be organized in this state."

Almost all states require a statement of purposes in the articles of organization. Some say that a general statement of purposes is sufficient—that is, "to engage in any lawful business for which limited liability companies may be organized in this state." Others states require a brief statement of the specific business purposes of the LLC—usually a short and straightforward description of the particular type of business to be operated by the LLC.

If a specific statement of business purposes is required, it is often a good idea to follow it with a general statement of purposes—allowing the LLC "to engage in any other lawful business for which limited liability companies may be organized in this state." Adding this general language helps make it clear to the organizers, future LLC members and others who may read your Articles that your LLC, while formed for one particular purpose, can engage in other business activities. The sample language in the sample above contains a dual-purpose statement of this sort.

Here are some other examples of how to complete this statement:

- "to open and operate a car stereo and security alarm sales and service facility, and to engage in any other lawful business for which limited liability companies may be organized in this state"
- "to purchase, sell and otherwise invest in real property and commercial interests in real property, and to engage in any other lawful business for which limited liability companies may be organized in this state," or
- "to provide financial consulting services to individuals and businesses, and to engage in any other lawful business for which limited liability companies may be organized in this state."

f.   Management of the LLC

Article 4. Management and Names and Addresses of Initial **"Members" or "Managers"**. The management of this limited liability company is reserved to the **"members" or "managers."** The names and addresses of its initial **"members" or "managers"** are: **names and addresses of members or managers.**

Articles of organization usually state whether the LLC will be member-managed or manager-managed (discussed in detail in Chapter 2, Section C). Here's a recap of what these terms mean:

- *Member-managed LLC.* Member management is the default rule in most states—if you don't specify how your LLC will be managed in your articles, your LLC will be managed by all the members.
- Manager-managed LLC. Some LLCs decide to specifically appoint some of the members and/ or nonmembers as managers of the LLC. If so, the articles must usually state that management is reserved to managers, and list the names and addresses of the specially designated managers. Normally, just one manager is required, but even smaller LLCs typically appoint more than one person to manage the company. If managers are listed, members' names and addresses usually are not required, but in some states, you may be asked to list the names and addresses of members and managers separately (even if some individuals function in both capacities— namely, members who are appointed as managers of a manager-managed LLC).

In each of the first sets of blanks, indicate whether your LLC will be run by "members" or "managers." In the indicated space, list the names and addresses of the LLC's initial members or managers. Normally, street (not post office box) addresses must be shown.

Number of members: All states allow an LLC to be formed with just one member. You may of course want more.

g. Principal Place of Business

Article 5. Principal Place of Business of the Limited Liability Company. The principal place of business of the limited liability company shall be: ___ **street address of principal office of LLC.** ___

The articles of organization often specify the principal place of business of the LLC. Normally, this location may be within or outside the state, but most LLCs will show the address of its main office located in the state. Technically, the principal place of business listed in the articles is one of the places where the business may be sued (brought to court), not necessarily the place where most of the business operations of the LLC are performed. For most smaller LLCs, there's only one place of business, and you will list it here.

h. Duration of the LLC

Article 6. Period of Duration of the Limited Liability Company. The period of duration of the limited liability company shall be: ___ **"perpetual" or "from the date these articles of organization are filed through and including (give future date or state a period of years)."** ___

In many states, the articles of organization must include a provision specifying the duration of the LLC. Your state's articles form, articles instructions or its statute for the contents of articles will tell you if this provision is required for your state, and, if so, how you must fill it in.

In some states, it's permissible to provide for a "perpetual" (unlimited) duration of the LLC in this provision. If you have this option, you probably will want to take it—this way your LLC automatically continues into the future until and unless your members vote to dissolve it.

Some states that require this provision won't let you provide a perpetual duration for your LLC. Instead, you must limit its duration to a number of years from the date the articles are filed or to a specific date in the future. Some states even say that this date can't be more than 30 or 50 years into the future. Don't worry about any of these limitations. If you must limit the life of your LLC in your articles under state rules, choose a date that is as far in the future as you can—either 30 or 50 years from the date of filing of your Articles, or even further into the future. If permitted, a good date to pick is the end of the 21st century: December 31, 2099. If your LLC is still around after the end of the next century—or whatever termination date you are forced to select—you or your LLC successors can file an amendment extending the legal life of the LLC for another 30, 50, or 100 years more.

i. Signatures of Persons Forming the LLC

In Witness Whereof, the undersigned organizer(s) of this Limited Liability Company has (have) signed these articles of organization on the date indicated.

Date: _____

Signature(s):

_____

 typed or printed name , Organizer

_____

 typed or printed name , Organizer

_____

 typed or printed name , Organizer

_____

 typed or printed name , Organizer

_____

 typed or printed name , Organizer

States have various signature requirements for LLC articles of organization. In most states, one person may act as organizer of the LLC by signing the form and submitting the articles for filing. The usual practice is to have one initial member listed in the articles of organization date and sign the form as the LLC organizer. If managers are listed instead of members in the articles, a manager will usually sign the form and act as organizer of the LLC.

If you have reserved your LLC's name. The person who reserved your LLC name with the state should sign your articles as one of its (or only) organizers. (If he or she is not available, check with your LLC filing office, which may allow you to file a transfer of reservation of name or similar form, signed by the person who reserved your LLC name.)

The signature statement on your state articles of organization may look a little different from the sample form, depending on your state. For example, in some states, people must sign under penalty of perjury with an assertion that the facts stated in the articles are true based upon the information and belief of the signers.

In a few states, the articles must be notarized—that is, signed in the presence of a notary public, who fills out a concluding notarization statement and impresses a notarial seal at the bottom of the form (notary statements vary from state to state). Notaries are found in real estate offices and other businesses, or simply by looking up the word "Notary" in a local telephone business directory. Notary fees are usually modest.

If your state does not provide a ready-to-use form, the articles instructions posted on your state's website should tell you who needs to sign your articles and how this should be done, including any required language or notary procedure.

LLC ORGANIZER DOES NOT HAVE TO BE A MEMBER OR MANAGER

Most states let you choose one person to act as the organizer of your LLC. The organizer can sign and file your articles on behalf of the LLC (instead of having all the initial members or managers sign the form). Typically, the organizer does not need to be a member or associated with the LLC in any way; in most states he or she must be at least 18 years of age.

What the states have in mind here is to allow a lawyer to prepare, sign and file your articles for you—but you will usually tend to this task yourself by selecting at least one of your initial members or managers as your organizer. Of course, you may want to let everyone join in on the action and have all founding members sign your articles as organizers of your LLC. This is not legally required, but fine to do if you want.

4. Sample Completed Articles of Organization

To help you tie all this information together, we include a sample completed articles of organization form below. The articles are prepared for a fictitious business, "Luxor Light LLC," a three-member LLC for a lighting fixture business. The sample is relatively standard; note that in Article 4 Luxor Light has opted to be managed by members (the option most LLCs will choose).

ARTICLES OF ORGANIZATION
OF
<u>LUXOR LIGHTING LLC</u>

The undersigned natural persons, of the age of eighteen years or more, acting as organizers of a limited liability company under the Anystate Limited Liability Company Act, adopt the following articles of organization for such limited liability company.

Article 1. Name of Limited Liability Company. The name of this limited liability company is **Luxor Light LLC.**

Article 2. Registered Office and Registered Agent. The initial registered office of this limited liability company and the name of its initial registered agent at this address are: **Robert Johnston, 1515 San Estudillo, Anycity, Anystate, 00000.**

Article 3. Statement of Purposes. The purposes for which this limited liability company is organized are:

to operate a custom home and commercial lighting and fixture store, and to

engage in any other lawful business for which limited liability companies

may be organized in this state.

Article 4. Management and Names and Addresses of Initial Members. The management of this limited liability company is reserved to the members. The names and addresses of its initial members are:

Robert Johnston, 1515 San Estudillo, Anycity, Anystate, 00000

Rebecca Johnston, 1515 San Estudillo, Anycity, Anystate, 00000

Gregory Luxor, 3021 Los Avenidos, Anycity, Anystate, 00000.

Article 5. Principal Place of Business of the Limited Liability Company. The principal place of business of the limited liability company shall be:

56 Rue de Campanille, Anycity, Anystate, 00000.

Article 6. Period of Duration of the Limited Liability Company. The period of duration of the limited liability company shall be: __**perpetual**__.

In Witness Whereof, the undersigned organizer of this Limited Liability Company has signed these articles of organization on the date indicated.

Date: **date**

Signature(s): *Gregory Luxor*

Gregory Luxor   , Organizer

5. Example of How to Prepare Articles From Scratch

As we've noted, not all states provide ready-to-use forms or sample articles of organization. If your state does not provide a ready-to-use or sample form, we list the required contents of articles or a certificate of organization in the "Special Instructions and Filing Requirements" portion of the Articles/Certificate of Organization section of your state sheet in Appendix A. Each list is drawn from each state's LLC statute which contains the technical requirements for articles or a certificate—we translate any technical or tricky terms for you in our list. Here is an example of how to use your state's list of requirements for articles, together with our sample articles (see section E4, above), to craft your own LLC articles of organization.

Hypothetical LLC articles statute:

Formation of a Limited Liability Company
To form a liability company, you must file articles of organization pursuant to Article 12.16 of the Hypothetical State Limited Liability Company Act. The articles of organization must minimally set forth:

1. The name of the limited liability company. The name must contain the words "Limited Liability Company" or "Limited Company" or the abbreviations "L.L.C.," "LLC," "LC," "L.C." or "Ltd. Co." The name of a limited liability company cannot be the same as or deceptively similar to that of another limited liability company, corporation, limited partnership, name reservation or registration.

2. The period of duration, which may be perpetual, or a specific date of termination.

3. The purpose for which the limited liability company is organized, which may be stated to be, or include, the transaction of any or all lawful business

for which limited liability companies may be organized.

4. The street address of its initial registered office in Texas and the name of its initial registered agent at such address.

5. If the limited liability company is to be managed by a manager or managers, a statement that the company is to be managed by a manager or managers and the names and addresses of the initial manager or managers. If the management of a limited liability company is reserved to the members, a statement that the limited liability company will not have managers and the names and addresses of its initial members.

6. The name and address of each organizer.

Here is a summary of how we used the sample articles of Section E4 to craft articles to meet the requirements of the hypothetical statute, above:

- The articles below use six of the sample articles from Section E4. We don't use sample Article 5, which specifies the principal place of business of the LLC, because the statute does not require it.

- In Article 4, below, we add a statement that the LLC shall not have managers. The statute says that this language is necessary if management is reserved to the members (normally, a statement that the management is reserved to members is enough). This is the only substantive change necessary to make our sample articles fit the hypothetical statute.

Finally, note that instructions for information to be supplied in blanks in our sample articles (from Section E4, above) are shown in bold. Additions to the language of our sample articles are noted in italics.

ARTICLES OF ORGANIZATION
OF

NAME OF LLC

The undersigned natural persons, of the age of eighteen years or more, acting as members of a limited liability company under the Hypothetical Limited Liability Company Act, adopt the following articles of organization for such limited liability company.

Article 1. Name of Limited Liability Company. The name of this limited liability company is

name of LLC.

Article 2. Registered Office and Registered Agent. The initial registered office of this limited liability company and the name of its initial registered agent at this address are:
name and address of registered agent and office.

Article 3. Statement of Purposes. The purposes for which this limited liability company is organized are:
"to engage in any lawful business for which limited liability companies

may be organized in this state."

Article 4. Management and Names and Addresses of Initial Members. The management of this limited liability company is reserved to the members, *and it shall not have managers.* The names and addresses of its initial members are:
names and addresses of initial members.

Article 5. Period of Duration of the Limited Liability Company. The period of duration of the limited liability company shall be: _____**"perpetual."**_____

Article 6. Names and Addresses of Organizers. The names and addresses of the organizers of this LLC are:
name and address of organizer(s), typically one or more of the initial members.

In Witness Whereof, the undersigned organizer(s) of this Limited Liability Company has (have) signed these articles of organization on the date indicated.

Date: **date**

Signature(s):   **signature(s) of organizer(s)**

typed or printed name   , Organizer

F. Finalize and File Your Articles of Organization

If you prepared a draft of your articles of organization, now's the time to transfer the information to a clean blank form. Again, if you're preparing your articles from scratch, they should be neatly typed or printed with a word processor on one side of letter-size pages (8½" x 11"). Check over your articles of organization one last time to make sure they're correct and have been properly signed.

If you downloaded an online articles form, it is normally provided in Adobe Acrobat pdf format. For most computer users, this means the form can only be printed (not filled in from) Adobe's Acrobat Reader program (available free from http://www.adobe.com). You will have to print the form, then fill in the blanks with a typewriter (if you can find one) or by printing neatly in the blanks. Type or print with black ink.

File your articles of organization with your state LLC filing office following the instructions in your state LLC materials. (Again, any special filing requirements or procedures are also listed in your state sheet.) Filing is usually done by mail, although many offices will accept articles in person. If you mail your articles, remember to keep an extra copy in case the original is lost in the mail.

Check your state website (See Appendix A)—some states now let you fill in and file your articles interactively online.

In Appendix C, we include a tear-out articles filing letter that you may wish to use to submit your articles of organization to the state LLC filing office (if you file by mail). Complete the tear-out form following the sample and Special Instructions below. The address of your state LLC filing office

and the amount of the required filing fee are shown on your state sheet in Appendix A. Your state website will have the most current fee information.

The articles filing letter is included on the CD-ROM at the back of this book.

If you have problems filing your articles. The filing office may return your articles and indicate which items need correction (your check should be held until you fix the problem). Often the problem is technical, not substantive, and easy to fix. If the problem is more complicated, such as an improper or insufficient LLC purpose clause, you may be able to solve the problem by rereading the instructions earlier in this chapter and those provided online for preparing articles. If you get stuck, you will need to do a little research or obtain further help from an LLC lawyer who's experienced in drafting and filing LLC articles of organization in your state. (See Chapter 8.)

SAMPLE LLC ARTICLES FILING LETTER

date _____

name and address of your state's LLC filing office _____

LLC Filings Office:

I enclose an original and ___**number**___ ❶ copies of the proposed articles of organization of ___**name of LLC**___, ❷ a proposed domestic limited liability company.

Please file the articles of organization and return a file-stamped copy of the original Articles or other receipt, acknowledgment or proof of filing to me at the address below.

A check/money order in the amount of $___**filing fee amount—see your state sheet**___, ❸ made payable to your office, for total filing and processing fees is enclosed.

☐ The above LLC name was reserved for my use ___**if applicable, insert "according to reservation number" and the reservation number**___, issued on ___**date of issuance**___. ❹

Sincerely,

your signature _____

your printed or typed name_____ , Organizer

your address and phone number ❺ _____

Enclosures: articles of organization; check

---

❶ In some states, you need only submit an original of the articles—the LLC office will file the original and send you a file-stamped copy or file receipt. In other states, you need to submit the original and one or more copies. The LLC filing office will file the original and file-stamp and return one or more copies to you.

Depending on the state, an additional fee may be charged for submitting more than one copy of your articles for file-stamping. One copy (plus the original) should be sufficient in most cases; you can always make copies of this file-stamped copy to keep in your LLC records book or give to others as the need arises.

❷ Show the proposed name for your LLC (the name stated in your articles of organization). As explained in Section C, above, it can be risky to file articles with a name that you haven't checked ahead of time. We recommend checking the availability of your proposed name before filing articles or reserving the name for your exclusive use. If you don't, and the desired name is unavailable, your articles will be returned unfiled.

❸ Include a check (or money order) for the total fees, made payable to the state or state office. Remember to consult your state sheet in Appendix A and your state website for particulars—a few states require payment by cashier's check or postal money order; some allow credit card payment.

❹ If you reserved your LLC name, check the box. Then fill in the blanks to show the certificate number and/or date of issuance of your reservation of LLC name. In some states, the LLC filing office simply sends you a file-stamped copy of your reservation letter—if so, just fill in the file-stamped date of the name reservation letter in the second blank, and include a copy of your file-stamped reservation certificate with this cover letter.

❺ The person (or one of the persons) who is acting as organizer of your LLC—by signing your articles—should sign this cover letter. If you reserved an LLC name, the person who reserved the name should sign this letter—and the articles of organization as well—since the LLC name is reserved for this person's use.

G. What to Do After Filing Articles of Organization

Once you've sent in your articles for filing, your next step is to wait. The LLC filing office will make sure the LLC name is available for use and that your articles of organization conform to law. If there are no problems, the office will mail you a file-stamped copy of your articles or a filing receipt. Don't forget to congratulate yourself. Once your articles of organization have been successfully filed, your business is a legally recognized limited liability company.

Before commencing LLC business, we want to issue a few words of advice. Although filing articles of organization is all you are legally required to do to establish the legal existence of your LLC, make sure you go at least one step further and prepare an operating agreement for your LLC—see Chapter 5 if your LLC is member-managed or Chapter 6 if your LLC is manager-managed. This agreement sets out the basic legal rules for operating your LLC.

Finally, don't miss Chapter 7, where we cover some of the ins and outs of tending to your new LLC.

Prepare an LLC Operating Agreement for Your Member-Managed LLC

If you've turned to this chapter, we assume you have already formed or are in the process of forming your LLC by preparing and filing articles of organization with your state LLC filing office, as explained in Chapter 4. Here, you'll learn how to prepare a fill-in-the-blanks operating agreement for a member-managed LLC.

Manager-managed LLCs. Most LLCs will be member-managed—that is, managed by all members. If, however, you plan to adopt a manager-managed LLC (one managed by only some LLC members and/or by nonmembers), you'll need an operating agreement that provides for manager-management. If yours is a manager-managed LLC, or you're unsure of the type of operating agreement to prepare for your LLC, start by turning to Chapter 6. Note that even if you create the management operating agreement covered in Chapter 6 (rather than the member-managed agreement in Section C of this chapter), you'll need to read all of Sections A and B below. Section A discusses areas of LLC operation not covered in either of our tear-out operating agreements, and Section B talks a little about making modifications to either agreement.

A. Scope of Our Basic LLC Operating Agreements

The tear-out operating agreements we supply in this book are relatively straightforward forms that cover all basic LLC issues. You may discover that our operating agreements are considerably shorter than the typically long-winded LLC agreements available commercially or from a lawyer. Our agreements help you set up your LLC under sensible ground rules and contain necessary reminders about restrictions that apply to most LLCs under state law.

There are two major areas of LLC operations that our agreements do not cover, however. Let's briefly look at each.

1. Special Capital Account Provisions

Capital account provisions set forth the types and amounts of capital contributed by your original members. If you read a lawyer- or accountant-prepared LLC operating agreement, you'll usually see lists of complicated capital account definitions and provisions (language that specifies how members' capital contributions and distributions are to be handled under a range of circumstances). This special language can be important if you decide to split profits and losses among your LLC members in ratios that are different from the percentage of capital each member contributes to your LLC. (Chapter 3, Section D2 gives a fuller discussion of this issue.)

For our purposes, and for most readers of this book, adding page upon page of special provisions to handle so-called "special allocations" of profits and losses will not be necessary, so we do not include them in our tear-out operating agreements. If you think you'd like to include special allocation provisions in your operating agreement, ask your tax advisor for help. (See Chapter 8 for suggestions on finding a legal or tax advisor.)

Consider getting help drafting other special financial provisions. Of course, a legal or tax advisor can also help you prepare special financial provisions of any sort—for example, to set up a special class of membership that gets a guaranteed share of LLC profits or losses or to establish a special schedule for distribution of LLC profits to members before liquidation.

2. Buy-Sell or Right of First Refusal Provisions

An important and sometimes complicated aspect of forming any business involves deciding whether and how to plan in advance to sell a member's interest in the business to outsiders or other owners. Here are some examples of the kinds of issues that may arise:

- *"Right of first refusal" issues.* Does an owner who wishes to sell out have to offer to sell his or her interest to the other owners before selling to an outsider? Must the other owners buy that interest for the amount an outsider is ready to pay?

- *Valuation questions.* When a member (or his or her estate) wishes to sell to other members, how will the interest be valued? At fair market value (whatever that is—it's often hard to tell with a small, privately held business)? Should an appraiser resolve this issue at the time of sale? Or should the value of membership interests be established ahead of time in the LLC operating agreement—if so, should the value be based upon the book (net asset) value of the business, a multiple of the earnings of the business or some other formula?

- *When and how should a departing LLC member be paid?* Should payment be made all in a lump sum or in installments? This is an important question, since your LLC or its other members may not have sufficient cash or borrowing power to come up with the needed buyout

funds right away, with the result that a cash sale could only be made to an outsider. On the other hand, a departing LLC member (or his or her estate) will want to be paid as soon as possible. Should interest be charged and paid by the LLC if the buyout is accomplished in installments?

- *Life insurance.* Should the buyout of a deceased owner be funded with life insurance purchased ahead of time by the LLC or each of the other members?

- *Does it matter why or when a member is being bought out?* For example, if a member calls it quits and wishes to transfer his or her interest back to the LLC after only six months with the LLC, should he or she receive a smaller buyback price than a member who stays with the LLC for five years? What about a member who is expelled? What about a member who suffers a debilitating illness or dies?

Just in case you find all these questions daunting, you should know that most businesses decide to tackle these issues down the road, hopefully with a few years of successful business operations under their belt. They reason that, for now, it's enough to know that an appraiser can be called in to establish a fair value of a member's interests if and when a member wishes to sell out. (You don't even need to say this in your operating agreement; just call in an appraiser when and if the time comes.) Similarly, most small LLCs decide that the basic transfer restrictions built into our operating agreements are adequate, at least in the short term. These provisions require the approval of all or a majority of the nontransferring members before admitting a new person as a member in the LLC.

However, other more detail-oriented business owners decide to ask and answer all these questions and spell out their conclusions as part of the membership restrictions in their initial operating agreement. Although we think each approach has its merits, we follow the first one here and do not add buy-sell provisions to our basic LLC operating agreements. One additional reason that we take this approach is that it could take a separate book to show you all the possible choices that can be included in buy-sell provisions.

If you want comprehensive buy-sell provisions. If you decide to go the extra distance and include buy-sell provisions for inclusion in your initial operating agreement, ask your LLC legal advisor to put together buy-sell provisions that will work for you. Alternately, you should be able to find several legal workbooks at the local law or business library that cover buy-sell or right of first refusal provisions. If you draft your own provisions, it makes sense to have your LLC legal advisor take a look at them to see if there are any glaring gaps or mistakes.

A Nolo Resource: Create a Buy-Sell Agreement for Your Business, by Bethany Laurence and Anthony Mancuso (Nolo), provides step-by-step instructions and forms for preparing your own agreement for an LLC, partnership or corporation.

B. Modifying Your LLC Operating Agreement

As you create your own LLC operating agreement, you will undoubtedly want to add or change provisions to suit your needs. Modifying or writing LLC operating agreement provisions is not akin to brain surgery, and you can ordinarily do much of it yourself—just use common sense and your own sound business judgment.

If you wonder whether state law has established any guidelines you must follow in an area of your LLC's operation, it is a simple matter to check your state's LLC Act (normally by following a link provided on your state filing office website to your state LLC act) to make sure your rule does not conflict with a specific statute. You may also choose to ask a legal or tax advisor for a second opinion on the validity or effect of your custom-crafted provisions. We think this second opinion is a good idea for any changes you feel are important—such as special voting rights to certain members, special vote requirements to amend your articles of organization or to approve the dissolution of the LLC. (For guidance on self-help research and finding an LLC legal or tax advisor, see Chapter 8.)

Will you need to retype your operating agreement? Minor changes to your operating agreement ordinarily can be accomplished simply by neatly crossing out a word or two, then typing or printing your changes between the lines or in the margins (with insertion marks, if necessary, to show where the new words go). Have all members initial each of these changes in the margin when they sign the agreement. For more comprehensive changes, you will need to retype one or more pages to substitute for the tear-out pages that you prepare. Don't worry if these "insert" pages don't cover a full page—they don't have to. Just be sure to consecutively renumber all pages of your operating agreement, including any inserted pages.

Here's a brief summary of the different types of changes you can make to the tear-out operating agreement, and a quick assessment of how safe you are in making them on your own:

• *Internal matters.* Happily, internal LLC housekeeping provisions are your own business. For example, you may choose to specify how and when member or manager meetings will be held, who qualifies to be an officer or employee in your LLC, and how to handle numerous other formalities. If you want to put rules such as these in your operating agreement, you should generally be safe doing so; state LLC statutes and the tax rules have little or nothing to say about internal issues of this sort.

- *Legal procedures.* If you wish to change a legal procedure—such as the number of votes necessary to dissolve your LLC, amend your articles of organization or effect a similar structural change to your LLC—you need to check to see if legal rules affect your desired change. If you browse your state's LLC Act online, it should take just a few minutes to see if state law has placed limitations or restrictions on the provisions you are thinking of adopting.

- *Tax matters.* Tax matters are a little oilier and may be harder to track down or grasp. We recommend showing your LLC tax advisor any changes to your operating agreement that may have tax effects—for example, provisions dealing with the sale of assets, allocation or distribution of profits, and the like. This person can tell you if your proposed operating agreement changes are good, bad or indifferent from a tax perspective.

Example 1: Hank forms an LLC with friend and former business partner Max. Hank has cash and Max doesn't. Max signs a note, promising to pay his investment to the LLC (together with interest) over time. It's decided that even though each person will contribute equally to the capitalization of the LLC, Hank should get an extra share of the profits for putting up cash in one lump sum at the start of the business operations. They ask their tax advisor to check their operating agreement, since special allocations (a disproportionate division) of profits may have tax consequences and require the addition of special provisions to their operating agreement. Their tax advisor adds IRS special allocations language to the agreement that restates technical tax regulations related to sharing profits and losses disproportionately. (See Chapter 3, Section D2, for more on this special allocations tax issue and adding provisions to your operating agreement to handle it.)

Example 2: Kenneth and Francine decide to lower the membership vote requirement in their LLC member-managed operating agreement to approve the transfer of LLC interests to outsiders. First, they check their state sheet in Appendix A, where we provide the basic state rules, and whether the state lets LLC organizers change these rules (they look under the heading "Operating Rules" and read the "Default Transfer Rule" found in the state's LLC law). To be doubly sure they have the latest rules, they ask their legal advisor to make sure their changes comport to any recent changes made to their state's LLC Act (or they go online to check the relevant code section in their state LLC Act themselves).*

C. How to Prepare a Member-Managed LLC Operating Agreement

Appendix D contains a basic Operating Agreement for a Member-Managed Limited Liability Company (the first of two agreements in Appendix D). If you wish to prepare this form, tear it out now, making sure that you don't miss any pages or inadvertently take pages from the other (manager-managed) operating agreement. You may want to photocopy the operating agreement before you get started, in case you make mistakes or want to modify it significantly.

The LLC Member-Managed Operating Agreement is included on the CD-ROM at the back of this book.

We'll start at the top of the agreement and work our way through it. We provide instructions for filling out items in the blanks of the sample agreement, below. To help you complete some of the more complicated information, we provide additional instructions in the Special Instructions that accompany the sample operating agreement. Special Instructions are numbered sequentially as they occur in the sample agreement.

OPERATING AGREEMENT FOR
MEMBER-MANAGED LIMITED LIABILITY COMPANY

I. PRELIMINARY PROVISIONS

Here we address preliminary matters, such as the effective date of the agreement, the name of the LLC and other basic information.

(1) Effective Date: This operating agreement of

_____**name of LLC,** ❶_____

effective_____**date**_____, ❷ is adopted by the members whose signatures appear at the end of this agreement. ❸

(2) Formation: This limited liability company (LLC) was formed by filing articles of organization, a Certificate of Formation or a similar organizational document with the LLC filing office of the state of _____**state of formation**_____ on ___**date of filing articles of organization, Certificate of Formation or similar organizational document.**___ ❹

A copy of this organizational document has been placed in the LLC's records book.

(3) Name: The formal name of this LLC is as stated above. However, this LLC may do business under a different name by complying with the state's fictitious or assumed business name statutes and procedures. ❺

(4) Registered Office and Agent: The registered office of this LLC and the registered agent at this address are as follows: _____
name and address of registered agent and office._____

The registered office and agent may be changed from time to time as the members may see fit, by filing a change of registered agent or office form with the state LLC filing office. It will not be necessary to amend this provision of the operating agreement if and when such a change is made. ❻

(5) Business Purposes: The specific business purposes and activities contemplated by the founders of this LLC at the time of initial signing of this agreement consist of the following: **state the specific business purposes and activities you foresee for your LLC.** ❼

It is understood that the foregoing statement of purposes shall not serve as a limitation on the powers or abilities of this LLC, which shall be permitted to engage in any and all lawful business activities. If this LLC intends to engage in business activities outside the state of its formation that require the qualification of the LLC in other states, it shall obtain such qualification before engaging in such out-of-state activities.

❶ Insert the name of your LLC exactly as shown in your articles of organization. (We discuss how to choose a name in Chapter 4, Section C.)

❷ The key is to insert a date that is on or after the date all your members sign this operating agreement (you'll have your operating agreement signed as the last step in preparing this form). If you aren't sure how long it will take to do this, simply insert the words "the last date of signing shown at the end of this agreement."

❸ All members will need to sign the agreement. Again, members will sign the operating agreement at the end of this process.

❹ Insert the date and year your articles of organization or Certificate of Formation were filed with your state LLC filing office. In most cases, this date will be shown as the "file-stamped" date on the first page of the filed Articles or Certificate, or on a filing receipt mailed to you from the state LLC filing office.

❺ This paragraph states that your LLC is allowed to do business under another name—one that is different from the formal LLC name stated in your articles of organization and operating agreement. In that event, you may need to register a fictitious or assumed business name with the state, as well as each county where you will use the fictitious business name. (See Chapter 7, Section D3, and call your state LLC filing office or check your state's website if you want more information.)

❻ Most articles of organization specify the LLC's registered office and agent—just copy the information from your articles of organization into the blank. (We cover this in Chapter 4, Section E3d.) Typically, the registered office address must be a street address (not a post office box) located in the state. Most states require the agent to be at least 18 years of age and a state resident. Typically, a founding member of the LLC will act as initial agent and show the principal office address of the LLC as the registered office address.

As this paragraph specifies, you may change your LLC's registered agent and office by filing a form with your state LLC filing office (and paying a small fee). If and when you do so, there is no need to go back and change this information in your operating agreement.

❼ In plain English, specify the business purposes of your LLC. You may have listed specific business purposes in your articles of organization (covered in Chapter 4, Section E3e). If so, you can copy that information in these blanks.

Mostly, this statement is meant to let your own members know what your plans are for the LLC's business operations, so feel free to expand your statement of purposes to provide as much detail as you want. Here are some examples:

- "to open and operate a car stereo and security alarm sales and service facility"
- "to purchase, sell and otherwise invest in real property and commercial interests in real property," or
- "to provide financial consulting services to individuals and businesses."

(6) Duration of LLC: The duration of this LLC shall be _____ **specify "perpetual" or any specific termination date or term of years for the LLC specified in the articles of organization**_____. Further, this LLC shall terminate when a proposal to dissolve the LLC is adopted by the membership of this LLC or when this LLC is otherwise terminated in accordance with law. ❽

II. MEMBERSHIP PROVISIONS

Here we cover provisions that deal with the rights and responsibilities of your LLC's members.

(1) Nonliability of Members: No member of this LLC shall be personally liable for the expenses, debts, obligations or liabilities of the LLC, or for claims made against it. ❾

(2) Reimbursement for Organizational Costs: Members shall be reimbursed by the LLC for organizational expenses paid by the members. The LLC shall be authorized to elect to deduct organizational expenses and start-up expenditures ratably over a period of time as permitted by the Internal Revenue Code and as may be advised by the LLC's tax advisor. ❿

(3) Management: This LLC shall be managed exclusively by all of its members. ⓫

(4) Members' Percentage Interests: A member's percentage interest in this LLC shall be computed as a fraction, the numerator of which is the total of a member's capital account and the denominator of which is the total of all capital accounts of all members. This fraction shall be expressed in this agreement as a percentage, which shall be called each member's "percentage interest" in this LLC. ⓬

(5) Membership Voting: Except as otherwise may be required by the articles of organization, Certificate of Formation or a similar organizational document, other provisions of this operating agreement, or under the laws of this state, each member shall vote on any matter submitted to the membership for approval in proportion to the member's percentage interest in this LLC. Further, unless defined otherwise for a particular provision of this operating agreement, the phrase "majority of members" means the vote of members whose combined votes equal more than 50% of the votes of all members in this LLC. ⓭

(6) Compensation: Members shall not be paid as members of the LLC for performing any duties associated with such membership, including management of the LLC. Members may be paid, however, for any services rendered in any other capacity for the LLC, whether as officers, employees, independent contractors or otherwise. ⓮

❽ Many states require the articles of organization to specify the duration of the legal existence of the LLC, as discussed in Chapter 4, Section E3h. If so, insert this same time period here. Remember, this duration requirement is a leftover state law provision meant to conform to old federal tax rules, and is no longer necessary as far as the IRS is concerned. Also, even if you must specify a limited duration for your LLC under state law, remember: you can always amend your Articles to extend the legal life of your LLC as the termination date approaches. (We cover the process of amending Articles in Chapter 7, Section D4.)

If your Articles are silent on this issue, your state most likely does not require you to limit the duration of your LLC's legal existence, and you can insert the word "perpetual" in the blank. Your state LLC materials should indicate if your state has any special rules for limiting the life of your LLC.

Finally, notice that the concluding sentence of this provision makes it clear that the LLC can always be terminated by a vote of the membership and as otherwise allowed by law. (See "VI. Dissolution Provisions: (1) Events That Trigger Dissolution of the LLC," in this operating agreement, and the corresponding Special Instructions ❸❽ through ❹❶, below.) We include this sentence as a reminder that members have the ultimate say as to when the LLC will wind up its affairs and dissolve.

❾ Although there is no legal requirement that you insert this statement of nonliability in your agreement, we think it's a good idea to include it as a basic restatement of this important state law protection.

❿ This paragraph authorizes the LLC to reimburse its founders for LLC formation expenses advanced by members, such as filing fees, legal fees and tax fees.

Also included is a reminder that the Internal Revenue Code allows businesses to amortize (deduct over a period of time, usually a 60-month period) organizational and start-up expenses paid or reimbursed by the LLC. (See Internal Revenue Code Sections 709 and 195.) Your tax advisor should tell you whether you can and should make either or both of these important tax elections, and how to implement each of them on your first LLC informational tax return. If you don't make these elections on your first LLC tax returns, you may not be able to deduct start-up expenses and organizational costs paid by the LLC. In other words, you may be forced to wait and deduct them later, when the LLC is sold or liquidated.

⓫ This provision makes it clear that all members will manage your LLC. This is exactly the structure and process founders of most smaller LLCs prefer, since it allows all members a hand in managing the business. If you want to provide for management by some, but not all, members, you need to adopt the management agreement covered in Chapter 6, not this agreement. For a discussion of this important management decision, see Chapter 2, Section C.

⓬ This paragraph defines an important LLC formula: the calculation of each member's percentage interest in the LLC. This percentage will be used later in the agreement to:

- allocate profits and losses of the LLC to members
- allocate voting rights among the members
- distribute assets of the LLC when it is liquidated, and
- value a member's interest when it is sold to an outsider or back to the LLC.

This percentage is arrived at by computing a fraction that reflects the proportion of each member's capital account to the total of all members' capital accounts. Each member's capital account starts with the amount of money or value of property he or she contributed at the outset of the LLC, plus any additions to, distributions from or other adjustments to this account.

Example: Barbara, Bill, Fred, Francis and Mike start their LLC by contributing $5,000 cash each. Each member's capital account currently shows a positive $5,000 balance. Each member has a 20% percentage interest in the LLC. This figure is the result of dividing each member's $5,000 capital account balance by the $25,000 total capital account balance for all members, resulting in the fraction 1/5, expressed in the operating *agreement as a percentage interest of 20%. (According to subsequent provisions in the agreement, each person is allocated 20% of the profits and losses of the LLC and is entitled to a 20% share of the LLC's total voting power.)*

If you want to change this standard approach. You may make changes to this provision and base percentage interests in your LLC disproportionately, or by some other formula. For example, you could decide that anyone who contributes cash to your LLC is entitled to a 10% increase in the standard percentage interest (with other members' interests reduced accordingly). If you wish to come up with your own method, ask your tax advisor to make sure that you will meet the requirements of IRS regulations relating to special allocations of profits and losses. Generally, Internal Revenue Code regulations under Section 704 of the Internal Revenue Code require that special allocations of LLC profits and losses have "substantial economic effect," meaning they are based upon a specific economic reality of your business—for example, perhaps one member devotes more time to a profit-making activity or is on the line for its losses. You can, however, pretty much do what you want if you adopt special allocation tax language in your agreement. See Chapter 3, Section D2, for more information on this special tax issue.

⓭ This provision gives each member voting power equal to his or her percentage interest in the LLC—for instance, a 10% member gets a 10% vote on any matter. This is standard practice, although you can base voting rights on some other measure if you wish. Here are some possibilities:

- each member gets one vote on all membership matters—known as per capita voting, or
- members get different numbers of votes each—you can even decide to make one or members nonvoting members by specifying that they have 0 votes,

- each member's vote depends on his or her share in the profits of the LLC (if profits interests differ from percentage interests).

If you decide to opt for your own membership voting scheme, delete this paragraph and substitute your own wording. For example, if a four-member LLC wishes to specify specific voting power for three members, and make the fourth a nonvoting member, it could replace the standard provision in the tear-out agreement with the following wording:

> Except as otherwise may be required by the articles of organization, Certificate of Formation or a similar organizational document, other provisions of this operating agreement, or under the laws of this state, the members of this LLC shall have the following voting power:
>
> Member 1: 1 vote
> Member 2: 2 votes
> Member 3: 2 votes
> Member 4: 0 votes
>
> Further, unless defined otherwise for a particular provision of this operating agreement, the phrase "majority of members" means the vote of members whose combined votes equal more than 50% of the votes of all members in this LLC.

Special voting rules. You'll see in later provisions that special membership voting rules are specified in your operating agreement to approve transfers of membership and to agree to continue the LLC after a member leaves. (Many states still require these specific membership approval procedures, even though they no longer matter under the federal tax rules—see Chapter 3, Section D1.) These special voting rules will take precedence if they conflict with any of the provisions of the basic LLC membership voting rule specified here. For example, this operating agreement's "V. Membership Withdrawal and Transfer Provisions: (2) Restrictions on the Transfer of Membership," requires the approval of all nontransferring members to approve the transfer of membership to a new member. This unanimous vote requirement will take precedence over the membership voting provisions contained in this paragraph.

⓮ This paragraph says that members will not be paid in their capacity as members or member-managers of the LLC. It does, however, allow compensation in any other capacity—for example, the LLC may pay members who also serve as LLC officers, staff, salaried personnel or independent contractors.

Example: Sally and Joe are the only two members of their member-managed LLC. Both actively operate the LLC, Sally as president and Joe as sales manager. They receive salaries for their day-to-day work, but don't receive any extra compensation simply for signing up and legally functioning as members (and member-managers) of their LLC.

⓯ Especially if you have previously been involved in a small corporation, you may be surprised that the operating agreement doesn't require regular membership meetings. We don't require meetings for two basic reasons:

- Most LLC members naturally will prefer to spend their time taking care of business, not holding and documenting formal LLC meetings. After all, you and your business associates can schedule and hold meetings for any purpose when and as you need, without having to treat them as formal LLC membership meetings.

- When you do need a formal meeting to approve an important legal formality that should be recorded in your LLC records, you can call one as provided in this clause.

Most state statutes are silent as to whether and how members' meetings are called and held. If your state law does deal with this, the state law LLC meeting provisions are usually default rules only—that is, you are usually free to change them in your LLC operating agreement. To learn what, if anything, your state has to say on this subject, scan your state's LLC Act. Particularly, look for a section

of law titled "Meetings of Members." Be aware, however, that many meeting requirements only concern meetings by managers in *manager*-managed LLCs (the type of LLC that uses the operating agreement covered in Chapter 6). Manager-meeting provisions of this sort do not apply to a member-managed LLC.

When it comes to calling meetings, we've kept things simple and in line with the kind of flexibility normally accorded LLCs under state law: members can decide to meet at any time with a minimum of pre-meeting formality. Further, our provision says that all members must either attend a meeting or, alternatively, that any nonattending members must agree in writing to the holding of the meeting ahead of time. This is the approach most small, closely held LLCs will wish to take—after all, the holding of a formal membership meeting is infrequent and is usually enough of a big deal to warrant attendance by everyone, or at least to require the pre-meeting consent of any member who can't attend.

We have also added an escape hatch in this provision, which allows the holding of a formal LLC membership meeting with a majority of the membership (percentage) interests in attendance, if it is a second postponed meeting (the second postponement of a members' meeting, whose time and date was announced at the first postponed meeting). You can change this postponement procedure to suit your tastes—for example, you could require two postponements (instead of one) before permitting a meeting with less than unanimous attendance or consent. Similarly, you may wish to change the quorum requirement of such a meeting, such as to two-thirds of the per capita membership in the LLC rather than our majority of percentage interests requirement.

Some LLCs will wish to provide for alternatives to face-to-face member meetings. For example, you can allow for membership action by unanimous written consent of the members (without a meeting), or provide for conference-call, computer bulletin-board or video hookups and other high-tech ways to hold virtual meetings over the phone

(7) Members' Meetings: The LLC shall not provide for regular members' meetings. However, any member may call a meeting by communicating his or her wish to schedule a meeting to all other members. Such notification may be in person or in writing, or by telephone, facsimile machine, or other form of electronic communication reasonably expected to be received by a member, and the other members shall then agree, either personally, in writing, or by telephone, facsimile machine or other form of electronic communication to the member calling the meeting, to meet at a mutually acceptable time and place. Notice of the business to be transacted at the meeting need not be given to members by the member calling the meeting, and any business may be discussed and conducted at the meeting.

If all members cannot attend a meeting, it shall be postponed to a date and time when all members can attend, unless all members who do not attend have agreed in writing to the holding of the meeting without them. If a meeting is postponed, and the postponed meeting cannot be held either because all members do not attend the postponed meeting or the nonattending members have not signed a written consent to allow the postponed meeting to be held without them, a second postponed meeting may be held at a date and time announced at the first postponed meeting. The date and time of the second postponed meeting shall also be communicated to any members not attending the first postponed meeting. The second postponed meeting may be held without the attendance of all members as long as a majority of the percentage interests of the membership of this LLC is in attendance at the second postponed meeting. Written notice of the decisions or approvals made at this second postponed meeting shall be mailed or delivered to each nonattending member promptly after the holding of the second postponed meeting. **❶❺**

Written minutes of the discussions and proposals presented at a members' meeting, and the votes taken and matters approved at such meeting, shall be taken by one of the members or a person designated at the meeting. A copy of the minutes of the meeting shall be placed in the LLC's records book after the meeting. **❶❻**

(8) Membership Certificates: This LLC shall be authorized to obtain and issue certificates representing or certifying membership interests in this LLC. Each certificate shall show the name of the LLC, the name of the member, and state that the person named is a member of the LLC and is entitled to all the rights granted members of the LLC under the articles of organization, Certificate of Formation or a similar organizational document, this operating agreement and provisions of law. Each membership certificate shall be consecutively numbered and signed by one or more officers of this LLC. The certificates shall include any additional information considered appropriate for inclusion by the members on membership certificates.

lines or the Internet. Frankly, we think worrying about all of this is probably a bit much for most smaller LLCs. Formal membership meetings are not commonly needed in the first place, unless big structural changes are in the works, such as amending the LLC articles of organization or approving a dissolution of the LLC. If you are considering approving a major proposal of this sort, meeting face-to-face makes the most sense anyway.

If the subject of LLC meetings sparks your interest and you want to include more detailed rules, you ordinarily can let your imagination and good sense be your guide. Following are some examples of issues you may want to address—but before you make any changes, do take a quick look at your state LLC act to be sure there are no special rules to consider:

- You can set a time limit for calling meetings (no more than 60 days or less than 10 days from the date of the call, for example).

- You may want to require verbal or written notice of meetings (our provision allows all sorts of methods for giving and acknowledging notice, including the use of fax machines and other electronic devices).

- You may limit the business to be conducted at a meeting to matters stated in the notice.

- You may wish to set lower quorum requirements to hold member meetings (less than the unanimous presence or consent of members), and the like.

16 In Chapter 7, Sections C2, C3 and C4, we show you how to document meetings, and we discuss the importance of keeping good records, preferably in a well-organized LLC records book. Of course, it's possible to create your own, or you may be interested in ordering an LLC records kit from Nolo. (See order page at the back of this book.)

17 There is no statutorily required form for LLC membership certificates, and you are not even legally required to issue them to your members. Many LLCs don't. However, if you prepare your own certificates, you can follow the basic format for the contents of the certificates as stated in this provision of the operating agreement, or you can modify the provision to require additional information on each certificate, such as the date of issuance and the percentage interest each member holds in the LLC. Remember to place a membership certificate legend on each of the certificates—see the sidebar, "How to Prepare a Membership Certificate Legend," below.

You do not have to obtain and impress a seal of the LLC on each certificate—and, in fact, seals are becoming a bit old-hat now that formal documents are routinely faxed or e-mailed to recipients. If you want to order an LLC seal from a local stamp maker, you can design one to your liking—state law does not contain mandatory requirements for LLC seals. Most in use are circular, and contain the name and year of formation of the LLC.

In addition to the above information, all membership certificates shall bear a prominent legend on their face or reverse side stating, summarizing or referring to any transfer restrictions that apply to memberships in this LLC under the articles of organization, Certificate of Formation or a similar organizational document and/or this operating agreement, and the address where a member may obtain a copy of these restrictions upon request from this LLC.

The records book of this LLC shall contain a list of the names and addresses of all persons to whom certificates have been issued, show the date of issuance of each certificate, and record the date of all cancellations or transfers of membership certificates. ⓱

(9) Other Business by Members: Each member shall agree not to own an interest in, manage or work for another business, enterprise or endeavor, if such ownership or activities would compete with this LLC's business goals, mission, profitability or productivity, or would diminish or impair the member's ability to provide maximum effort and performance in managing the business of this LLC. ⓲

III. TAX AND FINANCIAL PROVISIONS

*These provisions deal with tax and financial aspects
of organizing and running your LLC.*

(1) Tax Classification of LLC: The members of this LLC intend that this LLC be initially classified as a **"partnership" or "sole proprietorship of the sole member" or "corporation"** for federal and, if applicable, state income tax purposes. It is understood that all members may agree to change the tax treatment of this LLC by signing, or authorizing the signature of, IRS Form 8832, Entity Classification Election, and filing it with the IRS and, if applicable, the state tax department within the prescribed time limits. ⓳

(2) Tax Year and Accounting Method: The tax year of this LLC shall be **"the calendar year" or specify a noncalendar year period, such as "July 1 to June 30th"**. The LLC shall use the **"cash" or "accrual"** method of accounting. Both the tax year and the accounting period of the LLC may be changed with the consent of all members if the LLC qualifies for such change, and may be effected by the filing of appropriate forms with the IRS and state tax authorities. ⓴

(3) Tax Matters Partner: If this LLC is required under Internal Revenue Code provisions or regulations, it shall designate from among its members a "tax matters partner" in accordance with Internal Revenue Code Section 6231(a)(7) and corresponding regulations, who will fulfill this role by being the spokesperson for the LLC in dealings with the IRS as required under the Internal Revenue Code and Regulations, and who will report to the members on the progress and outcome of these dealings. ㉑

⓲ This provision limits the ability of members to own interests in, manage or work in competing outside businesses. We don't specify exactly what a competing business is, so you may want to add language that addresses this issue.

Example: Each member shall agree not to own an interest in, manage or work for another computer retail sales or service business, enterprise or endeavor…

You can be more liberal if you wish, and allow members to own, manage or be employed by competing businesses, but we think our provision states a basic restriction that will match the wishes of most smaller LLC owners.

If you wish to expand or otherwise change this provision. You may wish to take a look at noncompetition provisions for LLCs, partnerships, corporations and other businesses in a local law or business library. Noncompetition clauses can be found in various partnership and employment agreements contained in *Gordon's Modern Annotated Forms of Agreement*, by Saul Gordon, revised and updated by Stephen Kurzman (Prentice Hall, Englewood Cliffs, NJ). An overview of the court-developed rules in this area is contained in a legal reference book commonly found in law libraries: *ALR (American Law Reports)*, 3rd Edition, Volume 61, starting on page 397. Section 28 of this annotation discusses cases dealing specifically with agreements not to compete found in partnership agreements. Other places to look for specific noncompetition clauses are business buy-sell agreements, corporate bylaws, general and limited partnership agreements and employment contracts in legal and business practice books located in law and business libraries. Or, you may wish to ask your LLC legal advisor to help you craft a member noncompetition clause.

⓳ After rereading Chapter 3, Section A, fill in this blank to specify the IRS income tax classification you wish to obtain for your LLC. There are three choices for filling in this blank:

Choice #1: Insert "partnership" if you are forming an LLC with more than one member, and you do not wish to be classified as a corporation for income tax purposes—this is the response most multi-member LLCs will make.

Choice #2: Insert "sole proprietorship of the sole member" if you are forming a one-member LLC and do not wish to be classified as a corporation. This is the choice most one-member LLCs will make.

Choice #3: Insert "corporation" if you are forming a one- or a multi-member LLC and wish to be classified as a corporation for income tax purposes. Most LLC organizers will not wish to start out with their LLC classified as a corporation, but if you do, make sure to check the "A domestic eligible entity electing to be classified as an association taxable as a corporation" box on IRS Form 8832 and file it on time as explained in Chapter 3, Section A.

⓴ The tax year and accounting period options available to LLCs are the same as those available to partnerships. There are several places to look for the most current information on these rules, including IRS publications and commercial tax guides at the local law or business library. (See IRS Publication 538, *Accounting Periods and Methods*, and IRS Publication 541, *Tax Information on Partnerships*, available on the IRS website at http://www.irs.gov.) Of course, your tax advisor should be on top of any recent rules in these areas, and can help you make the right choices for your LLC tax year and its accounting method.

(4) Annual Income Tax Returns and Reports: Within 60 days after the end of each tax year of the LLC, a copy of the LLC's state and federal income tax returns for the preceding tax year shall be mailed or otherwise provided to each member of the LLC, together with any additional information and forms necessary for each member to complete his or her individual state and federal income tax returns. If this LLC is classified as a partnership for income tax purposes, this additional information shall include a federal (and, if applicable, state) Form K-1 (Form 1065— Partner's Share of Income, Credits, Deductions) or equivalent income tax reporting form. This additional information shall also include a financial report, which shall include a balance sheet and profit and loss statement for the prior tax year of the LLC. **㉒**

(5) Bank Accounts: The LLC shall designate one or more banks or other institutions for the deposit of the funds of the LLC, and shall establish savings, checking, investment and other such accounts as are reasonable and necessary for its business and investments. One or more members of the LLC shall be designated with the consent of all members to deposit and withdraw funds of the LLC, and to direct the investment of funds from, into and among such accounts. The funds of the LLC, however and wherever deposited or invested, shall not be commingled with the personal funds of any members of the LLC. **㉓**

(6) Title to Assets: All personal and real property of this LLC shall be held in the name of the LLC, not in the names of individual members. **㉔**

IV. CAPITAL PROVISIONS

These provisions deal with capital contributions, allocations and distributions by and to LLC members, as well as related matters.

(1) Capital Contributions by Members: Members shall make the following contributions of cash, property or services as shown next to each member's name below. Unless otherwise noted, cash and property described below shall be paid or delivered to the LLC on or by **_____final date or period for contributions_____**. The fair market values of items of property or services as agreed between the LLC and the contributing member are also shown below. The percentage interest in the LLC that each member shall receive in return for his or her capital contribution is also indicated for each member. **㉕**

Name	Contribution	Fair Market Value	Percentage Interest in LLC
_____	_____	$ _____	_____
_____	_____	$ _____	_____
_____	_____	$ _____	_____
_____	_____	$ _____	_____
_____	_____	$ _____	_____
_____	_____	$ _____	_____

HOW TO PREPARE A MEMBERSHIP CERTIFICATE LEGEND

If you adopt and use one of the two tear-out agreements included with this book without making modifications, you will require the vote of all nontransferring members to admit into membership a transferee of a selling member. See Special Instruction ㊱, below, which covers "V. Membership, Withdrawal and Transfer Provisions: (2) Restrictions on the Transfer of Membership," in this operating agreement.

This operating agreement's "II. Membership Provisions: (8) Membership Certificates," requires your LLC to put members on notice of the existence of these restrictions on transfer—as well as any others you may adopt in your operating agreement or Articles—by including a statement (a legend) on any membership certificates (if any) you issue. You don't need to spell out exact transfer restrictions in your LLC membership certificate legend. Instead, you can summarize the restrictions and tell people reading the certificate how to get a copy of the restrictions from the LLC.

Below is a sample of a simple membership certificate legend to accomplish these purposes. (This standard legend is printed on each LLC membership certificate included in the Nolo LLC records kit—see order page at the back of this book.) To use this legend, type or print the language below on the front of each membership certificate prior to issuing it to a member; printing it in all caps and/or in boldface is a good way to ensure that it is "conspicuous" and will be noticed and read by anyone who looks at the certificate:

THE MEMBERSHIP INTEREST REPRESENTED BY THIS CERTIFICATE IS SUBJECT TO RESTRICTIONS ON TRANSFER, AND MAY NOT BE OFFERED FOR SALE, SOLD, TRANSFERRED OR PLEDGED EXCEPT ACCORDING TO, AND ONLY IF ALLOWED BY, THESE TRANSFER RESTRICTIONS. TO OBTAIN A COPY OF THESE TRANSFER RESTRICTIONS, CONTACT AN OFFICER OF THIS LLC AT THE FOLLOWING ADDRESS: __**insert main address of LLC**__.

Here is the basic information you can use to delve deeper into tax options for your LLC:

- *Generally, LLCs that are treated as pass-through entities (partnerships or sole proprietorships) must select a tax year that is the same as a majority of its members* (members with a greater than 50% interest in the profits and capital of the LLC; or the sole member of a one-member LLC). For most LLCs, this means selecting a calendar tax year (from January 1 to December 31), which is the normal tax year for individual members.

- *If your LLC elects corporate tax treatment,* it should be able to choose a calendar tax year or a "fiscal year"—one which ends on the last day of any month except December.

- *An LLC classified as a partnership can also qualify for a fiscal tax year* if it can show a good business purpose, or if it results in the deferral of not more than three months of income for LLC members. For further information, see IRS Publication 538, *Accounting Periods and Methods.*

- *LLCs may elect a cash or accrual method of accounting.* Under the cash method, the business deducts expenses when paid and reports income when received. This is the way most individual taxpayers handle income and expenses on their tax returns. Under the accrual method, the business deducts expenses when it becomes legally obligated to pay them, and reports income when the LLC becomes legally entitled to receive the income. Small, closely held LLCs may benefit from the cash method of accounting because it may allow them to defer the reporting of income and give them added flexibility in claiming deductions, so most choose this option. However, your LLC may not be able to use the cash method of accounting if it has a corporation as a member (with some exceptions) or if it is considered a "tax shelter" under IRS rules. Tax shelters include businesses that sell securities that are registered with the SEC (your LLC should be exempt from registration—see Chapter 2, Section E); those set up with the principal purpose of avoiding the payment of federal income taxes (most LLC founders will have a primary purpose of making money from active business operations, not tax avoidance); and those that fall under the definition of a "syndicate" (your LLC will be considered a syndicate—and therefore unable to elect the cash accounting method—if more than 35% of its losses are allocable to members who do not actively participate in the business).

Select a tax year and accounting method with the help of your tax advisor. Because these are important tax decisions with significant financial and tax repercussions, it's important to check your conclusions on picking a tax year and accounting method with your tax advisor.

㉑ Generally, if you have ten or more LLC members (or if any member uses more than one percentage to figure his or her shares in LLC profits, losses, credits, deductions or other tax items—for example, a member with a 10% profits interest gets a 20% share of losses), you will need to select a "tax matters partner" and file a designation of tax matters partner form with the IRS. (Remember, LLCs are treated like partnerships under federal tax law.)

This provision simply reminds you that your LLC may have to designate a tax matters partner. Even if required, you do not have to specify in your operating agreement who will act in this capacity. You may designate someone later as a tax matters partner, and may change this designation when and as needed. There are technical rules on who may serve as a tax matters partner for an LLC (if interested, see Internal Revenue Code Regulation §301.6231(a)(7)-1, (a)(7)-2, found in Title 26 of the C.F.R. Ask your tax advisor to help you pick a tax matters partner if you are required to do so, and to make the appropriate IRS filing.

㉒ If an LLC is classified as a pass-through entity (partnership or sole proprietorship), LLC profits and losses are passed along to members, who will need these figures at the end of each year, as well as other LLC information, to prepare their individual income tax returns—see Chapter 3, Section B. To this end, we include a paragraph requiring that within 60 days after the end of each tax year, all members must be provided with:

- LLC income tax returns (partnership or corporate)
- If the LLC is classified as a partnership for income tax purposes, a completed IRS Form K-1 (Form 1065—*Partner's Share of Income, Credits, Deductions*), and
- LLC financial statements (you can dispense with the preparation of financial statements, but we think most members will regard this additional information as critical).

Important: Ask your tax advisor if you should add a provision to your agreement that requires the actual payout of a specified percentage of the profits allocated to each member at the end of the year. Members may need this money to pay their share of income taxes on profits allocated to them.

You can change the time frame for the LLC to provide this information—for example, within 30 days after the end of the LLC's tax year (instead of 60 days), but make sure to give your LLC enough time to prepare these forms and statements (Schedule K-1 must be given to each member of an LLC classified as a partnership on or by the date the LLC must file its annual 1065 partnership return—this means on or by April 15th for LLCs classified as partnerships with a calendar tax year).

㉓ This is a general authorization paragraph that allows the LLC to establish accounts with banks and other institutions. It allows one or more members to be designated to deposit and withdraw funds into and from these accounts, and to direct the investment of funds held in these accounts.

Note that unanimous consent is required to designate a person or persons to have this depositing/checkwriting authority, but you can lessen this requirement if you wish by simply deleting the words "with the consent of all members" from the second sentence of this paragraph.

Typically, each member of a small, closely held LLC will have depositing and checkwriting authority—although, for added fiscal control, multiple signatures may be required for withdrawals that exceed a specified amount. You don't need to specify these arrangements in your operating agreement. The details of these checkwriting and investment-directing arrangements will be spelled out on the signature cards and paperwork you must fill in when opening accounts on behalf of your LLC.

The final sentence in this paragraph is a reminder that personal funds of the LLC members may not be commingled (mixed) with the funds of the LLC. If you commingle funds, a state court may decide that you and the other members are not entitled to limited liability protection normally afforded an LLC, and may hold you personally liable for its debts and claims.

❷❹ This is another one of our "reminder" provisions to make it clear that the LLC will not commingle (mix) or confuse title to property. LLC property will only be owned by and in the name of the LLC.

❷❺ Here is an important provision in your agreement, where you specify who pays what to the LLC to get it started. Generally, there are no minimum capitalization requirements for LLCs under state law. You can start an LLC with a large amount of cash or property, or on a shoestring.

Most states allow members to contribute cash, property or a promise to pay cash or property in the future—for example, one member agrees to provide future services as a contribution and another to pay a specified amount of cash to the LLC within a certain time limit. The state sheets in Appendix A indicate if states place restrictions on the types of payment (consideration) that may be made for membership interests; a few prohibit the use of promises to pay money or provide future services as capital contributions.

Capital contributions may have tricky tax consequences. Particularly problematic are contributions of appreciated property and the contribution of future services to an LLC. We discuss potential problems that can occur with these types of capital contributions, such as increased personal income taxes for members, in Chapter 3, Section E1. To avoid problems, we strongly suggest you talk to your tax advisor before settling on the particular capital contribution scenario you will follow to fund your LLC if all members won't be paying cash up front.

Of course, even if your state says a promise to pay or to work for the LLC can't be used to set one up, you may be able to find a way around this limitation. For example, if a state prohibits using promissory notes (a promise to pay money) to capitalize an LLC, one of the cash-rich members may loan funds to another member for the latter to use as his or her capital contribution. Because the loan is made between the members on a personal basis only, and is off the books of the LLC, it should be fine.

Example: Warren has plenty of cash and will contribute $20,000 as his one-half interest in a new LLC. He makes a personal loan of another $20,000 to his buddy Carl, who turns around and pays this $20,000 as his contribution to the LLC. Warren trusts Carl to pay back the $20,000 (plus interest) with Carl's eventual shares in the LLC's profits. Warren asks Carl to sign a personal promissory note that carries an annual interest rate of 7%, and may even require that Carl pledge collateral for payback of the loan if he wants an extra measure of safety.

Use a promissory note for future cash payments. For future cash payments, you should have members sign a promissory note (with or without interest), payable on demand after a certain date or number of months or years, or payable in equal or unequal installments during the term of the note. For simple note forms to use for this purpose, see *Your Limited Liability Company: An Operating Manual,* by Anthony Mancuso (Nolo).

Once you've ironed out the details of members' contributions, you're ready to fill in the blanks. In the first blank, specify a date or period when capital contributions must be made by the members—such as "30 days from the signing of this agreement." (The date specified for members' contributions in the first paragraph of this provision applies only if you do not specify a later date for future payments on the individual contribution lines below this paragraph.)

Here's how to fill in the remaining blanks:

- *Name.* On separate lines, list the name of each contributing LLC member. We provide space for six members. If your LLC has seven or more members (or you simply find that you need more space), fill in the words "see Attachment 1" and provide the information on a separate sheet of paper that you label Attachment 1.
- *Contribution.* Describe each member's contribution. If a member is contributing cash, fill in the amount. Describe any contributions of property (personal property or real property) in plain language. If a member will make future payments of money, transfer property or contribute services to the LLC as a capital contribution, you must describe the timeline and general terms for those future payments or services. If you wish, you can insert the specifics of members' future payments here (again, the date specified for members' contributions in the first paragraph of this provision applies only if you do not specify a later date for payment here). If you need more room, which is likely, fill in the

words, "See the schedule/bill/promissory note attached to this agreement as Attachment 1" (or another numbered attachment, as the case may be). Then attach a separate document that spells out the details of each member's initial capital contribution to the LLC.

Example 1: Jeremy will contribute $10,000 in cash as his capital contribution. He can only come up with half the cash now, and agrees to pay the balance in six months. The description of his capital contribution reads as follows: "$5,000 cash on or by the date indicated above for contributions by members, and payment of an additional $5,000 on or by June 15, 200X."

Example 2: John contributes a promise to pay $10,000 in cash to his LLC as his capital contribution. The description of Tom's contribution is: "$10,000 to be paid per the terms of a promissory note attached to this agreement as Attachment 1."

Example 3: Tom will pay cash of $1,000 to his LLC, plus a promise to contribute $6,000 in future services as his capital contribution. The following statement is inserted: "$1,000 in cash; $6,000 in future services—see schedule of services attached to this agreement as Attachment 1." On an separate page, the following schedule of future services appears:

"Attachment 1—Schedule of Future Services Tom Chan will contribute a total of 300 hours of work for the LLC, for which he normally would be compensated at the hourly rate of $20. This contributed work shall be performed between January 1, 200X and December 31, 200X, and shall consist of services of at least 12 hours per week during this period."

- *Fair Market Value.* For noncash payments, show the fair market value of the property or services to be contributed. You may leave this item blank for cash payments.
- *Percentage Interest in LLC.* Here you specify the percentage interest each member will receive in return for his or her capital contribution. A member's percentage interest may be expressed as a percentage or a fraction—for example, either "50%" or "1/2." A percentage interest—also referred to as the member's capital interest—is the portion of the net assets of the LLC

(total assets minus liabilities) that each member is entitled to when the business is sold or used to value a member's interest when a member is bought out. This percentage interest figure is usually also used to determine other financial and managerial rights. In our agreement, it is used to determine each member's share of the LLC's profit and loss, as well as members' voting power in the LLC. In most cases involving smaller LLCs, members will each put up a proportionate amount of cash for a membership interest—that is, each will normally receive a percentage interest in the LLC that equals his or her proportionate cash capital contribution.

Example 1: Judy, Ed and Sharon each contribute $10,000 to their LLC to get it started, reasoning that $30,000 is just about right to begin operations until enough cash starts to flow into the business to make it self-supporting. Each person gets a one-third percentage interest in the LLC in return for his or her initial cash capital contributions.

Example 2: Gail and Lilian form their own LLC. Gail puts up $10,000 in cash, plus a used computer system that will be signed over to the LLC for a fair value of $5,000. Lilian puts up $7,500 in cash, plus signs over the pink slip to her paid-off Honda Accord with a middle blue book resale value of $7,500. Each has a 50% membership interest in the LLC.

Example 3: Sam and Jerry start an LLC. Sam has the cash, Jerry the expertise. Sam puts up $75,000. Jerry agrees to forego his first $25,000 in salary from the LLC as his capital contribution. Sam has a 75% interest in the LLC, and Jerry has a 25% interest. (In addition, Jerry will likely have to pay personal income taxes on the value of his LLC interest in the year the operating agreement is signed, as discussed in Chapter 3, Section D1.)

How much, if any, extra documentation do you need to prepare to back up your capital contributions? In most cases, just filling in these blanks in your operating agreement to describe the type, value and timing of each member's payment will be enough. For instance, stating that a member will contribute future services worth $10,000 to the LLC on or by a particular date, or that a member will pay $10,000 to the LLC within three years of signing the agreement, plus interest at an annual rate of 9%, will ordinarily make the other members comfortable. In some cases, you may feel the need to prepare additional documentation, such as a schedule of future services that describes when and what work a member will do for the LLC, or a promissory note that specifies the repayment terms of a future cash payment. Or you may wish to inventory and separately value various items of property that are being transferred by a member. Here are examples of how this provision can be completed.

Example 1: Jeff will pay $15,000 at an 8% interest rate per the terms of a two-year note to buy a one-quarter stake in a new LLC. His capital contribution is described as follows:

Name	Contribution	Fair Market Value	Percentage Interest in LLC
Jeff Billings	$15,000 per terms of note attached as Attachment 1		25%

Example 2: Mary plans to contribute $3,000 in cash and $3,000 in property over the first year of a new LLC's life for her 40% share. Here's how she completes this provision:

Name	Contribution	Fair Market Value	Percentage Interest in LLC
Mary Ranier	$3,000 in cash and $3,000 in property as described on schedule attached as Attachment 2	$6,000	40%

---

(2) Additional Contributions by Members: The members may agree, from time to time by unanimous vote, to require the payment of additional capital contributions by the members, on or by a mutually agreeable date. **26**

(3) Failure to Make Contributions: If a member fails to make a required capital contribution within the time agreed for a member's contribution, the remaining members may, by unanimous vote, agree to reschedule the time for payment of the capital contribution by the late-paying member, setting any additional repayment terms, such as a late payment penalty, rate of interest to be applied to the unpaid balance, or other monetary amount to be paid by the delinquent member, as the remaining members decide. Alternatively, the remaining members may, by unanimous vote, agree to cancel the membership of the delinquent member, provided any prior partial payments of capital made by the delinquent member are refunded promptly by the LLC to the member after the decision is made to terminate the membership of the delinquent member. **27**

(4) No Interest on Capital Contributions: No interest shall be paid on funds or property contributed as capital to this LLC, or on funds reflected in the capital accounts of the members. **28**

(5) Capital Account Bookkeeping: A capital account shall be set up and maintained on the books of the LLC for each member. It shall reflect each member's capital contribution to the LLC, increased by each member's share of profits in the LLC, decreased by each member's share of losses and expenses of the LLC, and adjusted as required in accordance with applicable provisions of the Internal Revenue Code and corresponding income tax regulations. **29**

26 This simple provision requires the unanimous vote of all members before members can be asked to contribute additional capital to the LLC. You may lower the vote requirement if you wish—for example, by specifying a majority vote (majority of members or of profits or capital interests), but if you do, be aware that some members may not be able to come up with the cash on time. What will you do then? Will you let the cash-rich members increase their percentage interests in the LLC while decreasing the percentage interests of the noncontributing members? This seems unfair, particularly to the members who want to contribute but can't come up with the additional capital on time. Especially for small LLCs, this is the reason we think unanimity is best when it comes to additional contributions.

27 This is a penalty provision for failure to pay contributions to the LLC on time. We don't address what "on time" means—it will follow the timelines established in your capital contributions clause unless you add language to this late payment provision specifying when its voting procedures kick in. For example, you may want this late payment provision to apply if a member fails to make a cash or property contribution within 30 days of its scheduled date. On the other hand, you may give a member who is to provide future services or make installment cash payments over the course of one or more years at least a month or two to remedy a missed installment payment before the late payment procedures go into effect.

You can also vary the penalty terms. Our provision requires a unanimous vote of remaining members to extend the terms for payment of a late capital contribution or terminate a delinquent member's membership. You may decide to require a lesser vote, eliminate entirely the alternate procedure of terminating a membership for failure to pay

a capital contribution on time, or make other changes or additions.

28 It is standard not to pay interest to members on their capital contributions—after all, members are investing money in the business with the hope of making more money, not banking it.

If, however, you wish to pay interest on members' capital contributions, you should delete this paragraph and provide for interest payments instead. You can make a general authorization, which lets members pin down the terms of the interest payments later by themselves, or spell out the terms—such as interest rate, dates and manner of payment:

> *Sample Language:* Interest on Capital Contributions: Interest shall be paid on funds or property contributed as capital to this LLC or on funds reflected in the capital accounts of the members **"as may be agreed by unanimous vote of the members" or specify terms (interest rate, dates and manner of payment).**

29 This tax language requires the LLC to set up capital accounts for each member, something that is required for federal income tax purposes. We state general rules here for LLC capital account bookkeeping. We don't cite specific sections of the Internal Revenue Code that may affect your LLC's bookkeeping or lay out all the special provisions that may apply to setting up and maintaining LLC capital accounts.

As discussed in Chapter 3, Section D2, if you decide to make special allocations of profits and losses, you (and your tax advisor) may decide to include (a significant amount of) additional language to make sure your allocations of profits and losses will go unchallenged by the IRS.

(6) Consent to Capital Contribution Withdrawals and Distributions: Members shall not be allowed to withdraw any part of their capital contributions or to receive distributions, whether in property or cash, except as otherwise allowed by this agreement and, in any case, only if such withdrawal is made with the written consent of all members. **30**

(7) Allocations of Profits and Losses: No member shall be given priority or preference with respect to other members in obtaining a return of capital contributions, distributions or allocations of the income, gains, losses, deductions, credits or other items of the LLC. The profits and losses of the LLC, and all items of its income, gain, loss, deduction and credit shall be allocated to members according to each member's percentage interest in this LLC. **31**

(8) Allocation and Distribution of Cash to Members: Cash from LLC business operations, as well as cash from a sale or other disposition of LLC capital assets, may be distributed from time to time to members in accordance with each member's percentage interest in the LLC, as may be decided by ____**"all" or "a majority"**____ of the members. **32**

(9) Allocation of Noncash Distributions: If proceeds consist of property other than cash, the members shall decide the value of the property and allocate such value among the members in accordance with each member's percentage interest in the LLC. If such noncash proceeds are later reduced to cash, such cash may be distributed among the members as otherwise provided in this agreement. **33**

(10) Allocation and Distribution of Liquidation Proceeds: Regardless of any other provision in this agreement, if there is a distribution in liquidation of this LLC, or when any member's interest is liquidated, all items of income and loss shall be allocated to the members' capital accounts, and all appropriate credits and deductions shall then be made to these capital accounts before any final distribution is made. A final distribution shall be made to members only to the extent of, and in proportion to, any positive balance in each member's capital account. **34**

V. MEMBERSHIP WITHDRAWAL AND TRANSFER PROVISIONS

These provisions deal with members deciding to leave the LLC. We specifically require a vote to admit a transferee (someone who buys or is otherwise transferred an LLC interest from a member) as a new member of the LLC. As you know from Chapter 3, Section D1, some states impose mandatory membership vote requirements to admit transferees into membership. Our transfer restriction language below is intended to help you meet the most stringent of any such rules in effect in your state.

(1) Withdrawal of Members: A member may withdraw from this LLC by giving written notice to all other members at least ____**number of days**____ days before the date the withdrawal is to be effective. **35**

(2) Restrictions on the Transfer of Membership: A member shall not transfer his or her membership in the LLC unless all nontransferring members in the LLC first agree to approve the admission of the transferee into this LLC. Further, no member may encumber a part or all of his or her membership in the LLC by mortgage, pledge, granting of a security interest, lien or otherwise, unless the encumbrance has first been approved in writing by all other members of the LLC. **36**

30 This provision reflects a standard practice of not allowing withdrawals of capital by LLC members prior to a dissolution of the company, unless approved in writing by all members. You can change this provision to allow premature withdrawals of capital in certain instances or with the consent of less than all members. For example, you may want to give yourself and the other members flexibility to withdraw part of the cash balance from positive capital accounts in times of personal financial emergency with less than unanimous membership consent as long as the LLC remains solvent and able to pay its bills. Your tax advisor can help you draft custom provisions of this sort.

31 This paragraph makes it clear that all members have equal participation rights in the tax items and capital returns of the LLC. The last sentence specifies that members will share in LLC profits and losses in accordance with their respective percentage interests in the business—the most common arrangement for smaller LLCs. These percentages, in turn, are established by the capital contributions listed in "IV. Capital Provisions: (1) Capital Contributions by Members" (the first paragraph of this section of the agreement).

As we've mentioned earlier, we think most smaller LLCs will not need or benefit by establishing a complex membership structure in their operating agreement, nor will they wish to adopt disproportionate profit or loss provisions. But if you have special needs and your tax advisor concurs, by all means replace this paragraph with special provisions of your own. For example, you may wish to give a member who contributes $25,000 in cash as capital a greater share of LLC profits than a member who promises to contribute $25,000 over the course of three years. Again, see Chapter 3, Section D2, and consult your tax advisor to make sure any disproportionate allocations of profits will have "substantial economic effect" under the IRS rules.

Example: Dwayne, Blaine and Jane agree to allocate their LLC profits and losses disproportionately. They change this paragraph to read: "No member shall be given priority or preference with respect to other members in obtaining a return of capital contributions, distributions or allocations of the income, gains, losses, deductions, credits or other items of the LLC. Items of its income, gain, loss, deduction and credit shall be allocated to members according to each member's percentage interest in this LLC, except as follows: [here they specify any special (disproportionate) allocations of profits, losses and any other items to particular members]. Their tax advisor adds a significant amount of additional language to have these special allocations respected by the IRS as explained in Chapter 3, Section D2.

Here are other changes you can make to this provision (again, get help from your tax advisor):
- You can adopt multi-class membership provisions, with some members being first in line to receive a return of their capital investment.
- If you want to go even further, you can decide that some LLC members will be entitled to their share of profits and losses (disproportionate or otherwise) before all other members and shall continue to receive the only distributions of LLC profits until they have been paid back their initial capital contribution. The following

sample provision, or one similar to it, will accomplish this.

Sample Language: Allocations of Profits and Losses: Notwithstanding any other provision in this agreement, the following members, called "priority members," shall receive all distributions of the LLC's profits and losses before any distributions are made to any other members of the LLC: ___**list priority members**___. Further, the other members of the LLC shall not receive any distributions until each of these priority members has received total distributions equal to each priority member's initial capital contribution to the LLC.

32 This provision gives members leeway to distribute cash profits or proceeds of the LLC to members if they vote to do so. Most smaller LLCs will specify a unanimous vote, but some may prefer to allow a majority of the membership to decide this issue—remember, a majority of members is defined earlier in this agreement ("II. Membership Provisions: (5) Membership Voting") as a majority of the percentage interests in the LLC.

Again, we assume that allocations of profits and proceeds will follow each member's percentage interest in the LLC, but you can vary who gets how much if you (and your tax advisor) decide to implement disproportionate (special) allocations of LLC profits.

33 This paragraph addresses how any noncash LLC property will be allocated among members. Basically, property gets allocated among the members in proportion to each member's percentage interest in the LLC. If reduced to cash later, it will be distributed to members according to an earlier provision in this operating agreement ("IV. Capital Provisions: (8) Allocation and Distribution of Cash to Members").

Example: Second-Hand Freight and Salvage, Ltd. Liability Co., a five-member company, decides to sell a truck and allocate the current value of this asset to the members, who own the LLC in equal percentages. The truck is worth $30,000, so the capital account of each member is increased by $6,000. The members can vote to distribute this cash according to the cash distribution provision in their agreement.

34 This paragraph sets up a special rule to handle a distribution of the cash and other assets of the LLC when the business itself liquidates or when a member's interest is liquidated. It applies the distribution to each member's capital account, then allows for credits and deductions that may need to be made prior to a final distribution. A final distribution of positive account balances is then made to members with positive account balances. Members with negative account balances owe the LLC money, not the other way around.

35 This is a liberal provision that lets a member bow out from the LLC by giving prescribed written notice. The period required is up to you—you can allow a quick departure, say in 30 days, or require many months' prior written notice. A typical advance notice period mentioned in LLC statutes is 180 days, but you may wish to shorten this period to 90 days or less.

If you want, you may modify this provision. For example, you may choose to limit the circumstances under which members may withdraw, or you may want to assess a monetary penalty if a member leaves too soon. (One way is to limit the price the member gets for his or her interest under mandatory buyout provisions in your agreement. We don't include buy-sell provisions of this sort in our simple agreement so you'll need to consult a lawyer or tax advisor; see Section A2 in this chapter.)

Problems with imposing significant penalties on departing members. Be careful if you decide to specify a substantial monetary penalty—for example, debiting a member's capital account prior to distributing the balance on departure. Courts can look askance on (decide not to enforce) limitations placed on individuals' abilities to come and go into and out of a business freely; they may decide that the limitations unduly restrict an individual's right to transfer an LLC interest or compete freely in the marketplace. Besides, lawyers love to sue, and your departing member may hook up with a litigious lawyer (or vice versa) upon leaving your LLC.

There are other issues you may want to address in this provision—for example, what will happen if a "service member" leaves the business before fully performing services promised in return for a share in the LLC.

Example: John received a 15% share in Fast Fries LLC in return for a promise to perform $15,000 worth of services for the LLC over a two-year period. However, John leaves prior to completing these promised capital contributions; when he gives notice of withdrawal, he has only worked off $7,500. Can John be forced to report to work for the LLC even though he is no longer a member? No—a court simply won't enforce this requirement. In short, if John is determined to leave, there is no legal remedy available to force him to keep working off his capital contribution.

The simple solution is to require departing "service members" to pay off in cash the amount of services left undone. This can be paid by way of a set-off against the departing member's capital account, with the member agreeing to pay any deficiency in cash or over time according to the terms of a promissory note.

Sample Language: If any member leaves this LLC prior to fully performing services promised as part of the member's capital contribution, his or her capital account shall be debited in an amount equal to the dollar amount of the value of the unpaid services prior to a distribution of any capital account balance to the member. If the capital account balance prior to this deduction is less than the full amount of the value of the unperformed services, the amount of the value of the unperformed services that exceeds the positive capital account balance of the member shall be paid by the departing member as follows:

<u>specify terms of repayment of any deficiency, for example "in cash within 30 days of departure by the member from the LLC" or "in accordance with the terms of a promissory note payable to the LLC by the departing member, the principal amount of which shall be the value of the unperformed services that were not satisfied from the member's positive capital account balance upon his or her departure from the LLC"</u>.

Example: Part of Sam's contribution to Sam & Pam's Sandblasting & Plastering LLC is a promise to perform future services worth $10,000. The LLC operating agreement requires departing service members to convert any unperformed services to a promissory note if they leave the LLC prior to performing all promised services. Sam decides to leave the LLC when he still owes $5,000, and his capital account balance is at $2,000. When he departs, Sam will either be required to pay the remaining $3,000 in cash or under the terms of a promissory note that he signs in favor of the LLC.

For departing members who received a share in the LLC in return for a promise to pay off a note on which they still owe money, you may choose to do nothing. Because these people are still legally bound to pay off the note, you can afford to simply let them leave (not try to renegotiate the note or convert it to a lump-sum payment).

You may, however, decide that any type of long-distance or extended payoff would be too tenuous or uncomfortable after a member leaves the business. Accordingly, you may wish to add language here requiring all persons who owe money on their initial capital contribution to make a lump sum cash payment to the LLC equal to the amount of the unpaid capital contribution at the time of their withdrawal from the LLC.

Sample Language: If a member departs this LLC prior to full payment of his or her capital

Notwithstanding the above provision, any member shall be allowed to assign an economic interest in his or her membership to another person without the approval of the other members. Such an assignment shall not include a transfer of the member's voting or management rights in this LLC, and the assignee shall not become a member of the LLC. **㊲**

VI. DISSOLUTION PROVISIONS

This section addresses the dissolution of the LLC, or events that may trigger a dissolution. In section 1(a), we specifically require the vote of all remaining members to continue the business of the LLC after a member is dissociated (loses his membership interest). Many states still require a vote in such cases, and our provision is intended to meet the most stringent of any such state rules in effect in your state.

The following events shall trigger a dissolution of the LLC, except as provided:

(a)   the death, incapacity, bankruptcy, retirement, resignation or expulsion of a member, except that within _____**number of days, typically a maximum of 90 under state LLC default rules**_____ of the happening of any of these events, all remaining members of the LLC may vote to continue the legal existence of the LLC, in which case the LLC shall not dissolve; **㊳**

(b)   the expiration of the term of existence of the LLC if such term is specified in the articles of organization, Certificate of Formation or a similar organizational document, or this operating agreement; **㊴**

(c)   the written agreement of all members to dissolve the LLC; **㊵**

(d)   entry of a decree of dissolution of the LLC under state law. **㊶**

VII. GENERAL PROVISIONS

These provisions cover general items concerning operation of the LLC. You'll also find standard provisions, normally found at the end of LLC agreements, dealing with the enforceability of the agreement.

(1) Officers: The LLC may designate one or more officers, such as a President, Vice President, Secretary and Treasurer. Persons who fill these positions need not be members of the LLC. Such positions may be compensated or noncompensated according to the nature and extent of the services rendered for the LLC as a part of the duties of each office. Ministerial services only as a part of any officer position will normally not be compensated, such as the performance of officer duties specified in this agreement, but any officer may be reimbursed by the LLC for out-of-pocket expenses paid by the officer in carrying out the duties of his or her office. **㊷**

(2) Records: The LLC shall keep at its principal business address a copy of all proceedings of membership meetings, as well as books of account of the LLC's financial transactions. A list of the names and addresses of the current membership of the LLC also shall be maintained at this address, with notations on any transfers of members' interests to nonmembers or persons being admitted into membership in the LLC.

contribution, whether the unpaid capital contribution consists of cash, payments under a promissory note, the performance of future services or the transfer of property, the member shall be bound to pay a lump sum to the LLC at the time of his or her departure equal to the amount or value of the unpaid cash, unpaid principal and interest under the note, value of unperformed services, or the value of the untransferred property. The lump sum shall be paid to this LLC no later than ____**period**____days after the departing member leaves the LLC, and payment of the lump sum within this period shall extinguish the liability of the departing member for the amount or value of his or her unpaid capital contribution to this LLC.

Our above examples and sample provisions are suggestions only. The best way to anticipate and come to terms with handling unpaid capital contributions upon the departure of a member is to talk with all members and your tax advisor (particularly if you plan to tinker with a member's capital account balance when he or she leaves). Reaching this kind of informed consensus before you add any language to your operating agreement can help avoid bad feelings and uncooperative behavior later—when, for example, a departing member complains he wasn't in on the discussions on how unpaid contributions would be handled when a member leaves, and therefore didn't realize he'd have to pay cash to be let out of the LLC.

This operating agreement provision deals only with a member packing up and quitting the LLC. It does not address a member who wants to sell his or her interest to a new member—we deal with this latter issue in the next provision in the agreement titled "Restrictions on the Transfer of Membership."

❸❻ This provision is intended to satisfy any "leftover" requirements in your state's LLC Act that impose mandatory approval of nontransferring

members when a members wishes to transfer her membership to a new member. As explained in Chapter 3, Section D1, these state law requirements are no longer necessary for your LLC to obtain a favorable tax classification with the IRS, but some states will keep these requirements on the books for at least a few more years.

This provision requires the approval of *all* nontransferring members to the sale of membership interests to a new member. This requirement should not only meet any requirement still found in your state's LLC Act, but it also helps protect your members from having to admit an incompatible person as a new member of your LLC. After all, the new member will have to get along and work closely with the other members. If any member doesn't like or is incompatible with the new member, the LLC's business may suffer significantly and the personal enjoyment the members derive from working together may be lost.

If you wish to alter this provision to allow a majority (or other lesser number) of nontransferring members to approve the sale of a membership to a new member, you need to make sure your state lets you adopt the lesser membership vote rule you have in mind. Your state's requirement on this vote is summarized in your state sheet in Appendix A, in the Operating Rules section, under the heading "Default Transfer Rule."

State Laws Are Expected to Change: Realize that this is a quick-changing area of the law, and your state may soon repeal this requirement altogether to go along with the flexible federal scheme (which lets LLCs make up their own rules on how and when membership interests may be transferred). If you want the transfer of membership in your LLC as unfettered as possible, check your state's LLC Act, or ask a lawyer to, to see exactly where the law stands on this issue in your state at the time of your LLC formation.

Copies of the LLC's articles of organization, Certificate of Formation or a similar organizational document, a signed copy of this operating agreement, and the LLC's tax returns for the preceding three tax years shall be kept at the principal business address of the LLC. A statement also shall be kept at this address containing any of the following information that is applicable to this LLC:

- the amount of cash or a description and value of property contributed or agreed to be contributed as capital to the LLC by each member;
- a schedule showing when any additional capital contributions are to be made by members to this LLC;
- a statement or schedule, if appropriate, showing the rights of members to receive distributions representing a return of part or all of members' capital contributions; and
- a description of, or date when, the legal existence of the LLC will terminate under provisions in the LLC's articles of organization, Certificate of Formation or a similar organizational document, or this operating agreement.

If one or more of the above items is included or listed in this operating agreement, it will be sufficient to keep a copy of this agreement at the principal business address of the LLC without having to prepare and keep a separate record of such item or items at this address.

Any member may inspect any and all records maintained by the LLC upon reasonable notice to the LLC. Copying of the LLC's records by members is allowed, but copying costs shall be paid for by the requesting member. ❹❸

(3) All Necessary Acts: The members and officers of this LLC are authorized to perform all acts necessary to perfect the organization of this LLC and to carry out its business operations expeditiously and efficiently. The Secretary of the LLC, or other officers, or all members of the LLC, may certify to other businesses, financial institutions and individuals as to the authority of one or more members or officers of this LLC to transact specific items of business on behalf of the LLC. ❹❹

(4) Mediation and Arbitration of Disputes Among Members: In any dispute over the provisions of this operating agreement and in other disputes among the members, if the members cannot resolve the dispute to their mutual satisfaction, the matter shall be submitted to mediation. The terms and procedure for mediation shall be arranged by the parties to the dispute.

Finally, note that this paragraph requires all members to agree before a member encumbers a membership, such as putting it up as collateral for a loan or pledging it as security for the performance of some other legal obligation. You can lessen the vote requirement for encumbrances, but we think unanimous written approval works best here too.

37 This paragraph states an exception recognized under state statutes. Namely, even in states that still require membership approval to a transfer of membership, a member is allowed to transfer *economic interests in a membership* without the approval of the nontransferring members. As long as the person getting the interest—the assignee or transferee—does not become a new member with management and voting rights, the transfer is of an economic interest only, and does not require membership approval under state law.

Example: Katherine owns a one-third interest in a lucrative LLC. She assigns one-quarter of her profits interest in her LLC to a trust set up for the benefit of her niece, Brenda. This transfer of economic rights only is not restricted under state law.

Of course, you can decide not to permit even these transfers of economic interests by members, simply by deleting this paragraph. (By the way, you don't need to be overly concerned about the possibility of outsiders buying an economic interest in your LLC—there generally is little interest by outsiders in buying a profits-only interest in an LLC without full membership rights.)

38 This provision covers what will happen when a member's interest in the LLC is terminated—legally, when a member is *dissociated*—because he resigns, retires, dies, is permanently incapacitated, goes bankrupt or is subject to any of the other conditions listed here. This is another one of those "leftover" state rules areas—many states still have requirements in their LLC Acts that require a membership vote to continue the legal existence of the LLC after a member is dissociated. There is no longer any tax reason for this requirement as explained in Chapter 3, Section D1, but

you will want to comply with any existing state law requirement on this issue.

State law generally requires the vote of at least a "majority in interest" of the remaining members to continue the legal existence of the LLC after a member's interest is terminated, but some states require a vote of all remaining members. To keep things simple, and to avoid a long-winded explanation of what "majority-in-interest" means, our provision requires the vote of all remaining LLC members to continue the legal life of your LLC after a member withdraws, sells his interest, becomes incapacitated, dies, or is expelled. This unanimous vote requirement satisfies the most stringent of any leftover legal requirement on this point still on the books in your state. We're sure you'll find it easy to comply with too—just meet with the remaining LLC members and ask if everyone is in agreement that the business of your LLC should continue without the dissociated member. With rare exceptions, everyone should agree (if someone doesn't, you will want to rethink your LLC business anyway, perhaps deciding to buy out the protesting member before continuing on with LLC business).

If you decide to modify the provision in the tear-out operating agreement and lessen the vote requirement, make sure your state lets you do so by checking the "Default Continuation Rule" listed in the Operating Rules section of your state sheet in Appendix A.

Check state law if this vote requirement is important to you: Again, also realize that your state may have decided to repeal all voting requirements in this area to conform to the new flexible federal tax rules as explained in Chapter 3D1. To find out, check your state's LLC Act online or in a law or business library, or ask a business lawyer to check for you.

If good-faith mediation of a dispute proves impossible or if an agreed-upon mediation outcome cannot be obtained by the members who are parties to the dispute, the dispute may be submitted to arbitration in accordance with the rules of the American Arbitration Association. Any party may commence arbitration of the dispute by sending a written request for arbitration to all other parties to the dispute. The request shall state the nature of the dispute to be resolved by arbitration, and, if all parties to the dispute agree to arbitration, arbitration shall be commenced as soon as practical after such parties receive a copy of the written request.

All parties shall initially share the cost of arbitration, but the prevailing party or parties may be awarded attorney fees, costs and other expenses of arbitration. All arbitration decisions shall be final, binding and conclusive on all the parties to arbitration, and legal judgment may be entered based upon such decision in accordance with applicable law in any court having jurisdiction to do so. **45**

(5) Entire Agreement: This operating agreement represents the entire agreement among the members of this LLC, and it shall not be amended, modified or replaced except by a written instrument executed by all the parties to this agreement who are current members of this LLC as well as any and all additional parties who became members of this LLC after the adoption of this agreement. This agreement replaces and supersedes all prior written and oral agreements among any and all members of this LLC. **46**

(6) Severability: If any provision of this agreement is determined by a court or arbitrator to be invalid, unenforceable or otherwise ineffective, that provision shall be severed from the rest of this agreement, and the remaining provisions shall remain in effect and enforceable. **47**

VIII. SIGNATURES OF MEMBERS AND SPOUSES

The final section of the agreement contains signature lines for the members, plus a series of lines for their spouses to sign.

(1) Execution of Agreement: In witness whereof, the members of this LLC sign and adopt this agreement as the operating agreement of this LLC.

Date: _____ **48**

Signature: _____

Printed Name: _____ , Member

Date: _____

Signature: _____

Printed Name: _____ , Member

Notice that you must fill in the blank in our provision to specify the deadline for voting to continue the legal existence of the LLC after the occurrence of a dissolution-triggering event. In most states, this vote must be taken within 90 days from the triggering event—again, see the "Default Continuation Rule" in your state sheet. If your state does not specify a deadline for taking this vote, or lets you override the state requirements (most states permit this), we suggest putting "90 days" in this blank anyway. You can always vote any time before the 90-day deadline (the language says "within [number of days]" of the happening of one of the membership terminating events). If, however, you are set on a shorter period, we recommend specifying no less than 30 days to give your members a chance to meet and approve the continuance of your LLC.

39 Some states require the articles of organization to limit the legal existence of the LLC to a specified term of years or until a particular date. This provision simply states that the LLC will dissolve if a termination date or period is specified in the articles of organization or this operating agreement. (See our earlier discussion on filling in "I. Preliminary Provisions: (6) Duration of LLC," Special Instruction **8**, above.)

40 Your LLC may decide to call it quits at any time by the unanimous approval of all members to dissolve. We think this makes sense—and most LLC owners wouldn't want it any other way. (In fact, most state LLC laws say you can do this even if your operating agreement doesn't specify it.)

41 State statutes may provide for the involuntary dissolution of an LLC should the members reach an impasse or in the case of fraud, illegality or nonpayment of state taxes. This provision simply recognizes that the LLC may dissolve by order of a state court.

42 This paragraph allows, but does not require, the LLC to appoint one or more persons as officers of the LLC, who may be members or nonmembers. Some state LLC statutes mention the officer positions of president, vice president, secretary and

treasurer, but even those states don't require that the positions be filled or define the job duties and responsibilities of these offices.

We suggest you not worry too much about specific officer titles ("Treasurer" vs. "Chief Financial Officer" vs. "Chief Poobah in Charge of Payroll"). Pay attention instead to making sure each LLC employee knows the scope and responsibilities of his or her position with your LLC, whether it is as a formal officer or in a regular staff position.

Feel free to modify this provision to have it reflect how you want to handle the designation and compensation of any officers in your LLC. We suggest not being too specific, to allow you to have the maximum leeway to appoint various types of LLC salaried and nonsalaried officers and personnel. Note that you do not need to say that your LLC has the power to hire employees and compensate them for their services; this type of employment authority goes without saying.

43 Your state LLC statute may allow you to restrict when or why members are allowed to look at LLC records, or permit you to restrict access to particular types of LLC legal or financial records. We don't nitpick here, and simply give all members an unrestricted right to view all records at any time.

If you want to restrict membership inspection rights, take a look at your state LLC statute to see how restrictive you are allowed to be under state law, then insert your own provisions.

Sample Language: Any member may inspect the financial or other records of this LLC for a purpose reasonably related to the member's interest in this LLC. The Treasurer of this LLC shall make the determination within one week of the member's request and, if the Treasurer finds that the member's request is related to his or her interest in the LLC, the requesting member shall be allowed to inspect the records during regular business hours of the LLC at its principal place of business.

Date: _____

Signature: _____

Printed Name: _____ , Member

Date: _____

Signature: _____

Printed Name: _____ , Member

(2) Consent of Spouses: The undersigned are spouses of members of this LLC who have signed this operating agreement in the preceding provision. These spouses have read this agreement and agree to be bound by its terms in any matter in which they have a financial interest, including restrictions on the transfer of memberships and the terms under which memberships in this LLC may be sold or otherwise transferred. **49**

Date: _____

Signature: _____

Printed Name: _____

Spouse of: _____

Date: _____

Signature: _____

Printed Name: _____

Spouse of: _____

Date: _____

Signature: _____

Printed Name: _____

Spouse of: _____

Date: _____

Signature: _____

Printed Name: _____

Spouse of: _____

④④ This housekeeping provision says that the secretary of the LLC, or other LLC officers or its members, may sign a statement that certifies to other businesses or to outside persons the capacity of one or more LLC members or officers to engage in particular business on behalf of the LLC. A bank, escrow or title company, or outside person or business may wish to obtain a statement certifying such authority prior to entering into a contract or business transaction with an LLC member or officer. (We provide a Certification of Authority form to use for this purpose in Chapter 7, Section D7c; a tear-out form is also provided in Appendix D.)

④⑤ A mediation approach, followed if necessary by arbitration, is a relatively quick and inexpensive way to settle disputes among members—for example, arguments over the valuation of LLC interests incident to a buyout or disagreements over who gets to use the LLC's name after the business is formally dissolved.

This bare-bones provision says unresolved disputes among LLC members should first be submitted to mediation. Mediation is a voluntary, nonbinding process, in which an impartial mediator tries to get the parties to agree to a settlement. (For an excellent, in-depth coverage of the mediation process, see *How to Mediate Your Dispute,* by Peter Lovenheim (Nolo).)

In our provision, if mediation cannot be undertaken or is unsuccessful, the dispute may be submitted to binding arbitration by the parties. This procedure is voluntary, and all parties to the dispute must agree to arbitration. Even this procedure—an out-of-court, informal hearing before an impartial arbitrator that produces a legally enforceable decision—is a better dispute resolution process than a full-blown lawsuit. Arbitration is both quicker and less expensive than going to court.

You may want to make some minor changes, such as choosing a different association as a model for the arbitration rules, requiring three arbitrators instead of one (opposing sides of a dispute each pick one arbitrator, and these two arbitrators pick a third), and other changes you deem appropriate.

④⑥ This is a boilerplate legal provision that negates any prior agreements among the members, whether oral (spoken) or written. This can be important because the general rule is that LLCs, like partnerships, may legally be based on oral agreements.

This provision also requires future changes to the agreement, or the adoption of a new operating agreement, to be signed by all original parties to the agreement who are current members of the LLC, plus any new members. You can change this provision to allow less than unanimous approval of operating agreement changes, but we think these changes are usually important enough to warrant unanimous approval of all current members. (We cover how to amend your operating agreement in Chapter 7, Section C1.)

④⑦ This is a standard legal provision that directs a court or arbitrator to enforce the balance of the agreement even if one or more provisions are held invalid, ambiguous or otherwise unenforceable.

④⑧ Before the members sign the agreement, remember that they must initial crossed-out language and changes that were made to the agreement, if any. (However, they don't need to initial filled-in lines.)

Have each member date and sign the operating agreement. Type or print the name of each member under the corresponding signature line, after the words "Printed Name." Make sure each member signs the operating agreement.

Get assistance from a tax advisor. Before you settle on your final agreement, let your tax advisor review your choices, particularly those related to the financial (capital) provisions and tax options (for example, whether to have your LLC taxed as a pass-through entity or as a corporation, and whether to require minimum payouts of a percentage of profits each year to help members pay income taxes they owe on LLC profits allocated to them at the end of the year).

49 Here is another standard provision that shows spousal consent to the provisions of the operating agreement. We strongly suggest that each married LLC member have his or her spouse date and sign on one of the sets of lines following this spousal consent provision. Doing this can help avoid disputes later, should spouses separate, divorce or die, or should one spouse decide to sell or transfer his or her membership in the LLC.

Leaving interests by means of estate planning devices. You may add provisions that permit spouses of members to use a will or other estate planning device, such as a living trust, to leave their half- or other co-interest in an LLC membership to outsiders. See your tax or legal advisor for guidance if you wish to address issues of this sort in your agreement.

D. Distribute Copies of Your Operating Agreement

Congratulations! You are done with another important organizational task, and your LLC is well on its legal way. Make photocopies of the completed, signed operating agreement and give each member a copy. Finally, place the original, signed operating agreement in your LLC records book.

CHAPTER 6

Prepare an LLC Operating Agreement for Managers

Some LLCs wish to set up a special management structure that does not consist of all LLC members. The management team may be made up of:

- some—but not all—LLC members
- both outside managers and some—but not all—LLC members, or
- only outside managers.

In this chapter, we show you how to prepare an alternate operating agreement for a manager-managed LLC. We assume you are in the process of forming, or have already formed, your LLC by preparing and filing Articles of Organization with your state LLC filing office, as explained in Chapter 4.

If yours is a member-managed LLC, turn to Chapter 5. In Chapter 5, we cover the first LLC operating agreement contained in Appendix D, which provides for management of the LLC by all members. If you're unsure of the type of agreement you will need, read on.

A. Choosing a Manager-Managed LLC

Although most smaller LLCs will choose to be managed by all members (not by managers, as provided in the agreement covered in this chapter), a minority will find a manager-managed LLC more suitable. LLCs usually decide on manager-management for one or both of these reasons:

- At least one member wishes to be a "passive" investor and to hand over the reins and responsibilities of management to others.

  *Example: Sole Sisters is a shoe design and distribution partnership owned and operated by three sisters, Julie, Laurie and Ginny. Ginny contributed the cash to get the partnership started, leaving all business man-*agement and day-to-day operations to Julie and Laurie, who contributed as their capital contributions portions of past (unpaid) services performed for the partnership. All three sisters decide that converting the business to an LLC makes sense, but they wish to keep the same management arrangement among themselves. What's the solution? Simple: They decide to adopt a manager-management agreement—the kind discussed in this chapter—with Julie and Laurie designated as the managers of the LLC. Ginny will be a nonmanaging member, thus avoiding all management responsibilities.

- The members believe that the LLC will be handled better by outsiders (nonmembers) who have special expertise in managing the business.

  Example: Power-Packed Peanut Products LLC, a food wholesaler, is formed and funded by Tina and Kay, entrepreneurs with an eye for a promising business venture, but with little expertise or interest in managing or running it on a day-to-day basis. They decide to shell out substantial salaries to experienced food wholesalers Jason and Charlotte, who will manage and run the business as its nonmember managers. Jason and Charlotte bring years of prior experience to the newly formed business, having just sold their co-owned food distribution business, J & C Wholesalers, at a substantial profit. They are ready to get involved growing another successful company in exchange for chunky salaries on PPPP's payroll.

Possible self-employment tax savings: Setting up a manager-managed LLC may also help to lower self-employment taxes of the nonmanaging members of the LLC—see Chapter 3, Section C.

1. Limited Liability for All Members of Manager-Managed LLC

In their roles as LLC members, all members—whether managing or nonmanaging—qualify for personal legal immunity from business debts and legal claims made by outsiders against the LLC.

2. Limited Liability for Managers of Manager-Managed LLC

State law may impose slightly stricter standards on LLC managers (regardless of whether or not they're also members). That is, managers will receive the normal personal immunity from business debts and liabilities that the LLC provides, but they may suffer exposure to personal liability if they participate in making exceptionally bad or illegal business decisions in their roles as managers.

Don't get too concerned here if you plan to be an LLC manager. The circumstances where a manager may be found personally liable are the exceptions, not the rule. Circumstances that breed such personal liability tend to involve decisions that are self-interested (where a manager takes personal advantage of a business deal with the LLC without proper disclosure of his or her interest) or situations where the manager acts in an extremely reckless or illegal manner.

*Example 1: Suits of Amoré, Limited Liability Company, a haberdasher of formal men's attire for weddings, parties and other black-tie affairs, is on the lookout for top quality Italian suits it can offer to its customers. In the course of his research, Fredo, an LLC manager, spots a phenomenal opportunity to purchase top-of-the-line Santoro suits (normally $2,500 plus retail per unit) at an unheard of discount. He decides to cash out his personal bank account savings and buy up the suits, rather than mention his find to the other LLC managers, who would jump at the chance to acquire the merchandise. Fredo will either find a private buyer or store the suits until he can set himself up in a sideline business selling suits. If another LLC manager gets wind of Fredo's find, and the LLC sues him for lost profits—the amount the LLC could have made had it been allowed to buy and resell the suits—a court would likely find Fredo personally liable. The normal rule is that a manager has a duty of loyalty to disclose oppor-*tunities *discovered in the course of his or her work that might benefit the business (unless it is obvious that the business would have no interest in the opportunity); only after the business decides not to act is the manager allowed to go ahead and personally pursue the opportunity.*

Example 2: The managers of Lowball Construction Ltd. Liability Co. are warned repeatedly by the VP of operations that an electrical panel box installation being performed by the company at one of its worksites is not up to code. The LLC managers disregard his advice to order the substandard work to be redone, insisting that the company can't afford to miss another performance deadline under its contract with the owner of the building. After Lowball completes the installations, the owner rents the building to a computer manufacturer, which moves in and sets up sensitive electronic measurement and test equipment it uses in its operation. When the computer firm flips the switch to fire up its equipment, a short circuit due to faulty ground wiring in the service panel box sends a voltage spike through the outlets on the circuit—and destroys all the computer maker's expensive test equipment. The building owner is sued for the loss, and she immediately sues the LLC and its managers. The LLC's lawyer advises the managers that it is unlikely that their commercial insurance carrier will cover this loss—the electrical panel box at fault was never inspected and approved by the local building inspector. The managers may be held personally liable for the loss due to their gross negligence (and illegality) in not heeding the warnings of their VP to redo the faulty service panel wiring.

Of course, these are fanciful or extreme examples, mostly used to make the following points. First, the LLC will protect you and your co-managers personally for normal negligence—the kind of business judgment errors humans without 20-20 foresight may make. You'll even be protected if outsiders inadvertently suffer a financial loss due to such faulty decisions (of course, the LLC itself can be forced to pay for these losses). Second, don't be lulled into an unassailable sense of security by the normal limited liability protection afforded by the

LLC form. If you engage in truly foolish conduct that is obviously reckless to the safety of other people or their property, or you act illegally or underhandedly in your own self-interest, then the mantle of personal protection that your LLC normally provides may be lifted. In that case, you and the other LLC managers will be exposed to personal liability for the reckless or illegal decisions.

Provide managers with indemnification and/or insurance. If you want to attract outside managers to help run your LLC, you may need to take extra measures to make them feel more comfortable in these lawsuit-happy times. One way is to offer an LLC indemnity agreement, which guarantees direct payment by the LLC for any legal expenses or judgments managers may be asked to pay arising out of their work for the LLC. Another personal safeguard is to cover managers personally with an errors and omissions insurance policy for their managerial duties. The two can be combined for complete legal coverage: indemnification can kick in for all amounts not covered by insurance.

One final point about managers: state law typically invests each manager of a manager-managed LLC with "agency" authority. That is, each manager has legal authority to bind the LLC to contracts and business deals made with outsiders. You will want to make sure to select managers you can trust.

Exception: State law normally says a manager's acts will not bind the LLC if 1) the business was the type the LLC normally would not transact or, 2) even if it was the type of business the LLC would normally transact, the manager did not have the actual authority to enter into the deal and the outsider knew the manager didn't. These are exceptional exceptions—don't expect to be able to rely on either them if a manager commits your LLC to a bad business deal.

3. Compliance With Old-Fashioned State LLC Laws

The same state law issues arise when adopting a manager-managed operating agreement as those discussed in Chapter 3, Section D1. Namely, many states still have old-fashioned laws in their LLC acts, intended to help you meet old federal tax rules, that require a membership vote of nontransferring members to approve a transfer of membership by a member to a new member. These same states often also require a membership vote to continue the business of the LLC after a member is dissociated—when a member's interest in the LLC is terminated because of her departure from the LLC, disability, death or expulsion. We show you how to comply with any such "leftover" state requirements in our discussion below.

B. How to Prepare an LLC Management Operating Agreement

Now let's look at the LLC management operating agreement. Note that this is the second operating agreement in Appendix D, titled Limited Liability Company Management Operating Agreement. Make sure you pick the right agreement and don't miss any pages or inadvertently take pages from the other (member-managed) agreement. You may want to photocopy the management operating agreement before you get started, in case you make mistakes or want to modify it significantly.

The LLC Manager-Managed Operating Agreement is included on the CD-ROM at the back of this book.

1. Read Chapter 5 Material on Basic Operating Agreement Issues

The management operating agreement is similar to the operating agreement provided in Chapter 5, but it is customized to include LLC manager provisions. Before you begin filling in your LLC management operating agreement, spend a few minutes to learn more about these important matters:

- *Scope of our basic LLC operating agreements.* Read Chapter 5, Section A. There you'll find information about capital account provisions and buy-sell and right of first refusal provisions.
- *Modifying your operating agreement.* Also read Chapter 5, Section B, which covers general rules on when and how to make changes to your agreement.

- *Lettered references* accompany provisions that are unique to this operating agreement. Special Instructions **A** through **N** accompany the management operating agreement in this chapter.
- *Numbered references* apply to provisions that are the same as (or almost identical to) those found in the Chapter 5 agreement. Special Instructions **1** through **49** are contained in Chapter 5, Section C. Note that some numbered references will be missing from this agreement. This is because certain provisions in Chapter 5 apply only to member-managed LLCs, so they are not carried over to this management operating agreement.

While this may sound complicated, it really isn't, and you'll get the idea with no trouble at all as you read the provisions below.

2. Where to Find Instructions for LLC Management Operating Agreement

Below, we provide instructions in the sample agreement to help you fill in the blanks. In addition, we use two different kinds of references to alert you to Special Instructions:

3. Line-by-Line Instructions for Management Operating Agreement

We'll start at the top of the Limited Liability Company Management Operating Agreement and work our way through it.

LIMITED LIABILITY COMPANY
MANAGEMENT OPERATING AGREEMENT

I. PRELIMINARY PROVISIONS

Here we address preliminary matters, such as the effective date of the agreement, the name of the LLC and other basic information. These provisions are almost identical to those provided in the basic LLC operating agreement in Chapter 5. Again, where indicated, the numbered Special Instructions for these provisions are in Chapter 5, Section C.

(1) Effective Date: This operating agreement of
_____
name of LLC, ❶

effective _____**date**_____, ❷ is adopted by the members whose signatures appear at the end of this agreement. ❸

(2) Formation: This limited liability company (LLC) was formed by filing Articles of Organization, a Certificate of Formation or a similar organizational document with the LLC filing office of the state of _____**state of formation**_____ on __**date of filing Articles of Organization, Certificate of Formation or similar organizational document**__.
❹ A copy of this organizational document has been placed in the LLC's records book.

(3) Name: The formal name of this LLC is as stated above. However, this LLC may do business under a different name by complying with the state's fictitious or assumed business name statutes and procedures. ❺

(4) Registered Office and Agent: The registered office of this LLC and the registered agent at this address are as follows:
name and address of registered agent and office.
_____

The registered office and agent may be changed from time to time as the members or managers may see fit, by filing a change of registered agent or office form with the state LLC filing office. It will not be necessary to amend this provision of the operating agreement if and when such a change is made. ❻

(5) Business Purposes: The specific business purposes and activities contemplated by the founders of this LLC at the time of initial signing of this agreement consist of the following:
state the specific business purposes and activities you foresee for your LLC. ❼
_____

It is understood that the foregoing statement of purposes shall not serve as a limitation on the powers or abilities of this LLC, which shall be permitted to engage in any and all lawful business activities. If this LLC intends to engage in business activities outside the state of its formation that require the qualification of the LLC in other states, it shall obtain such qualification before engaging in such out-of-state activities.

(6) Duration of LLC: The duration of this LLC shall be___**specify "perpetual" or any specific termination date or term of years for the LLC specified in the Articles of Organization**_. Further, this LLC shall terminate when a proposal to dissolve the LLC is adopted by the membership of this LLC or when this LLC is otherwise terminated in accordance with law. **❽**

II. MANAGEMENT PROVISIONS

These provisions address the unique management structure of a manager-managed LLC. The lettered Special Instructions for these provisions accompany the agreement in this chapter.

(1) Management by Managers: This LLC will be managed by the managers listed below. All managers who are also members of this LLC are designated as "members"; nonmember managers are designated as "nonmembers." **Ⓐ**

Name: _____ ☐ Member ☐ Nonmember
Address: _____

Name: _____ ☐ Member ☐ Nonmember
Address: _____

Name: _____ ☐ Member ☐ Nonmember
Address: _____

Name: _____ ☐ Member ☐ Nonmember
Address: _____

Name: _____ ☐ Member ☐ Nonmember
Address: _____

Name: _____ ☐ Member ☐ Nonmember
Address: _____

(2) Nonliability of Managers: No manager of this LLC shall be personally liable for the expenses, debts, obligations or liabilities of the LLC, or for claims made against it. **B**

(3) Authority and Votes of Managers: Except as otherwise set forth in this agreement, the Articles of Organization, Certificate of Organization or similar organizational document, or as may be provided under state law, all management decisions relating to this LLC's business shall be made by its managers. Management decisions shall be approved by ___ **"all" or "a majority"** ___ of the current managers of the LLC, with each manager entitled to cast one vote for or against any matter submitted to the managers for a decision. **C**

(4) Term of Managers: Each manager shall serve until the earlier of the following events:

(a) the manager becomes disabled, dies, retires or otherwise withdraws from management;

(b) the manager is removed from office; or **D**

(c) the manager's term expires, if a term has been designated in other provisions of this agreement.

Upon the happening of any of these events, a new manager may be appointed to replace the departing manager by ___ **"a majority of the members of the LLC" or "a majority of the remaining managers"** ___ . **E**

(5) Management Meetings: Managers shall be able to discuss and approve LLC business informally, and may, at their discretion, call and hold formal management meetings according to the rules set forth in the following provisions of this operating agreement.

Regularly scheduled formal management meetings need not be held, but any manager may call such a meeting by communicating his or her request for a formal meeting to the other managers, noting the purpose or purposes for which the meeting is called. Only the business stated or summarized in the notice for the meeting shall be discussed and voted upon at the meeting.

The meeting shall be held within a reasonable time after a manager has made the request for a meeting, and in no event, later than ___ **period** ___ days after the request for the meeting. A quorum for such a formal managers' meeting shall consist of ___ **"all" or "a majority of"** ___ managers, and if a quorum is not present, the meeting shall be adjourned to a new place and time with notice of the adjourned meeting given to all managers. An adjournment shall not be necessary, however, and a managers' meeting with less than a quorum may be held if all nonattending managers agreed in writing prior to the meeting to the holding of the meeting. All such written consents to the holding of a formal management meeting shall be kept and filed with the records of the meeting.

The proceedings of all formal managers' meetings shall be noted or summarized with written minutes of the meeting and a copy of the minutes shall be placed and kept in the records book of this LLC. **F**

A Fill in the name(s) and address(es) of the manager(s) of the LLC—you only need one, but many LLCs wish to have more than one person on their management team. Check the appropriate box to show whether each manager is a member or nonmember. Remember, managers can be either members or nonmembers.

B This paragraph reiterates the basic legal rule that managers (like members) are not personally liable for LLC debts and claims.

C In the blank, specify the number of management votes necessary to pass or approve decisions submitted to the managers. You may select "all" or "a majority," or specify a particular number or percentage of votes needed to make a management decision, such as "two-thirds, "51%" or "three." We recommend specifying percentages or fractions, rather than numbers, because a specified number may turn out to be too small if you increase the size of your management team later. For example, if you require three management votes for a management team currently consisting of five persons, this number will represent less than a majority if you later add one more manager to your LLC.

Note that this provision states the standard rule that each manager gets one vote, regardless of any percentage interest he or she may hold in the LLC as a member.

D You may wish to use your operating agreement to give procedures for the removal of LLC managers. You may want to specify the membership votes needed for removal of a manager, or the automatic grounds for such removal. You can even specify a procedure to have a vote of the managers themselves decide the removal of a manager. (You'll need to retype at least one page of the tear-out form to add this new language.)

Sample Language: Removal of Managers: Managers may be removed by the vote of **"a majority of the members" or "all of the members"**, not counting the vote of any member-manager to be removed. **You may specify one or more automatic reasons for removal of a manager, for example: "A member-manager shall be removed automatically from office upon missing two or more consecutive meetings of the managers without giving reasonable notice of such expected absence to the other managers of the LLC prior to the meeting."**

E Our provision gives an unspecified term for managers—that is, it doesn't contain a periodic election procedure for managers. This provision does specify a procedure to fill a vacancy on the management team. In the blank, indicate the vote requirement necessary for the remaining managers or members to accomplish this. If you require a majority vote of members, keep in mind that this is defined in "III. Membership Provisions: (4) Membership Voting," as the vote of a majority of the percentage interests of the members—unless you provide a special formula to use for filling a vacancy by members. A majority of managers under paragraph (3) of this section of the agreement means the per capita (one person, one vote) majority vote of the current LLC managers (the managers remaining on the management team who are appointing someone to fill the vacancy).

You may wish to limit the terms of managers by providing for their periodic election. Here is an optional management election provision you can add to this provision to require the annual election of managers by the members. (You'll need to retype at least one page of the tear-out form to add this new language.)

Sample Language: Election of Managers: The membership of this LLC shall meet every year on _____**date**_____ to nominate and elect _____**number**_____ member-managers and _____**number**_____ nonmember-managers of the LLC. **You may specify a procedure for voting and how the number of votes to be cast are to be calculated [for example: "Voting by the membership at this election shall be as follows: according to _____ "capital interests," "per capita voting" (one person, one vote) or specify your own method for calculating votes]". You may want to exclude member-managers from voting in this election or add other provisions to suit your needs.**

Written or electronic notice of this annual membership meeting, its purpose, and the name of anyone nominated as of the date of the notice, shall be mailed, delivered or personally given to each member of this LLC no later than _____**period, typically "30 days"**_____ prior to the date of the annual meeting.

The term of office for each manager so elected shall be for one year, and until his or her successor is elected by the membership at the next annual membership meeting and such successor accepts his or her office.

F This provision explains that management decisions may be made either informally or at a formal meeting of managers. This is a flexible provision with the following key points:

- *Managers don't have to call formal meetings to make ordinary business decisions.* A formal meeting is only necessary if you want the managers to meet in person at a prearranged time or if you want to make a written record of the decisions reached by your managers.
- *Formal management decisions—those you wish to record in your LLC records book—should be approved by the vote requirement specified in the manager voting provision of your agreement.* The vote requirement is covered in "II. Management Provisions: (3) Authority and Votes of Managers."
- *Formal management meetings may be called by any manager.* Formal meetings must be held "within a reasonable time" of the call for the meeting, subject to a final date (no later than a specified number of days after the request for the meeting—for example, 30 or 60 days from the request by a manager for a meeting). You may change these provisions to specify minimum and maximum timelines—for example, requiring the holding of a meeting no less than 10 or more than 60 days after a request for a meeting.

- *You can set the quorum requirement—the number or percentage of managers who must be present to hold a formal management meeting.* You may specify "all," "a majority" or some other portion of the managers. If you specify a quorum requirement, and a quorum is not in attendance, the meeting must be adjourned unless all nonattending managers sign off on the holding of the meeting ahead of time (sign a written consent before the meeting that says they agree to the holding of the meeting for one or more specified purposes even though they can't attend; a simple signed note to this effect is enough to comply with this formal written consent procedure).

- *Only the business communicated in the call for the formal meeting by the manager may be taken up at the meeting.* We think this makes sense for formally called and held management meetings, but you can be more expansive and change our language to allow any business to be discussed and voted upon at a formal meeting. For example, "Any business may be discussed and voted upon at a formal managers' meeting, whether or not stated or summarized in the notice for the meeting or written consent signed by a nonattending member."

![book icon]

More about manager meetings. See Chapter 7, Section C2, for details on when and how to conduct and document formal LLC meetings.

Our provisions are adequate for most smaller LLCs. If the formal management meeting provisions don't suit your needs, you are free to change them. For example, even though the managers of most smaller LLCs should normally talk, meet and make decisions face-to-face at a formal managers' meeting, you can add language that recognizes state-of-the-art ways for managers to meet and formally make decisions at a distance—such as over the Internet, on other computer bulletin boards, via e-mail, video or telephone conferences and the like. You also can allow your managers to make decisions by written consent of all managers (unanimity is typically required for written management decisions under state law, so check your state LLC Act if this interests you).

Again, bear in mind that if an issue is important enough to require the time and consideration of your managers to make and record a formal decision, it's probably best for the managers to talk with one another in person, not just to mail, fax or e-mail in their votes.

(6) Managers' Commitment to LLC: Managers shall devote their best efforts and energy working to achieve the business objectives and financial goals of this LLC. By agreeing to serve as a manager for the LLC, each manager shall agree not to work for another business, enterprise or endeavor, owned or operated by himself or herself or others, if such outside work or efforts would compete with the LLC's business goals, mission, products or services, or would diminish or impair the manager's ability to provide maximum effort and performance to managing the business of this LLC. **G**

(7) Compensation of Managers: Managers of this LLC may be paid per-meeting or per-diem amounts for attending management meetings, may be reimbursed actual expenses advanced by them to attend management meetings or attend to management business for the LLC, and may be compensated in other ways for performing their duties as managers. Managers may work in other capacities for this LLC and may be compensated separately for performing these additional services, whether as officers, staff, consultants, independent contractors or in other capacities. **H**

III. MEMBERSHIP PROVISIONS

The membership provisions are nearly identical to those provided in the basic LLC operating agreement; where indicated, see the corresponding instructions in Chapter 5, Section C.

(1) Nonliability of Members: No member of this LLC shall be personally liable for the expenses, debts, obligations or liabilities of the LLC, or for claims made against it. **9**

(2) Reimbursement for Organizational Costs: Members shall be reimbursed by the LLC for organizational expenses paid by the members. The LLC shall be authorized to elect to deduct organizational expenses and start-up expenditures ratably over a period of time as permitted by the Internal Revenue Code and as may be advised by the LLC's tax advisor. **10**

(3) Members' Percentage Interests: A member's percentage interest in this LLC shall be computed as a fraction, the numerator of which is the total of a member's capital account and the denominator of which is the total of all capital accounts of all members. This fraction shall be expressed in this agreement as a percentage, which shall be called each member's "percentage interest" in this LLC. **12**

G This provision expresses the desire of the LLC to obtain maximum energy and effort from each LLC manager, and prohibits managers from working in or for outside businesses that compete with the LLC's business or in any business if doing so detracts from the manager's ability to perform properly for the LLC.

This is a general provision, and you may wish to tighten it up a little. For example, we've carefully avoided saying that managers must work full-time for the LLC (as managers or in other capacities), since this is not always the case. You can add language that requires such full-time effort, or go the other way and permit involvement with outside businesses or personal projects by your managers as long as they don't compete with the LLC's business.

Example: Bird Nest Bed & Breakfast, LLC, is founded by Ted and Jill. They have the money and energy to buy, set up and maintain a few scenically situated bed and breakfast cottages in their home town—a suburban location outside a major metropolitan area. Their community is overrun with summer and spring tourists seeking comfortable accommodations from which to base shopping and sightseeing sorties into the neighboring city. The two members are new to the B & B business and decide to bring in Elaine, an experienced B & B consultant, to help organize and operate the LLC. Elaine will work part-time on a consulting basis, plus be given a small stake in LLC profits for joining Ted and Jill as formal managers of the LLC. They decide to modify this provision in their operating agreement to allow Elaine (the provision can be stated to apply generally to all managers or can worded to specifically apply to manager Elaine) to do consulting work for other businesses, whether in the B & B or unrelated areas of operation, as long as this outside work does not interfere with a manager's ability to provide best management efforts for the LLC.

Whatever changes you make to this provision, don't go overboard. Courts are often reluctant to enforce overreaching restrictions on the abilities of individuals to decide how hard to work, and for whom. You may be able to sue a manager who strays from the fold in contravention of your operating agreement provisions or for nonperformance of his or her duties under an employment agreement, but don't expect a court to order a person to return to work for you, or work harder for your LLC—this just won't happen.

Also realize that provisions of this sort are really best viewed as an expression of the parties' expectations, rather than ironclad legal language. If a manager wishes to stray or stay away from your LLC, your best solution is to acquiesce—and find a more suitable replacement on your management team for the errant manager.

H This broad provision says managers may receive per-meeting, per-diem, or other payment or compensation for serving as managers. It allows managers to serve and be paid for performing work for the LLC in other capacities as officers, employees and independent contractors.

Even though this provision allows for a multitude of arrangements, the normal situation for smaller LLCs is that the managers also work for the LLC on a day-to-day basis in an officer or employee position (as president, sales manager, chief financial officer) and do not receive payment for also serving as managers of the LLC. But you may wish to make other arrangements if you bring in nonmember managers who only work part-time for your LLC as managers. If they do not work in other capacities for your LLC, you may want to pay your managers as managers. The details of these arrangements are up to you; this provision allows you to pay managers in any capacity you wish.

Note that managers may not wish to receive direct payment for managing an LLC. If the manager is an investor in the LLC, for example, she can look to her capital and/or profits interest in the LLC for a payback, rather than to direct payment for intermittent or part-time management services.

(4) Membership Voting: Except as otherwise may be required by the Articles of Organization, Certificate of Formation or a similar organizational document, other provisions of this operating agreement, or under the laws of this state, each member shall vote on any matter submitted to the membership for approval in proportion to the member's percentage interest in this LLC. Further, unless defined otherwise for a particular provision of this operating agreement, the phrase "majority of members" means the vote of members whose combined votes equal more than 50% of the votes of all members in this LLC. **⓭**

(5) Compensation: Members shall not be paid as members of the LLC for performing any duties associated with such membership. Members may be paid, however, for any services rendered in any other capacity for the LLC, whether as officers, employees, independent contractors or otherwise. **⓮**

(6) Members' Meetings: The LLC shall not provide for regular members' meetings. However, any member may call a meeting by communicating his or her wish to schedule a meeting to all other members. Such notification may be in person or in writing, or by telephone, facsimile machine, or other form of electronic communication reasonably expected to be received by a member, and the other members shall then agree, either personally, in writing, or by telephone, facsimile machine or other form of electronic communication to the member calling the meeting, to meet at a mutually acceptable time and place. Notice of the business to be transacted at the meeting need not be given to members by the member calling the meeting, and any business may be discussed and conducted at the meeting.

If all members cannot attend a meeting, it shall be postponed to a date and time when all members can attend, unless all members who do not attend have agreed in writing to the holding of the meeting without them. If a meeting is postponed, and the postponed meeting cannot be held either because all members do not attend the postponed meeting or the nonattending members have not signed a written consent to allow the postponed meeting to be held without them, a second postponed meeting may be held at a date and time announced at the first postponed meeting. The date and time of the second postponed meeting shall also be communicated to any members not attending the first postponed meeting. The second postponed meeting may be held without the attendance of all members as long as a majority of the percentage interests of the membership of this LLC is in attendance at the second postponed meeting. Written notice of the decisions or approvals made at this second postponed meeting shall be mailed or delivered to each nonattending member promptly after the holding of the second postponed meeting. **⓯**

Written minutes of the discussions and proposals presented at a members' meeting, and the votes taken and matters approved at such meeting, shall be taken by one of the members or a person designated at the meeting. A copy of the minutes of the meeting shall be placed in the LLC's records book after the meeting. **⑯**

(7) Membership Certificates: This LLC shall be authorized to obtain and issue certificates representing or certifying membership interests in this LLC. Each certificate shall show the name of the LLC, the name of the member, and state that the person named is a member of the LLC and is entitled to all the rights granted members of the LLC under the Articles of Organization, Certificate of Formation or a similar organizational document, this operating agreement, and provisions of law. Each membership certificate shall be consecutively numbered and signed by each of the current members of this LLC. The certificates shall include any additional information considered appropriate for inclusion by the members on membership certificates.

In addition to the above information, all membership certificates shall bear a prominent legend on their face or reverse side stating, summarizing or referring to any transfer restrictions that apply to memberships in this LLC under the Articles of Organization, Certificate of Formation or a similar organizational document and/or this operating agreement, and the address where a member may obtain a copy of these restrictions upon request from this LLC.

The records book of this LLC shall contain a list of the names and addresses of all persons to whom certificates have been issued, show the date of issuance of each certificate, and record the date of all cancellations or transfers of membership certificates. **⑰**

IV. TAX AND FINANCIAL PROVISIONS

The tax and financial provisions below are very similar to those provided in the basic LLC operating agreement, but they are extended to apply to LLC managers. Where indicated, see the corresponding numbered instructions in Chapter 5, Section C.

(1) Tax Classification of LLC: The members of this LLC intend that this LLC be initially classified as a **"partnership" or "sole proprietorship of the sole member" or "corporation"** for federal and, if applicable, state income tax purposes. It is understood that all members may agree to change the tax treatment of this LLC by signing, or authorizing the signature of, IRS Form 8832, Entity Classification Election, and filing it with the IRS and, if applicable, the state tax department within the prescribed time limits. **⑲**

(2) Tax Year and Accounting Method: The tax year of this LLC shall be **"the calendar year" or specify a noncalendar year period, such as "July 1 to June 30th"**. The LLC shall use the **"cash" or "accrual"** method of accounting. Both the tax year and the accounting period of the LLC may be changed with the consent of all members or all managers if the LLC qualifies for such change, and may be effected by the filing of appropriate forms with the IRS and state tax authorities. **❷⓿**

(3) Tax Matters Partner: If this LLC is required under Internal Revenue Code provisions or regulations, it shall designate from among its members or member-managers a "tax matters partner" in accordance with Internal Revenue Code Section 6231(a)(7) and corresponding regulations, who will fulfill this role by being the spokesperson for the LLC in dealings with the IRS as required under the Internal Revenue Code and Regulations, and who will report to the members and managers on the progress and outcome of these dealings. **❷❶**

(4) Annual Income Tax Returns and Reports: Within 60 days after the end of each tax year of the LLC, a copy of the LLC's state and federal income tax returns for the preceding tax year shall be mailed or otherwise provided to each member of the LLC, together with any additional information and forms necessary for each member to complete his or her individual state and federal income tax returns. If this LLC is classified as a partnership for income tax purposes, this additional information shall include a federal (and, if applicable, state) Form K-1 (Form 1065—Partner's Share of Income, Credits, Deductions) or equivalent income tax reporting form. This additional information shall also include a financial report, which shall include a balance sheet and profit and loss statement for the prior tax year of the LLC. **❷❷**

(5) Bank Accounts: The LLC shall designate one or more banks or other institutions for the deposit of the funds of the LLC, and shall establish savings, checking, investment and other such accounts as are reasonable and necessary for its business and investments. One or more employees of the LLC shall be designated with the consent of all managers to deposit and withdraw funds of the LLC, and to direct the investment of funds from, into and among such accounts. The funds of the LLC, however and wherever deposited or invested, shall not be commingled with the personal funds of any members or managers of the LLC. **❶**

(6) Title to Assets: All personal and real property of this LLC shall be held in the name of the LLC, not in the names of individual members or managers. **❷❹**

Example: Sals' Berry Farms, a two-person LLC owned and operated by a married couple, Salvatore and Sally, owns and operates a California berry growing business. The spouses bought the business from the prior owners, who have been kept on as managers of the LLC. Sally and Sal are on the management team too, but they receive compensation as vice presidents of operations, not as managers. The prior owners sold the business for a lump-sum buyout payment, plus a 20% share in future profits for the next five years. These nonmember managers of the LLC are not paid in their capacities as managers—they are content to let their management efforts pay off in a more important and lucrative fashion—namely, by boosting the value of their 20% profits interest in the business.

Finally, note that managers of smaller management-run LLCs normally approve the amount of payment, if any, each person gets for performing management duties. You may, however, let LLC members decide the compensation issue. By adding the sample language that follows to the end of this provision, you allow members who are not managers to approve payments to managers. The managers are still allowed to approve smaller amounts, such as reimbursements or per-meeting or per-diem payments.

> *Sample Language:* Except for per-meeting or per-diem amounts, or reimbursement of actual expenses paid to managers, the nonmanaging members of this LLC shall approve compensation and other payments to managers for performing management duties for this LLC.

❶ This is a general authorization paragraph that allows the LLC to establish accounts with banks and other institutions. It allows the managers to unanimously designate one or more LLC employees to deposit and withdraw funds into and from these accounts, and to direct the investment of funds held in these accounts.

Note that unanimous consent is required to designate a person or persons to have this depositing/checkwriting authority, but you can lessen this requirement if you wish by simply deleting the words "with the consent of all managers" from the second sentence of this paragraph.

In many businesses, multiple signatures may be required for withdrawals that exceed a specified amount. You don't need to specify these arrangements in your operating agreement. The details of these checkwriting and investment-directing arrangements will be spelled out on the signature cards and paperwork you must fill in when opening accounts on behalf of your LLC.

The final sentence in this paragraph is a reminder that personal funds of the LLC members and managers may not be commingled (mixed) with the funds of the LLC. If you commingle funds, a state court may decide that you and the other members and/or managers are not entitled to limited liability protection normally afforded an LLC, and may hold members and managers personally liable for LLC debts and claims.

❿ This provision gives members or managers leeway to distribute cash profits or proceeds of the LLC to members if they vote to do so. You can give authority to approve cash distributions exclusively to members and/or managers. Many smaller LLCs will trust their managers to make these allocations and distributions, but some may wish to leave important financial decisions of this sort strictly to the members themselves, or require the approval of both managers and members.

Most smaller LLCs will specify a unanimous vote, but some may prefer to allow a majority of the members and/or managers to decide this issue. Remember, a majority of members is defined in "III. Membership Provisions: (4) Membership Voting," as a majority of the percentage interests in the LLC, whereas a majority of managers is determined on a per capita basis (according to "II. Management Provisions: (3) Authority and Votes of Managers").

V. CAPITAL PROVISIONS

Most of the capital provisions in the tear-out management agreement are almost identical to those provided in the basic LLC operating agreement in Chapter 5, Section C. These provisions should work fine for smaller manager-run LLCs.

(1) Capital Contributions by Members: Members shall make the following contributions of cash, property or services as shown next to each member's name below. Unless otherwise noted, cash and property described below shall be paid or delivered to the LLC on or by **_final date or period for contributions_**. The fair market values of items of property or services as agreed between the LLC and the contributing member are also shown below. The percentage interest in the LLC that each member shall receive in return for his or her capital contribution is also indicated for each member. ㉕

Name	Contribution	Fair Market Value	Percentage Interest in LLC
_____	_____	$ _____	_____
_____	_____	$ _____	_____
_____	_____	$ _____	_____
_____	_____	$ _____	_____
_____	_____	$ _____	_____
_____	_____	$ _____	_____

(2) Additional Contributions by Members: The members may agree, from time to time by unanimous vote, to require the payment of additional capital contributions by the members, on or by a mutually agreeable date. ㉖

(3) Failure to Make Contributions: If a member fails to make a required capital contribution within the time agreed for a member's contribution, the remaining members may, by unanimous vote, agree to reschedule the time for payment of the capital contribution by the late-paying member, setting any additional repayment terms, such as a late payment penalty, rate of interest to be applied to the unpaid balance, or other monetary amount to be paid by the delinquent member, as the remaining members decide. Alternatively, the remaining members may, by unanimous vote, agree to cancel the membership of the delinquent member, provided any prior partial payments of capital made by the delinquent member are refunded promptly by the LLC to the member after the decision is made to terminate the membership of the delinquent member. ㉗

(4) No Interest on Capital Contributions: No interest shall be paid on funds or property contributed as capital to this LLC, or on funds reflected in the capital accounts of the members. **㉘**

(5) Capital Account Bookkeeping: A capital account shall be set up and maintained on the books of the LLC for each member. It shall reflect each member's capital contribution to the LLC, increased by each member's share of profits in the LLC, decreased by each member's share of losses and expenses of the LLC, and adjusted as required in accordance with applicable provisions of the Internal Revenue Code and corresponding income tax regulations. **㉙**

(6) Consent to Capital Contribution Withdrawals and Distributions: Members shall not be allowed to withdraw any part of their capital contributions or to receive distributions, whether in property or cash, except as otherwise allowed by this agreement and, in any case, only if such withdrawal is made with the written consent of all members. **㉚**

(7) Allocations of Profits and Losses: No member shall be given priority or preference with respect to other members in obtaining a return of capital contributions, distributions or allocations of the income, gains, losses, deductions, credits or other items of the LLC. The profits and losses of the LLC, and all items of its income, gain, loss, deduction and credit shall be allocated to members according to each member's percentage interest in this LLC. **㉛**

(8) Allocation and Distribution of Cash to Members: Cash from LLC business operations, as well as cash from a sale or other disposition of LLC capital assets, may be distributed from time to time to members in accordance with each member's percentage interest in the LLC, as may be decided by ___**"all" or "a majority"**___ of the ___**"members," "managers,"** **"members and managers" or "members or managers"**___. **Ⓙ**

(9) Allocation of Noncash Distributions: If proceeds consist of property other than cash, the ___**"members," "managers," "members and managers" or "members or** **managers"**___ shall decide the value of the property and allocate such value among the members in accordance with each member's percentage interest in the LLC. If such noncash proceeds are later reduced to cash, such cash may be distributed among the members as otherwise provided in this agreement. **Ⓚ**

(10) Allocation and Distribution of Liquidation Proceeds: Regardless of any other provision in this agreement, if there is a distribution in liquidation of this LLC, or when any member's interest is liquidated, all items of income and loss shall be allocated to the members' capital accounts, and all appropriate credits and deductions shall then be made to these capital accounts before any final distribution is made. A final distribution shall be made to members only to the extent of, and in proportion to, any positive balance in each member's capital account. **㉞**

VI. MEMBERSHIP WITHDRAWAL AND TRANSFER PROVISIONS

These provisions, which are the same as those in the Chapter 5 member-managed operating agreement, deal with members deciding to leave the LLC. We specifically require a vote to admit a transferee (someone who buys or is otherwise transferred an LLC interest from a member) as a new member of the LLC. As you know from Chapter 3, Section D1, some states impose mandatory membership vote requirements to admit transferees into membership. Our transfer restriction language below is intended to help you meet the most stringent of any such state rules in effect in your state. For further information, see the discussion to the special instructions noted below in Chapter 5.

(1) Withdrawal of Members: A member may withdraw from this LLC by giving written notice to all other members at least ___**number of days**___ days before the date the withdrawal is to be effective. ㉟

(2) Restrictions on the Transfer of Membership: A member shall not transfer his or her membership in the LLC unless all nontransferring members in the LLC first agree to approve the admission of the transferee into this LLC. Further, no member may encumber a part or all of his or her membership in the LLC by mortgage, pledge, granting of a security interest, lien or otherwise, unless the encumbrance has first been approved in writing by all other members of the LLC. ㊱

Notwithstanding the above provision, any member shall be allowed to assign an economic interest in his or her membership to another person without the approval of the other members. Such an assignment shall not include a transfer of the member's voting or management rights in this LLC, and the assignee shall not become a member of the LLC. ㊲

VII. DISSOLUTION PROVISIONS

This section addresses the dissolution of the LLC, or events that may trigger a dissolution. In section 1(a), we specifically require the vote of all remaining members to continue the business of the LLC after a member is dissociated (loses his membership interest). Many states still require a vote in such cases, and our provision is intended to meet the most stringent of any such state rules in effect in your state. For further information, see the discussion to the special instructions noted below in Chapter 5.

(1) Events That Trigger Dissolution of the LLC: The following events shall trigger a dissolution of the LLC, except as provided:

Again, we assume that allocations of profits and proceeds will follow each member's percentage interest in the LLC, but you can vary who gets how much if you (with help from your tax advisor) decide to implement disproportionate (special) allocations of LLC profits.

K This paragraph addresses how any noncash LLC property will be allocated among members. As with the previous provision, you may want to leave these decisions to just members or managers, or have either or both approve them.

Whoever decides, this provision says that property gets allocated among members in proportion to each member's percentage interest in the LLC. If reduced to cash later, it will be distributed to members according to the previous provision in this operating agreement.

Example: Second-Hand Freight and Salvage, Ltd. Liability Co., a five-member company with three member-managers, decides (by a unanimous manager vote as provided in its operating agreement) to sell a truck and allocate the current value of this asset to all five members, who own the LLC in equal percentages. The truck is worth $30,000, so the capital account of each member is increased by $6,000. The members and/or managers can vote to distribute this cash according to the cash distribution provision in their agreement.

L Your state LLC statute may allow you to restrict when or why members or managers are allowed to look at LLC records, or restrict access to particular types of LLC legal or financial records. We don't nitpick here, and simply give all members and managers an unrestricted right to view all records at any time.

If you want to restrict inspection rights, take a look at your state LLC statute to see how restrictive you are allowed to be under state law, then insert your own provisions. Normally, you will not wish to limit manager's rights—managers may need to look at LLC legal or financial records on a moment's notice to make a management decision—but you may wish to restrict members' inspection rights. Here's some sample language to accomplish this:

Sample Language: Any member may inspect the financial or other records of this LLC for a purpose reasonably related to the member's interest in this LLC. The Treasurer of this LLC shall make the determination within one week of the member's request and, if the Treasurer finds that the member's request is related to his or her interest in the LLC, the requesting member shall be allowed to inspect the records during regular business hours of the LLC at its principal place of business.

M Have each of your managers (one or more) sign and date at the bottom of the form. If a manager is also a member, she should sign and date the operating agreement in two places: once as member on the members' lines (section 1), and a second time here as a manager on the manager lines (section 3).

(a) the death, permanent incapacity, bankruptcy, retirement, resignation or expulsion of a member, except that within ___**number of days, typically a maximum of 90 under state LLC default rules**___ of the happening of any of these events, all remaining members of the LLC may vote to continue the legal existence of the LLC, in which case the LLC shall not dissolve; **38**

(b) the expiration of the term of existence of the LLC if such term is specified in the Articles of Organization, Certificate of Formation or a similar organizational document, or this operating agreement; **39**

(c) the written agreement of all members to dissolve the LLC; **40**

(d) entry of a decree of dissolution of the LLC under state law. **41**

VIII. GENERAL PROVISIONS

The housekeeping and miscellaneous provisions are almost identical to those provided in the basic LLC operating agreement; see the corresponding instructions in Chapter 5, Section C.

(1) Officers: The managers of this LLC may designate one or more officers, such as a President, Vice President, Secretary and Treasurer. Persons who fill these positions need not be members or managers of the LLC. Such positions may be compensated or noncompensated according to the nature and extent of the services rendered for the LLC as a part of the duties of each office. Ministerial services only as a part of any officer position will normally not be compensated, such as the performance of officer duties specified in this agreement, but any officer may be reimbursed by the LLC for out-of-pocket expenses paid by the officer in carrying out the duties of his or her office. **42**

(2) Records: The LLC shall keep at its principal business address a copy of all proceedings of membership meetings, as well as books of account of the LLC's financial transactions. A list of the names and addresses of the current membership of the LLC also shall be maintained at this address, with notations on any transfers of members' interests to nonmembers or persons being admitted into membership in the LLC. A list of the current managers' names and addresses shall also be kept at this address.

Copies of the LLC's Articles of Organization, Certificate of Formation or a similar organizational document, a signed copy of this operating agreement, and the LLC's tax returns for the preceding three tax years shall be kept at the principal business address of the LLC. A statement also shall be kept at this address containing any of the following information that is applicable to this LLC:

- the amount of cash or a description and value of property contributed or agreed to be contributed as capital to the LLC by each member;
- a schedule showing when any additional capital contributions are to be made by members to this LLC;
- a statement or schedule, if appropriate, showing the rights of members to receive distributions representing a return of part or all of members' capital contributions; and

- a description of, or date when, the legal existence of the LLC will terminate under provisions in the LLC's Articles of Organization, Certificate of Formation or a similar organizational document, or this operating agreement.

If one or more of the above items is included or listed in this operating agreement, it will be sufficient to keep a copy of this agreement at the principal business address of the LLC without having to prepare and keep a separate record of such item or items at this address.

Any member or manager may inspect any and all records maintained by the LLC upon reasonable notice to the LLC. Copying of the LLC's records by members and managers is allowed, but copying costs shall be paid for by the requesting member or manager. **🅛**

(3) All Necessary Acts: The members, managers and officers of this LLC are authorized to perform all acts necessary to perfect the organization of this LLC and to carry out its business operations expeditiously and efficiently. The Secretary of the LLC, or other officers, or one or more managers or all members of the LLC, may certify to other businesses, financial institutions and individuals as to the authority of one or more members, managers or officers of this LLC to transact specific items of business on behalf of the LLC. **④④**

(4) Mediation and Arbitration of Disputes Among Members: In any dispute over the provisions of this operating agreement and in other disputes among the members, if the members cannot resolve the dispute to their mutual satisfaction, the matter shall be submitted to mediation. The terms and procedure for mediation shall be arranged by the parties to the dispute.

If good-faith mediation of a dispute proves impossible or if an agreed-upon mediation outcome cannot be obtained by the members who are parties to the dispute, the dispute may be submitted to arbitration in accordance with the rules of the American Arbitration Association. Any party may commence arbitration of the dispute by sending a written request for arbitration to all other parties to the dispute. The request shall state the nature of the dispute to be resolved by arbitration, and, if all parties to the dispute agree to arbitration, arbitration shall be commenced as soon as practical after such parties receive a copy of the written request.

All parties shall initially share the cost of arbitration, but the prevailing party or parties may be awarded attorney fees, costs and other expenses of arbitration. All arbitration decisions shall be final, binding and conclusive on all the parties to arbitration, and legal judgment may be entered based upon such decision in accordance with applicable law in any court having jurisdiction to do so. **④⑤**

(5) Entire Agreement: This operating agreement represents the entire agreement among the members of this LLC, and it shall not be amended, modified or replaced except by a written instrument executed by all the parties to this agreement who are current members of this LLC as well as any and all additional parties who became members of this LLC after the adoption of this agreement. This agreement replaces and supersedes all prior written and oral agreements among any and all members of this LLC. **④⑥**

(6) Severability: If any provision of this agreement is determined by a court or arbitrator to be invalid, unenforceable or otherwise ineffective, that provision shall be severed from the rest of this agreement, and the remaining provisions shall remain in effect and enforceable. **47**

IX. SIGNATURES OF MEMBERS, MEMBERS' SPOUSES AND MANAGERS

The execution provisions and signatures lines for members and their spouses are the same as those provided in the basic LLC member-managed operating agreement (see the corresponding instructions in Chapter 5, Section C), but we also include date and signature lines for your manager(s).

(1) Execution of Agreement: In witness whereof, the members of this LLC sign and adopt this agreement as the operating agreement of this LLC.

Date: _____ **48**

Signature: _____

Printed Name: _____ , Member

Date: _____

Signature: _____

Printed Name: _____ , Member

Date: _____

Signature: _____

Printed Name: _____ , Member

Date: _____

Signature: _____

Printed Name: _____ , Member

Date: _____

Signature: _____

Printed Name: _____ , Member

Date: _____

Signature: _____

Printed Name: _____ , Member

(2) Consent of Spouses: The undersigned are spouses of members of this LLC who have signed this operating agreement in the preceding provision. These spouses have read this agreement and agree to be bound by its terms in any matter in which they have a financial interest, including restrictions on the transfer of memberships and the terms under which memberships in this LLC may be sold or otherwise transferred. **49**

Date: _____

Signature: _____

Printed Name: _____

Spouse of: _____

Date: _____

Signature: _____

Printed Name: _____

Spouse of: _____

Date: _____

Signature: _____

Printed Name: _____

Spouse of: _____

Date: _____

Signature: _____

Printed Name: _____

Spouse of: _____

Date: _____

Signature: _____

Printed Name: _____

Spouse of: _____

Date: _____

Signature: _____

Printed Name: _____

Spouse of: _____

(3) Signatures of Managers: The undersigned managers of this limited liability company have read this agreement and agree to be bound by its terms in discharging their duties as managers. **Ⓜ**

Date: _____

Signature: _____

Printed Name: _____ , Manager

Date: _____

Signature: _____

Printed Name: _____ , Manager

Date: _____

Signature: _____

Printed Name: _____ , Manager

Date: _____

Signature: _____

Printed Name: _____ , Manager

Date: _____

Signature: _____

Printed Name: _____ , Manager

C. Distribute Copies of Your Operating Agreement

Congratulations! You are done with another important organizational task, and your LLC is well on its legal way. Make photocopies of the completed, signed management operating agreement and give each member and manager a copy. Finally, place the original, signed agreement in your LLC records book.

●

CHAPTER 7

After Forming Your LLC

In this chapter, we discuss legal and procedural formalities that you may need to tend to after setting up your limited liability company. We suggest you skim through the chapter and get a general sense of the work you may need to do. If any topic seems pertinent, make sure you carefully read the discussion.

It's important to keep in mind that LLCs are relatively new, so trying to anticipate the ongoing issues and concerns particular to LLCs is a bit of a guessing game. For now, we cover operational tasks and issues we believe are most likely to apply. We're sure you'll be on the lookout for other LLC matters, and should be able to handle them successfully using common sense and good business judgment (backed up, if necessary, by a consultation with a small business legal or tax advisor, as discussed in Chapter 8).

General business information. This book can't possibly cover all the ins and outs of small business law. You'll find a wealth of helpful information in *Legal Guide for Starting & Running a Small Business*, by Fred S. Steingold (Nolo). For tax guidance, see *Tax Savvy for Small Business*, by Frederick W. Daily (Nolo).

A. If You Converted an Existing Business to an LLC

If you converted an existing sole proprietorship or partnership to an LLC, you'll need to take a few extra steps, as discussed in this section. (The aftermath of converting a corporation to an LLC is beyond the scope of this book.)

If yours is a new business. If you did not convert a pre-existing business to an LLC, skip to Section B, below.

1. Notify Agencies and Businesses That You're Now an LLC

Make sure you notify the IRS, your state taxing authority and other governmental agencies that you've changed your legal status to an LLC, and provide your new LLC name. As part of this process, you may need to obtain some of the following in your new LLC name:

- federal Employer Identification Number (EIN)
- state employer identification number
- fictitious or assumed business name statement if you run your LLC under a name different from its formal name listed in its Articles (see Section D3, below)
- sales tax permit
- business license, and
- professional license or permit, if the LLC members engage in a licensed profession.

Of course, you'll want to immediately get to work changing your stationery, business cards, brochures, advertisements, signs and other marketing and business miscellany to reflect your new LLC name. In addition, let your bank, suppliers, customers and business associates know your new business name and LLC status.

Review your files and other papers. If you go through the tax returns and other papers for your prior business, you'll likely discover the names and addresses of other agencies and businesses that should be notified of your new business name and form.

2. Special Procedures for Converting a Partnership to an LLC

If you converted an existing general or limited partnership to an LLC, you will probably need to do a little extra paperwork to end the legal existence of the partnership. If you neglect to take these steps, the general partner(s) may remain personally liable for any unpaid partnership business debts (we assume your LLC will pay off any unpaid debts of the prior business anyway; see the sidebar, "Liability for Previous Partnership Debts"):

- *Converting a general partnership to an LLC.* State law may require the publication of a notice of dissolution of partnership. Newspapers handle this requirement as a matter of routine, so call a local paper that publishes legal notices and ask if it provides this service. Not only should the newspaper be able to tell you whether a notice of dissolution of partnership applies in your state, it should be able to mail you a summary of your state's notice requirements in this area if you want to read them yourself. Once you publish your notice, the newspaper should send you a copy of the published notice and an affidavit of publication to place in your files. (If you can't get a satisfactory answer from a newspaper, a law or business library should contain information on terminating the legal existence of a partnership in your state; look up "partnerships" in the card catalog or ask a research librarian for help.)
- *Converting a limited partnership to an LLC.* The conversion usually is not legally effective until you file a cancellation or termination of limited partnership form with your Secretary of State's office. The state filing office should have a fill-in-the-blanks or sample form you can order by phone to use for this purpose, similar to the sample provided below. You generally must attend to this formality even if your state LLC office supplied a special form of Articles to convert a partnership to an LLC. (See your state sheet in Appendix A. Your LLC filing office will normally handle the filing for terminating a limited partnership.)

LIABILITY FOR PREVIOUS PARTNERSHIP DEBTS

If your general or limited partnership has outstanding claims or debts owing at the time of its conversion to an LLC, the general partners of the pre-existing partnership will remain personally liable for these debts. Of course, your new LLC probably plans to assume and pay these bills as they come due. As a courtesy, and to make sure all partnership creditors have personal notice of your new business form, we recommend you send a personal letter to notify each one of the conversion of the partnership to an LLC, and provide the LLC's name and business address where future correspondence may be sent.

If there are significant disputed debts or claims of your prior partnership that your LLC will not automatically pay when it begins doing business, we strongly urge you to check with a business lawyer. You will obviously want to know your legal rights and responsibilities as to these disputed amounts.

SAMPLE CANCELLATION OF LIMITED PARTNERSHIP

Prescribed by
Bob Taft, Secretary of State
30 East Broad Street, 14th Floor
Columbus, Ohio 43266-0418
Form LPC (July 1994)

Registration # _____
Approved _____
Date _____
Fee $10

CERTIFICATE OF CANCELLATION OF
LIMITED PARTNERSHIP

Pursuant to the provisions of Ohio Revised Code Section 1782.10(B), the undersigned,_____

(name of limited partnership)

bearing registration number _____, does hereby certify the following:

1.   The name of the limited partnership:_____

_____

2.   The registration number of the limited partnership:_____

3.   The date of the initial filing of its certificate of limited partnership:_____

month   day   year

4.   The date of the filing of its certificate of limited partnership with the Ohio Secretary of State (if different from the date listed in line #3):_____

month   day   year

5.   The reason for filing the certificate of cancellation is as follows:

(If insufficient space for this item, please attach a separate sheet)

6.   The effective date of cancellation: (please check/complete one of the following)

[   ] Upon Filing of Certificate of Cancellation   [   ]_____

month   day   year

(Please note that the effective date of cancellation cannot precede or be earlier than the date of filing)

7.   Is a person other than any general partner reflected on the certificate of limited partnership winding up the limited partnership's affairs?

[   ] Yes   [   ] No   *(please check the applicable box)*

Prescribed by
Bob Taft, Secretary of State
30 East Broad Street, 14th Floor
Columbus, Ohio 43266-0418
Form LPC (July 1994)

Registration #_____
Approved_____
Date_____
Fee $10

CERTIFICATE OF CANCELLATION OF
LIMITED PARTNERSHIP

Pursuant to the provisions of Ohio Revised Code Section 1782.10(B), the undersigned,_____

(name of limited partnership)

bearing registration number _____, does hereby certify the following:

1.   The name of the limited partnership:_____

_____

2.   The registration number of the limited partnership:_____

3.   The date of the initial filing of its certificate of limited partnership:_____

                                                       month   day   year

4.   The date of the filing of its certificate of limited partnership with the Ohio Secretary of State (if different from the date listed in line #3):_____

                                          month   day   year

5.   The reason for filing the certificate of cancellation is as follows:

(If insufficient space for this item, please attach a separate sheet)

6.   The effective date of cancellation: (please check/complete one of the following)

[   ] Upon Filing of Certificate of Cancellation   [   ]_____

                                                      month   day   year

(Please note that the effective date of cancellation cannot precede or be earlier than the date of filing)

7.   Is a person other than any general partner reflected on the certificate of limited partnership winding up the limited partnership's affairs?

[   ] Yes   [   ] No   *(please check the applicable box)*

3. Certain Businesses Must File Notice of Bulk Sales

Most states require the publication and mailing of a Notice of Bulk Sales when certain types of businesses—such as retail, wholesale and manufacturing businesses—are sold or converted to another form. The idea behind these notice requirements is to prevent debtor businesses (those owing money when they "go out of business") from changing their business form without arranging to pay their debts.

A local paper that publishes legal notices should know the rules for making this publication if it is required in your state. Ask the newspaper for a copy of your state's bulk sales act rules if you want to read them yourself. If the newspaper can't help you, again, a business or law library should have information and forms that you can use to handle any state requirements.

Your conversion to an LLC may be exempt from notice of bulk sales rules. In many states, bulk notice requirements are simplified or even waived if a business is simply being converted to a new form—such as the conversion of a partnership or sole partnership to an LLC—and the new business will assume and pay off the prior business's debts.

B. Basic Tax Forms and Formalities

Let's look at some tax issues and tasks you will need to keep in mind and tend to when the time comes (and tax time inevitably comes much too soon for most of us).

1. Federal Income Taxes

If you wish your LLC to start out being treated by the IRS as a corporation, make sure to file IRS Form 8832 on time (within 75 days of the formation of your LLC). A tear-out Form 8832 is provided in the Appendix. For further information, see Chapter 3, Section A.

If your LLC is classified as a partnership or a corporation (and not as the sole proprietorship of your sole-member), it will need to file partnership or corporate tax returns each year—see Chapter 3, Section B. If it is classified as a partnership, make sure to provide Schedule K-1s to each member on your LLC on tax after the close of the LLC tax year as well.

Like many small business owners, you may plan to turn your annual tax preparation work over to your tax advisor, rather than handle this task yourself. If you're like many LLC owners, you may also decide to keep yourself informed of tax matters that may affect your business.

Whether you plan to prepare your own tax returns or simply want more information, you'll want to take advantage of the free tax forms and publications provided by the IRS. Go to www.irs.gov and download the forms and publications, or call 1-800-TAX-FORM and request copies of:

• the federal *U.S. Return of Partnership Income,* IRS Form 1065

• 1065 Schedule K-1, and

• IRS Publication 334, *Tax Guide for Small Business.* This is one of the best guides for finding and filling in the latest annual tax return form for different types of business, including LLCs (which are treated as partnerships). The final part of this publication contains filled-in sample forms for all types of businesses. Look at the partnership return and schedules, as these apply to your LLC.

2. State Income Taxes

Most states follow the federal lead and will classify your LLC the same as the IRS does. This normally means you avoid the payment of any entity (business) level income tax charged in your state, unless your file IRS Form 8832 and elect to have your LLC classified and taxed as a corporation. In other words, if you haven't made this filing, just the members pay state income taxes on LLC profits and salaries, assuming the state has a personal income tax scheme. Even if your LLC is exempt from payment of state income taxes, it may have to file a state informational return, or annually submit a copy of the federal partnership (or corporation) tax return.

If your state doesn't impose corporate or personal income taxes. The states of Nevada, South Dakota, Washington and Wyoming do not impose either personal or corporate state income taxes. Alaska, Florida, New Hampshire, Tennessee and Texas do not impose state tax on individual income (although New Hampshire and Texas impose a special personal tax on interest and dividend income). Being treated as a partnership in a state without a personal income tax ordinarily means that the LLC and its members do not pay state income tax on LLC profits. However, don't forget that even if your LLC and members avoid paying income taxes on profits earned in your state, out-of-state taxes may be imposed if profits are earned in other states. This is a technical issue, and subject to state-by-state variations. Ask your tax advisor or check the tax section of a business or law library if you are forming an LLC with multi-state operations.

Some state tax offices require LLCs to pay a minimum annual tax each year, sometimes euphemistically called an LLC "renewal fee." Some states go whole hog and subject LLCs to the same or similar business income or franchise tax that is levied on corporations. The best source for current information on how your state handles the income taxation of LLCs is your state tax office. The main office is usually located in the state capital city and can be reached in-state through a toll-free telephone number. Your state sheet in Appendix A will tell you if your state is one of the few that charges a separate LLC income or renewal fee each year (other than the small annual report fee typically required in most states).

If your LLC must pay a minimum or full state franchise or income tax, make sure you make required estimated payments. Franchise and income taxes must usually be prepaid in four installments during the tax year, with the first payment consisting of any minimum amount charged. If you miss estimated tax payments, you will be charged penalties and interest. In some states, your LLC can be suspended if you fail to pay these taxes for a few years.

3. Employment Taxes

Your LLC will need to register as an employer. For salaried workers, your LLC must withhold, report and pay:

- federal and, if applicable, state incomes taxes
- federal employment taxes (unemployment and social security taxes), and
- state payroll taxes (state unemployment, disability, workers' compensation insurance).

And don't forget, LLC members may have to pay self-employment taxes on their share of your LLC's profits—see Chapter 3, Section C.

For more information on ongoing federal payroll tax requirements. Go to http://www.irs.gov or call 1-800-TAX-FORM and download or request IRS Form SS-4 (to get a federal Employer Identification Number for your LLC), IRS Publication 15, *Circular E, Employer's Tax Guide* and the IRS Publication 15 Supplement (for federal payroll tax information). For state payroll tax requirements, go to the state tax office online (typically, the Department of Revenue) or call the state tax office at its main information number—usually a toll-free number for use within the state—and ask to be transferred to the state employment tax division.

4. Other State and Local Taxes

State sales, use and county property tax payments apply to LLCs. Counties and cities also may impose local and regional taxes in an effort to stay above the red line and provide basic services to residents. Check with your county and city tax offices for current information.

C. Ongoing LLC Legal Paperwork and Procedures

Now let's cover a few legal formalities that may come up from time to time during the life of your LLC.

1. Changing Your Operating Agreement

During the life of your LLC, you may want to make changes to your operating agreement or draw up a new agreement—for example:

- If a new member joins the LLC, you will want a new agreement to include the new member's capital, profits and losses and voting percentages, and have it signed by new and old members.
- A prospective new member, or his or her legal or tax advisor, may ask for a change to one or more provisions in your old agreement to suit the needs of the new member.

Of course, you can decide to update your operating agreement at any time, not just when a new member joins your LLC. Generally, we think it's a good idea to sit down with your fellow LLC members at least once every two or so years and go over your agreement to see if it continues to meet your needs. If it doesn't, perhaps now is the time to make a few changes.

Example: The Pig in a Poke Ltd. Liability Company, a mail order lottery subscription and award notification service, wants to enlarge its membership base. The current members reason that it will be easier to attract new LLC members if they can be allowed to transfer their membership to others more easily under provisions of their operating agreement. They meet and decide to lessen the current unanimous vote requirement in their agreement to allow transfers to new members by a per capita majority vote of the members. They then amend their operating agreement to reflect this change.

a. How to Update Your Operating Agreement

There are three steps to updating an LLC operating agreement:

- First, have your members formally meet, discuss and formally approve the changes you plan to make to the operating agreement. (We cover LLC meetings in Section C2, below.)
- Next, prepare a new operating agreement. Simply recreate your old agreement, revising it to reflect your LLC's new needs.
- Finally, have all members sign the updated operating agreement, which contains the new provisions plus all unchanged provisions carried over from your previous agreement.

WATCH OUT FOR STATE LAW RESTRICTIONS ON CHANGES TO YOUR AGREEMENT

Your state's LLC Act may contain restrictions or requirements. For example, some states may prevent you from lowering the voting requirements necessary for the members to amend the Articles or Certificate of Organization, or to approve the transfer of a membership to a new member.

We alert you to your state's statutory rule on membership approval of transfers, and whether you can change it, in the "Default Transfer Rule" paragraph of the Operating Rules section of your state Sheet in Appendix A. We do the same for your state's voting requirements when a member is dissociated (when a member retires, dies, is disabled, expelled or otherwise loses his membership interest) in the "Default Continuation Rule" paragraph of the same section. For other state rules, scan your state's LLC Act, particularly the section of law titled "Articles (or "Certificate") of Organization," to see what basic LLC operating rules cannot be changed or lowered.

b. How to Prepare a New Agreement for a New Member

As we've said, preparing and signing a new LLC operating agreement is essential to make sure a new member agrees to all rights and responsibilities of LLC membership, and to make sure each current member agrees to the new division of capital, profits, losses and voting that results from bringing in a new member.

To prepare a new operating agreement, you can simply recreate your old agreement, making sure to change the capital contributions clause and other provisions that are affected by admitting the new member. All current members plus the new member sign the new agreement. Place the original in your LLC records book.

Example: Shortly after its formation, Tried & True Triad Music Promotions LLC, a three-owner company, decides to admit a fourth member. The new member will pay $20,000 to the LLC, the same amount each of the original members paid. The company adopts a new operating agreement and changes the ownership percentages of the original three members in the capital contribution clause from 33-1/3% to 25%, also showing a 25% interest for the newly admitted fourth member. No other changes are required, because splitting of profits and losses and voting rights follow the percentage interests shown in the capital contributions clause. The three initial members and the new member sign the new agreement and place it in the LLC records book.

2. Minutes of Meetings of Members and Managers

If your LLC wishes to approve and formally document an important legal, tax or business transaction, you'll normally hold a meeting of your members (or managers, if you have opted for manager control by adopting the operating agreement covered in Chapter 6).

Your members or managers may decide to hold a formal LLC meeting to take actions such as the following:
- vote on any matters that require a membership (or manager) vote, as set out in your operating agreement
- change your LLC operating agreement (even in manager-managed LLCs, the members normally are asked to ratify any changes to the operating agreement proposed by managers)
- amend the LLC's articles of organization (see Section D4, below)
- make significant capital outlays, such as to purchase real property
- fund a major, recurring LLC expense, such as contributions to an employee pension or profit-sharing plan
- sell real estate or other major capital items

- sell or purchase an operating division within the company, or expand or discontinue a product line or services
- pursue or settle a lawsuit, or
- approve other important legal, business, financial or tax decisions.

You should prepare minutes of formal LLC meetings during or after the meeting, recording the discussions and decisions made. After the meeting, place the signed minutes in your LLC records book.

You don't always have to meet face-to-face to record a formal LLC decision. Even if your LLC operating agreement requires that all or a certain percentage of members or managers approve a particular decision formally, you don't usually need to get together in person to do so. You may hold meetings on paper if all members or managers agree. You do this by preparing minutes that record a decision as though it had been made at a formal meeting. You then circulate these minutes for formal approval (signing and dating) by each member or manager. This sort of "paper meeting" is fine if everyone agrees to approve a decision this way.

a. Give Adequate Notice of Meeting to All Members or Managers

We don't cover all the ins and outs of calling, providing notice of and holding formal LLC meetings in our standard operating agreement. Most state laws are very flexible and allow LLCs to handle these matters in any way the members or managers wish. If, however, you have specified meeting rules in your operating agreement or articles of organization, make sure you follow them.

To make sure everyone involved knows the time, date and purpose of each upcoming meeting, make sure you tell, write, fax, phone or otherwise notify all members or managers (or both groups if both will attend the meeting) well in advance. Normally, two to four weeks' mailed notice is adequate. Providing adequate notice is particularly important if some members are not active in the LLC and not part of your LLC's normal network of memos, discussions and verbal feedback. Taking the extra step to provide notice of an upcoming meeting may not be legally necessary under your operating agreement or state law, but it can avoid a lot of aggravation later—for example, if a controversial decision is adopted at a meeting without the approval of one or more members or managers.

See *Your Limited Liability Company: An Operating Manual,* by Anthony Mancuso (Nolo), for a comprehensive treatment of LLC meetings, with tear-out and CD-ROM minutes forms plus more than 80 resolutions to show approval of various legal, tax and business transactions by LLC members and managers.

b. How to Complete Minutes of Meeting

On the next page, we provide a sample of the simple, ready-to-use LLC Minutes of Meeting form included in Appendix C. Make a copy of the tear-out form and fill it in as you follow the sample and instructions.

The LLC Minutes form is included on the CD-ROM at the back of this book.

MINUTES OF MEETING OF THE
"MEMBERS" OR "MANAGERS" ❶ OF
NAME OF LLC

A meeting of the _____ **"members" or "managers"** _____ of the above named limited liability company was held on _____ **date, including year** _____, at _____ **time** _____ __.M., at

_____ **address,** _____

State of _____ **state** _____, for the following purpose(s):

list the items of business discussed or considered by the members or managers. ❷

_____

_____ **name and title** _____ acted as chairperson, and

_____ **name and title** _____ acted as secretary of the meeting. ❸

The chairperson called the meeting to order.

The following _____ **"members" or "managers"** _____, were present at the meeting:

names of members or managers. ❹ _____

The following persons were also present at the meeting, and any reports given by these persons are noted next to their names below: ❺

Name and Title	Reports Presented, If Any
_____	_____
_____	_____
_____	_____
_____	_____

After discussion, on motion duly made and carried by the affirmative vote of

"all," "a majority of the percentage interests" or "a majority of the number,"
or whatever voting requirement is used for members or managers in your LLC
of _____ **the "members" or "managers"** _____, the following resolution(s) was/were adopted:

insert language of proposal(s) passed by members or managers. ❻

There being no further business to come before the meeting, it was adjourned on motion duly made and carried.

Date: **date** _____

Signature(s): **signature of LLC Secretary, officer or member** ❼

typed or printed name _____

Title: **LLC title or status** _____

❶ In the first blank, indicate whether the minutes are being prepared for a meeting of members or managers. Remember, most smaller LLCs are managed by members (not managers), so formal meetings will usually be constituted and convened as membership meetings.

❷ Include a brief statement of the nature of the resolutions that are raised for approval at the meeting. For example: "to approve the purchase of property by the LLC" or "to approve a proposed employment contract to be offered to the CEO of the LLC" or "to accept the terms of a construction loan obtained by the Treasurer of the LLC."

❸ Insert the name and title of the persons designated as chairperson and secretary of the meeting. Normally, the CEO or President of the LLC acts as chairperson. The person preparing these minutes will typically be the secretary of the meeting (often the Secretary of the LLC).

If you have not designated officers for your LLC (see the operating agreement instructions in Chapter 5, Section C, Special Instruction ㊷), simply appoint one of the attending members or managers to serve in each of these capacities.

❹ This paragraph indicates which members or managers attended the meeting. Check your operating agreement to see if it states that a specific number of members or managers must attend meetings—technically, this number is called a "quorum." Our standard operating agreement provisions require:

• *Member-managed LLC:* All members must attend meetings unless a nonattending member agrees in writing prior to the meeting that it may be held in his or her absence (or unless the meeting is a second postponed meeting; see Chapter 5, Section C, Special Instruction ⓯).

• *Manager-managed LLC:* You may pick the number of managers who must attend an LLC managers' meeting—see Chapter 6, Section B3, Special Instruction ❻).

❺ List any nonmembers or nonmanagers who attend the meeting. Also show to the right of an attendee's name any report presented by this person (such as an annual written financial report by the LLC Treasurer, an insurance availability and premium quote report by a Vice President or an oral report by the President on the negotiations that led to the drafting of a proposed lease agreement being presented at the meeting for approval by members). Attach to your minutes a copy of any written reports handed out at the meeting.

❻ Here you take care of the primary reason for preparing minutes of your meeting: to show the vote taken and the language of the proposals approved by your members or managers. If different votes are obtained on different resolutions, repeat the wording of this preliminary paragraph before each resolution.

LLC members are normally given voting power equal to their percentage interests in the LLC; see Chapter 5, Section C, Special Instruction ⓭. So, for example, a member who owns 25% of the LLC will normally have 25% of the voting power of the LLC. Managers, on the other hand, normally are given one vote per person in reaching management decisions; see Chapter 6, Section B3, Special Instruction ❻. Check your operating agreement to be sure of your voting rules for members and managers.

Show the vote obtained in favor of the proposal in the first blank. For more significant or controversial decisions, where members or managers dissent or abstain, you may wish to insert a paragraph that shows how each person voted on every individual proposal—for, against or abstained.

On special matters, your operating agreement may have stricter voting requirements. For example, unanimous voting approval of members or managers may be required for:

- the approval of structural changes to the LLC, such as a sale of assets
- the admission or departure of members (covered in Section C3, below)
- continuance or dissolution of the business after a member leaves (discussed in Section C3, below), or
- amendments to the articles of organization (covered in Section D4).

In the last blanks of the vote-specification paragraph, insert the wording of each resolution approved at the meeting. The language should be nontechnical and clearly state the decision the members or managers reached. If you wish to back up your brief description of the decision, you can attach additional information to your minutes and refer to the attachments here.

Example of Contract Approval: "The members approved a long-term contract for the supplying of goods to the LLC by [name of company]. A copy of the contract approved is attached." (Although routine business contracts are normally not formally approved at a membership meeting, such approval may be sought to avoid the appearance of a conflict of interest—for example, if the supply company is owned or managed by a member's spouse).

Example of Lease Approval: "The managers approved the terms of a ten-year lease of premises by the LLC. A copy of the lease agreement is attached."

Approval of Tax Matter: "The members approved the following tax proposal, recommended for passage by the LLC's accountant, [name of accountant]. Copies of correspondence with the accountant and other relevant documents considered by members before approval of this proposal are attached."

❼ Have the secretary of the meeting, or any other designated LLC officer or member, date and sign the minutes. Type or print the person's name and title under the signature line. Finally, place a copy of the signed minutes in your LLC records book together with any attachment pages.

3. Special Approvals for New or Departing Members

When a member joins or leaves an LLC, it is important to comply with the voting requirements in the LLC's operating agreement. As explained in Chapter 3, these voting requirements must be met under state statutes. This means making sure to obtain the formal approval of members to:

- continue the legal existence of the LLC after a member's interest is terminated, either voluntarily or involuntarily, and
- admit new members who have been transferred an interest in the LLC from a prior member.

The specific vote requirements for each of these events is specified in your operating agreement, as discussed below.

a. Check Vote Required to Approve Transfer or Continuance of LLC

You'll need to determine who has to vote, when, and by how many votes, to approve the transfer of membership by a former member to a new member, or to continue the existence of the LLC after a member dies, retires, resigns, goes bankrupt or insane or is expelled.

The accompanying sidebar, "Standard Voting Requirements in Our LLC Operating Agreements," lists the requirements for these two formal matters under provisions in our tear-out operating agreements in Appendix C. Check your operating agreement to make sure of your exact requirements for these matters.

STANDARD VOTING REQUIREMENTS IN OUR LLC OPERATING AGREEMENTS

Here's how the two operating agreements in Appendix C address voting requirements for these two important tax-related LLC matters:

CONTINUANCE OF LLC AFTER DISSOCIATION OF A MEMBER

• **Who Votes:** Remaining members.

• **When:** Typically within 90 days of dissociation of member.

• **Vote Required:** Typically, approval by all remaining members.

• **Where to Look for More Information:** Chapter 5, Section C, Special Instruction **38**.

TRANSFER OF MEMBERSHIP BY FORMER MEMBER TO NEW MEMBER

• **Who Votes:** Typically, nontransferring members.

• **When:** Varies; see your operating agreement.

• **Vote Required:** Typically, approval by all nontransferring members. Some LLCs may opt for approval by another method, if allowed under state law: by majority of capital and profits interests, by majority of capital *or* profits interests, or simply by a per capita (one vote per person) majority of nontransferring members.

• **Where to Look for More Information:** See Chapter 5, Section C, Special Instruction **36**.

---

b. Prepare Minutes Approving Transfer of Membership or Continuance of LLC

Once you know the voting rules you must follow, hold a meeting and obtain the required membership (or member-manager) approval. Then prepare written minutes of the meeting to place in your LLC records book. (Instructions for holding and documenting meetings are in Section C2, above).

Here is language you can use in your minutes to show the approval of either of these formal matters at a membership or member-manager meeting:

Sample Language: The members of _____**name of LLC**_____ met to approve the ____**"transfer of membership by (name of former member) to (name of new member)" or "continuance of the LLC following the (insert dissociation event, such as "resignation," "retirement," "death," "bankruptcy," "mental incompetence" or "expulsion") of (name of dissociated member)"**___, which occurred on ___**date of transfer of membership or dissociation of member**___. The ___**"nontransferring" (use this word to approve transfers) or "remaining" (use this word instead to approve a continuance of the LLC)**___ ___**"members" or "member-managers"**___ of the LLC voted to approve the matter by the following vote:

Name of Member	LLC Interest ❶	Vote
list each nontransferring or remaining member		**"approve," "against" or "abstain"**

---

❶ If your agreement requires (as ours do) a per capita vote to approve these special matters (this means a simple head count for each member or member-manager), leave this "LLC Interest" column blank.

If your operating agreement requires voting approval of these matters by capital and/or profits interests in the LLC, indicate in this column the appropriate percentage(s) for each member. If, for instance, your agreement requires a majority of the LLC's capital and profits interests to approve the continuance of your LLC after a member resigns, you would fill out this column to show these two percentages for each remaining member who attends the meeting and votes. For example, if a remaining voting member holds both a 50% capital and profits interest in your LLC, this column would state "50% capital and 50% profits interest" for the member.

c.   Prepare New Operating Agreement

Follow the instructions in Section C1, below, and have all members (old and new) sign the new agreement.

4.   Keep LLC Records

You will want to keep your important LLC documents in a safe, convenient place. We recommend setting up an organized system for keeping your LLC records, whether in manila envelopes, file folders or a specially ordered LLC records book. Nolo offers the Nolo LLC Records Kit, an LLC records book that includes the following materials:

- a three-ring binder, with a slipcase cover
- labeled index dividers for LLC articles of organization, Operating Agreement, Membership Register, Minutes of LLC Meetings and Membership Certificates, and
- 20 customized membership certificates with stubs, with your LLC's name printed on the face of each certificate.

If you're interested in purchasing a Nolo LLC records kit, call our Customer Service desk, 800-992-NOLO.

D. Other Ongoing LLC Formalities

In this section, we cover a number of additional ongoing legal, tax and practical formalities that apply to LLCs.

1. How to Sign Papers on Behalf of Your LLC

We're sure the separate legal existence of your LLC is important to you, particularly as a means of avoiding personal liability for business debts and claims. To make sure you and other LLC members will enjoy limited liability, members should always sign LLC papers, documents, contracts and other commitments clearly in the name of the LLC, not in their own names.

The best way to do this is to first state the name of the LLC, then sign your name on its behalf.

Example: Tom is one of two members of Park Place Plasterers, Ltd. Liability Co. He enters into a long-term contract for the refurbishing of apartments in a high-rise condominium. Tom signs the contract as follows:

Date: November 3, 199X
Park Place Plasterers, Ltd. Liability Co.
By: _____[Tom's signature]_____,
    Tom Park, LLC Member/Manager

If you sign contracts in your own name. If you don't follow our advice, the other company or party may be able to hold you personally liable under the contract you've signed. To avoid confusion and legal problems, make this simple signing procedure a regular part of your day-to-day business routine.

SAMPLE STATE LLC ANNUAL REPORT

STATE OF MONTANA

Prepare, sign and submit with fee.

(For use by the Secretary of State only)

ANNUAL LIMITED LIABILITY COMPANY REPORT

Filing Fee: Before April 15 $10 -- After April 15 $20
After September 1 $30   Form: ART-L

MAIL TO: **MIKE COONEY**
Secretary of State
PO Box 202801
Helena, MT 59620-2801
Phone: (406)444-3665

In compliance with Section 35-8-208, MCA, the undersigned limited liability company submits the following report:
Exact Name of Limited Liability Company: _____

Registered Agent Information

Name of Registered Agent: _____

Street Address of Registered Office: _____

PO Box or Mailing Address: _____

City, State, Zip: _____

If there is any change in the registered agent or registered office location, please complete a statement of change form and send an additional $5 filing fee. (A PO Box number may be added without the form or fee.)

1. **State of Organization:** _____

2. **Address of Principal Office** in state of organization: _____

3. **Limited liability company is managed by** *(members or member/managers):* _____

4. **The last date when the limited liability company will be dissolved:** _____

5. **Names and addresses** (street name and number) **of Individual Managers or Member/Managers of company:**

_____   _____
_____   _____
_____   _____
_____   _____
_____   _____
_____   _____
_____   _____
_____   _____

6. **Names and addresses of registered business** *(managers or member/managers):* **These businesses must be registered with the Montana Secretary of State's Office.**

_____   _____
_____   _____
_____   _____
_____   _____
_____   _____
_____   _____
_____   _____
_____   _____
_____   _____
_____   _____

7. ☐ **Professional Limited Liability Companies only.** *(Please check)* All the members and not less than one-half of the managers are qualified with the proper licensing authority in Montana or meet higher standards as specified by that licensing authority.

8. By my signature below, I, a member of the above limited liability company authorized to execute documents on its behalf, do state that any and all statements contained herein are true and based upon actions taken by the LLC in accordance with the statutes or its articles of organization or operating agreement.

   And I further state that the LLC remains in existence and has taken the necessary actions during the past year to preserve the status.

_____
Exact Name of Limited Liability Company

✓_____   _____
Signature of Member   Printed Name of Member Signing

_____
Address of Member Signing Report

2. File Annual State LLC Reports

Most states require the yearly filing of one-page annual report forms. These forms are filed with the state LLC filing office where you filed your LLC articles of organization, typically, the Secretary of State's office in the state capitol. Annual report forms are printed and supplied by the LLC filing office, and should be mailed out annually (although not necessarily on a calendar-year basis).

You usually need to provide minimal information on this form, such as the names and addresses of current LLC members and/or managers, and the name and address of the LLC's registered agent and office for service of legal process. Often, you can leave items blank if there is no change in the information from the previous annual report filing.

Typically, a small fee, in the $10 to $50 range, must be mailed with this form, but some states require significantly more. For example, expect higher LLC annual report fees in Illinois—$300, Pennsylvania—$300, and Wyoming. We alert you on your state sheet in Appendix A if your state asks for more than a small amount for this annual report filing.

3. Filing a Fictitious or Assumed Business Name Statement

You may wish to operate your LLC locally under a name that's different from the formal name of your LLC listed in your articles of organization.

Example: The Solar Plexus Flex and Fitness Center Ltd. Liability Co. decides to operate its three franchise locations under the fictitious name Flex and Fitness Center. The LLC owners want to continue to keep the formal name stated in the state-filed LLC articles of organization, but prefer operating their fitness centers under this second, shortened version.

Most states let you use a new name by filing a fictitious or assumed business name statement form and paying a small fee. You normally file this paperwork with the Secretary of State's office or the local county clerk or another county office. In some states, both a state and county filing are required. Find out your state's rules by checking your state's LLC filing office website or calling your Secretary of State (see your state sheet in Appendix A) or a local county clerk's office.

Some states also require that a notice of use of, or intention to use, the fictitious name be published in a newspaper of general circulation one or more times in each county where the name is or will be used. Newspapers with legal notice classified sections will perform the required publications for you at a moderate fee and file any statements of publication required under your state's fictitious business name statute. Calling a local newspaper is generally your best way to discover whether your state requires the publication of a fictitious name statement, and how to satisfy any state requirements.

4. Amending Articles of Organization

Your original LLC articles of organization contain basic information and ordinarily will stay the way they are for a long time to come. But if you need to make a major change to your LLC that alters the information in this document—such as changing the formal name of your LLC or changing whether your LLC is managed by members or managers—you will need to file amended articles of organization with your state's LLC filing office. The filing fee for amended Articles is typically the same as the fee paid to file original articles of organization.

Most LLC filing provide an amendment form online, which you can fill in—doing so is usually an easy task. Below is a standard amendment form, typical of the type of filing necessary to register amendments to LLC articles of organization with the state.

Hold formal membership meeting to approve amendment. Before filing an amendment with the state, your membership should approve any amendment to the LLC's articles of organization at a formal meeting. See Section C2, above, on how to hold and prepare minutes of an LLC meeting.

SAMPLE AMENDMENT OF ARTICLES

ARTICLES AMENDING OR RESTATING ARTICLES OF ORGANIZATION
DOMESTIC LIMITED LIABILITY COMPANY
LLC   Rev. 10/93

Secretary of the State
30 Trinity Street
Hartford, CT 06106

1. Name of the limited liability Company:

    _____

2. Date of filing Articles of Organization (month, day, year): _____

3. The Articles of Organization Are: (Check One Only)

    _____A. Amended only, pursuant to P.A. No. 93-262 §12(b).

    _____B. Amended and Restated, pursuant to P.A. No. 93-262 §12(c).

    _____C. Restated only, pursuant to P.A. No. 93-262 §12(c).

If 3A or 3B checked, complete #4.

4. The amendment is as follows: (Attach plain sheet of 8½x11 paper, if additional
    space required)

If 3C is checked, read #5.
5. If the Articles of Organization are restated set forth each article including
    all prior amendments. (Attach plain sheet of 8½x11 paper, if additional space
    required.)

EXECUTION

6. Dated this_____day of_____, 19_____

7. _____ 8. _____
    Name and capacity of signatory (print or type   Signature

_____
For Official Use Only |Rec; CC:
                                 |_____
                                 |
                                 |_____
                                 |
                                 |_____
                                 |
                                 |_____
                                 |
                                 |_____
                                 |
                                 |_____

J150.6

5. Changing Registered Agent or Office

The initial registered agent and office of your LLC are usually specified in your articles of organization filed with the state LLC filing office, covered in Chapter 4, Section E3d. The registered agent is the person your LLC authorizes to receive legal documents from the state as well as the public on behalf of the LLC. The registered address is the business address of the agent where legal papers may be served.

If you change the name or address of the registered agent, you are normally required to notify the state. In most states, the LLC filing office provides a standard fill-in-the-blanks form (titled "Change of Registered Agent or Address" or something similar) online. There may be a small filing fee.

It's in your LLC's best interests that the state have the most current registered agent and office information—you don't want to miss any important legal papers sent by the state to an old address. So take care of this small task when and if you change your LLC's registered agent name or registered office address.

Note that the change of registered agent or office is a routine task. In other words, you don't need to hold a formal LLC meeting to approve these changes, nor do you need to amend your articles of organization or revise your operating agreement—besides, your operating agreement specifically lists only the name of your first initial agent and registered office, not subsequent agents or offices. Just fill in and file the state-supplied form—that's all there is to it.

6. Certification of LLC Existence

Outside businesses, financial institutions, creditors and individuals may want to see formal legal paperwork to establish the existence of your LLC before deciding to transact other business with it (enter into a contract, sign a lease, agree to sell or buy property or the like). You can normally show these status-seekers a copy of your articles of organization or a copy of your operating agreement to help satisfy them that your LLC has handled all the necessary organizational formalities.

Occasionally, you may have to be even more formal and show a certified copy of your LLC articles of organization. A certified copy, which should be available for a small fee from your state LLC filing office (typically the Secretary of State), may not only show the file stamp of the office, but may even contain formal language stating that your LLC has met all necessary state formalities to begin doing business in your state.

Some outsiders may be sticklers for detail and may insist that you show them that your legal status is still valid—after all, articles of organization and operating agreements only show that you met legal requirements on a past date. Most states will help you with this. One way is to call the status or legal section of the LLC filing office and ask if you can obtain a current certificate of status or good standing for your LLC. Some states provide a standard certification form, which shows your LLC meets all state legal and tax requirements on the date of the status request. This should be enough to satisfy most outsiders that your LLC is a bona fide business. (See the state sheets in Appendix A for the website URL and address and phone number of your state's LLC filing office.)

SAMPLE CHANGE OF REGISTERED AGENT OR ADDRESS

State of Tennessee

Department of State
Corporations Section
18th Floor, James K. Polk Building
Nashville, TN 37243-0306

**CHANGE OF REGISTERED
AGENT/OFFICE
(BY A LIMITED LIABILITY COMPANY)**

For Office Use Only

Pursuant to the provisions of § 48A-8-102(a) of the Tennessee Limited Liability Company Act, the undersigned Limited Liability Company hereby submits this application:

1. The name of the Limited Liability Company is: _____

   _____

2. The street address of its current registered office is: _____

   _____

3. If the current registered office is to be changed, the street address of the new registered office, the zip code of such office, and the county in which the office is located is: _____

   _____

4. The name of the current registered agent is: _____

   _____

5. If the current registered agent is to be changed, the name of the new registered agent is: _____

   _____

6. After the change(s), the street addresses of the registered office and the business office of the registered agent will be identical.

_____
Signature Date

_____
Signer's Capacity

_____
Name of Limited Liability Company

_____
Signature

_____
Name (typed or printed)

SS-4225   RDA Pending

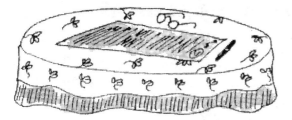

7. Certification of Authority of LLC Members or Officers

It's possible that an outsider may raise a question about the legal authority of your LLC members, managers and/or officers, and want to be sure they really have official status or specific authority for a transaction before proceeding. Typically, this occurs with real estate transactions involving title (and escrow companies that are paid to be fussy), particularly if the property is located in another state.

Complying with a request of this sort involves more than simply checking the legal status of your LLC as discussed in Section D6, just above. You also will need to document the fact that the person acting on behalf of the LLC is properly authorized by the LLC to enter into the transaction. There are a few ways to handle this, as discussed in detail below, namely by providing a:

- copy of your articles of organization
- copy of your operating agreement
- certification of authority, or
- state certification form.

 Let's look at each of these options.

a. Copy of articles of organization

In most states, your articles of organization list the *initial* members of your LLC and state whether or not the members will manage the LLC. If your LLC has adopted a manager-managed operating agreement, these individuals should be listed as managers in your articles of organization, along with the fact that the LLC is manager-run. To obtain certified copies of articles of organization (available for a small fee), contact your state LLC filing office—see your state sheet in Appendix A for the phone number and address.

b. Copy of Operating Agreement

If you need to certify the authority of a member or manager who assumed this role after your articles of organization were filed, you can provide a copy of the amended operating agreement signed by the new member or manager.

c. Certification of Authority

If you want to keep your operating agreement private, an alternative approach is to prepare a simple form to certify the authority of any members or managers. We include a tear-out Certification of Authority in Appendix C for this purpose. Below is a sample of this tear-out form, along with instructions.

The Certificate of Authority form is included on the CD-ROM at the back of this book.

SAMPLE CERTIFICATION OF AUTHORITY

This LLC is managed by its ___**"members" or "managers"**___. The names and addresses of each of its current ___**"members" or "managers"**___ as of ___**date of certification**___ are listed below. Each of these persons has managerial authority of the LLC and is empowered to transact business on its behalf.

Name of ___**"Member" or "Manager"**___   Address

_____   _____
_____   _____
_____   _____
_____   _____

Further, each of the following ___**"members" or "managers"**___ is specifically authorized to transact the following business on behalf of the LLC:

describe the specific business transaction. ❶ _____

date of signing—on or after certification date shown above

name of LLC _____

by   **signature** _____

typed or printed name of signer _____

LLC title or status ❷ _____

SPECIAL INSTRUCTIONS

❶ Here is a specific designation of authority you can fill in to underscore the member's or manager's authority to transact specific business for your LLC. In the blanks, describe the specific transaction for which the certification is being sought, such as:

• "the signing of a lease for the premises located at [address]"
• "entering into a contract with [name of company or individual] for [specify product or services under consideration]"

• if you don't want to limit the person's authority in any way, "any and all LLC business," or
• if you don't want to complete this blank, insert "N/A" instead.

❷ You can have your LLC Secretary, President or another designated officer prepare and sign this form, or you can have it signed by all current LLC members or managers. These signing procedures are authorized under the standard provisions in the tear-out operating agreements included in this book. (See Chapter 5, Section C, Special Instruction ㊽.) Simply fill in the appropriate title, such as "Secretary," "President," "Member" or "Manager."

d. State Certification Form

Some states let you file a form with the state LLC filing office, which certifies the names and authority of your LLC members and/or managers. They do this because LLCs are a relatively new type of business and the state recognizes that an official form may look better than an internal certification form provided by the LLC. To find out if your state has a form of this type, check your state website or call your state LLC filing office—see your state sheet in Appendix A for the URL and phone number.

Once filed with the state, file-stamped copies of the statement of authority form can be provided to outside businesses and individuals to let them know who is in charge and has authority to act on behalf of the LLC. Note that some state forms allow the LLC to specify limitations on the members' or managers' authority. Such a statement can come in handy if you want outsiders to know that they must deal with *all* LLC members to transact specific business.

Below is a sample state certification form. This particular form certifies the authority of LLC members and/or managers to transfer real property on behalf of the LLC. This is the typical language found in state-sponsored forms, needed for the typical case where such certification may be necessary—for example, to set up an escrow account or record a real property document on behalf of the LLC.

SAMPLE STATE CERTIFICATION FORM

**DOMESTIC
LIMITED LIABILITY COMPANY**

STATE OF MAINE

**STATEMENT OF LIMITED LIABILITY
COMPANY AUTHORITY**

_____
(Name of Limited Liability Company)

Filing Fee $20.00

```
                                    _____
                                    Deputy Secretary of State

            A True Copy When Attested By Signature

                                    _____
                                    Deputy Secretary of State
```

Pursuant to 31 MRSA §626.1., the undersigned limited liability company executes and delivers for filing this statement of limited liability company authority:

FIRST: The street address of its principal place of business:

_____
(physical location - street (not P.O. Box), city, state and zip code)

_____
(mailing address if different from above)

SECOND: The street address of an office in this State: (if no office, so indicate)

_____
(physical location - street (not P.O. Box), city, state and zip code)

_____
(mailing address if different from above)

THIRD: ("X" one box only)

☐ A.   The names of the members or, if management is vested in a manager or managers, the names of the managers, authorized to execute an instrument transferring real property held in the name of the limited liability company are:

_____	_____
(name and capacity)	(mailing address)
_____	_____
(name and capacity)	(mailing address)
_____	_____
(name and capacity)	(mailing address)

☐ Names of additional members/managers with such authority are attached hereto as Exhibit ____, and made a part hereof.

☐ B.   The name of an agent maintaining a list of the names and mailing addresses of members or managers, authorized to execute an instrument transferring real property held in the name of the limited liability company is:

_____	_____
(name)	(mailing address)

Lawyers, Tax Specialists and Legal Research

Much of the work involved in organizing and running an LLC (or other small business) is routine. Any knowledgeable and motivated business person can competently do the work. But there's no way around it—from time to time you are bound to need help from outside sources. One good way to learn more about tax matters and legal issues is to read up on them yourself. You've already taken a big step in this direction by using this book.

Quite likely, you will want to supplement your understanding of the legal and tax consequences of forming an LLC by asking a lawyer or tax professional to double-check your decisions and review your paperwork or advise you on complex areas of law or taxation. At times, you may want to run important business decisions by an experienced advisor who has a mix of business, tax and legal savvy.

Throughout this book, we have flagged instances where a lawyer or tax advisor can provide valuable assistance, such as to:

- review the legal options in your operating agreement
- add special provisions to satisfy the IRS if you will split profits and losses among members disproportionately to capital contributions, or
- customize buy-sell provisions (requirements for transferring interests in your LLC, discussed in Chapter 5, Section A2).

In the sections below, we provide a few tips to help you locate this sort of competent expert assistance and advice. Finally, if you want to do your own research, you'll find valuable suggestions on how to get started.

Consider joining one or more trade groups related to your business. These groups often track legislation in particular areas of business—such as LLC legal and tax developments—and provide sample contracts and other useful legal forms. Some also retain law firms for trade association purposes, which may be able to refer you to competent local lawyers.

A. Finding the Right Tax Advisor

You know that forming an LLC involves understanding and choosing among various tax options. Among these technical issues is finding out if it makes sense at some time in your LLC's life to elect corporate tax treatment with the IRS by filing Form 8832, "Entity Classification Election." Another important, and changing, area of tax law is how your individual state will treat your LLC for state income tax purposes. Most go along with the federal classification scheme, but some don't or will be slow to update their tax law to conform to the federal rules. A tax person who is on top of tax developments in your state can help you immensely in these and other areas. (We discuss the various LLC tax issue in Chapter 3)

Other LLC business decisions involve tax issues and advice: selecting a tax year and accounting period, setting up financial books and bookkeeping procedures, withholding and reporting payroll taxes, preparing tax returns and schedules that allocate profits, losses, credits and deductions among LLC members. To accomplish these tasks and make informed decisions in these and other tax areas may require help from a tax advisor. Depending on the tax or financial issue, this advisor may be a certified public accountant, financial or investment advisor, loan officer at a bank, pension plan specialist or bookkeeper trained in employment tax reporting and return requirements. To keep costs down, you may be able to take advantage of lower rates offered by newer firms or practitioners.

The best way to find a knowledgeable and helpful tax advisor is to shop around for someone recommended by small business people whose judgment you trust, or someone who is otherwise known to you as qualified for the task. Your tax person should be available over the phone to answer routine questions, or by mail or fax to handle paperwork and correspondence, with a minimum of formality. It is likely that you will spend much more time dealing with your tax advisor than your legal advisor (discussed in Section B, below), so be particularly attentive to the personal side of this relationship.

Tax issues are often cloudy and subject to a range of interpretations and strategies, particularly in the new LLC legal arena, so it is absolutely essential that you discuss and agree to the level of tax-aggressiveness you expect from your advisor. Some LLC owners want to live on the edge, saving every possible tax dollar. Others are content to forego contestable tax deductions to gain an extra measure of peace of mind. Whatever your tax strategy, make sure you find a tax advisor who feels the same way you do, or is willing to defer to your more liberal or conservative tax tendencies.

It pays to spend some time learning about LLC and employment taxation. Not only will you have to buy less help from tax professionals, but you'll be in a good position to make good financial and tax planning decisions. IRS publications, business and law library materials, trade groups and countless other sources should provide a growing body of LLC tax information as more businesses avail themselves of this unique business structure. Your accountant or other tax advisor should be able to help you put your hands on good LLC materials. (See the accompanying sidebar, "Resources for Tax and Financial Information.")

RESOURCES FOR TAX AND FINANCIAL INFORMATION

Your tax advisor isn't your only tax and financial resource. For example, banks are an excellent source of general financial advice, particularly if they will be creditors—after all, they will have a stake in the success of your business. The Small Business Administration can be an ideal source of financial and tax information and resources (as well as financing, in some cases).

Following are just a few suggestions for finding additional tax and financial information relevant to operating a business. If you want to get copies of free IRS publications, you can find them online at http://www.irs.gov or at your local IRS office, or you can order them by phone (call the toll-free IRS forms and publications request telephone number at 1-800-TAX-FORM).

- Start by obtaining IRS Publication 509, *Tax Calendars*, prior to the beginning of each year. This pamphlet contains tax calendars showing the dates for business and employer filings during the year.

- You can find further information on withholding, depositing, reporting and paying federal employment taxes in IRS Publication 15, *Circular E, Employer's Tax Guide*, and the Publication 15 Supplement. Also helpful is IRS Publication 334, *Tax Guide for Small Business*.

- IRS Publication 538, *Accounting Periods and Methods*, and IRS Publication 583, *Starting a Business and Keeping Records*, provide helpful information on accounting methods and bookkeeping procedures.

B. How to Find the Right Lawyer

Most small businesses can't afford to put a lawyer on retainer. Even when consulted on an issue-by-issue basis, lawyer's fees mount up fast—usually way too fast for all but the most pressing legal issues. Just as with individuals, more small businesses are trying to at least partially close this legal affordability gap by doing as much of their own legal research and form preparation as possible. Often a knowledgeable self-helper can sensibly accomplish the whole task. This is one of the reasons we refer to various sections of your state's LLC throughout the book—by spending a few minutes time reading a section of your state's LLC Act from time to time, you can save yourself lawyers' fees. Other times, it makes sense to consult briefly with a lawyer at an interim stage, or have your paperwork or conclusions reviewed, particularly for decisions that are complex or have significant legal consequences.

1. The "Legal Coach" Arrangement

Most readers will not want a lawyer who is programmed to take over all legal decision-making and form-drafting—this just builds up billable hours that few can afford. Instead, we suggest you find someone we call a "legal coach": a professional who is willing to work with you—not just for you—in establishing your LLC and helping with ongoing LLC legal formalities. Under this model, the lawyer helps you take care of many routine legal matters yourself, also being available to consult on more complicated legal issues as the need arises.

Not all lawyers will be comfortable with your taking an active role in your LLC's legal life, so you may need to interview several people before finding a compatible legal advisor. When you call a lawyer, announce your intentions in advance—that you are looking for someone who is willing to review your LLC formation papers or to handle ongoing legal work from time to time. Mention that you are looking for someone who is willing to be flexible,

point you in the right direction as the need arises, serve as a legal advisor as circumstances dictate, and tackle particular legal problems if necessary. In exchange for this, let the lawyer know you are willing to pay promptly and fairly.

Some lawyers may find a "legal coach" model unappealing—for example, they may not feel comfortable reviewing documents you have drafted using self-help materials. If so, thank the person for being frank and keep interviewing other lawyers, unless you are willing and able to pay to have a lawyer do all the work for you, from start to finish.

When you find a lawyer who seems agreeable to the arrangement you've proposed, ask to come in to meet for a half hour or so. Expect to pay for this initial consultation. At the in-person interview, reemphasize that you are looking for a "legal coach" relationship. You'll also want to discuss other important issues in this meeting, such as the lawyer's customary charges for services, as explained further below. Pay particular attention to the rapport between you and your lawyer. Remember, you are looking for a legal advisor who will work with you. Trust your instincts and seek a lawyer whose personality and business sense are compatible with your own.

Look elsewhere for tax advice. When it comes to special tax questions, such as when and if you should elect corporate tax treatment with the IRS, we think a tax advisor with LLC experience is the best person to ask for help. For other tax and financial decisions, such as the best tax year, accounting period, or employee benefit plan for your LLC, you'll find that accountants, financial planners, pension plan specialists and bank officers often have a better grasp of the issues than lawyers. And an added bonus is that although tax advice doesn't come cheap, it usually costs less than legal advice.

WHY TO HIRE A SMALL BUSINESS LAWYER

There is a lawyer surplus these days, and many newer lawyers, especially, are open to nontraditional business arrangements. In your quest for a lawyer, remember:

- *You don't need a big-time business lawyer.* Look for a lawyer with some small business experience, preferably in your field or area of operations. For the most part, you don't want a lawyer who works with big businesses (publicly held corporations, large limited partnerships or investment pools and the like). Not only will this person deal with issues that are far from your concerns, but he or she is almost sure to charge too much.

- *You don't need a legal specialist.* What if you have a very technical legal question? Should you start by seeking out a legal specialist in an area such as insurance, banking or securities law? For starters, the answer is probably no. First, find a good small business lawyer to act as your coach. Then rely on this person to suggest specialized materials or experts as the need arises. Again, finding a lawyer with LLC experience is helpful, but specialized legal involvement in narrower realms of business practice can wait until you actually need advice on a particular legal issue or problem.

2. How to Find a Lawyer

When you're ready to look for a lawyer, talk to people in your community who own or operate businesses of comparable size and scope. Try to get a personal recommendation of a knowledgeable and helpful lawyer. If possible, ask someone who has successfully formed an LLC for the name of the lawyer who helped get the LLC started and what he or she thinks of that person's work.

If you talk to half a dozen business people, chances are you'll come away with several good leads. Other people, such as your banker, accountant, insurance agent or real estate broker may be able to provide the names of lawyers they trust to help them with business matters. Friends, relatives and business associates also may have names of possible lawyers.

How shouldn't you search for a lawyer? Don't conduct a random search of phone books, legal directories or advertisements. Lawyer referral services operated by bar associations are usually equally unhelpful. Often, these simply supply the names of lawyers who have signed onto the service, often accepting the lawyer's word for what types of skills he or she has.

Don't wait until a legal problem arises before seeking out a lawyer. Even if you have all your LLC formation work covered, it's not too early to find a lawyer to use later for ongoing business consultations. Once enmeshed in a crisis, you may not have time to hire a lawyer at affordable rates. Chances are you'll wind up settling for the first person available at a moment's notice—almost a guarantee you'll pay too much for possibly poor service.

3. Set the Extent and Cost of Services in Advance

When you hire a lawyer, get a clear understanding about how fees will be computed. For example, if you call the lawyer from time to time for general advice or to be steered to a good information source, how will you be billed? Some lawyers bill a flat amount for a call or a conference; others bill to the nearest 6-, 10- or 20-minute interval. Whatever the lawyer's system, you need to understand it.

Especially at the beginning of your relationship, when you bring a big job to a lawyer, ask specifically about what it will cost. If you feel it's too much, don't hesitate to negotiate; perhaps you can do some of the routine work yourself, thus reducing the fee.

It's a good idea to get all fee arrangements in writing—especially those for good-sized jobs, such as reviewing your operating agreement. In several states, fee agreements between lawyers and clients must be in writing only if the expected fee is $1,000 or more or is contingent on the outcome of a lawsuit. But whether required or not, it's a good idea to get a written agreement.

Use nonlawyer professionals to cut down on legal costs. Often, nonlawyer professionals perform some tasks better and at less cost than lawyers. For example, look to management consultants for strategic business planning, real estate brokers or appraisers for valuation of properties, financial planners for investment advice, accountants for preparation of financial proposals, insurance agents for advice on insurance protection, independent paralegals for routine legal form-drafting, and CPAs for the preparation of tax returns. Each of these matters is likely to have a legal aspect, and you may eventually want to consult your lawyer, but normally you can wait until you've gathered information on your own.

4. Confront Problems Head-On

If you have any questions about a lawyer's bill or the quality of his or her services, speak up. Buying legal help should be just like purchasing any other consumer service. If you are dissatisfied, seek a reduction in your bill or make it clear that the work needs to be redone properly (a more comprehensive lease, a better contract). If the lawyer runs a decent business, he or she will promptly and positively deal with your concerns. If you don't get an acceptable response, find another lawyer pronto. If you switch lawyers, you are entitled to get your important documents back from the first lawyer.

Even if you fire your lawyer, you may still feel unjustly wronged. If you can't get satisfaction from the lawyer, write to the client grievance office of your state bar association (with a copy to the lawyer, of course). Often, a phone call from this office to your lawyer will bring the desired results.

C. How to Do Your Own Legal Research

Law is information, not magic. If you can look up necessary information yourself, you need not purchase it from a lawyer—although if it involves important issues, you may wish to check your conclusions with a lawyer or use one as a sounding board for your intended course of action.

Much of the research necessary to understand your state's LLC law can be done without a lawyer by spending some time online or in a local law or business library browsing your state's LLC Act. Even if you need to go to a lawyer for help in preparing an LLC legal form or to discuss the legal implications of a proposed business transaction, you can give yourself a leg up on understanding the legal issues by reading practice manuals prepared for lawyers and law students.

In doing legal research online or in a law library, there are a number of sources for legal rules, procedures and issues that you may wish to examine. Here are a few:

• *State limited liability company statutes.* These state laws should be your primary focus for finding the rules for organizing and operating your LLC.

• *Other state laws, such as the Corporations, Partnerships, Securities, Commercial, Civil, Labor and Revenue Codes.* These and other laws govern the operation of other types of businesses or specific business transactions; the content, approval and enforcement of commercial contracts; employment practices and procedures, employment tax requirements, and other aspects of doing business in your state. Depending on the type of business operations you engage in, you also may want to research statutes and regulations dealing with legal topics such as environmental law, products liability, real estate, copyrights and so on.

HOW LAWYERS CHARGE FOR LEGAL SERVICES

You can expect your lawyer to bill you in one of these ways:

• *By the hour.* In most parts of the United States, you can get competent services for your small business for $150 to $250 an hour, and often less. Newer attorneys still in the process of building a practice may be available for paperwork review, legal research and other types of legal work at lower rates.

• *Flat fee for a specific job.* Under this arrangement, you pay an agreed-upon amount for a given project, regardless of how much or how little time the lawyer spends. Particularly when you begin working with a lawyer and are worried about hourly costs getting out of control, it can make sense to negotiate a flat fee for a specific job, such as doing a pre-filing review of your LLC paperwork. For example, the lawyer may review your articles of organization and operating agreement for $300, or prepare special buy-sell provisions to control the transfer of LLC interests for $500.

• *Retainer.* Some businesses can afford to pay relatively modest amounts, perhaps $1,000 to $2,000 a year, to keep a business lawyer on retainer for ongoing phone or in-person consultations or routine business matters during the year. Of course, your retainer won't cover a full-blown legal crisis, but it may take care of routine contract and other legal paperwork preparation and reviews.

• *Contingent fee based upon settlement amounts or winnings.* This type of fee typically occurs in personal injury, products liability, fraud and employment discrimination disputes, where a lawsuit will likely be filed. The lawyer gets a percentage of the recovery (often 33% to 40%) if you win and nothing if you lose (of course, if your business is the defendant, not the plaintiff, expect to pay an hourly rate to defend the case or settle the dispute—ouch!). Since most small business legal needs involve advice and help with drafting paperwork, a contingency fee approach doesn't normally make sense. However, if you are seeking an award based upon a personal injury claim or lawsuit involving fraud, unfair competition or the infringement of a patent or copyright, you may want to explore the possibility of a contingency fee approach.

- *Federal laws.* These include the tax laws and procedures found in the Internal Revenue Code and Treasury Regulations implementing these code sections; regulations dealing with advertising, warranties and other consumer matters adopted by the Federal Trade Commission; and equal opportunity statutes such as Title VII of the Civil Rights Act administered by the Justice Department and Equal Employment Opportunities Commission.

- *Administrative rules and regulations (issued by federal and state administrative agencies charged with implementing statutes).* State and federal statutes are often supplemented with regulations that clarify specific statutes and contain rules for an agency to follow in implementing and enforcing them. For example, most states have enacted special administrative regulations under their securities statutes that provide exemptions for businesses registering the offer and sale of interests to others within the state.

- *Case law.* This consists of decisions of federal and state courts interpreting statutes—and sometimes making law, known as "common law," if the subject isn't covered by a statute. Annotated state legal codes contain not only the statutes, but references to court cases interpreting and implementing specific provisions of the states' legal provisions.

- *Secondary sources.* Also important in researching business law are sources that provide background information on particular areas of law. One example is this book. Others are commonly found in the business, legal or reference section of your local library or bookstore.

How to locate state statutes online. Go to Nolo's website at http://www.nolo.com. On the state laws page, you'll find links to the statutes of each state.

NOLO RESOURCES

Below are a few titles published by Nolo that we believe offer valuable business information for LLCs:

• *LLC Maker.* An interactive Windows program that produces the articles to form an LLC in each state. LLC maker can be ordered and downloaded from http://www.nolo.com.

• *Your Limited Liability Company: An Operating Manual,* by Anthony Mancuso. This book with CD-ROM provides ready-to-use minutes forms for holding formal LLC meetings; it also contains forms and information for formally approving legal, tax and other important business decisions that arise in the course of operating an LLC.

• *Legal Guide for Starting & Running a Small Business,* by Fred S. Steingold. This book is an essential resource for every small business owner, whether just starting out or already established. Find out the basics about forming a business, negotiating a favorable lease, hiring and firing employees, writing contracts and resolving business disputes.

• *Tax Savvy for Small Business,* by Frederick W. Daily. This book gives business owners information about federal taxes and explains how to make the best tax decisions for business, maximize profits and stay out of trouble with the IRS.

• *The Employer's Legal Handbook,* by Fred Steingold. Here's a comprehensive resource that compiles all the basics of employment law in one place. It covers safe hiring practices, wages, hours, tips and commissions, employee benefits, taxes and liability, insurance, discrimination, sexual harassment and termination.

• *How to Write a Business Plan,* by Mike McKeever. If you're thinking of starting a business or raising money to expand an existing one, this book will show you how to write the business plan and loan package necessary to finance your business and make it work. Includes updated sources of financing.

• *Web and Software Development: A Legal Guide* (book with CD-ROM), by Stephen Fishman. A reference bible for people in the software industry, this book explores the legal ins and outs of copyright, trade secrets and patent protection, employment agreements, working with independent contractors and employees, development and publishing agreements and multimedia developments. Sample agreements and contracts are included on disk.

Small business owners often find that they need to learn more about intellectual property issues (patent, copyright, trademark and trade secret law). Whether you're a do-it-yourselfer or simply wish to expand your knowledge of intellectual property law, here are some helpful resources:

• *Patent, Copyright and Trademark: An Intellectual Property Desk Reference,* by Stephen Elias and Richard Stim. Written for anyone who needs to understand the terminology of intellectual property law, this book provides overviews and straightforward explanations of the protections offered by patent, copyright, trademark and trade secret laws.

• *Trademark: Legal Care for Your Business & Product Name,* by Stephen Elias. This book shows small business owners how to choose, use and protect the names and symbols that identify their services and products. Provides step-by-step instructions and all the official forms necessary to register a trademark with the U.S. Patent and Trademark Office.

• *Patent It Yourself,* by David Pressman. This state-of-the-art guide is a must for any inventor who wants to get a patent—from the patent search to the actual application. Patent attorney and former patent examiner David Pressman covers use and licensing, successful marketing and infringement. This best-selling book is also available in software (system requirements: mouse and hard disk, 4 MB RAM, Windows 3.1 or higher, VGA or higher monitor).

• *The Copyright Handbook: How to Protect and Use Written Works,* by Stephen Fishman. Provides fill-in-the-blanks forms and detailed instructions for protecting all types of written expression under U.S. and international copyright law. It also explains copyright infringement, fair use, works for hire and transfers of copyright ownership.

State Sheets

The state sheets in this appendix provide the essential, state-specific information necessary to comply with state requirements to form an LLC.

Locate the material in this appendix for the state in which you plan to form your LLC (the states are listed alphabetically). You'll refer to this information as you prepare your LLC forms according to the instructions in Chapters 4 and 5 or 6 of this book.

Note that your state sheet is divided into four main headings, which we summarize just below:

- LLC Filing Office
- Articles of Organization (or Certificate of Formation)
- State Tax Status, and
- Operating Rules.

LLC Filing Office

Here you'll find the Web address, physical address and phone number (subject to change) of the state office that deals with LLCs and other business entities formed in the state. As discussed in Chapter 4, Section A, you'll go online or contact the LLC filing office to download or request state-supplied LLC forms and information. The Secretary of State, Corporations Division, is the office that generally handles LLC forms and filings, but some states have a different name for this office.

- *Forms and Statutes:* In this section, we indicate whether your state's LLC filing office or website provide a sample or ready-to-use Articles of Organization form or publish guidelines for preparing your own form.

⚠

Get up-to-date state materials. State-specific information changes frequently and may not always be current on all points in every state. The state LLC filing information office will update you on your state's latest legal requirements and tax rules.

Articles of Organization (or Certificate of Formation)

This section contains information you'll need to complete fill-in-the-blanks articles of organization or to prepare your own articles. When you file this form with the state LLC filing office, your LLC begins its legal existence. (See Chapter 4, Section F.) The Articles of Organization section has several subheadings:

- *Name Requirements.* Each state requires certain words to be included in an LLC's formal name—typically "Limited Liability Company," "Ltd. Liability Co.," "LLC" or "L.L.C." We also indicate the fee and time period for which you may reserve an available LLC name prior to filing your articles. Typically, the state LLC office supplies a form you may use to apply for a name reservation, but a simple written name reservation request will normally work just as well. (We cover name reservations in Chapter 4, Section C5.)

- *Filing Fee.* We list the fee you'll need to pay to file your LLC articles, plus, if applicable, any special rules for computing and paying the filing fee.

- *Annual Fees.* In some states, we add this section to cover any special (unusually costly) annual fee requirements. For example, in a few states, annual fees in excess of $100 must be paid to the LLC filing office to maintain your LLC's legal status. (See Chapter 7, Section D2.)

- *Special Instructions and Filing Requirements.* This section tells you how many copies of the articles to send to your state LLC office for filing. It also covers any additional forms that must be filed along with your articles, as well as any special requirements for preparing and filing articles of organization in your state. If you form an LLC in a state that does not provide a printed or sample articles form, you'll find the statutory requirements for the contents of articles. In states such as these, we give sample wording if the required information seems particularly tricky or technical. (See Chapter 4, Section E5, for more on preparing articles from scratch.)

State Tax Status

This is a short heading with two tax-related items:

- *State Tax Treatment of LLCs.* We fill you in on how your state is expected to treat an LLC for state tax purposes. Most states follow the federal tax scheme, and will treat your LLC the way the IRS does—as a partnership for a multi-member LLC; as a sole proprietorship for a one-member LLC (assuming your state allows the formation of one-member LLCs); or as a corporation if your LLC has filed IRS Form 8832 and elected

to be taxed by the IRS as a corporation. For further information on state and federal tax treatment of LLCs, see Chapter 3.

- *State Tax Office.* We list the location, telephone number and Web address of your state's revenue and taxation (or similar) office. We recommend you go to this website or call the tax office number early in the LLC formation process, and obtain tax forms and other tax materials relevant to forming and operating an LLC in your state.

Operating Rules

Each state sheet covers several important statutory requirements:

- *Default Transfer Rule* and *Default Continuation Rule.* We address each state's rules for how members must vote to approve the transfer of membership to a new member or to continue the legal life of the LLC after a member is dissociated (leaves, dies, is expelled or otherwise loses a membership interest). We summarize and give the legal citation to sections of each state's Limited Liability Company Act that govern these technical LLC operating options. In most cases, the rules shown are "default" rules—that is, they apply only if you do not come up with a different voting or approval rule in your LLC operating agreement. In some states, however, the state rules for these options are mandatory—and we point out when this is the case. Generally, the information given in these sections is essential if you wish to lower the unanimous-vote rule that we supply for each of these options in our tear-out operating agreements. (See Chapters 5 and 6.)

Note: These default rules are in a state of flux. Even if your state is listed as requiring a vote to admit new members or to continue the LLC after a member leaves, it may have repealed or changed the listed vote requirement, or be on the brink of doing so, by the time a member is admitted to or leaves your LLC. The best way to check is to look up the section of the state LLC

Act given (using the State LLC Act link listed in your state sheet) to see if it still requires a vote or if it has been changed or repealed.

- *Special Statutory Rules.* Some state sheets list uncharacteristic legal operating rules that apply (those that vary significantly from LLC operating rules found in most other states). For example, if a state limits the type of payment that may be made as a capital contribution to an LLC, we mention the special capital contribution rule here.

●

ALABAMA

LLC Filing Office

Secretary of State
  Corporate Section
  P.O. Box 5616
  Montgomery, AL 36103

Telephone: 334-242-5324

http://www.sos.state.al.us/business/corporations.cfm

Forms and Statutes: Alabama Secretary of State provides an LLC formation summary sheet together with a fill-in-the-blanks articles of organization form and a Report of Domestic Limited Liability Company. (See "Special Instructions and Filing Requirements" below.)

Internet Forms: Guidelines for Alabama articles, LLC report forms and other statutory forms can be downloaded from the state website. Additional links let you browse the state LLC act and other Alabama laws.

The Alabama LLC Act is contained in Title 10, Chapter 12 of the Alabama statutes, and is browseable from the following Web page (select Title 10, then Chapter 12):

http://www.legislature.state.al.us/CodeofAlabama/1975/coatoc.htm

Minimum Number of Members: One.

Articles of Organization

Name Requirements: Must contain the words "Limited Liability Company" or the abbreviation "L.L.C." The Alabama LLC filing office currently does not reserve LLC names.

Filing Fee: $40, payable to "Secretary of State" plus a separate check for $35 for "Probate Court Judge," who receives and records the original articles. (See "Special Instructions and Filing Requirements" below.)

Special Instructions and Filing Requirements: Have initial member(s) sign the articles. Submit an original plus two copies of completed and signed articles to the nearest Probate Court judge (check local governmental telephone listing and call for address). The judge will record the original articles of organization and forward a copy with fees to the Secretary of State.

After filing articles of organization, fill in the Domestic LLC Company Report form and send the original plus two copies of the completed form, together with a check for $5, to the Secretary of State.

Tax Status

State Tax Treatment of LLCs: Follows IRS classification.

State Tax Office: Department of Revenue, Montgomery, telephone 334-242-1170.

http://www.ador.state.al.us

Operating Rules

Default Transfer Rule: Unless otherwise provided in operating agreement, by unanimous written consent of all nontransferring members. [Section 10-12-33.]

Default Continuation Rule: Vote to continue LLC after dissociation of member not required.

Special Statutory Rules: Unless provided otherwise in operating agreement, managers, if chosen, must be appointed by a vote of at least one-half the number of members. [Section 10-12-22(b)(1).]

ALASKA

LLC Filing Office

Department of Commerce & Economic Development
  Division of Banking, Securities & Corporations
  Corporations Section
  P.O. Box 110808
  Juneau, AK 99811-0808

Telephone: 907-465-2530

http://www.dced.state.ak.us/bsc/corps.htm

Forms and Statutes: State provides fill-in-the-blanks articles of organization with instructions, plus an information booklet with requirements for organizing and operating an Alaska LLC.

Internet Forms: Alaska LLC articles and other statutory forms can be downloaded from the state website. Current Alaska LLC Act provisions and the status of pending LLC bills may be searched on the Alaska website.

The Alaska LLC Act is contained in Title 10, Chapter 10.50 of the Alaska statutes, starting at section 10.50.010, and is browseable online. Go to the Web page listed below (the corporations section home page), select the link to "Alaska Statutes and Regulations," then select "The Current Alaska Statutes." Expand the Title 10 heading and select "Chapter 10.50" to view the LLC Act.

http://www.dced.state.ak.us/bsc/corps.htm

Minimum Number of Members: One.

Articles of Organization

Name Requirements: Must contain the words "Limited Liability Company" or the abbreviations "LLC" or "L.L.C." The word "Limited" may be abbreviated as "Ltd." and the word "Company" as "Co." The name may not contain the words "city" or "borough" or otherwise imply that the company is a municipality. An LLC name may be reserved for 120 days for $15. A proposed LLC name may be registered (kept on the rolls of the LLC filing office) by paying an annual fee of $25.

Filing Fee: $250 fee (includes $100 biennial license fee—due every two years), payable to "State of Alaska."

Special Instructions and Filing Requirements: Articles need not state a limit on the duration of the LLC. Specify in Article VI of the fill-in-the-blanks form any terms restricting members' ability to transfer their interests. If you adopt the standard language contained in our operating agreements for controlling the transfer of membership rights, you may use the following sentence to sum up the restrictions on assignments of LLC interests: "The unanimous vote of nonassigning members of this LLC is necessary to admit an assignee of a member as a new member of this LLC. Upon such approval, the assignee shall be accorded all rights associated with membership in this LLC."

The articles must also give a primary and secondary standard industrial code (SIC) that describes the type of business to be operated by the LLC. A list of SIC codes is included in the Alaska LLC filing office materials. File the original and one copy of articles of organization.

If you are converting an existing partnership to an LLC, prepare and attach Form 08-431, Application for Certificate of Conversion to your LLC articles. This is a simple form, available for downloading from the state LLC office website, that contains general information on the prior partnership.

Tax Status

State Tax Treatment of LLCs: Follows IRS classification.

State Tax Office: Department of Revenue, telephone: Juneau 907-465-5887, Fairbanks 907-451-2830, Anchorage 907-269-6900.

http://www.revenue.state.ak.us

Operating Rules

Default Transfer Rule: Unless otherwise provided in agreement, by unanimous consent of nontransferring members. [Section 10.50.165.]

Default Continuation Rule: After the loss of a member, the LLC continues—a vote to continue the LLC is not required. [Section 10.50.400.]

Special Statutory Rules: Memberships can be issued to persons in exchange for a promissory note or promise to contribute property or services in the future only if the person has also paid in some property or services to the LLC. [Section 10.50.275.]

ARIZONA

LLC Filing Office

Arizona Corporation Commission
  Corporation Filing Section
  1300 West Washington
  Phoenix, AZ 85007-2996

Telephone: 800-345-5819 (in AZ only)
  or 602-542-3135

Tucson Branch Office: 520-628-6560 (accepts LLC filings)

http://www.cc.state.az.us/corp/index.htm

Forms and Statutes: State provides fill-in-the-blanks articles of organization.

Internet Forms: The latest Arizona LLC articles of organization with instructions, plus other Arizona LLC statutory forms (Notice of Filing, Application for Reservation of LLC Name and others) can be downloaded from the state LLC filing office website. General Instructions for forming an LLC plus a checklist of steps to take to form an Arizona LLC also are available for downloading.

The Arizona LLC Act is contained in Title 29, Chapter 4 of the Arizona statutes, starting at section 29.601, and is browseable from the following Web page:

http://www.azleg.state.az.us/ars/29/title29.htm

Minimum Number of Members: One.

Articles of Organization

Name Requirements: Must contain the words "Limited Liability Company" or "Limited Company" or the abbreviations "L.L.C." or "L.C." Call the LLC filing office to check name availability. An available LLC name may be reserved for 120 days for $10.

Filing Fee: $50, payable to "Arizona Corporation Commission."

Special Instructions and Filing Requirements: The address of the LLC's statutory agent stated in the articles must be a street address, and the statutory agent must sign the articles in the space provided to indicate acceptance of this position. Submit the original and one copy of the articles for filing. Providing a specific duration date for the LLC is optional—most LLCs will want a "perpetual" existence and can leave this item blank, or insert "perpetual."

After filing articles of organization, you must publish a Notice of Filing as follows: Within 60 days of filing, publish a Notice of Filing three times in a newspaper of general circulation that publishes legal notices in the county where the LLC has its place of business. The LLC filing office materials contain a Notice of Filing form to use to meet the publication requirement. Within 90 days of filing articles, an Affidavit of Publication—a form supplied by the newspaper that verifies the Notice was published—must be filed with the Corporation Commission (no fee). The newspaper will handle this requirement.

Tax Status

State Tax Treatment of LLCs: Follows IRS classification.

State Tax Office: Department of Revenue, Phoenix, telephone 602-542-2076.

http://www.revenue.state.az.us

Operating Rules

Default Transfer Rule: By consent of all nontransferring members, but operating agreement can give authority to admit new members to one or more members. [Section 29-731(B)(2).]

Default Continuation Rule: Vote to continue LLC after dissociation of member not required. [Section 29-781(A)(3).]

ARKANSAS

LLC Filing Office

Arkansas Secretary of State
   Corporations Division
   State Capitol
   Little Rock, Arkansas 72201-1094

Telephone: 888-233-0325

http://www.sosweb.state.ar.us/corp_forms/forms.html

Forms and Statutes: State provides fill-in-the-blanks articles of organization (Form LL-01) with instructions.

Internet Forms: The latest LLC articles of organization with instructions, plus other Arkansas LLC statutory forms (Application for Reservation of LLC Name and others) can be downloaded from the state LLC filing office website.

The Arkansas LLC Act (called the "Small Business Entity Tax Pass Through Act"), is located in Title 4 (Business and Commercial Law), Subtitle 3 (Corporations and Associations), Chapter 32, starting with section 4-32-101, and is browseable from the following Web page (choose HTML or Java version, then click to open the "arcode folder" to see a list of title headings; then drill down through the Title 4 folders until you reach the Small Business Entity Tax Pass Through Act in Title 4, Subtitle 3, Chapter 32):

http://170.94.58.99sdcodejul2002lpext.dll?f=templates &fn=default.htm

Minimum Number of Members: One.

Articles of Organization

Name Requirements: Must contain the words "Limited Liability Company," "Limited Company" or the abbreviation "L.L.C.," "L.C.," "LLC" or "LC." LLCs that perform professional services must have the words "Professional Limited Liability Company," "Professional Limited Company" or the abbreviations

"P.L.L.C.," "P.L.C.," "PLLC" or "PLC" in their name. In any of these name variations, the word "Limited" may be abbreviated as "Ltd." and the word "Company" may be abbreviated as "Co." An LLC name may be reserved for 120 days for $25.

Filing Fee: $50 fee, payable to the "Arkansas Secretary of State."

Special Instructions and Filing Requirements: The initial registered agent must accept the designation by signing on the signature line provided in the third article of the fill-in-the-blanks form. Send an original and one copy of completed articles for filing. A file-stamped copy will be returned to you.

Note: If you are converting an existing partnership into an LLC, obtain the "Form for Conversion of Partnership to an LLC," available for downloading from the state website. Complete and attach it to your completed articles.

Tax Status

State Tax Treatment of LLCs: An LLC with two or more members will be treated as a partnership for state tax purposes. An LLC with only one member will be treated as a sole proprietorship. [Section 4-32-1313.] This state classification conforms to federal default classification rules for LLCs. Presumably, an Arkansas LLC that elects corporate tax treatment with the IRS will be treated as a corporation for state tax purposes as well.

State Tax Office: Department of Finance & Administration, Revenue Division, Little Rock, telephone 501-682-7250.

http://www.ark.org/dfa

Operating Rules

Default Transfer Rule: Unless otherwise stated in operating agreement, by unanimous consent of nontransferring members. [Section 4-32-706.]

Default Continuation Rule: After a member withdraws, the LLC continues—a vote to continue the LLC is not required. [Section 4-32-901.]

Special Statutory Rules: Default membership approval rule is by a vote of one-half or more of the number of members; operating agreement may change this requirement, and special statutory rules may require a greater vote in some matters (unanimous membership is the default rule to amend the operating agreement). [Section 4-32-403.]

CALIFORNIA

LLC Filing Office

California Secretary of State
  Limited Liability Company Unit
  P.O. Box 944228
  Sacramento, CA 94244-2280

Telephone: 916-653-3795

http://www.ss.ca.gov/business/business.htm

Branch offices of the Secretary of State are located in Fresno, Los Angeles, San Diego and San Francisco. Currently, branch offices provide LLC forms over-the-counter only, and do not accept LLC filings.

Forms and Statutes: State provides fill-in-the-blanks articles of organization (Form LLC-1) with instructions, plus a summary of the California LLC Act (called the Beverly-Killea LLC Act). The basic articles form is all that is legally needed, although you may attach extra provisions to the state-provided form if you wish. The LLC filing office also provides an annual LLC Statement of Information form, which must be filed within 90 days of forming the LLC.

Internet Forms: The latest California LLC articles of organization with instructions, plus other California LLC statutory forms (Reservation of LLC Name and others) can be downloaded from the Secretary of State's website.

The California Beverly-Killea Limited Liability Company Act is contained in the California Corporations Code, Title 2.5 (Limited Liability Companies), starting with Section 17000, and is browseable from the following Web page (check the "Corporations Code" box, then click the search button at the bottom of the page; then scroll down to section 17000 to find the LLC Act Sections):

http://www.leginfo.ca.gov/calaw.html

Note for Professionals: The practices of specially licensed California professions, such as lawyers, accountants, doctors and other health professionals (the same professions which, if they are incorporated, must be set up as special California "professional" corporations), cannot be organized as LLCs. However, lawyers, accountants and architects may form a Registered Limited Liability Partnership (ask the Secretary of State for RLLP forms and instructions). If you are unsure whether you can form a California LLC to render professional services, call your state licensing board.

Minimum Number of Members: One.

Articles of Organization

Name Requirements: Must contain the words "Limited Liability Company" or the abbreviation "LLC." The word "Limited" may be abbreviated as "Ltd." and the word "Company" as "Co." The LLC name may contain the names of one or more members, but may not include the words "Bank," "Insurance," "Trust," "Trustee," "Incorporated" or "Corporation," or the abbreviations "Inc." or "Corp."

An available LLC name may be reserved for 60 days for a $10 fee. Name availability cannot be checked by phone unless you have set up a prepaid account with the LLC office. The best way to secure a name is to reserve it by mail with the LLC filing office (list one or more alternate names in case your first choice for a corporate name is not available for reservation).

Filing Fee: $70 filing fee, payable to "Secretary of State."

Annual Fees: California charges LLCs (as well as C— regular—corporations, S corporations and limited partnerships) a minimum annual tax of $800, payable to the Franchise Tax Board (but corporations do not have to pay the minimum tax for the first tax year). You must pay this minimum amount within three months after forming your LLC. (If LLC elects corporate tax treatment, this minimum payment is made to the Secretary of State when articles are filed.) LLCs with total annual incomes of $250,000 or more must also estimate and pay the following additional annual amounts (check the California Tax Office website for the latest LLC tax information—see Tax Office Web address, below):

Annual Total Income Reportable to California	*Additional Annual LLC Fee*
$250,000–$499,999:	$900
$5,000–$999,999:	$2,500
$1,000,000–$4,999,999:	$6,000
$5,000,000 or more:	$11,790

Special Instructions and Filing Requirements: Send only original articles of organization to the LLC office in Sacramento, together with a check for the filing fee. You will receive a certified copy from the LLC filing office.

Tax Status

State Tax Treatment of LLCs: Follows IRS classification rules.

State Tax Office: Franchise Tax Board, Sacramento, telephone 800-852-5711.

http://www.ftb.ca.gov

Operating Rules

Default Transfer Rule: Except as otherwise provided in articles or operating agreement, by consent of majority interest nontransferring members. Presumably, this means a "majority in interest," defined as members entitled to more than 50% of LLC profits. [Section 17303.]

Default Continuation Rule: After a member withdraws, the LLC continues—a vote to continue the LLC is not required. [Section 17350.]

COLORADO

LLC Filing Office

Secretary of State
1560 Broadway, Suite 200
Denver, CO 80202

Telephone: 303-894-2251

http://www.sos.state.co.us/pubs/business/main.htm

Forms and Statutes: Provides fill-in-the-blanks articles of organization with instructions for new businesses. Provides special articles of organization to convert existing general or limited partnership to a Colorado LLC.

Internet Forms: The latest LLC articles of organization, plus other Colorado LLC statutory forms (Reservation of LLC Name and others) can be downloaded from the state LLC filing office website. Forms are provided in WordPerfect and Adobe Acrobat format. A publication called the Citizen's Guide to the Business Division is browseable and downloadable, with helpful information on forming LLCs and other types of Colorado businesses.

The Colorado LLC Act is contained in Title 7, Chapter 80 of the Colorado Statutes, starting with Section 7-80-101, and is browseable from the following Web page:

www.michie.com/colorado.html

Minimum Number of Members: One.

Articles of Organization

Name Requirements: Name must include the words "Limited Liability Company," "Company" or the abbreviation "LLC." The word "Limited" may be abbreviated as "Ltd." and the word "Company" as "Co." For name availability, call the LLC filing office. The Secretary of State provides an Application for Reservation of Name form; the reservation fee is $10 for a 120-day reservation.

Filing Fee: $50, payable to "Secretary of State." Expedited (quick) filing costs $50 extra. Papers returned to you by fax cost $7 more.

Special Instructions and Filing Requirements: Type or print the information in the blanks on the state-provided form and supply a stamped, self-addressed envelope for the return of file-stamped articles to you (or have file-stamped articles faxed back to you for an additional charge). File the original and one copy of articles of organization.

Tax Status

State Tax Treatment of LLCs: Follows IRS classification.

State Tax Office: Revenue Department, Denver, telephone 303-866-3091.

http://www.taxcolorado.com

Operating Rules

Default Transfer Rule: By written consent of all nontransferring members, unless otherwise provided in operating agreement. If unanimous consent is not obtained, transferee gets only an economic interest in the LLC (rights to profits and losses and return of capital contribution of transferring member), but no voting or management rights. [Section 70-80-702.]

Default Continuation Rule: Vote to continue LLC not required.

Special Statutory Rules: LLC Act provides for annual meetings of members; if managers are chosen, they are elected or reelected by majority vote of the number of members at each annual meeting of members. [Section 7-80-402.] In the absence of a provision in the operating agreement, profits and losses and distributions of capital are allocated and distributed to members according to the value of each member's capital contribution. [Sections 7-80-503 and 7-80-504.]

LLC Filing Office

Connecticut Secretary of State
  30 Trinity Street
  P.O. Box 150470
  Hartford, CT 06106

Telephone: 860-509-6001

http://www.sots.state.ct.us

Forms and Statutes: Provides fill-in-the-blanks articles of organization, Domestic Limited Liability Company. Cannot form an LLC for a bank, trust, insurance, building and loan, utility (except telephone) or cemetery company.

LLC Forms Requests: 860-509-6079

Internet Forms: The latest LLC articles of organization with instructions, plus other Connecticut LLC statutory forms (Reservation of LLC Name and others) can be downloaded from the state LLC filing office website.

The Connecticut LLC Act is contained in Title 34, Chapter 613 of the Connecticut Statutes, starting with section 34-100, and is browseable from the following Web page (click "Title 34," then click "Chapter 613"):

http://www.cga.state.ct.us/2001/pub/titles.htm

Minimum Number of Members: One.

Articles of Organization

Name Requirements: Must contain the words "Limited Liability Company" or the abbreviations "LLC" or "L.L.C." The word "Limited" may be abbreviated as "Ltd." and the word "Company" as "Co." To reserve an LLC name for 120 days, mail the state form Application for Reserved Name, Limited Liability Company, with $30 fee, to Secretary of State.

Filing Fee: $60, payable to "Secretary of State." Add $25 extra to request a certified copy of your articles; add $20 for each plain copy of articles you wish to receive.

Special Instructions and Filing Requirements: You only need to send the original articles. The Secretary of State will return a mailing receipt to you.

Tax Status

State Tax Treatment of LLCs: Follows IRS classification. [Sec. 34-113.]

State Tax Office: Department of Revenue Services, Hartford, telephone 203-566-8520.

http://www.drs.state.ct.us

Operating Rules

Default Transfer Rule: Unless otherwise provided in the operating agreement, by approval of a "majority in interest" of the members, not counting the interests of the transferring member. [Section 34-172.] The term "majority in interest" is not defined in the Connecticut LLC Act, but probably follows the definition found in IRS Revenue Procedure 95-10, namely the vote of remaining members holding a majority of both the capital and profits interests in the LLC.

Default Continuation Rule: Vote to continue LLC after dissociation of member not required.

Special Statutory Rules: Profits and losses are allocated to members according to the value of their capital contributions, unless otherwise stated in the operating agreement. [Section 34-152.]

DELAWARE

LLC Filing Office

Department of State
Division of Corporations
P.O. Box 898
Dover, DE 19903

Telephone: 302-739-3073

http://www.state.de.us/corp/index.htm

Forms and Statutes: When you ask for LLC information, Delaware will send you its corporate formation package. Included in this package is a fill-in-the-blanks "Certificate of Formation" (Delaware's version of articles of organization).

Internet Forms: The latest LLC Certificate of Formation, plus other LLC statutory forms (Reservation of LLC Name and others) can be downloaded from the state LLC filing office website (as part of the complete online forms package).

The Delaware LLC Act is contained in Title 6 (Commerce and Trade), Chapter 18 of the Delaware Statutes, starting with section 18-101, and is browseable from the following Web page:

http://www.michie.com

Minimum Number of Members: One.

Certificate of Formation

Name Requirements: Must contain the words "Limited Liability Company" or the abbreviation "L.L.C." May contain the words "Club," "Foundation," "Fund," "Institute," "Society," "Union," "Syndicate," or "Trust." Name availability may be checked by calling 302-727-7283.

An LLC name may be reserved for 120 days by sending two copies of an Application for Reservation of Name together with a fee payment of $75 to the Delaware Division of Corporations. (Delaware LLCs cannot use Delaware's 900-line to reserve a name—a convenience afforded incorporators in Delaware.)

Filing Fee: $70, payable to "Delaware Department of State." The Department of State, Division of Corporations, also accepts major credit cards.

Annual Fees: A Delaware LLC must pay a flat annual franchise tax of $100. Contact the Franchise Tax Office of the Division of Corporations for more information and for tax forms; telephone 302-739-4225.

Special Instructions and Filing Requirements: Send the Department of State an original plus one copy, and request that the copy be certified and returned to you. Use letter-sized paper only and black ink printer, ribbon or pen to fill in forms. Sign all forms with black ink pen. You may leave the third article of the state-provided Limited Liability Company Certificate of Formation blank; you do not have to specify a dissolution date for your LLC.

Tax Status

State Tax Treatment of LLCs: Follows IRS classification.

State Tax Office: Delaware Franchise Tax Office, Dover, telephone 302-739-4225.

http://www.state.de.us/revenue

Operating Rules

Default Transfer Rule: In addition to any rule stated in the operating agreement, by vote of all nontransferring members of the LLC. [Section 18-704(a).]

Default Continuation Rule: Vote to continue LLC after dissociation of member not required.

Special Statutory Rules: Unless otherwise stated in the operating agreement, members are vested with management power according to their percentage interests in the LLC, and are given voting power equal to these interests. A vote of more than 50% of the membership interests is the default rule to approve members' decisions. [Section 18-402.] Profits and losses, and distributions of cash, are allocated to members according to the value of their respective capital contributions, unless otherwise stated in the operating agreement. [Sections 18-503 and 18-504.]

DISTRICT OF COLUMBIA

LLC Filing Office

Department of Consumer & Regulatory Affairs
    Business Regulation Administration
    Corporations Division
    941 North Capitol Street, N.E.
    Washington, DC 20002
    Telephone: 202-442-4400

http://dcra.dc.gov/main.shtm

Forms and Statutes: Provides guidelines and sample form for articles of organization. Use this information to type your own articles document according to the instructions.

Internet Forms: The latest District of Columbia LLC forms and information are available for viewing and downloading at the LLC filing office website.

The DC LLC Act is contained in Title 29 (Corporations), Chapter 10 of the DC Code, starting with section 29-1001, and is browseable from the following Web page (click "DC," then click "Division 5," then "Title 29," then "Chapter 10"):

http://www.michie.com

Minimum Number of Members: One.

Articles of Organization

Name Requirements: Must contain the words "Limited Liability Company" or the abbreviation "L.L.C." If a professional practice is being organized, the name must include the words "Professional Limited Liability Company" or the abbreviation "P.L.L.C." Name availability may be checked by calling 202-727-7283. Available LLC names may be reserved for 60 days for $25.

Filing Fee: $100, payable to "D.C. Treasurer."

Annual Fees: Domestic and registered foreign LLCs must pay an annual registration fee of $50.

Special Instructions and Filing Requirements: Type articles of organization on letter- or legal-sized paper. Submit two originally signed copies (sign each form with a pen) and attach a consent of the registered agent—a fill-in-the-blanks consent form to use for this purpose is included in materials sent out by the LLC filing office. Don't be confused by instructions to the articles that discuss your LLC operating agreement; you *do not* have to submit a copy of this agreement when you file articles of organization.

Tax Status

State Tax Treatment of LLCs: Follows IRS classification. Also note: DC LLCs are subject to 9.975% tax on income earned in DC.

State Tax Office: Finance & Revenue Department, telephone 202-727-6083.

http://cfo.dc.gov/etsc/main.shtm

Operating Rules

Default Transfer Rule: Unless otherwise restricted by the articles or operating agreement (see Section 29-1037 for rules on permissible restrictions), with consent of nontransferring members holding a majority of the interests in profits of the LLC. [Section 29-1036.]

Default Continuation Rule: In addition to any procedure or vote required by articles or operating agreement, by the unanimous consent of the remaining members with voting rights within 90 days of the dissociation of a member. [Section 29-1047.]

Special Statutory Rules: Unless otherwise stated in articles or the operating agreement, members vote according to their interests in the profits of the LLC, with the vote of a majority of the profits interests required to approve a membership decision. [Section 29-1017(d).]

A majority of the profits interests of members is also the default vote requirement for filling a vacant manager position. [Section 29-1019(e).] The default rule for allocating profits and losses, and distributing cash of LLC, is according to the value of each member's capital contribution to the LLC. [Sections 29-1024 and 29-1025.]

FLORIDA

LLC Filing Office

Florida Department of State
  Division of Corporations
  P.O. Box 6327
  Tallahassee, FL 32314

Telephone: 850-245-6051

http://www.dos.state.fl.us/doc/index.html

Forms and Statutes: Provides fill-in-the-blanks articles of organization with instructions.

Internet Forms: LLC forms, including articles and other statutory forms, are available for downloading from the Division of Corporation's website. Note: The state provides an online filing service that allows you to fill in and file your articles online.

The Florida LLC Act is contained in Title XXXVI (Business Organizations), Chapter 608 of the Florida Statutes, starting with section 608.401, and is browseable from the following Web page (click "Statutes and Constitution" tab, then select "Title XXXVI," then "chapter 608" from the index):

http://www.leg.state.fl.us/Welcome/index.cfm

Minimum Number of Members: One.

Articles of Organization

Name Requirements: Must end with the words "Limited Company" or the abbreviation "L.C." Names for use by LLCs (and other business entities) cannot be reserved. A preliminary name availability request can be handled over the phone by calling the state LLC filing office. You can also search name availability at the Division's website. Once you have determined that a name is available, quickly submit your proposed articles for filing. If the name is not available, you will be notified by the filing office.

Filing Fee: $100 for filing articles, plus $25 for designation of registered agent (included in articles) for a total of $125, payable to "Florida Department of State." The department will send you a letter of acknowledgment upon filing. You can add $30 to receive a certified copy of your articles from the LLC filing office, and/or add $5 for a "Certificate of Status" certifying that your LLC is an active Florida LLC as of its filing date. These extra copies and fees are optional.

Special Instructions and Filing Requirements: If you file articles by mail (instead of filing articles online), submit the signed original and one copy of articles of organization to the LLC filing office.

If you are converting an existing partnership to an LLC, complete and attach a "Certificate of Conversion," Form INHS11, to your articles. Also include an additional $25 in your filing fee check. This form can be downloaded from the state filing office website.

Tax Status

State Tax Treatment of LLCs: Follows IRS classification.

State Tax Office: Revenue Department, Tallahassee, telephone 1-800-352-3671.

http://sun6.dms.state.fl.us/dor

Operating Rules

Default Transfer Rule: Unless otherwise stated in the articles, by unanimous consent of nontransferring members. [Section 608-433.]

Default Continuation Rule: Except as may be provided in the articles, vote to continue the LLC after dissociation of a member (cessation or termination of a membership interest) not required. [Section 608.441.]

Special Statutory Rules: In manager-managed LLCs, managers must be elected annually. [Section 608.422.]

GEORGIA

LLC Filing Office

Secretary of State
  Corporations Division
  Suite 315, West Tower
  2 Martin Luther King Jr. Drive
  Atlanta, GA 30334

Telephone: 404-656-2817

http://www.sos.state.ga.us/corporations

Forms and Statutes: Provides sample articles of organization with two articles. Type or word-process articles on letter-sized paper following the format and content of the sample form. This short format produces minimal, though legally sufficient, articles of organization to form a Georgia LLC.

Internet Forms: LLC forms, including sample articles, transmittal of articles form (BR231), and other statutory forms, are available for downloading from the state LLC filing office website.

The Georgia LLC Act starts with section 14-11-100 of the Georgia Code, and is browseable from the following Web page:

http://www.ganet.org/cgi-bin/pub/ocode/ocgsearch?docname=OCode/G/14/11/100

Minimum Number of Members: One.

Articles of Organization

Name Requirements: Must contain the words "Limited Liability Company" or "Limited Company" or one of the following abbreviations: "L.L.C.," "LLC," "L.C.," or "LC." The word "Limited" may be abbreviated as "Ltd." and the word "Company" may be abbreviated as "Co." The name must not exceed 80 characters, including spaces and punctuation.

Important: The proposed LLC name must be reserved before filing articles. Call the LLC filing office at the above telephone number to check the availability and reserve your LLC name over the phone (there is no fee for an LLC name reservation). If name reservation approval is given, you will be mailed a name reservation certificate and a Transmittal Form—these documents must be filed with your articles (as explained in "Special Instructions and Filing Requirements," below).

Filing Fee: $75, payable to "Secretary of State." Attach check to completed Transmittal Form.

Special Instructions and Filing Requirements: File original and one copy of articles of organization. Include the original name reservation certificate with your papers. Also include a completed Transmittal Form, with a check for the filing fee attached. The Transmittal Form should be completed to show the name of your LLC and your name reservation number. If your papers are in order, the LLC filing office will attach a certificate of organization to the file copy of your articles and mail them to you.

Tax Status

State Tax Treatment of LLCs: Follows IRS classification.

State Tax Office: Department of Revenue, Atlanta, telephone 404-656-4071.

http://www2.state.ga.us/departments/dor

Operating Rules

Default Transfer Rule: Except as otherwise stated in articles or operating agreement, by unanimous consent of nontransferring members. [Section 14-11-503.]

Default Continuation Rule: Except as may be provided in the articles, vote to continue the LLC after dissociation of a member (cessation or termination of a membership interest) not required [for LLCs formed on or after July 1, 1999]. [Section 14-11-602.]

HAWAII

LLC Filing Office

Dept. of Commerce and Consumer Affairs
Business Registration Division
Kamamalu Bldg.
1010 Richards St.
P.O. Box 40
Honolulu, HI 96810

Telephone: 808-586-2727

http://www.businessregistrations.com

Forms and Statutes: Provides fill-in articles of organization with instructions.

Internet Forms: LLC forms, including sample articles with separate instructions, are available for downloading from the state LLC filing office website. The state provides an online filing service that allows you to fill in and file your articles online. If you prefer to mail articles for filing, the site posts a form you can complete online, print with your browser and mail to the state LLC filing office.

The Hawaii LLC Act is contained in Chapter 428 of the Hawaii Statutes, starting with section 428-101, and is browseable from the following Web page (select "Legal Info" at the bottom of the page; click "Statutes"; then select "Uniform Limited Liability Company Act"):

http://www.businessregistrations.com

Minimum Number of Members: One.

Articles of Organization

Name Requirements: The name must contain the words "Limited Liability Company," "Limited Company" or the abbreviation "LLC" or "L.L.C." The word "Limited" may be abbreviated as "Ltd." and the word "Company" may be abbreviated as "Co." An available LLC name may be reserved for 120 days for $25.

Filing Fee: $100 fee, payable to "Department of Commerce and Consumer Affairs."

Special Instructions and Filing Requirements: The state provides an online filing service that allows you to fill in and file your articles online. If you prefer to mail articles for filing, the site posts a form you can fill in online, print with your browser and mail to the state LLC filing office. Mailed articles instructions: Only one person is required to sign the articles as the LLC's organizer. Submit original articles, plus the number of copies you want file-stamped and returned to you (one copy is sufficient). In Article V, most organizers will check the "at-will" box to give their LLC an unlimited duration. Of course, you will want to check the box under Article VII that specifies your members are not liable for the debts of your LLC.

Tax Status

State Tax Treatment of LLCs: Follows IRS classification.

State Tax Office: Hawaii Tax Department, Honolulu 808-587-4242.

http://www.state.hi.us/tax/tax.html

Operating Rules

Default Transfer Rule: Except as otherwise stated in operating agreement, by unanimous consent of nontransferring members. [Section 428-503(a).]

Default Continuation Rule: Vote to continue LLC after dissociation (withdrawal or loss) of a member not required. [Section 428-801.]

IDAHO

LLC Filing Office

Idaho Secretary of State
  Corporations Division
  P.O. Box 83720
  Boise, ID 83720-0080

Telephone: 208-334-2300

http://www.idsos.state.id.us/corp/corindex.htm

Forms and Statutes: State provides fill-in-the-blanks articles of organization with instructions.

Note for Professionals: State also provides articles for organizing a professional limited liability company (under Section 53-615 of the Idaho LLC Act). This special professional form applies to LLCs formed to render licensed professional services in the fields of architecture, chiropractic, dentistry, engineering, landscape architecture, law, medicine, nursing, occupational therapy, optometry, physical therapy, podiatry, professional geology, psychology, certified or licensed public accountancy, social work, surveying and veterinary medicine.

Internet Forms: LLC forms, including articles and other statutory forms, are available for downloading from the state LLC filing office website.

The Idaho LLC Act is contained in Title 53 (Partnership), Chapter 6 of the Idaho Statutes, starting with section 53-601, and is browseable from the following Web page:

http://www3.state.id.us/idstat/TOC/53006KTOC.html

Minimum Number of Members: One.

Articles of Organization

Name Requirements: An LLC name may be reserved for four months for $20. The name must contain the words "Limited Liability Company," "Limited Company" or the abbreviation "L.L.C.," "L.C.," "LLC" or "LC." The word "Limited" may be abbreviated as "Ltd." and the word "Company" may be abbreviated as "Co." A professional services limited liability company name must *end* with the words "Professional Company" or the abbreviation "P.L.L.C." or "PLLC."

Filing Fee: $100 fee, payable to "Idaho Secretary of State."

Special Instructions and Filing Requirements: Submit the original and two copies for filing to the Corporations Division. The filing fee is increased to $120 if articles of organization are not typed or if they include attachments. (To save money, type your responses on the fill-in-the-blanks articles form.)

Tax Status

State Tax Treatment of LLCs: Follows IRS classification.

State Tax Office: State Tax Commission, telephone 208-334-7660.

http://www2.state.id.us/tax/home.htm

Operating Rules

Default Transfer Rule: Unless otherwise stated in the operating agreement, by unanimous written consent of nontransferring members. [Section 53-638.]

Default Continuation Rule: Unless otherwise stated in the operating agreement, by unanimous consent of remaining members within 90 days of the dissociation (loss of membership rights) of a member. [Section 53-642(3).]

ILLINOIS

LLC Filing Office

Illinois Secretary of State
   Department of Business Services
   Limited Liability Company Division
   Room 359, Howlett Building
   Springfield, IL 62756

Telephone: 800-252-8980

Branch Office: Chicago, telephone 312-793-3380 (for questions and info only; not LLC filings).

http://www.sos.state.il.us/departments/business_services/business.html

Forms and Statutes: State provides fill-in-the-blanks articles of organization.

Internet Forms: The latest Illinois LLC articles of organization (Form LLC-5.5), plus other Illinois LLC statutory forms (Reservation of LLC Name and others) can be downloaded from the state LLC office website.

The Illinois LLC Act is contained in Chapter 805 (Business Organizations), starting with section 180/1-1, and is browseable from the following Web page:

http://www.legis.state.il.us/ilcs/ch805/ch805act180articles/ch805act180artstoc.htm

Minimum Number of Members: One.

Articles of Organization

Name Requirements: Must contain the words "Limited Liability Company" or the abbreviation "L.L.C." The abbreviations "Ltd." and "Co." are *not* allowed in Illinois LLC names. Call 217-782-9520 to check availability of up to three proposed LLC names.

An available LLC name may be reserved for 90 days for a whopping $300! A corporate name may be reserved for $25 in Illinois, so why so much for an LLC name

reservation? We don't know, but this is what the statute currently requires. Perhaps this fee will be lowered to a more modest amount by future LLC legislation, but for now, you may want to skip reserving your name; just check name availability by calling the above number, then take your chances by promptly filing articles with your proposed name.

Filing Fee: $400, payable to the "Secretary of State." Payment must be made by certified check, cashier's check, money order or Illinois attorney's or CPA's check (don't send a personal check).

Annual Fees: LLCs do not pay state franchise taxes, but must pay an annual LLC renewal fee of $300.

Special Instructions and Filing Requirements: Submit the original and one copy of the signed articles of organization form. The fill-in-the-blanks articles form must be completed with a typewriter.

* *Article 2:* Attach Form LLC-1.20, available from the LLC Division, to your articles if you will do business under a name other than the one stated in the articles (under an assumed business name).

* *Article 6:* A Standard Industrial Code (SIC) sheet is included with state materials to specify principal activity of LLC in Article 6. You may also wish to include a statement in this Article that says, "The purpose of this company is to transact any or all lawful business for which limited liability companies may be organized under the Illinois Limited Liability Company Act."

* *Article 7:* Leave Article 7 blank to give your LLC a perpetual existence.

If you are converting an existing general or limited Illinois partnership to an LLC, read the requirements posted on the state filing office website. Follow the additional requirements posted there if you wish to convert a partnership to an LLC in Illinois. You will need to include an attachment page with your articles and pay $100 extra for the conversion.

Tax Status

State Tax Treatment of LLCs: Follows IRS classification.

State Tax Office: For annual tax information, contact the Department of Business Services at 217-782-7808. For other tax information, contact the Department of Revenue, Springfield, at 217-785-3336.

http://www.revenue.state.il.us

Operating Rules

Default Transfer Rule: Unless otherwise stated in articles or operating agreement, by unanimous consent of nontransferring members. [Section 180/30-10.]

Default Continuation Rule: Vote to continue LLC after dissociation of member not required.

INDIANA

LLC Filing Office

Indiana Secretary of State
   Corporations Division
   302 W. Washington, Room E018
   Indianapolis, IN 46204

Telephone: 317-232-6576

http://www.in.gov/sos/business/index.html

Forms and Statutes: Provides articles and other statutory forms.

Internet Forms: Articles of Organization and other standard statutory forms, such as a request to reserve a name, are downloadable from the state LLC filing office website.

The Indiana LLC Act (also called the "Indiana Business Flexibility Act") is contained in Title 23 (Business and Other Associations), Article 18 of the Indiana Code, starting with section 23-18-1-1, and is browseable from the following Web page (select Title 23, then Article 18):

http://www.in.gov/legislative/ic/code

Minimum Number of Members: One.

Articles of Organization

Name Requirements: Must include "Limited Liability Company" or abbreviations "L.L.C." or "LLC." Name availability can be checked by phone, and an available name may be reserved for 120 days for $20.

Filing Fee: $90, payable to "Secretary of State" (staple check to articles).

Special Instructions and Filing Requirements: File original and one copy of articles; file-stamped copy will be returned to you.

Tax Status

State Tax Treatment of LLCs: Follows IRS classification.

State Tax Office: Department of Revenue, Indianapolis, telephone 317-232-2189.

http://www.state.in.us/dor

Operating Rules

Default Transfer Rule: Unless otherwise stated in operating agreement, by unanimous written consent of nontransferring members. [Section 23-18-6-4.]

Default Continuation Rule: For LLCs formed after June 30, 1999, a membership vote to continue the LLC after dissociation of a member (cessation or termination of a membership interest) is not required. [Section 23-18-9-1.1.]

IOWA

LLC Filing Office

Iowa Secretary of State
   Corporations Division
   Hoover Building, 2nd Floor
   Des Moines, IA 50319

Telephone: 515-281-5204

http://www.sos.state.ia.us/business

Forms and Statutes: Does not provide fill-in-the-blanks articles of organization, but provides Section 490A.303 of the Iowa LLC law, which lists the required contents of articles (see "Special Instructions and Filing Requirements," below).

Internet Forms: Section 490A.303 of the Iowa LLC law, which lists the required contents of articles, is posted online. The Secretary of State provides reservation of name and other statutory forms on its website.

The Iowa LLC Act is contained in Title XII (Business Entities), Chapter 490A of the Iowa Code, starting with section 490A.100, and is browseable from the following Web page:

http://www.legis.state.ia.us/IACODE/1999SUPPLE-MENT/490A

Minimum Number of Members: One.

Articles of Organization

Name Requirements: Must contain the words "Limited Company" or the abbreviation "L.C." An available LLC name may be reserved for 120 days for $10.

Filing Fee: $50, payable to the "Iowa Secretary of State."

Special Instructions and Filing Requirements: Type or word-process articles in black ink. You need to file the original articles only. The Secretary will return the document, endorsed as filed, to you together with a receipt for payment of the filing fee.

Below is a summary of the requirements for the contents of Iowa articles of organization, taken from the Iowa LLC Act. (See Chapter 4, Section E5, for an example of how to draft your own articles based upon similar state statutory requirements.)

Section 490A.303.

1. The articles of organization must set forth all of the following:

   a. A name that satisfies the requirements of section 490A.401 (see "Name Requirements," above).

   b. The street address of the LLC's initial registered office and the name of its initial registered agent at that office.

   c. The street address of the principal office of the LLC, which may be the same as the registered office, but need not be within the state.

   d. The period of the LLC's duration, which may not be perpetual.

Additional information must be provided in articles if you are converting an existing partnership to an LLC. See the state website or call the state LLC filing office for instructions on adding this additional information to your articles.

Tax Status

State Tax Treatment of LLCs: Follows IRS classification.

State Tax Office: Department of Revenue & Finance, Des Moines, telephone 515-281-3135.

http://www.state.ia.us/government/drf/index.html

Operating Rules

Default Transfer Rule: Unless otherwise stated in articles or operating agreement, by unanimous written consent or vote at meeting of nontransferring members. [Section 490A.903.]

Default Continuation Rule: Vote to continue LLC after dissociation of member not required.

KANSAS

LLC Filing Office

Kansas Secretary of State
   Corporation Division
   First Floor, Memorial Hall
   120 S.W. 10th Ave.
   Topeka, KS 66612

Telephone: 913-296-4564

http://www.kssos.org

Forms and Statutes: Provides articles plus other statutory forms.

Internet forms: Kansas LLC articles (Form DL), instructions for articles, plus other forms can be downloaded from the LLC office website.

The Kansas LLC Act is contained in Chapter 17 of the Kansas Statutes, Article 76, starting with section 17-7662 (ignore sections 17-7601 to 17-7661; this is the prior LLC Act), and is browseable from the Web page listed below. Use the arrow keys to highlight "Chapter 17, Corporations," in the center box, then press "Get Articles in Chapter." Then use the arrow keys to highlight "Article 76, Limited Liability Companies," and press "List Statutes in Article" to see a list of the LLC Act statutes.

http://www.kslegislature.org/cgi-bin/statutes/index.cgi

Minimum Number of Members: One.

Articles of Organization

Name Requirements: Must contain the words "Limited Liability Company" or "Limited Company" or the abbreviation "LLC," "L.L.C.," "LC" or "L.C."

Filing Fee: $150 fee, payable to "Kansas Secretary of State."

Special Instructions and Filing Requirements: Submit original signed articles and one copy.

Tax Status

State Tax Treatment of LLCs: Follows IRS classification. But note: Kansas LLCs are subject to state's franchise tax on net capital accounts.

State Tax Office: Department of Revenue, Topeka, telephone 913-296-3909.

http://www.ink.org/public/kdor

Operating Rules

Default Transfer Rule: Unless otherwise provided in the operating agreement, the admission of a transferee as a member must be approved by majority of nontransferring members. [Section 17-7618.]

Default Continuation Rule: Vote to continue LLC after dissociation of member not required.

KENTUCKY

LLC Filing Office

Kentucky Secretary of State
  Business Filings
  P.O. Box 718
  Frankfort, KY 40602

Telephone: 502-564-2848

http://www.sos.state.ky.us

Forms and Statutes: Secretary of State articles (SOS LAOO) with instructions and other statutory forms for LLCs ("Amendment of Articles," "Change of Registered Agent or Office," "Certificate of Existence or Authorization," "Articles of Dissolution").

Internet Forms: Kentucky articles plus other statutory LLC forms can be downloaded from the state LLC Office website.

The Kentucky LLC Act is contained in Title XXIII (Private Corporations and Associations), Chapter 275 of the Kentucky Statutes, starting with section 275.001, and is browseable from the following Web page:

http://162.114.4.13/krs/275-00/CHAPTER.HTM

Minimum Number of Members: One.

Articles of Organization

Name Requirements: Must contain the words "Limited Liability Company" or "Limited Company" or the abbreviation "LLC" or "LC." Professional LLCs must contain the words "Professional Limited Liability Company" or "Professional Limited Company" or "PLLC" or "PLC." The word "Limited" may be abbreviated as "Ltd." and the word "Company" may be abbreviated as "Co." in any limited liability company name. An available LLC name can be reserved for $15. Professional LLCs are those whose members will practice one of the following professions: certified public or public accountant, architect or landscape architect, attorney, chiropractor, dentist, engineer, nurse, occupational therapist, optometrist, osteopath, pharmacist, physical therapist, physician, podiatrist, psychologist, veterinarian.

Filing Fee: $40, payable to "Secretary of State."

Special Instructions and Filing Requirements: Type or print articles in black ink. Form can be signed by one or more members or managers or by an organizer of the LLC. Submit signed original plus *two* copies for filing. After filing, make sure to file a copy of the file-stamped articles with the county clerk of the county where your LLC's registered office is located.

Note for Professionals: Professional LLCs are those which will practice, through members, one of the following professions: certified public or public accountant, architect or landscape architect, attorney, chiropractor, dentist, engineer, nurse, occupational therapist, optometrist, osteopath, pharmacist, physical therapist, physician, podiatrist, psychologist, veterinarian. If you are forming a professional Kentucky LLC, use Form SOS PLLC, available for downloading from the state LLC filing office website, to form your LLC.

Tax Status

State Tax Treatment of LLCs: Follows IRS classification.

State Tax Office: Kentucky Revenue Cabinet, Frankfort, telephone 502-564-3658.

http://revenue.state.ky.us

Operating Rules

Default Transfer Rule: Unless otherwise provided in operating agreement, by unanimous written consent of a majority-in-interest of (majority of capital interests held by) members. [Section 275.265.]

Default Continuation Rule: Vote to continue LLC after
dissociation of member not required.

LOUISIANA

LLC Filing Office

Louisiana Secretary of State
　Commercial Division
　P.O. Box 94125
　Baton Rouge, LA 70804-9125

Telephone: 504-925-4704

http://www.sec.state.la.us/comm/comm-index.htm

Forms and Statutes: State provides a fill-in-the-blanks
articles of organization (Form 365) with instructions,
as well as a "Limited Liability Company Initial Report,"
which must be filed with the articles.

Internet Forms: The above forms, plus other statutory
forms, such as a Reservation of LLC Name form, can
be downloaded from the state LLC office website.

The state LLC filing office publishes a "Corporation Law
Book," which includes limited liability company,
partnership, trademark and trade name laws of the
state. The fee for a copy is $10.

The Louisiana LLC Law is contained in Chapter 22, Title
12 of the Louisiana Statutes, starting with section
12:1301. See the following Web page to browse the
Law (click "Louisiana Laws" in the left panel, then
select "RS" inside the "Law Body" box to search the
Revised Statutes, then insert in the search box the
section number you wish to view:

http://www.legis.state.la.us

Minimum Number of Members: One.

Articles of Organization

Name Requirements: Must contain the words "Limited
Liability Company" or the abbreviation "L.L.C." or
"L.C." Check LLC name availability by calling the
Corporations Division. LLC names may be reserved for
60 days for $20.

Filing Fee: $60, payable to "Secretary of State."

Special Instructions and Filing Requirements: Have one of
your initial members (or managers) sign the articles in
the presence of a notary. A "Limited Liability Company
Initial Report" must accompany your articles when
submitted for filing. This form must be signed by each

person who signs your articles, and by a person whom
you designate to act as your LLC's registered agent.
Sign this form in the presence of a notary (have your
articles notarized at the same time).

Mail the completed initial report plus your original
signed and notarized articles, with any additional
copies of articles you wish certified (for an additional
$10 charge per copy) to the LLC filing office. You can
request expedited (one-day) filing service for an
additional $20 fee.

Note: If your articles are filed within five working days of
the date of notarization of the initial report form,
which is submitted with your articles, the legal date of
existence begins on the date of notarization (prior to
the actual date the articles are filed).

Tax Status

State Tax Treatment of LLCs: Follows IRS classification.

State Tax Office: Department of Revenue & Taxation,
Baton Rouge, telephone 504-925-7537.

http://www.rev.state.la.us

Operating Rules

Default Transfer Rule: Unless otherwise stated in articles
or operating agreement, by unanimous written consent
of nontransferring members. [Section 1332.]

Default Continuation Rule: Vote to continue LLC after
dissociation of member not required.

MAINE

LLC Filing Office

Secretary of State
　Bureau of Corporations, Elections & Commissions 101
　State House Station
　Augusta, ME 04333-0101
　ATTN: Corporate Examining Section

Telephone: 207-624-7740

http://www.state.me.us/sos/cec/cec.htm

Forms and Statutes: State provides fill-in-the-blanks forms
for most LLC statutory filings, including articles of
organization.

Internet Forms: The latest LLC articles of organization
with instructions, plus other LLC statutory forms

(Reservation of LLC Name and others) can be downloaded from the state's website.

The Maine LLC Act is contained in Title 31 (Partnerships and Associations), Chapter 13 of the Maine Statutes, starting with section 601, and is browseable from the following Web page:

http://janus.state.me.us/legis/statutes/31/title31sec601.html

Minimum Number of Members: One.

Articles of Organization

Name Requirements: Must contain the words "Limited Liability Company." If a professional LLC, must contain the word(s) "Chartered," "Professional Association" or abbreviation "P.A." Use the state-furnished LLC Application for Reservation of Name form and include $20 fee to reserve an LLC name.

Filing Fee: $125, payable to the "Secretary of State."

Special Instructions and Filing Requirements: If you are forming a professional service LLC, check the box at the beginning of the fill-in-the-blanks articles of organization. Have the initial registered agent named in the articles date and sign in the space provided on the articles form.

Tax Status

State Tax Treatment of LLCs: Follows IRS classification.

State Tax Office: Bureau of Taxation, Augusta, telephone 207-287-2076.

http://www.state.me.us/revenue

Operating Rules

Default Transfer Rule: By unanimous written consent of nontransferring members and as may otherwise be provided in articles or operating agreement. [Section 687.]

Default Continuation Rule: A vote to continue the LLC after withdrawal of a member is not required. [Section 701.]

MARYLAND

LLC Filing Office

Maryland Department of Assessments & Taxation
  Corporate Charter Division
  Room 801
  301 West Preston Street
  Baltimore, MD 21201-2395

Telephone: 410-767-1184

http://www.dat.state.md.us/sdatweb/charter.html

Forms and Statutes: State provides articles and instructions.

Internet Forms: The latest Maryland LLC articles of organization and guidelines for preparing this form plus other Maryland LLC statutory forms (such as Reservation of LLC Name) can be downloaded from the state filing office website.

The Maryland LLC Act is contained in the Corporations and Associations heading, Title 4A, starting with section 4A-101, and is browseable from the following Web page (currently, sections of the Act must be browsed one at a time from this page—click the "Statutes" check box, enter the section number in the search box, then click the search button):

http://mgasearch.state.md.us/verity.asp

Minimum Number of Members: One.

Articles of Organization

Name Requirements: Must contain the words "Limited Liability Company" or one of the following abbreviations: "LLC," "LC," "L.L.C." or "L.C." Call the LLC filing office at 410-225-1340 to check name availability. An available name may be reserved for 30 days for a $7 fee.

Filing Fee: $50, payable to "SDAT" (this is the acronym for the State Department of Assessments & Taxation). If you ask for a certified copy, it costs $6 plus $1 per page extra.

Annual Filing: Every five years, the LLC must file a statement (by September 15th) affirming that it is still actively engaged in the business for which it was formed. (Presumably, you may change or expand the original line of business stated in your articles.)

Special Instructions and Filing Requirements: Blanks in articles must be typed or printed, not handwritten. Submit the signed original for filing.

You may ask for a certified copy of the original articles to be returned to you by including an additional $6 plus $1 per page in your filing fee check.

Tax Status

State Tax Treatment of LLCs: Follows IRS classification.

State Tax Office: Department of Assessments & Taxation, Baltimore, telephone 410-225-1340.

www.comp.state.md.us/default.asp

Operating Rules

Default Transfer Rule: By unanimous written consent of nontransferring members and as may otherwise be specified in the operating agreement. [Section 4A-604.]

Default Continuation Rule: Vote to continue LLC after dissociation of member not required.

MASSACHUSETTS

LLC Filing Office

Commonwealth of Massachusetts
    Corporations Division
    One Ashburton Place, 17th Floor
    Boston, MA 02108

Telephone: 617-727-9640

www.state.ma.us/sec/cor

Forms and Statutes: The name of the document filed in Massachusetts to form an LLC is the "Certificate of Organization." Massachusetts does not provide a form, but does allow you to prepare and file the Certificate of Organization online from the filing office website. If you wish to prepare and mail a Certificate for filing, below we explain the statutory requirements for forming and operating a Massachusetts LLC (contained in Section 112.03 of the Massachusetts LLC regulations) (see "Special Instructions and Filing Requirements").

Note for Professionals: Existing Massachusetts professional practice general partnerships can register as Registered Limited Liability Partnership instead of converting their general partnerships to LLCs (the registration process is simple and provides limited liability protection to the LLP partners). For more information, see the Massachusetts Secretary of the Commonwealth LLP regulations, available upon request.

Internet Forms: Massachusetts does not provide a form, but does allow you to prepare and file the Certificate of Organization online from the filing office website. The required contents for the LLC Certificate of Organization also are posted on the state website.

The Massachusetts LLC Act is contained in Title XXII (Corporations), Chapter 156C of the Massachusetts General Laws, starting with section 1, and is browseable from the following Web page:

www.magnet.state.ma.us/legis/laws/mgl/156C-1.htm

Minimum Number of Members: One (beginning in March 2003).

Certificate of Organization

Name Requirements: Must contain the words "Limited Liability Company," "Limited Company" or the abbreviation "LLC," "LC," "L.L.C." or "L.C." Available LLC names may be reserved for 30 days for $15.

Filing Fee: $500 fee, payable to "Commonwealth of Massachusetts."

Annual Fees: You must file an annual report and pay a fee of $500 per year (ouch!).

Special Instructions and Filing Requirements: Massachusetts does not provide a form, but does allow you to prepare and file the Certificate of Organization online from the filing office website. If you wish to prepare and mail a Certificate, prepare and submit an original and one copy of a completed, signed Certificate of Organization (the Massachusetts name for articles of organization). Type or print on only one side of 8½" x 11" paper.

If you do prepare your Certificate form, here is a list of the required contents of the Certificate of Organization for Massachusetts LLCs (see Chapter 4, Section E5, for an example of how to draft your own articles based upon similar state statutory requirements):

1. Federal Employer Identification Number (EIN), if available. To apply for an EIN, file IRS Form SS-4—

available by calling 800-TAX-FORM or going to the IRS website (www.irs.gov). In some areas, you can obtain a federal EIN over the phone; call your local IRS tax office to find out if this phone service is available. If you have not yet received your federal EIN, just state in this paragraph of your articles: "The federal Employer Identification Number of this limited liability company has been applied for, but has not yet been assigned."

2. The name of the LLC. (See "Name Requirements," above.)

3. The street address in Massachusetts where LLC records will be maintained. (Normally, this is the principal business office of the LLC.)

4. The general nature of the LLC's business. A statement that you plan to engage in any and all lawful business allowed LLCs under state law is not enough. You must indicate the nature of the LLC's actual business—for example, "The general nature of the business of this LLC is real estate sales" or "securities investments."

If your LLC plans to render licensed professional services, such as law, medicine or accounting, you must include the following information: (1) the service to be rendered; (2) the names and addresses of each member or manager who will render the service; and (3) a statement that "The limited liability company will abide by and be subject to any conditions or limitations established by any applicable regulating board, including the provisions of liability insurance required under state law." A professional service LLC also must obtain a certificate from the state board that regulates the profession, which states that each member or manager who will render a professional service is duly licensed. Your state professional board should be able to provide this statement and help you prepare a Certificate of Organization for your professional LLC if you have any questions about these requirements.

5. The date the LLC will dissolve, if applicable. If your LLC wishes to have a perpetual existence (to dissolve only when the members or managers decide), simply don't include this statement in your Certificate.

6. The name and business address of the agent for service of process of the LLC. (If an individual, the agent must be a Massachusetts resident.)

7. If the LLC is manager-managed, the name and the business address of each LLC manager (member-managed LLCs should ignore this item). The business address of a manager may be omitted if it is identical to the LLC's address.

8. The names and business addresses (again, only non-LLC business office addresses are required) of any nonmanagers who are authorized to execute documents on behalf of the LLC for filing with the Corporations Division of the Secretary of the Commonwealth. If you have a member-managed LLC, you must list at least one person here. Normally, member-managed LLCs will show the name of the member who prepares and files the Certificate of Organization—for example, "The name and business address of the person who is authorized to execute documents to be filed with the Corporations Division of the Secretary of the Commonwealth is [name and address of member who is preparing the Certificate]."

9. If desired, the name and business address (again, if different from the LLC business address) of any person specifically authorized to execute, acknowledge, deliver and record any recordable instrument purporting to affect an interest in real property. Include this optional statement if your LLC may engage in real property transactions. (The LLC filing office will, for a fee, prepare a Certificate of Good Standing, which shows the names of persons listed in this clause as persons authorized to sign real property papers for your LLC.) You may use wording such as: "The names and addresses of persons who are authorized to execute, acknowledge, deliver and record any recordable instrument affecting an interest in real property are: [names and business addresses of one or more managers and/or members]."

10. The Certificate can contain any additional information you wish to include—for example, the names and addresses of the initial members of your LLC.

The Certificate of Organization may be signed by any manager (if the LLC is manager-managed), any other person authorized to file papers for the LLC with the Corporations Division (see Item 8 above) or the organizer of the LLC (the person who is forming the LLC, whether or not listed in the Certificate). Generally, member-managed LLCs will list one of the members under Item 8 in the Certificate as a person who may make filings with the Division, and this member will sign the Certificate immediately after an execution paragraph included at the end of the Certificate:

In Witness Whereof, the undersigned affirms, under penalty of perjury, that the facts stated in this Certificate of Organization are true.

Dated: _____

Signed: _____,

[show capacity as "Manager," "Member" or "Organizer"]

Tax Status

State Tax Treatment of LLCs: Follows IRS classification.

State Tax Office: Department of Revenue, Boston, telephone 617-626-2299.

www.dor.state.ma.us/Dorpg.htm

Operating Rules

Default Transfer Rule: By unanimous consent of nontransferring members or as provided in operating agreement. [Sections 39 & 41.]

Default Continuation Rule: By unanimous consent of nontransferring members within 90 days of dissociation event or as provided in operating agreement. [Section 43(4).]

Special Statutory Rules: The certificate of organization or operating agreement may eliminate or limit the personal liability of a manager for breach of any duty to the limited liability company [Section 8(b)]. If you set up a manager-managed LLC and wish to add general language to do this, you can do so by adding the following provision to your operating agreement: "Any and all personal liability of all managers of this limited liability company is eliminated in accordance with Section 8(b) of the Massachusetts Limited Liability Act." Of course, if you want to find out just how effective this "magic" language will be in the event of a claim or lawsuit involving one of your LLC managers, you will want to check this language ahead of time with an experienced Massachusetts LLC lawyer.

MICHIGAN

LLC Filing Office

Department of Consumer & Industry Services
   Bureau of Commercial Services

Corporation Division
7150 Harris Drive
P.O. Box 30054
Lansing, MI 48909

Telephone: 517-241-6470

www.michigan.gov/cis

Forms and Statutes: State provides fill-in-the-blanks articles of organization (Form 700) with instructions. Use Form 753 instead if converting a partnership to an LLC. Use Form 701 instead to file articles for an LLC rendering licensed professional services of public accountant, dentist, osteopathic physician, physician, surgeon, doctor of divinity or other clergy, or attorney, or use Form 753p instead if converting a professional partnership in one of these professions to an LLC. The latest versions of all of these forms, plus instructions and the state's guidelines for approving each form, are contained on the department's website.

Internet Forms: The latest versions of all of Michigan LLC forms, plus instructions and the state's guidelines for approving each form, are contained on the bureau's website. Note that articles can be filed electronically after filling out an application (by telephone at 517-214-6400 or online) for a filer number.

The Michigan LLC Act is contained in Chapter 450 (Corporations) of the Michigan Compiled Laws, Act 23 of 1993, starting with section 450.4101, and is browseable from the following Web page (select "Chapter Index" under "Michigan Compiled Laws Information," then select Chapter 450, then select "Act 23 of 1993" at the bottom of the page, which is the LLC Act):

www.michiganlegislature.org

Minimum Number of Members: One.

Articles of Organization

Name Requirements: Must contain the words "Limited Liability Company" or the abbreviation "LLC," "LC," "L.L.C.," or "L.C." A Professional Limited Liability Company (see list of professions above who must use Form 701 or 753p) name must, instead, include the words "Professional Limited Liability Company" or the abbreviation "PLLC," "PLC," "P.L.L.C." or "P.L.C."

Filing Fee: $50 nonrefundable fee, payable to "State of Michigan."

Special Instructions and Filing Requirements: You are only required to submit original articles. This document will be returned to you after it is copied and stored in the bureau's LLC database.

Use Form C & S 753 instead of standard C & S Form 700 if converting a partnership to an LLC. Use Form C & S 701 to file articles for an LLC rendering licensed professional services of public accountant, dentist, osteopathic physician, physician, surgeon, doctor of divinity or other clergy or attorney, or use Form C & S 753p instead if converting a professional partnership in one of these professions to an LLC.

Tax Status

State Tax Treatment of LLCs: Michigan imposes a 4.2% tax on LLC tax base.

State Tax Office: State Treasurer's Office, Revenue Bureau, Lansing, telephone 517-373-3196.

http://www.michigan.gov/treasury

Operating Rules

Note: Michigan uses two section-number reference systems for its Limited Liability Company Act. Below, we use the section numbers that correspond to the MCL (Michigan Corporations Law).

Default Transfer Rule: By unanimous consent of nontransferring members. [Section 450.4501.]

· *Default Continuation Rule:* Vote to continue LLC after dissociation of member not required.

You can lower the above default voting rules in your operating agreement, but to do so requires coordinating your vote requirements for approval of transfers and continuance of the LLC with each other—see Sections 450.4506 & 450.4801 for the details.

MINNESOTA

LLC Filing Office

Minnesota Secretary of State
  Business Services Division
  180 State Office Building
  100 Constitution Avenue
  St. Paul, MN 55155-1299

Telephone: 1-877-551-6SOS (6767)

http://www.sos.state.mn.us/business/index.html

Forms and Statutes: State provides fill-in-the-blanks articles of organization with instructions.

Internet Forms: Articles and other statutory forms are available for downloading from the state LLC filing office website.

The Minnesota LLC Act is contained in Chapter 322B of the Minnesota Statutes, starting with section 322B.01, and is browseable from the following Web page:

http://www.revisor.leg.state.mn.us/stats/322B

Minimum Number of Members: One.

Articles of Organization

Name Requirements: Must contain the words "Limited Liability Company" or the abbreviation "LLC." Cannot include the words "incorporated" or "corporation" or their abbreviations. Check name availability by calling 612-296-2803. An LLC name may be reserved for a fee of $35.

Filing Fee: $135, payable to "Minnesota Secretary of State." For fee questions, call 612-296-2803.

Special Instructions and Filing Requirements: Articles must be filled in black ink only (use a black-ink pen or black-ribbon typewriter). The person who signs the articles must be at least 18 years of age. Send original and copy of signed articles to the LLC filing office.

Here's how to address several particulars in the state articles form:

  • *Articles 2 and 3:* Although you must specify a registered office in Article 2, designating a registered agent at this address in Article 3 is optional.

  • *Article 5:* If you leave this article blank, the duration of the LLC will be presumed to be perpetual.

  • *Article 6:* If your LLC will own or lease agricultural or farm land, look at Minnesota Statutes Section 500.24 to make sure you meet the legal requirements before checking the "Yes" box.

Tax Status

State Tax Treatment of LLCs: Follows IRS classification.

State Tax Office: Department of Revenue, St. Paul, telephone 800-297-5309.

http://www.taxes.state.mn.us

Operating Rules

Default Transfer Rule: Unless otherwise stated in articles, by unanimous written consent of nontransferring members. [Section 322B.313.]

Default Continuation Rule: For LLCs formed on or after August 1, 1999, the LLC automatically dissolves upon the occurrence of an event that terminates the continued membership of an LLC member, but only if: (a) the articles of organization or a member control agreement specifically provide that the termination causes dissolution and in that event only as provided in the articles or member control agreement; or (b) the membership of the last or sole member terminates and the legal representative of that last or sole member does not cause the LLC to admit at least one member within 180 days after the termination. [Section 322B.80.]

Special Statutory Rules: The Minnesota LLC scheme presupposes management by a board of governors (management by governors is an anachronistic concept carried over by older nonprofit statutes still in force in some states). The LLC law specifies that LLCs must have one or more governors, elected by the members, who serve for an indefinite term of office. Section 322B.606 of the Minnesota LLC Act, however, recognizes that LLCs may wish to adopt membership management. That section says that the LLC members may act in the place of the governors as long as they make management decisions by unanimous vote; this is usually easy to achieve in smaller LLCs and we assume most smaller Minnesota LLCs will opt for membership management. To make sure you satisfy this vote requirement, you'll need to specify a unanimous membership vote requirement in your member-managed LLC operating agreement in Chapter 5.

Note: To make matters more confusing, Minnesota law requires the appointment or election of two persons who function as the LLC president and treasurer, but who are called "managers" (one is called the "chief manager," the other is called the "treasurer"—see Minn. LLC Act Sec. 322B.673). If you go through the Minnesota LLC Act, don't be confused by this nonstandard nomenclature. Simply decide which of your members (or managers, in a manager-managed LLC) will be "chief manager" and function as the LLC president, and pick a member or manager as treasurer.

By the way, you may decide to go along with the statutory scheme and opt for management by governors. Use the manager-management operating agreement in Chapter 6, but change all occurrences of the word "manager" to "governor" and "managers" to "board of governors." Although our general management provisions should work fine (in most cases, you can override the state law management rules with management rules of your own in your operating agreement), take a look at the Board of Governors section of the Minnesota LLC Act to learn more about the default statutory management scheme.

MISSISSIPPI

LLC Filing Office

Mississippi Secretary of State
  Corporate Division
  P.O. Box 136
  Jackson, MS 39205

Telephone: 601-359-1633 (toll-free: 1-800-256-3494)

http://www.sos.state.ms.us

Forms and Statutes: The Mississippi Secretary of State provides a fill-in "Certificate of Formation" to use to create a Mississippi LLC. This is a special form designed to be scanned by a computer.

Internet Forms: You can fill in the Mississippi LLC Certificate of Formation (Form F100) online on the state filing office website.

The Mississippi LLC Act is contained in Title 79 (Corporations, Associations and Partnerships) of the Mississippi Code, Chapter 29, starting with section 79-29-101, and is browseable from the following Web page:

http://www.michie.com

Minimum Number of Members: One.

Certificate of Formation

Name Requirements: Must contain the words "Limited Liability Company" or the abbreviation "LLC" or "L.L.C." An available LLC name can be reserved for $25.

Filing Fee: $50, payable to the "Secretary of State."

Tax Status

State Tax Treatment of LLCs: Follows IRS classification.

State Tax Office: Mississippi State Tax Commission, Jackson 601-359-1141.

http://www.mstc.state.ms.us

Operating Rules

Default Transfer Rule: By unanimous consent of all nontransferring members or as provided in Certificate of Formation or operating agreement. [Section 79-29-704.]

Default Continuation Rule: For LLCs formed on or after July 1, 1998, a membership vote to continue the LLC after dissociation of a member (cessation or termination of a membership interest) is not required. [Section 79-29-801.]

Special Statutory Rules: The certificate of formation or operating agreement may eliminate or limit the personal liability of a manager for money damages except for a few types of acts, which include intentional infliction of harm or criminal acts [Section 79-29-403]. If you wish to do this, you can do so by adding the following provision to your operating agreement: "Liability of all members and managers of this limited liability company for money damages for any action taken, or any failure to take any action, is eliminated in accordance with Section 79-29-403 of the Mississippi Limited Liability Act." Of course, if you want to find out just how effective this language will be in the event of a claim or lawsuit involving one of your LLC members or managers, you will want to check this language ahead of time with an experienced Mississippi LLC lawyer.

MISSOURI

LLC Filing Office

Secretary of State
    Corporation Division
    P.O. Box 778
    Jefferson City, MO 65102

Telephone: 573-751-2359 or 4544

http://www.sos.state.mo.us

Forms and Statutes: State provides fill-in-the-blanks articles of organization with instructions. Professionals should form a Limited Liability Partnership (LLP) instead of an LLC; ask the filing office for the LLP organization form.

Internet Forms: The Missouri articles of organization form (LLC-1), plus other statutory forms, are available for downloading from the state LLC office website.

Other information: Visit the state's one-stop-shopping site (available from the Secretary of State's home page, which is linked to the state filing office site), for tax and other state business formation information.

The Missouri LLC Act is contained in Title XXIII (Corporations, Associations and Partnerships) of the Missouri Statutes, Chapter 347, starting with section 347.010, and is browseable from the following Web page:

http://www.moga.state.mo.us/STATUTES/C347.HTM

Minimum Number of Members: One.

Articles of Organization

Name Requirements: Must contain the words "Limited Liability Company," "Limited Company" or the abbreviations "L.L.C." or "L.C." It may not contain the abbreviation "Ltd." To reserve a name, submit an Application for Reservation of Name (available from the LLC filing office), together with a check for $25. To check on name availability, call 314-751-3317.

Filing Fee: $105, payable to "Director of Revenue."

Special Instructions and Filing Requirements: Submit completed articles in duplicate. Note these instructions for the Missouri articles:

- *Article 5:* You can insert "perpetual" in this blank to give your LLC an unlimited life.

- *Article 7:* Check the "No" box in response to the question, "For tax purposes, is the limited liability company considered a corporation?" unless you have decided to elect corporate taxation for your LLC by filing IRS Form 8832—see the discussion in Chapter 3, Section A (if you file this IRS form to elect corporate tax treatment, check the "Yes" box in Article 7 instead).

Tax Status

State Tax Treatment of LLCs: Follows IRS classification.

State Tax Office: Department of Revenue, Jefferson City, telephone 314-751-4450.

http://dor.state.mo.us/tax

Operating Rules

Default Transfer Rule: Unless otherwise stated in the operating agreement, by unanimous written consent of nontransferring members. [Section 347.113.]

Default Continuation Rule: A vote to continue the LLC after dissociation (cessation or termination of a membership interest) of a member is not required. But, except as provided in the operating agreement, a majority (in number) of the remaining members are allowed to vote to dissolve the LLC within 90 days of the dissociation. [Section 347.137.]

Special Statutory Rules: A promise by a member to make a contribution to the LLC must be in writing to be enforceable [Section 347.099(1)]. Therefore, make sure to execute a written promissory note or written contract to perform future services if a member promises to pay or perform future services as his or her capital contribution to your Missouri LLC.

MONTANA

LLC Filing Office

Montana Secretary of State
   Corporation Bureau
   P.O. Box 202801
   Helena, MT 59620-2801

Telephone: 406-444-2034

http://sos.state.mt.us/css/index.asp

Forms and Statutes: State provides fill-in-the-blanks form for articles of organization plus LLC fact sheet booklet containing instructions on forming a Montana LLC. LLC office also provides an annual limited liability company report form.

Internet Forms: The latest version of the Montana LLC articles of organization (Form DLC-1), plus other statutory forms, can be downloaded from the state LLC filing office website.

The Montana LLC Act is contained in Title 35 (Corporations, Partnerships and Associations) of the Montana Code, Chapter 8, starting with section 35-8-101, and is browseable from the following Web page (select Title 35, then Chapter 8):

http://data.opi.state.mt.us/bills/mca_toc/index.htm

Minimum Number of Members: One.

Articles of Organization

Name Requirements: Must contain the words "Limited Liability Company" or "Limited Company" or, if formed to render licensed professional services, "Professional Limited Liability Company." Permitted abbreviations are "LLC," "L.L.C.," "LC" or "L.C." An available LLC name may be reserved for $10.

Filing Fee: $70 fee, payable to "Montana Secretary of State."

Special Instructions and Filing Requirements: Submit original signed articles and one copy.

Tax Status

State Tax Treatment of LLCs: Follows IRS classification.

State Tax Office: Department of Revenue, Helena, telephone 406-444-3696.

http://discoveringmontana.com/revenue/css/default.asp

Operating Rules

Default Transfer Rule: Unless otherwise stated in articles or operating agreement, by unanimous consent of nontransferring members. [Section 35-8-706.]

Default Continuation Rule: A membership vote to continue the LLC after the dissociation of a member (cessation or termination of a membership interest) is not required. [Section 35-8-901.]

NEBRASKA

LLC Filing Office

Nebraska Secretary of State
   Corporate Division
   P.O. Box 94608
   Lincoln, NE 68509-4608

Telephone: 402-471-4079

http://www.sos.state.ne.us//corps/corpform.htm

Forms and Statutes: State provides a fill-in-the-blanks form, "Articles of Organization Limited Liability Company."

Internet Forms: The latest version of the Nebraska LLC articles of organization (Form 2606), plus other statutory LLC forms, can be downloaded from the state LLC filing office website.

The Nebraska LLC Act is contained in Chapter 21 (Corporations and Other Companies) of the Nebraska Statutes, starting with section 21-2601. It is browseable from the Web page listed below (click on "Laws of Nebraska," "Statutes & Constitution," then the "Statutes" folder; open the "Chapter 21" folder, then click the "View Chapter" link under the search box and scroll down to Section 21-2601 to begin browsing the LLC Act:

http://www.unicam.state.ne.us/index.htm

Minimum Number of Members: One.

Articles of Organization

Name Requirements: Must contain the words "Limited Liability Company" or the abbreviation "L.L.C." An available LLC name may be reserved for 120 days for $20.

Filing Fee: $100, plus $5 per page, plus $10 to receive a certificate of organization from the Secretary of State after filing, payable to "Secretary of State."

Special Instructions and Filing Requirements: Submit original and copy of signed articles for filing.

Following is specific information for filling in the state-provided form. If a particular item in the fill-in-the-blanks form does not apply, fill in "N/A" in the blank.

- *Article 2:* Insert "perpetual" to give your LLC an unlimited life.

- *Article 3:* Show the purpose of the LLC. You can simply indicate "to transact any or all lawful business for which limited liability companies may be organized in this state."

- *Article 5:* In the first blank, show the total amount of cash all initial members will contribute as capital to the LLC. (If no cash will be contributed, show "0"; if you are unsure whether all initial cash contributions will be reflected in the stated capital account in the LLC's books, ask your tax advisor.) In the second part of this article, describe any noncash capital contributions to be made by the initial members and state the fair market value of these noncash contributions.

- *Article 6:* If LLC members will be required to make additional contributions after your LLC is formed (beyond the initial contributions listed in Article 5), list them here. Indicate the dates or circumstances when the additional contributions must be made.

- *Article 7:* If you adopt the standard language in our operating agreements, you may check the box that says members shall have the right to admit additional members. Then, you can use the following sentence to sum up the rights of members to admit additional members: "The existing

members of this LLC must approve the admission of new members by a unanimous vote. Upon such approval, new members shall be accorded all rights associated with membership in this LLC."

Instead of standard articles, professional LLCs should use "Application for Registration as a Professional Limited Liability Company" to form an LLC. This form is available from the state LLC filing office or its website.

Tax Status

State Tax Treatment of LLCs: Follows IRS classification.

State Tax Office: Department of Revenue, Lincoln, telephone 800-742-7474.

http://www.revenue.state.ne.us/index.html

Operating Rules

Default Transfer Rule: By written consent of two-thirds of a majority in interest (presumably, a majority of capital and profits interests in the LLC) of nontransferring members. Statute allows operating agreement to set its own rules for the transfer of memberships, but apparently withholds voting and management rights associated with membership from transferees until the two-thirds vote of remaining members is obtained. [Section 21-2621.]

Default Continuation Rule: Vote to continue LLC after dissociation of member not required.

NEVADA

LLC Filing Office

Secretary of State
New Filings Section
202 North Carson Street
Carson City, NV 89701

Telephone: 775-684-5708

Filings may also be made at the Secretary of State satellite office in Las Vegas (702-486-2880).

http://sos.state.nv.us/comm_rec/index.htm

Forms and Statutes: State provides fill-in-the-blanks articles of organization with instructions.

Internet Forms: Provides downloadable articles of organization with instructions (either as a separate document or as part of a "Limited Liability Packet").

The Nevada LLC Act is contained in Title 7 (Business Associations; Securities; Commodities), Chapter 86 of the Nevada Statutes, starting with section 86.011, and is browseable from the following Web page (select "Nevada Revised Statutes" then click on "NRS Chapter 86 Limited Liablility Companies").

http://sos.state.nv.us/comm_rec/index.htm

Minimum Number of Members: One.

Articles of Organization

Name Requirements: Must contain the words "Limited Liability Company," "Limited Company" or "Limited" or the abbreviations "L.L.C.," "L.C.," "LLC" or "LC." The word "Company" may be abbreviated as "Co." To check name availability or reserve a name for 90 days, call the LLC filing office.

Filing Fee: $125, payable to "Secretary of State."

Special Instructions and Filing Requirements: Your LLC's initial agent named in the articles must sign on the signature line provided at the bottom of the articles (in the certificate of acceptance section). The LLC organizer also signs in Article 6 on the first signature line. Submit two copies of the completed, signed articles.

Tax Status

State Tax Treatment of LLCs: Nevada does not have a state income tax scheme, and there is no special state entity tax levied on LLCs.

State Tax Office: Department of Taxation, Carson City, telephone 702-687-4892.

http://tax.state.nv.us

Operating Rules

Default Transfer Rule: By unanimous written consent of majority in interest of (majority of profits interests held by) nontransferring members, unless otherwise provided in articles of operating agreement. [Section 86:351 & 86.065.]

Default Continuation Rule: Vote to continue LLC after dissociation of member not required.

NEW HAMPSHIRE

LLC Filing Office

New Hampshire Secretary of State
　State House, Room 204
　107 North Main Street
　Concord, NH 03301-4989

Telephone: 603-271-3244

http://www.state.nh.us/sos/corporate/index.htm

Forms and Statutes: State provides fill-in-the-blanks "Certificate of Formation" (Form LLC 1) with instructions, and "Addendum to Certificate of Formation" (Form LLC-1-A).

Internet Forms: The New Hampshire LLC Certificate of Formation, which includes the required addendum to certificate, and other statutory forms are available on the state LLC filing office website.

The New Hampshire LLC Act is contained in Title XXVIII (Partnerships), Chapter 304C of the New Hampshire Statutes, starting with section 304-C:1. It is browseable from the Web page listed below (select "Browse Index," then scroll down the index and click "Title XXVIII Partnerships"; then click "Chapter 304-C" to see a listing of the LLC Act sections):

http://sudoc.nhsl.lib.nh.us/rsa/default.htm

Minimum Number of Members: One.

Certificate of Formation

Name Requirements: Must contain the words "Limited Liability Company" or the abbreviations "LLC" or "L.L.C." The state specifically says that an additional space may be inserted between the letters or periods in each of these abbreviations—namely, "L. L. C." and "L L C" are also allowed. The name may contain the words "company," "association," "club," "foundation," "fund," "institute," "society," "union," "syndicate," "limited" or "trust" or abbreviations of these words. An available LLC name may be reserved for 120 days for $15. The name of a professional LLC in New Hampshire must end with the words "Professional Limited Liability Company" or the abbreviation "P.L.L.C."

Filing Fee: $85, payable to the "Secretary of State." This fee includes $50 for filing an Addendum form, discussed in "Special Instructions and Filing Requirements," which follows below.

Annual Fees: LLCs must pay an annual report fee of $100.

Special Instructions and Filing Requirements: When completing the fill-in-the-blanks Certificate of Formation, keep the following points in mind:

- *Second Article:* Be precise and state the nature of your LLC's specific business—for example, "real estate sales" or "automotive repair." You may add a general statement to your specific purposes if you wish: "and to engage in any lawful businesses permitted to limited liability companies under state law." New Hampshire LLCs may be formed for any lawful business purpose except banking, the construction or maintenance of railroads (unless a special permit is granted), the business of making contracts for the payment of money (loan agreements) or the business of a trust, surety, indemnity or safe deposit company.

- *Fourth Article:* Insert the word "None" in this blank if, as is usually the case, you do not want to specify an automatic dissolution date for your LLC.

- *Fifth Article:* Most smaller LLCs—those without specially designated managers—will insert the words "is not" in the blank in this article.

Submit original and copy of signed Certificate for filing. You must include an "Addendum to Certificate of Formation" form that is signed by all LLC members. This form states that the offer and sale of interests in the LLC will be made according to specific New Hampshire security law requirements. Most smaller LLCs will be able to fill in Item 1 on the form, which shows that the LLC is eligible for the exemption summarized near the top of the form. This is the state securities exemption under RSA 421-B:17 II (k) that allows sales of ownership interests to be made to ten or fewer members within 60 days of the start of businesses by a new LLC. The members must be purchasing for investment purposes (not for resale), sales commissions cannot be paid and advertising for buyers of the membership interests is prohibited. This exemption is "self-executing"—that is, no form has to be filed with the State Securities Bureau to rely on this exemption. Otherwise, you must complete Item 2 or 3 and you should call the New Hampshire Division of Securities Regulation or a lawyer for help in preparing this form.

Tax Status

State Tax Treatment of LLCs: Follows IRS classification.

State Tax Office: Revenue Administration Department, Concord, telephone 603-271-6121.

http://webster.state.nh.us/revenue/index.htm

Operating Rules

Default Transfer Rule: Unless otherwise stated in operating agreement, by unanimous consent of nontransferring members. [Section 304-C:48.]

Default Continuation Rule: Vote to continue LLC after dissociation of member not required.

NEW JERSEY

LLC Filing Office

Department of State
Division of Revenue/Corporate Filing Unit
P.O. Box 308
Trenton, NJ 08625-0308

Telephone: 609-292-9292

http://www.state.nj.us/njbgs/index.html

Forms and Statutes: New Jersey provides an online LLC formation and business registration service (click "Services/Online Services" on the state LLC filing office home page, then scroll to the list of Online Services and select "One-Stop Business Filing and Registration"). If you do not have an Internet connection or prefer to file paperwork to form your LLC, you can complete the New Jersey Business Registration Package (Form NJ-REG provided online or by telephone), which includes a two-page "Public Record Filing for New Business Entity" portion that can be used to form an LLC. Unless you do not have an Internet connection, we recommend you form your LLC online rather than by mail.

The New Jersey LLC Act is contained in Title 42 (Partnerships and Partnership Associations), Chapter 2B of the New Jersey Statutes, starting with section 42:2B-1, and is browseable from the following Web page (select "Statutes," then select "Browse by Table of Contents," then expand Title 42, and scroll to section 42:2B-1):

http://www.njleg.state.nj.us

Minimum Number of Members: One.

Certificate of Formation

Name Requirements: Must include "Limited Liability Company" or the abbreviation "L.L.C."

Filing Fee: Check or money order for $100, payable to "Secretary of State."

Special Instructions and Filing Requirements: See "Forms and Statutes," above. If you form your LLC by mail, complete the "Public Record Filing for New Business Entity" portion of the New Jersey Business Registration Package (Form NJ-REG provided online or by telephone).

Tax Status

State Tax Treatment of LLCs: Follows IRS classification, but one-member LLC, treated as sole proprietorship by IRS, not allowed at present.

State Tax Office: Division of Taxation, Trenton, telephone 609-292-5185.

http://www.state.nj.us/treasury/taxation

Operating Rules

Default Transfer Rule: By unanimous written consent of nontransferring members and by any other procedure provided in the operating agreement. [Section 42:2B-46.]

Default Continuation Rule: Vote to continue the LLC after termination of a membership not required. But note, the LLC automatically dissolves 90 days after the date on which the LLC has no remaining members unless a member is admitted within the 90 days. [Section 42:2B-48.]

NEW MEXICO

LLC Filing Office

State Corporation Commission
    Corporation Department
    Chartered Documents Bureau
    P.O. Drawer 1269
    Santa Fe, NM 87504-1269

Telephone: 1-800-947-4722

http://www.nmprc.state.nm.us

Forms and Statutes: Provides fill-in-the-blanks articles of organization with instructions.

Internet Forms: LLC articles (Form NMSCC DLLC-CD) with instructions and an "Affidavit of Acceptance of Appointment of Registered Agent" (which must be completed and filed with the articles), plus other statutory forms, are available for downloading from the state LLC filing office website.

The New Mexico LLC Act is contained in Chapter 53 (Corporations), Article 19 of the New Mexico Statutes, starting with section 53-19-1, and is browseable from the following Web page (drill down the folder headings in the left panel by going to the New Mexico Statutes Annotated, then Chapter 53, then Article 19 to view the LLC Act):

http://www.michie.com

Minimum Number of Members: One.

Articles of Organization

Name Requirements: Must contain the words "Limited Liability Company" or "Limited Company." The word "Limited" may be abbreviated as "Ltd." and the word "Company" may be abbreviated as "Co." An available LLC name may be reserved for 120 days for $20.

Filing Fee: $50, payable to "State Corporation Commission."

Special Instructions and Filing Requirements: Member-managed LLCs should leave Article Four of the state-provided articles of organization blank. Submit the original and one copy of articles for filing.

A signed affidavit of the LLC's initial registered agent showing acceptance of the position must be included; this form is provided by the LLC filing office. The affidavit must be signed by the agent in the presence of a notary.

Tax Status

State Tax Treatment of LLCs: Follows IRS classification.

State Tax Office: Taxation & Revenue Department, Santa Fe, telephone 505-827-0700.

http://www.state.nm.us/tax

Operating Rules

Default Transfer Rule: Unless otherwise stated in articles or operating agreement, by unanimous written consent of nontransferring members. [Section 53-19-33.]

Default Continuation Rule: Unless otherwise provided in articles or operating agreement, written consent of majority-in-interest (presumably, this means a majority of capital and profits interests held by) remaining members within 90 days of dissociation event. [Section 53-19-39(3).]

NEW YORK

LLC Filing Office

Department of State
 Division of Corporations
 State Records and Uniform Commercial Code
 41 State Street
 Albany, NY 12231

Telephone: 518-473-2492

http://www.dos.state.ny.us/corp/corpspub.html

Forms and Statutes: State provides sample articles of organization (Form DOS-1336) with instructions.

Internet Forms: The New York Department of State (DOS) provides its statutory forms for downloading on its website, including standard LLC articles of organization (DOS-1336), articles of conversion of a partnership to an LLC and articles of organization for a professional service LLC. Note: New York provides a fill-in-the-blanks Adobe Acrobat (PDF) articles form on its state filing office website. The state office also provides a booklet titled "Forming a Limited Liability Company in NY," which can be downloaded from the site. We recommend you obtain this guide—it contains specific instructions to the state articles form, plus useful LLC legal and tax information.

If you wish to change a general or limited partnership to a New York LLC, the state provides a special "Certificate of Conversion" form (Form DOS-1363). Use this form instead of the standard LLC articles. (If converting a limited partnership, you must also file a certificate of cancellation for the limited partnership with the Department of State.)

Note for Professionals: Use the state-provided articles of organization for a Professional Service Company (Form DOS-1374) instead of the standard New York LLC articles document if your LLC will perform licensed legal or medical professional services. Other licensed professionals, such as those licensed in the field of education, also need to use this special form. The state website proves a link to the list of professions that must use this special form to form a professional LLC.

The New York LLC Law is contained in Chapter 34 of the New York Consolidated Laws, starting with section 101, and is browseable from the following Web page (click "New York State Laws," then "New York State Consolidated Laws," then "Limited Liability Company

Law," then select article headings to view each part of the law):

http://assembly.state.ny.us/leg

Minimum Number of Members: One.

Articles of Organization

Name Requirements: Must contain the words "Limited Liability Company" or the abbreviations "LLC" or "L.L.C." An available LLC name may be reserved for 60 days for $20.

Words related to the finance, banking, trust or insurance business cannot be used without prior approval (see Section 204 of the New York LLC Law). Here is a partial list of such restricted words: acceptance, annuity, assurance, bank, benefit, bond, casualty, endowment, exchange, fidelity, finance, guaranty, indemnity, insurance, investment, loan, mortgage, savings, surety, title, trust, underwriter.

Filing Fee: $200, payable to the "Department of State." If you wish to receive a certified copy of your articles (optional), include $10 for each certified copy requested. Fee may be paid by check or money order. If a check is for an amount over $500, it must be a certified check.

Special Instructions and Filing Requirements: You may leave these articles in form DOS-1336 blank:

- *Third Article:* automatic dissolution date of LLC. Leave this item blank to give your LLC a perpetual existence.

- *Fifth Article:* street address of registered agent (the Second Article designates the Secretary of State as the LLC agent for service, so this item is not required).

- *Sixth Article:* If you leave this optional article blank, your LLC will come into existence on the date your articles are filed.

- *Seventh Article:* states that one or more members of the LLC will be personally liable for LLC debts! Do not fill this in.

When you mail your articles for filing, if you reserved your LLC name prior to filing your articles, include a copy of the certificate of name reservation you received from the Department of State.

After filing, the state filing office sends a receipt of filing. Keep this receipt in your LLC records.

Within 120 days of filing your articles, you must publish a copy of the information in your articles for six successive weeks in two newspapers in the county where your LLC principal office is located. A local newspaper can help you make this filing (the county clerk in your area has a list of approved newspapers to use when making this publication). After publication, an affidavit of publication must be mailed to the state LLC filing office for filing. The filing fee for each affidavit is $25.

Conversion of Limited Partnership: If you are converting an existing New York limited partnership to an LLC, the conversion does not become effective until a "Certificate of Cancellation" form (available from the Department of State) is filed for the limited partnership with the DOS. Make sure to use DOS Form 1363 instead of the standard LLC articles (DOS-1336) to form your LLC. Note: There is a "Certificate of Conversion" form also posted on the state website. This is for use by LLCs that first file standard articles, then file a "Certificate of Conversion" (DOS Form 1364) that shows the date of filing of the original articles. We suggest you use Form 1363 instead, rather than using this alternate procedure. The two procedures are contained in Section 1006 of the NY LLC Act, which can be browsed through a link on the state LLC filing office website.

Formation of Professional Service LLC: If you are forming an LLC to engage in a licensed New York profession (including law, accounting, engineering, medicine and the like—for a complete list, see the link to the Office of the Professions provided on the form download page of the state LLC filing office website), you must obtain a certificate from the New York licensing board that regulates your profession, which states that all LLC members and managers must hold valid licenses to practice the professional service rendered through the LLC. A copy of this certificate must be attached to your original articles filed with the Department of State. Also, a certified copy of the articles must be filed with the New York licensing board for the profession within 30 days after filing with the DOS. Make sure to use DOS Form 1374 to form your LLC instead of the standard LLC articles.

Tax Status

State Tax Treatment of LLCs: Follows IRS classification. State assesses a tax based upon the number of LLC members.

State Tax Office: Taxation & Finance Department, Albany, telephone 518-438-8581.

http://www.tax.state.ny.us

Operating Rules

Default Transfer Rule: Unless otherwise stated in the operating agreement, by vote or written consent of a majority in interest (under Section 102(o), this is a majority of profits interests, (unless the operating agreement contains a different definition) of nontransferring members. [Section 604.] Note: Notwithstanding anything to the contrary under applicable law, an operating agreement may provide that a membership interest may not be assigned prior to the dissolution and winding up of the LLC. [Section 606.]

Default Continuation Rule: Membership vote to continue the LLC after dissociation of a member (cessation or termination of a membership interest) not required. [Section 701.]

NORTH CAROLINA

LLC Filing Office

North Carolina Department of the Secretary of State Corporations Division
P.O. Box 29622
Raleigh, NC 27626-0622

Telephone: 919-807-2225

(toll-free: 888-246-7636)

http://www.secretary.state.nc.us/corporations

Forms and Statutes: Provides fill-in-the-blanks articles of organization.

Internet Forms: North Carolina LLC articles with instructions, plus other statutory forms, are available for downloading from the state LLC filing office website. A guide to LLCs, which includes helpful name, trademark and securities law information applicable to LLCs, plus state business and licensing office listings, is also available for downloading.

The North Carolina LLC Act is contained in Chapter 57C of the North Carolina Statutes, starting with section 57C-1-01, and is browseable from the following Web page (click "NC General Statutes" at the bottom of the page, then click "Chapters 1-168A," then "Chapter 57C, North Carolina Limited Liability Company Act"):

http://www.secstate.state.nc.us

Minimum Number of Members: One.

Articles of Organization

Name Requirements: Must end with the words "Limited Liability Company" or the abbreviation "LLC" or "L.L.C." The words "Limited" and "Company" may be abbreviated to "Ltd." and "Co." An available LLC name may be reserved for $10.

Filing Fee: $125, payable to "Secretary of State."

Annual Fees: LLCs must pay an annual report fee of $200.

Special Instructions and Filing Requirements: Submit original and one copy of state articles form (Form L-01).

A different articles form (Form PLLC-02), available from the state's website, should be used to form a professional LLC in North Carolina. Also, if you are converting an existing general or limited partnership to an LLC, use state articles Form L-01A instead of standard LLC articles.

Tax Status

State Tax Treatment of LLCs: Follows IRS classification.

State Tax Office: Department of Revenue, Raleigh, telephone 919-733-3991.

http://www.dor.state.nc.us

Operating Rules

Default Transfer Rule: Unless otherwise stated in articles or operating agreement, by unanimous vote at a members' meeting or by unanimous written consent of nontransferring members. [Section 57C-5-04.]

Default Continuation Rule: Membership vote to continue the LLC after dissociation of a member (cessation or termination of a membership interest) not required. [Section 57C-6-01.]

NORTH DAKOTA

LLC Filing Office

North Dakota Secretary of State
  Corporations Division
  600 East Boulevard Avenue, Dept. 108
  Bismarck, ND 58505-0500

Telephone: 701-328-4284 (toll-free: 800-352-0867 ext. 4284)

http://www.state.nd.us/sec/Business/ businessinforegmnu.htm

Forms and Statutes: State provides sample articles of organization form that you can use to prepare your own form, along with a Registered Agent Consent to Serve form and a brochure summarizing state LLC requirements. LLCs formed to render licensed professional services should obtain and file articles of organization for a Professional Limited Liability Company; a sample form is available from the LLC filing office together with a separate law summary brochure.

Internet Forms: Sample articles are available for downloading from the Secretary of State's website.

The North Dakota LLC Act is contained in Title 10-32 of the North Dakota Century Code, starting with section 10-32-01, and is browseable from the Web page listed below (select "State Laws" in the left pane, then "ND Century Code," then click "10 Corporations" to open the pdf file, then select "Chapter 10-32" in the left-panel table of contents):

http://www.state.nd.us/lr

Minimum Number of Members: One.

Articles of Organization

Name Requirements: Must contain the words "Limited Liability Company" or the abbreviation "L.L.C." Cannot contain the words "bank," "banker" or "banking." An available LLC name may be reserved for $10.

Filing Fee: $135 ($125 for filing articles, plus $10 for filing Registered Agent Consent to Serve form), payable to the "Secretary of State."

Special Instructions and Filing Requirements: Follow the sample format provided by the Secretary of State's office when preparing articles (call the office for a copy of sample articles or follow the sample form available online from the state filing office website). Submit completed Registered Agent Consent to Serve form with the articles (a consent form, Form SFN 7974, is available from the office or online from the state filing office website).

Tax Status

State Tax Treatment of LLCs: Follows IRS classification.

State Tax Office: Office of State Tax Commission, Bismarck, telephone 701-328-3700.

www.state.nd.us/taxdpt

Operating Rules

Default Transfer Rule: By unanimous written consent of nontransferring members. [Section 10-32-32(2).]

Default Continuation Rule: Except as otherwise provided in the articles, a vote to continue the LLC after termination of a membership not required. [Section 10-32-109.] Note: This section requires dissolution when the LLC has no remaining members unless the last member or his or her legal representative admits a member within 180 days after the last member's termination.

In the North Dakota LLC Act, the member-managers of an LLC are called the "board of governors." (The president and treasurer of the LLC—two officers that ND LLCs must appoint—are called "managers" in the Act.) You can change the standard LLC operating agreements to reflect this nonstandard terminology, or you can simply decide that any reference in your agreement to managers of a manager-managed LLC is the same as a reference to your LLC's "board of governors." The most significant real-life difference to keep in mind is the following North Dakota rule (under Section 10-32-69 of the ND LLC Act: All members of a member-managed LLC must approve decisions that are specially assigned by the North Dakota statutes to the board of governors. In other words, if you run a member-managed North Dakota LLC, make sure to obtain and record the unanimous votes of all members regarding any important LLC decisions. This makes good business sense anyway, and should not be difficult to obtain for the average smaller-sized LLC.

OHIO

LLC Filing Office

Ohio Secretary of State
Business Services Division
P.O. Box 670
Columbus, OH 43216

Telephone: 614-466-3910

Toll-free: 1-877-SOS-FILE (1-877-767-3453)

www.state.oh.us/sos/business_services_information.htm

Forms and Statutes: State provides fill-in-the-blanks articles of organization (Form 533) with instructions.

Internet Forms: Downloadable articles and other statutory forms are provided online at the state LLC filing office website.

The Ohio LLC Act is contained in Title XVII (Corporations-Partnerships), Chapter 1705 of the Ohio Statutes, starting with section 1705.01, and is browseable from the following Web page (click "Revised Code," select "Title 17" in the left pane, click "Chapter 1705," then select each section of the Act you wish to view):

http://onlinedocs.andersonpublishing.com

Minimum Number of Members: One.

Articles of Organization

Name Requirements: Must contain the words "Limited Liability Company" or "Limited" or the abbreviation "Ltd" or "Ltd." Call the LLC filing office for name availability. Names may be reserved for 60 days for a $5 fee.

Filing Fee: $125 fee, payable to the "Ohio Secretary of State."

Special Instructions and Filing Requirements: In the Second Article, you may show a "perpetual" or "indefinite" duration for your LLC (alternatively, if you leave this Article blank, the law assumes your LLC has a perpetual duration).

You need to file original articles only (copies are not required).

Tax Status

State Tax Treatment of LLCs: Follows IRS classification.

State Tax Office: Taxation Department, Columbus, telephone 614-466-2166.

www.state.oh.us/tax

Operating Rules

Default Transfer Rule: Unless otherwise stated in articles or operating agreement, by unanimous consent of nontransferring members. [Section 1705:20.]

Default Continuation Rule: By unanimous consent of remaining members and as may be stated in the operating agreement. [Section 1705:43(4).]

OKLAHOMA

LLC Filing Office

Oklahoma Secretary of State
  2300 N. Lincoln Blvd.
  Room 101
  State Capitol Building
  Oklahoma City, OK 73105-4897

Telephone: 405-522-4560

http://www.sos.state.ok.us

Forms and Statutes: Provides sample articles of organization with instructions.

Internet Forms: LLC statutory forms, including articles of organization, are available for downloading from the state LLC filing office website.

Professional LLCs: Licensed professionals should use SOS Form 01, "Professional Articles of Organization," instead of the standard Oklahoma LLC articles to form their LLC. A downloadable form is available from the state LLC filing office website.

The Oklahoma LLC Act is contained in Title 18 (Corporations) Oklahoma Statutes, starting with section 18-2000. It is browseable from the Web page listed below. To limit your browse time, it's best to restrict your search of Oklahoma statutes to Title 18 (Corporations). Type "18-2000" (without quotes) in the Search Oklahoma Statutes Database box to find section 18-2000 (the start of the LLC Act). Note that the text of each statute is provided in rtf format, and you must download rtf files section by section.

http://www2.lsb.state.ok.us/tsrs/os_oc.htm

Minimum Number of Members: Beginning 11/1/97, Oklahoma LLCs can be formed with one member.

Articles of Organization

Name Requirements: Must contain the words "Limited Liability Company" or "Limited Company" or the abbreviations "L.L.C." or "L.C." The word "Limited" may be abbreviated as "LTD." and "Company" may be abbreviated as "CO." Call the LLC filing office to check name availability. An available LLC name may be reserved for 60 days for $10.

Filing Fee: $100, payable to "Secretary of State."

Special Instructions and Filing Requirements: Send one signed original version of your articles plus one copy.

Professional LLCs: Licensed professionals should use SOS Form 01, "Professional Articles of Organization," instead of the standard Oklahoma LLC articles to form their LLC. A downloadable form is available from the state LLC filing office website.

Tax Status

State Tax Treatment of LLCs: Follows IRS classification.

State Tax Office: Tax Commission, Oklahoma City, telephone 405-521-2035.

http://www.oktax.state.ok.us

Operating Rules

Default Transfer Rule: Either as stated in operating agreement, or by consent of majority of capital interests held by nontransferring members. [Section 2035.]

Default Continuation Rule: Vote to continue LLC after dissociation of member not required.

OREGON

LLC Filing Office

Oregon Secretary of State
  Corporate Division
  255 Capitol Street, NE, Suite 151
  Salem, OR 97310-1327

Telephone: 503-986-2200

http://www.sos.state.or.us/corporation

Forms and Statutes: State provides articles of organization (Form CR151) with instructions.

Internet Forms: Oregon LLC articles, plus other statutory forms, are available on the state LLC filing office website.

The Oregon LLC Act is contained in Chapter 63 of the Oregon Statutes, starting with section 63.001, and is browseable from the following Web page:

http://www.leg.state.or.us/ors/063.html

Minimum Number of Members: One.

Articles of Organization

Name Requirements: Must contain the words "Limited Liability Company" or the abbreviation "L.L.C." May not contain the words "Cooperative," "Limited Partnership" or the abbreviation "L.P." An available LLC name may be reserved for 120 days for $10.

Filing Fee: $20, payable by check to the "Corporation Division" or by charging to a credit card (include card information on an attachment page to the articles of organization).

Special Instructions and Filing Requirements: Most organizers will check the box in Article 2 that specifies a perpetual duration for the LLC.

If you are forming an LLC to practice one of a number of special professions (such as law, accounting or medicine), Article 8 of your articles must specify the type of professional services your LLC will perform. The state licensing board that regulates your profession can tell you if your profession must comply with this requirement (and others relating to Oregon professional LLCs).

Mail one signed original of the articles plus one copy for filing.

Tax Status

State Tax Treatment of LLCs: Follows IRS classification.

State Tax Office: Department of Revenue, Salem, telephone 503-945-8738.

http://www.dor.state.or.us

Operating Rules

Default Transfer Rule: Unless otherwise stated in articles or operating agreement, by consent of majority of nontransferring members. [Section 63.245.]

Default Continuation Rule: Vote to continue LLC after dissociation of member not required.

PENNSYLVANIA

LLC Filing Office

Commonwealth of Pennsylvania
  Department of State
  Corporation Bureau
  P.O. Box 8722
  Harrisburg, PA 17105-8722

Telephone: 717-787-1057

http://www.dos.state.pa.us/dos/site/default.asp

Forms and Statutes: State provides fill-in-the-blanks "Certificate of Organization—Domestic Limited Liability Company" with instructions, as well as an LLC office Docketing Statement.

Internet Forms: The "Certificate of Organization" with instructions, plus the Entity Docketing Statement and other statutory forms, are available for downloading from the state LLC filing office.

The Pennsylvania LLC Act is contained in Title 19 (Corporations and Business Associations), Chapter 89 of the Pennsylvania Statutes, starting with section 8901. Chapter 89 (the LLC Act) had not been added to the browseable chapter list in Title 19 at the time of our research. Please check the following Web page to see if it has been added to the Title 19 list:

http://www.pacode.com/secure/data/019/019toc.html

Minimum Number of Members: One.

Certificate of Organization

Name Requirements: Must contain the words "Company," "Limited" or "Limited Liability Company," or an abbreviation of one of these three choices. The statute does not provide examples of acceptable abbreviations for these words—our guess is that "Ltd." and "Co." can be used, but not "Liab."

Filing Fee: $100 fee, payable to the "Department of State."

Annual Fees: An annual registration fee of $330, payable to the Department of State.

Special Instructions and Filing Requirements: Here's how most LLCs will complete these blanks on the state-provided form:

- *Article 4:* Smaller LLCs normally will not issue membership certificates and can strike out this language.

- *Article 5:* Most smaller LLCs will be managed by members and should strike out this language.

- *Article 6:* Insert "Not Applicable" in the blank unless you want the LLC office to file your articles on a particular day after your articles are received by the office for filing. This would only be applicable if you want to start the legal life of your LLC on a particular day—for example, the first of the month.

- *Article 7:* Strike out the language of this article unless you are forming an LLC to render licensed professional services. In the latter case, you may need to submit written approval of the state professional board that oversees your profession with your articles. Such a requirement applies to the following types of practices: chiropractic, dentistry, law, medicine and surgery, optometry, osteopathic medicine and surgery, podiatric medicine, public accounting, psychology and veterinarian medicine. It may also apply to others—so if you are forming an LLC to practice a licensed profession, check with your state board and make sure you can form a Pennsylvania LLC and how to deal with this Article (whether to strike it out or fill it in).

Submit an original Certificate of Organization form and one copy of the state docketing statement (DCSB: 15-134A). Also enclose a stamped, self-addressed post-card (or envelope with an additional copy of the certificate enclosed) to obtain a receipt (or file-stamped copy of your certificate) from the LLC filing office.

Professional LLCs: If you are forming one of the special restricted professional LLCs, you may be required to attach a consent form to your certificate, which shows the approval from the board that regulates your profession of the formation of your LLC (the board first checks to make sure all members/managers are licensed). If a professional association is being converted to an LLC, a "Certificate of Election by Professional Association of Limited Liability Company," available for downloading from the state LLC filing office website, may be required to be filed. Check with the Corporation Bureau or your professional association board.

Tax Status

State Tax Treatment of LLCs: State generally follows the IRS classification.

State Tax Office: Department of Revenue, Harrisburg, telephone 717-783-3682.

http://www.revenue.state.pa.us

Operating Rules

Default Transfer Rule: Unless otherwise stated in articles or operating agreement, by unanimous written consent of nontransferring members. [Section 8924.]

Default Continuation Rule: Either as provided in the operating agreement or by unanimous consent of remaining members within 90 days of the dissociation event. [Section 8971(4).]

RHODE ISLAND

LLC Filing Office

Rhode Island Secretary of State
  Corporations Division
  100 North Main Street
  Providence, RI 02903-1335

Telephone: 401-277-3040

http://155.212.254.78/corporations.htm

Forms and Statutes: Provides fill-in-the-blanks form for articles of organization.

Internet Forms: LLC articles plus other statutory forms can be downloaded from the state LLC filing office website.

The Rhode Island LLC Act is contained in Title 7 (Corporations, Associations and Partnerships), Chapter 7-16 of the Rhode Island General Laws, starting with section 7-16-1, and is browseable from the following Web page:

http://www.rilin.state.ri.us/Statutes/TITLE7/7-16/
  INDEX.HTM

Minimum Number of Members: One.

Articles of Organization

Name Requirements: Must *end* with the words "Limited Liability Company" or the abbreviations "LLC" or "L.L.C." (upper or lower case are specifically permitted). Call the LLC filing office to check name availability. An available name may be reserved for 120 days for a fee of $50.

Filing Fee: $150, payable to "Secretary of State."

Special Instructions and Filing Requirements: File two original, signed articles forms. The Secretary will return a file-stamped copy to you, together with a Certificate of Organization.

Follow these guidelines when preparing your articles:

- *Article 3:* Most multi-member LLCs will check the box in Article 3 that indicates the LLC intends to be treated as a partnership for federal income tax purposes. If your LLC has just one member, you will want to change this selection, moving the "X" to the third box in this article, which reads "disregarded as an entity separate from its member" (this means that your LLC will be taxed as a sole proprietorship). If your single- or multi-member LLC wishes to be taxed as a corporation (and plans to file a business entity classification election with IRS Form 8832 for this purpose), you will move the "X" to the second box (the corporation box) instead. For further guidance with selecting the best tax classification for your LLC, ask your tax advisor.

Tax Status

State Tax Treatment of LLCs: Follows IRS classification.

State Tax Office: Division of Taxation, Providence, telephone 401-277-3934.

http://www.tax.state.ri.us

Operating Rules

Default Transfer Rule: Unless otherwise stated in operating agreement, by unanimous consent of nontransferring members obtained by written consent or vote at members' meeting. [Section 7-16-36.]

Default Continuation Rule: Vote to continue LLC after dissociation of member not required.

SOUTH CAROLINA

LLC Filing Office

South Carolina Secretary of State
  Corporations Department
  P.O. Box 11350
  Columbia, SC 29211

Telephone: 803-734-2158

http://www.scsos.com/Corporations.htm

Uniform LLC Act: South Carolina is one of just a handful of states that have updated their LLC statutes to incorporate the Uniform Limited Liability Company Act, proposed as a standard body of law for adoption by the states by the National Conference of Commissioners on Uniform State Laws.

Forms and Statutes: State LLC office provides fill-in-the-blanks articles of organization, articles of organization for professional LLCs and other LLC forms.

Internet Forms: LLC Articles are available for downloading from the state LLC filing office website.

The South Carolina LLC Act is contained in Title 33 (Corporations, Partnerships and Associations), Chapter 44 of the South Carolina Code, starting with section 33-44-101, and is browseable from the Web page listed below. Note that the prior LLC Act (Chapter 43) also is available for downloading (repealed January 1, 2001).

http://www.lpitr.state.sc.us/code/t33c044.htm

Minimum Number of Members: One.

Articles of Organization

Name Requirements: Must contain the words "Limited Liability Company" or "Limited Company" or the abbreviations "L.L.C.," "LLC," "LC" or "L.C." The word "Limited" may be abbreviated as "Ltd." and the word "Company" may be abbreviated as "Co." An LLC name may be reserved for 120 days by filing two copies of an Application to Reserve an LLC Name along with a $25 fee.

Filing Fee: $110 fee, payable to "South Carolina Secretary of State."

Special Instructions and Filing Requirements: File original and one copy of articles. Most LLC organizers will not wish to limit the life of their LLC by specifying a term for its existence, and will therefore not check the box or fill in the blank in Article 5 of the state's official form. We assume no member of the LLC wishes to be personally liable for LLC debts, and therefore Box 7 and the lines in this article should be left blank.

Conversion of Partnership to LLC: If you are converting an existing partnership to an LLC, obtain a special articles form, "Conversion of Partnership or Limited Partnership to Limited Liability Company Articles of Organization," instead of the standard LLC articles to form your LLC. This special articles form is available for downloading from the state LLC filing office website.

Tax Status

State Tax Treatment of LLCs: Follows IRS classification.

State Tax Office: Tax Commission, Columbia, telephone 803-737-9881.

http://www.sctax.org/DOR/default.htm

Operating Rules

Default Transfer Rule: By unanimous consent of nontransferring members, and as may be provided in the LLC operating agreement. [Section 33-44-503(a).]

Default Continuation Rule: A membership vote to continue the LLC after dissociation of a member (cessation or termination of a membership interest) is not required. [Section 33-44-801.]

SOUTH DAKOTA

LLC Filing Office

South Dakota Secretary of State
  State Capitol
  500 East Capitol Ave.
  Pierre, SD 57501-5070

Telephone: 605-773-4845

http://www.state.sd.us/sos/sos.htm

Forms and Statutes: State provides fill-in-the-blanks "Articles of Organization for Domestic Limited Liability Company" with instructions.

Internet Forms: LLC articles, plus other statutory forms, are available for downloading online at the state LLC filing office website.

The South Dakota LLC Act is contained in Title 47 (Corporations), Chapter 34 of the South Dakota Codified Laws, starting with section 47-34-1, and is browseable from the following Web page (drill down through the folder headings in the left pane, as follows: 'South Dakota Codified Laws,' 'Title 47,' 'Chapter 47-34'):

http://www.michie.com

Minimum Number of Members: One.

Articles of Organization

Name Requirements: Must contain the words "limited liability company" or "limited company" or the abbreviation "LLC," "LC," "L.L.C." or "L.C." "Limited" may be abbreviated as "Ltd." and "Company" as "Co."

Filing Fee: $90, if the initial LLC capital is $50,000 or less, payable to the "Secretary of State." Fees increase if the LLC has additional capital, as follows: $50,001 to $100,000 capital—$150 filing fee; in excess of $100,000 capital—filing fee of $150 for the first $100,000 plus 50 cents for each additional $1,000 of capital (maximum fee = $16,000).

Special Instructions and Filing Requirements: The original and one copy of the articles are filed. The LLC's first annual report must accompany the articles. The office will return a file-stamped copy attached to a Certificate of Organization.

Tax Status

State Tax Treatment of LLCs: South Dakota does not implement a state income tax.

State Tax Office: Department of Revenue, Pierre, telephone 605-773-3311.

http://www.state.sd.us/revenue/revenue.html

Operating Rules

Default Transfer Rule: Unless otherwise provided in operating agreement, by unanimous consent of nontransferring members. [Section 47-34A-502.]

Default Continuation Rule: Vote to continue LLC after dissociation of member not required.

TENNESSEE

LLC Filing Office

Tennessee Department of State
  Division of Business Services
  Corporations Section
  312 Eighth Avenue North
  6th Floor, William R. Snodgrass Tower
  Nashville, TN 37243

Telephone: 615-741-2286

http://www.state.tn.us/sos/service.htm#corporations

Forms and Statutes: State provides fill-in-the-blanks articles of organization with instructions. Existing general or limited partnerships convert to a Tennessee LLC by filing special Form SS-4248, "Articles of Conversion of Limited Liability Company."

Internet Forms: LLC articles with instructions, articles of conversion and other statutory forms are available from the state LLC office website. A "Limited Liability Companies Filing Guide" is also available for viewing and downloading.

Note: You can ignore the "Certificate of Formation" form listed in the index to downloadable forms. It is an optional form that can be filed to show that the LLC began its legal existence on a date after filing of the articles (if you request a delayed effective date for your articles).

The Tennessee LLC Act is contained in Title 48 (Corporations and Associations), Chapters 201-248 of the Tennessee Code, starting with section 48-201-101, and is browseable from the following Web page (drill down through the folder headings in the left pane, as follows: 'Tennessee Code,' 'Title 48,' 'Chapter 201' to view the first chapter of the LLC Act, then select other chapters to continue browsing the remaining sections of the Act):

http://www.michie.com

Minimum Number of Members: One.

Articles of Organization

Name Requirements: Must contain the words "Limited Liability Company" or the abbreviations "L.L.C." or "LLC." An available LLC name may be reserved for $10.

Filing Fee: $50 per LLC member as of the date of filing, with a minimum fee of $300 (maximum fee is $3,000). Make check payable to the "Tennessee Secretary of State."

Special Instructions and Filing Requirements: Submit an original and one copy of the articles of organization. If you are converting an existing partnership to an LLC, use the special state-provided articles of conversion instead of the standard LLC articles to form your LLC (articles of conversion are available for downloading from the state LLC filing office website).

Here's how to complete specific articles:

- *Article 4:* Check the appropriate box to indicate whether your LLC is member-managed (this is normally the case) or "board-managed." In Tennessee, persons selected for a special management team are called "governors," not "managers" as is normally the case. If you plan to select a special management team to run your LLC (and will adopt the management operating agreement covered in Chapter 6), check the "board managed" box. (By the way, in the Tennessee LLC Act, the term "manager" is used to refer to two special officer—not management—positions. For more on this odd use of LLC nomenclature, see "Special Statutory Rules," below.)

- *Article 8:* Insert "Perpetual" unless you wish to insert a date or term of years to limit the duration of your LLC.

- *Article 10:* We assume you will form a profit-making LLC, and, therefore, will not check the box that applies to special Tennessee nonprofit LLCs.

Articles should be signed by a member or manager; show the person's title as member or manager in the line marked "signer's capacity."

Tax Status

State Tax Treatment of LLCs: Follows IRS classification.

State Tax Office: Department of Revenue, Nashville, telephone 615-741-2461.

http://www.state.tn.us/revenue

Operating Rules

Default Transfer Rule: Unless the articles allow transfers by a majority of the voting power of the LLC (including the votes of parties to any contribution agreements), by unanimous written consent of nontransferring members (including the consent of parties to any contribution agreements). [Section 48-218-102.]

Default Continuation Rule: Unless otherwise provided in articles or operating agreement, by vote of a majority in interest of remaining members (majority of remaining members having right to profits and capital distributions in the LLC). Approval must be obtained within 90 days of a dissociation event, and there must be at least two remaining members. [Section 48-245-101.]

Special Statutory Rules: Tennessee has an unusual statutory scheme and nomenclature for management of the LLC. As with all other states, it allows for management of the LLC by all members—you elect this standard management option by checking the "Member Managed" box in Article 4 of the state-provided articles of organization.

Now, here is where it begins to get complicated. Member-managed (and other) LLCs are expected to appoint at least two "managers": a chief manager and a secretary. In reality, these are officer—not manager—positions. The chief manager functions as president of the LLC, and is charged under Section 48A-41-102 with making sure that management orders are carried out (a typical CEO day-to-day responsibility). The secretary is charged with maintaining the records of the LLC (again, a typical day-to-day officer job).

The people who can be selected in place of the members to manage the LLC are not called managers as they are in most other states—they are called "governors" and they are selected to serve on the board of governors. If you want to select a special management team not consisting of all members, you check the "board managed" box in Article 4 of the state form as explained above.

Where does this nonstandard statutory terminology leave you when selecting and filling in the tear-out operating agreements in this book? Here's what we suggest.

If you opt, as most smaller LLCs do, for member management, the standard tear-out operating agreement covered in Chapter 5 will work fine for you, with two minor changes.

First, make it clear in your agreement that your members are taking the place of the board of governors as allowed under law in managing your LLC. To do this, add a second sentence to Provision II(3), Management, so that it reads in full as follows (the new sentence is italicized):

> **(3) Management:** This LLC shall be managed exclusively by all of its members. *Any action that would require the action of the Board of Governors under law shall be made by the members.*

Second, change Provision VII(1), Officers, of the standard agreement so that it requires the two "manager" (officer) positions to be filled as required under the LLC Act. You do this by replacing the first sentence with the italicized material below:

> **(1) Officers:** *The LLC shall designate persons to fill the officer positions of Chief Manager and Secretary. The duties associated with these positions shall include those responsibilities listed under law for these officers, plus any additional duties the members shall prescribe for these offices. The duties of the office of Chief Manager shall include seeing that all orders and resolutions of the members are carried into effect. The duties of the office of Secretary shall include keeping accurate membership records and records of the proceedings of meetings of members of this LLC. This LLC may have such other officers, such as President, Vice President and Treasurer, with such duties as the members shall decide.*
>
> Persons who fill these positions need not be members of the LLC. Such positions may be compensated or noncompensated according to the nature and extent of

the services rendered for the LLC as a part of the duties of each office. Ministerial services only as a part of any officer position will normally not be compensated, such as the performance of officer duties specified in this agreement, but any officer may be reimbursed by the LLC for out-of-pocket expenses paid by the officer in carrying out the duties of his or her office.

If you form a manager-managed LLC by preparing the management operating agreement covered in Chapter 6, make the following changes to the tear-out agreement.

First, change Provision II(1) so to make it clear that your managers will act as "governors" under Tennessee law (again, changes are noted below in italics):

> **(1) Management by Managers:** This LLC will be managed by the managers listed below. *Managers shall function under law as the "governors" of this LLC as this term is defined and used in the Tennessee Limited Liability Company Act.* All managers who are also members of this LLC are designated as "members"; nonmember managers are designated as "nonmembers."

Second, add a new paragraph to the officer provision—Provision VIII(1)—in your agreement, as shown in italics below:

> **(1) Officers:** The managers of this LLC may designate one or more officers, such as a President, Vice President, Secretary and Treasurer. Persons who fill these positions need not be members or managers of the LLC. Such positions may be compensated or noncompensated according to the nature and extent of the services rendered for the LLC as a part of the duties of each office. Ministerial services only as a part of any officer position will normally not be compensated, such as the performance of officer duties specified in this agreement, but any officer may be reimbursed by the LLC for out-of-pocket expenses paid by the officer in carrying out the duties of his or her office.
>
> *The LLC shall designate persons to fill the officer positions of Chief Manager and Secretary. The Chief Manager shall be an officer, not a "manager" of this LLC as the term "manager" is used in Provision II(1) of this agreement, and shall not, as Chief Manager, take part in the management of this LLC. The duties associated with these officer positions shall include those responsibilities*

listed under law for these officers, plus any additional duties the managers shall prescribe for these offices. The duties of the office of Chief Manager shall include seeing that all orders and resolutions of the managers are carried into effect. The duties of the office of Secretary shall include keeping accurate membership records and records of the proceedings of the meetings of members and managers of this LLC.

TEXAS

LLC Filing Office

Texas Secretary of State
  Statutory Filings Division
  Corporations Section
  P.O. Box 13697
  Austin, TX 78711-3697

Telephone: 512-463-5583

www.sos.state.tx.us/corp/index.shtml

Forms and Statutes: State provides articles of organization (Form 205) plus other statutory forms.

Internet Forms: "Articles of Organization" (Form 205), "Articles for a Professional LLC" (Form 206), other statutory forms and a "Filing Guide" are available for downloading from the state LLC filing office website.

The Texas LLC Act is contained in Title 32 (Corporations), Part 3 of the Vernon's Texas Civil Statutes, starting with Article 1.01, and is browseable from the following Web page (click "Vernon's Texas Civil Statutes" at the bottom of the page; next, under "Title 32—Corporations," select "Chapter 18—Miscellaneous;" then at the bottom of the list, select "'Article 1528n—Texas Limited Liability Company Act"):

www.capitol.state.tx.us/statutes/statutes.html

Minimum Number of Members: One.

Articles of Organization

Name Requirements: Must contain the words "Limited Liability Company" or "Limited Company" or the abbreviations "L.L.C.," "LLC," "LC," "L.C." or "Ltd. Co." Name availability may be checked over the phone by calling 512-463-5555. An available LLC name may be reserved for 120 days for $25.

Filing Fee: $200, payable to "Secretary of State."

Special Instructions and Filing Requirements: Submit an original and one copy of the articles of organization. You will be mailed a file-stamped copy after the original is filed.

If you are forming a professional LLC, download and use Form 206, Articles for a Professional LLC, instead of the standard LLC articles to form your LLC.

If you are converting a partnership to an LLC, your articles must include additional language. Here is the summary of additional information required to be added to your articles to convert a partnership to an LLC (from the Filing Guide, available for viewing and downloading from the state LLC filing office website): "The organizational documents of a converted domestic entity must include the following statements in addition to the statements normally required in its formation documents: 1) The statement that the corporation, limited liability company or limited partnership is being incorporated, organized or formed pursuant to a plan of conversion and 2) A statement providing the name, address, prior form of organization and its date of formation, and jurisdiction of incorporation, formation or organization of the converting entity."

Tax Status

State Tax Treatment of LLCs: Texas LLCs are subject to payment of the state corporate franchise tax and are subject to the Texas intangibles tax. (Texas has no personal income tax scheme.)

State Tax Office: Comptroller of Public Accounts, Austin at 800-252-1381.

www.window.state.tx.us

Operating Rules

Default Transfer Rule: By unanimous consent of nontransferring members or as the operating agreement may provide. [Section 4.07.]

Default Continuation Rule: By unanimous vote of remaining members within 90 days of a dissociation event. Articles or the operating agreement may specify a different vote requirement or date by which the vote must be made, or the operating agreement may say that the dissociation of a member does not trigger dissolution of the LLC at all. [Section 6.01(5).]

Special Statutory Rules: Texas LLC law refers to operating provisions adopted by an LLC as its "regulations." [Section 2.09.] In other words, references in the Texas LLC Act to "regulations" mean the provisions contained in your operating agreement. An amendment of articles to continue the LLC's existence beyond a duration ending date for the LLC specified in the articles must be filed with the Secretary of State within three years of the duration ending date. [Section 6.01(B).]

UTAH

LLC Filing Office

Utah Division of Corporations & Commercial Code
160 East 300 South, 2nd Floor
Box 146705
Salt Lake City, UT 84114-6705

Telephone: 801-530-4849 (toll-free: 877-526-3994)

http://www.commerce.state.ut.us/corporat/corpcoc.htm

Forms and Statutes: State provides sample articles of organization.

Internet Forms: Sample LLC articles of organization are provided on the website—plus statutory forms, such as a Reservation of Business Name (which can be used by an LLC).

The Utah LLC Act is contained in Title 48 (Partnership), Chapter 2c of the Utah Code, starting with section 48-2c-101, and is browseable from the Web page listed below (select search by 'Keyword,' then expand the left pane index to select Title 48, Chapter 2c):

http://www.le.state.ut.us/Documents/code_const.htm

Minimum Number of Members: One.

Articles of Organization

Name Requirements: Must contain the words "Limited Liability Company," "Limited Company" or the abbreviation "LLC," "LC," "L.L.C." or "L.C."

Filing Fee: $50, payable to "State of Utah."

Special Instructions and Filing Requirements: To prepare articles, follow the format and content of the sample LLC articles provided online at the state filing office website. Submit a signed original and one photocopy of the articles for filing.

Tax Status

State Tax Treatment of LLCs: Follows IRS classification.

State Tax Office: Utah State Tax Commission, Salt Lake City, telephone 801-530-4848.

http://www.tax.ex.state.ut.us

Operating Rules

Default Transfer Rule: Except as otherwise provided in operating agreement, by consent of a majority of the profits interests in the LLC of nontransferring members. [Section 48-2b-131.]

Default Continuation Rule: Vote to continue LLC after dissociation of member not required.

VERMONT

LLC Filing Office

Vermont Secretary of State
81 River Street, Drawer 09
Montpelier, VT 05609-1104

Telephone: 802-828-2386

http://www.sec.state.vt.us/corps/corpindex.htm

Uniform LLC Act: Vermont is one of just a handful of states that have updated their LLC statutes to incorporate the Uniform Limited Liability Company Act, proposed as a standard body of law for adoption by the states by the National Conference of Commissioners on Uniform State Laws.

Forms and Statutes: Provides fill-in-the-blanks articles of organization with instructions and background information on the Vermont LLC Act and how it affects the formation and operation of Vermont LLCs.

Internet Forms: Vermont LLC statutory forms, including articles of organization, are available for downloading (in Microsoft Word, WordPerfect and text format) from the state LLC filing office website.

The Vermont LLC Act is contained in Title 11 (Corporations, Partnerships and Associations), Chapter 21 of the Vermont Statutes, starting with section 3001, and is browseable from the following Web page (select the "Vermont Statutes" link in the left pane, then select "Title 11," then "Chapter 21"):

http://www.leg.state.vt.us

Minimum Number of Members: One.

Articles of Organization

Name Requirements: Must contain the words "Limited Liability Company" or "Limited Company" or the abbreviations "LLC," "LC," "L.L.C." or "L.C." "Limited" may be abbreviated as "Ltd." and "Company" as "Co." An LLC name, if available, may be reserved for 120 days for a $20 fee.

Filing Fee: $75, payable to "Vermont Secretary of State."

Special Instructions and Filing Requirements: Mail an original and one copy of the articles to the Secretary of State.

The articles ask if the company will be a "term" company (one whose duration is limited to a definite term of years). If the LLC answers "No," its duration is perpetual, and it is called an "at-will" company under the Vermont LLC Act. Articles must also indicate if any members have agreed to assume personal liability for LLC debts and obligations (this assumption of liability is specifically allowed under Section 3043(b) of the Vermont LLC Act). Since one of the benefits of forming an LLC is immunity for all members from personal liability for LLC debts, the usual answer to this question is "No."

Tax Status

State Tax Treatment of LLCs: Follows IRS classification.

State Tax Office: Vermont Department of Taxes, Montpelier, 802-828-2551.

http://www.state.vt.us/tax

Operating Rules

Default Transfer Rule: By unanimous consent of nontransferring members; it appears the operating agreement can provide an alternate means of admission of transferees as new members (for example, by saying that any transferee who has been transferred an LLC interest together with all membership rights automatically becomes a new member). Most LLCs will want to stay with the default rule to allow existing members to affirmatively vote on the admission of future transferees. [Section 3073(a).]

Default Continuation Rule: By vote of a "majority in interest" of remaining members within 90 days of the dissociation (termination of membership rights) of a member (or a member-manager, if any, of a manager-managed LLC), or as may additionally be provided in the operating agreement. [Section 3101(3).] Note: The vote of a "majority in interest" is not defined in the definitions section of Act—our guess, by analogy to federal tax rules, is that this term means the vote of remaining members holding a majority of both the capital and profits interests in the LLC.

LLC Filing Office

Clerk of the State Corporation Commission
P.O. Box 1197
First Floor
Richmond, VA 23218

Telephone: 804-371-9733 (toll-free: 866-SCC-CLK1)

http://www.state.va.us/scc/division/clk/corp.htm

Forms and Statutes: Provides fill-in-the-blanks "Articles of Organization," "Articles of Organization to Convert Existing Partnership to an LLC" and "Articles of Organization for a Professional LLC" with instructions for each form. Persons forming an LLC practice in medicine, law, dentistry, accounting, pharmacy, optometry, behavioral sciences, veterinary medicine or insurance consulting should form a professional LLC. All others should form a regular LLC.

Internet Forms: Virginia LLC statutory forms, including articles of organization (both regular LLCs—Form 1011—and professional LLCs—Form 1103, as well as Form 1010.1 for the conversion of a partnership into an LLC), are available for downloading from the state LLC office website in Microsoft Word and Adobe Acrobat (PDF) formats. A helpful "Business Registration Guide," which contains statutory forms plus tax, licensing and other state information, also is available for downloading.

The Virginia LLC Act is contained in Title 13.1 (Corporations) of the Virginia Code, Chapter 12, starting with section 13.1-1000, and is browseable from the following Web page (click "Code of Virginia," then click "Table of Contents" on the search page; select the "Title 13" heading, then click "Chapter 12, Virginia Limited Liability Company Act" to see a list of the sections in the LLC Act):

http://legis.state.va.us/codecomm/codehome.htm

Minimum Number of Members: One.

Articles of Organization

Name Requirements: Must contain the words "Limited Liability Company" or "Limited Company" or the abbreviations "LLC," "LC," "L.L.C." or "L.C." To reserve an LLC name, mail state form LLC-1013, Application for Reserved Name, with a $10 fee.

Filing Fee: $100, payable to "State Corporation Commission."

Special Instructions and Filing Requirements: You only need to send original articles for filing. Type or print in blanks of state form in black ink only.

To form a professional LLC, download and use Form 1103 from the state LLC office website. For the conversion of an existing partnership into a new LLC, use Form 1010.1 (also available from the state website).

Tax Status

State Tax Treatment of LLCs: Follows IRS classification.

State Tax Office: Department of Taxation, Richmond, telephone 804-367-2062.

http://www.tax.state.va.us

Operating Rules

Default Transfer Rule: Unless otherwise provided in operating agreement, by consent of majority-in-interest of (majority of capital and profits interests held by) nontransferring members. [Section 13.1-1040 & 13.1-1002.]

Default Continuation Rule: Vote to continue LLC after dissociation of member not required.

WASHINGTON

LLC Filing Office

Washington Secretary of State
Corporations Division
801 Capitol Way S.
P.O. Box 40234
Olympia, WA 98504-0234

Telephone: 360-753-7115

http://www.secstate.wa.gov/corps

Forms and Statutes: State provides a fill-in-the-blank Certificate of Formation form.

Internet Forms: Washington LLC statutory forms, including the Certificate of Formation, are available for downloading from the state LLC office website.

The Washington LLC Act is contained in Title 25.15 (Partnerships) of the Washington Code, starting with section 25.15.005, and is browseable from the following Web page:

http://search.leg.wa.gov/wslrcw/
RCW%20%2025%20%20TITLE/
RCW%20%2025%20.%2015%20%20CHAPTER/
RCW%20%2025%20.%2015%20%20chapter.htm

Minimum Number of Members: One-member LLCs can be formed starting 9/1/97.

Certificate of Formation

Name Requirements: Must contain the words "Limited Liability Company," "Limited Liability Co." or the abbreviation "LLC" or "L.L.C." The fee to reserve an available LLC name for 180 days is $30.

Filing Fee: $175, payable to "Secretary of State."

Special Filing Instructions and Requirements: Most LLCs will insert "Not Applicable" in the "Date of Dissolution" box to give their LLC a perpetual existence. Make sure the registered agent signs the Certificate in the space provided. Submit original and one copy of the Certificate of Formation to the LLC filing office.

Tax Status

State Tax Treatment of LLCs: State applies a gross income tax on LLCs (which also applies to partnerships). State has no personal income tax.

State Tax Office: Department of Revenue, Olympia, telephone 800-647-7706.

http://dor.wa.gov

Operating Rules

Default Transfer Rule: Unless otherwise stated in articles or operating agreement, by unanimous consent of nontransferring members. [Section 25.15.250.]

Default Continuation Rule: Membership vote to continue the LLC after dissociation of a member (cessation or termination of a membership interest) not required. [Section 25.15.270.]

WEST VIRGINIA

LLC Filing Office

West Virginia Secretary of State
  Corporations Division
  Bldg. 1, Suite 157-K
  1900 Kanawha Blvd. East
  Charleston, WV 25305-0770

Telephone: 304-558-8000

http://www.wvsos.com

Uniform LLC Act: West Virginia is one of just a handful of states that have updated their LLC statutes to incorporate the 1995 Uniform Limited Liability Company Act, proposed as a standard body of law for adoption by the states by the National Conference of Commissioners on Uniform State Laws.

Forms and Statutes: Provides standard fill-in articles of organization (Form LLD-1).

Internet Forms: Articles (Form LLD-1) that can be filled in online, then printed and mailed to the state, plus other statutory forms such as an application to reserve an LLC name, are available for downloading from the state LLC filing office website.

The West Virginia LLC Act is contained in Chapter 31B of the West Virginia Code, starting with section 31B-1-101, and is browseable from the following Web page (select "State Code" from the WV Code folder in the left pane, then scroll down the browse box until you select "Chapter 31B," then press "Browse" and click the link to "Chapter 31B" to browse the LLC Act):

http://www.legis.state.wv.us/legishp.html

Minimum Number of Members: One.

Articles of Organization

Name Requirements: The name of a West Virginia LLC must contain the words "Limited Liability Company" or "Limited Company" or the abbreviations "L.L.C.," "LLC," "LC" or "L.C." The word "Limited" may be abbreviated as "Ltd." and the word "Company" may be abbreviated as "Co." An available LLC name may be reserved for 120 days for $5.

Professional Service LLCs: If you are forming a "professional service LLC" (for example, a law, accounting or medical practice LLC) your LLC name must, instead, include the words "Professional Limited Liability Company" or the abbreviations "Professional L.L.C." or

"P.L.L.C." A professional LLC must have at least two members, and must carry at least $1 million in professional liability insurance coverage. Call your state board to determine if a licensed profession is subject to these special professional service LLC requirements.

Filing Fee: $100, plus an "Attorney-in-Fact" fee (it has nothing to do with attorneys) based on the month when articles are filed (see the state website to compute your total filing fee), payable to the "Secretary of State."

Special Instructions and Filing Requirements: Use the fill-in-the-blanks articles online if you can. Print the completed form from your browser, then mail the articles to the state filing office. Submit one original copy of the articles, plus a manually signed copy, which will be date- and time-stamped and returned to you at no charge. Your organizer must sign the articles of organization in the presence of a notary public (in the blank immediately following the acknowledgment—Article 14). The Notary will complete the other blanks in the Acknowledgment Section.

Note: We assume you will check "No" in Article 9 to show that no member is individually liable for LLC debts.

Form LLD-1 contains a box to check if you are forming a professional LLC (one engaged in the practice of accounting, architecture, chiropody, chiropractic, dentistry, law, medicine, osteopathy, podiatry or veterinary medicine). Articles for a professional LLC will not be filed until the LLC filing office receives a confirmation from the state licensing board that all LLC members have current licenses and have met the professional requirements of the board.

If you are converting a general or limited partnership to an LLC, attach a completed Form LLD/F-6, "Statement of Conversion" (available from the LLC filing office), to your Form LLD-1.

Tax Status

State Tax Treatment of LLCs: Follows IRS classification.

State Tax Office: Department of Tax & Revenue, Charleston, telephone 304-558-3333.

http://www.state.wv.us/taxdiv

Operating Rules

Default Transfer Rule: By unanimous consent of nontransferring members, and as may be provided in the LLC operating agreement. [Section 31B-5-503(a).]

Default Continuation Rule: By consent of members entitled to receive a majority of current or future distributions within 90 days of dissociation (termination of membership rights) of member; and as may be provided in operating agreement. Note: This statutory majority-of-distributions voting rule to continue the LLC applies in manager-managed LLCs only when a member who is also a manager is dissociated—vote is not required when a nonmanaging member's interest is terminated in a manager-managed LLC (of course, your operating agreement can provide otherwise). [Section 31B-8-801(b)(3).]

WISCONSIN

LLC Filing Office

Wisconsin Secretary of State
Department of Financial Institutions
P.O. Box 7846
Madison, WI 53707-7846

Telephone: 608-261-7577

http://www.wdfi.org/corporations/default.htm

Forms and Statutes: Provides fill-in-the-blanks articles of organization with instructions.

Internet Forms: Fill-in-the-blanks articles of organization, which can be filled in and printed from your browser, plus other statutory forms, are available from the state LLC office website. Note: You can prepare and file your LLC articles online with the Wisconsin Quickstart LLC service (see below).

The Wisconsin LLC Act is contained in Chapter 183 of the Wisconsin Statutes, starting with section 183.0102, and is browseable from the following Web page (click "Statutes"):

http://folio.legis.state.wi.us

Minimum Number of Members: One.

Articles of Organization

Name Requirements: Must contain the words "Limited Liability Company" or "Limited Liability Co." or end with the abbreviations "LLC" or "L.L.C." You may specify a second name in the blank in the instructions to Article 1 (on the back page of the printed form) in case the name you show in Article 1 is not available for your use. An available LLC name may be reserved for 120 days by calling the LLC filing office at the telephone number shown above for $30 or by mail for $15.

Filing Fee: $170, payable to "Department of Financial Institutions." Note: You pay a lower $130 fee to form your LLC online with the Wisconsin Quickstart LLC service.

Special Instructions and Filing Requirements: The state LLC filing office provides an online LLC formation service called Quickstart LLC. We recommend you use this online service to form your LLC instead of the state-provided paper articles from the state filing office because 1) the online service costs less ($130 instead of the $170 charge for filing paper articles) and 2) the online service is fast and easy to use and includes a name availability search prior to the acceptance of your online application.

If you do not have an Internet connection or prefer to prepare and file paper articles, submit both pages of the state-provided Articles form to the LLC filing office. Mail one signed original of the articles plus one copy for filing. A file-stamped copy will be returned to you.

Tax Status

State Tax Treatment of LLCs: Follows IRS classification.

State Tax Office: Department of Revenue, Madison, telephone 608-266-6466.

http://www.dor.state.wi.us

Operating Rules

Default Transfer Rule: Unless otherwise stated in the operating agreement, by unanimous written consent of nontransferring members. [Section 183.0706.]

Default Continuation Rule: By unanimous consent of remaining members within 90 days of a dissociation event or as may otherwise be provided in the operating agreement. [Section 183.0901(4).]

WYOMING

LLC Filing Office

Wyoming Secretary of State
　Corporations Division
　The State Capitol Building
　Cheyenne, WY 82002-0020

Telephone: 307-777-7311

http://soswy.state.wy.us/corporat/corporat.htm

Forms and Statutes: State provides fill-in-the-blanks
　articles of organization.

Internet Forms: Articles of Organization, as well as other
　statutory forms, are available from the state LLC filing
　office website.

The Wyoming LLC Act is contained in Title 17 of the
　Wyoming Statutes, Chapter 15, starting with section
　17-15-101, and is browseable from the following Web
　page (click the link to the "Limited Liability Company
　Act"):

http://soswy.state.wy.us/corporat/statutes.htm

Minimum Number of Members: One member permitted if
　LLC elects "flexible limited liability company" status in
　its articles of organization (see below). Otherwise, two
　members are required.

Articles of Organization

Name Requirements: Must contain the words "Limited
　Liability Company," "Limited Company," the abbrevia-
　tions "LLC," "L.L.C.," "LC" or "L.C." or one of the
　following combination forms: "Ltd. Liability Com-
　pany," "Ltd. Liability Co." or "Limited Liability Co."
　(Any of these nine forms is acceptable.) The fee to
　reserve an LLC name is $30.

Filing Fee: $100.

Annual Fees: Annual LLC tax (called the Annual Report
　License tax) is $50 or $.0002 of every dollar of the
　company's assets located and employed in Wyoming,
　whichever is greater.

Special Instructions and Filing Requirements: Submit an
　original plus one copy of articles for filing.

Here are instructions for some of the less straightforward
　articles:

- *Article II:* State the period of duration of the LLC.
　You can specify a date, or a term of years, such as 50
　or 75. If no duration is given in this blank, the law

says your LLC's duration is 30 years from the date of
filing.

- *Article III:* Fill in the purpose(s) of your LLC. Rather
　than referring to the specific business of the LLC (for
　example, "real estate sales"), you can provide a
　general statement—but you must specifically
　exclude the banking and insurance business in such
　a statement. For example, the following general
　statement of purpose will work fine: "Any lawful
　business except the business of banking or
　insurance."

- *Article V:* Specify the cash and value of property to
　be contributed to start up the LLC.

- *Article VI:* Indicate the amount or circumstances for
　any additional contributions required of members of
　your LLC.

- *Article VII:* If you adopt the standard language
　contained in our operating agreements, you can use
　the following sentence to sum up the rights of
　members to admit additional members, and the
　terms of such admission: "The existing members of
　this LLC must approve the admission of new
　members by a unanimous vote. Upon such
　approval, new members shall be accorded all rights
　associated with membership in this LLC."

- *Article VIII:* If you adopt the standard language
　contained in our operating agreements, the
　following sentence will sum up the rights of
　remaining members to continue the LLC after
　dissociation of a member: "The unanimous approval
　of the remaining members is required to continue
　the business of this LLC upon the death, retirement,
　resignation, expulsion, bankruptcy or dissolution of
　a member or the occurrence of any other event that
　terminates the continued membership of a member
　in this limited liability company."

If you wish to form a one-member LLC, you must
　retype the standard articles, and add an article (you
　can add it to the end of your articles and label it
　"Article 10"). In this article you must elect "flexible
　LLC" status (Wyoming flexible LLCs can say in their
　operating agreement that they will have just one
　member). See the specific instructions in "Special
　Statutory Rules," below.

The written consent of the registered agent to his or her
　appointment in this capacity must accompany the
　articles. Simply use the "Consent of Agent" form

included as the last page of the articles in the downloadable form provided on the state filing office website.

Tax Status

State Tax Treatment of LLCs: No state income tax.

State Tax Office: Department of Revenue, Cheyenne, telephone 307-777-7961.

http://revenue.state.wy.us

Operating Rules

Default Transfer Rule: By unanimous written consent of nontransferring members; this consent requirement is mandatory (unless the LLC elects "flexible" LLC status—see "Special Statutory Rules" below). [Section 17-15-122.]

Default Continuation Rule: By unanimous consent of remaining members; this right of remaining members to consent to continue the LLC after the dissociation of a member must be stated in the articles (see "Special Instructions and Filing Requirements," above, Article VIII); this unanimous consent requirement and its inclusion in the articles is mandatory (unless the LLC elects "flexible" LLC status—see "Special Statutory Rules" below). [Section 17-15-123(a)(iii).]

Special Statutory Rules. Section 17-15-144 of the Wyoming LLC Act allows the articles to contain a provision which elects "flexible Limited Liability Company" status. This means that the LLC can have only one member (regular Wyoming LLCs must have at least two members). It also means that special provisions for the assignment of membership interests and for continuance of the LLC after a member is dissociated can be adopted by the LLC in its operating agreement; that is, the LLC can waive the otherwise mandatory default rules listed in the preceding two paragraphs. If you wish to form a flexible LLC, do the following:

1. Add a new Article X to the bottom of your articles just before the date and signature lines (you'll have to

retype the last page of the state's fill-in Article form), which reads as follows: "Article X: Article 10. Pursuant to W.S. 17-15-107(a)(x), this limited liability company elects to be a flexible limited liability company, and is thereby authorized to adopt provisions within its operating agreement as authorized by W.S. 17-15-144."

2. Next, use the following as your response in Article VII (admission of new members) of your articles of organization (instead of the language given above in the "Special Instructions and Filing Requirements" section): "Except as may be permitted in the operating agreement of this limited liability company, the existing members of this LLC must approve the admission of new members by a unanimous vote. Upon such approval, new members shall be accorded all rights associated with membership in this LLC."

3. Finally, use the following as your response to Article VIII (continuance of the LLC): "Except as may be permitted in the operating agreement of this limited liability company, the unanimous approval of the remaining members is required to continue the business of this LLC upon the death, retirement, resignation, expulsion, bankruptcy or dissolution of a member or the occurrence of any other event that terminates the continued membership of a member in this limited liability company."

The result of making these changes to your articles is that you can have just one member and you are allowed to override the default transfer and continuation rules noted above—that is, you can provide in your operating agreement for the admission of new members (including those who have been transferred a membership from a prior member) and the continuance of the LLC after a member's interest is terminated by less than unanimous approval of nontransferring or remaining members. Again, we think going with the default unanimous rules makes the most sense—in small LLCs, obtaining full membership approval is usually best, but you can adopt these provisions and make up your own less-than-unanimous rules if you wish.

APPENDIX B

Tax Regulations

REVENUE RULING 88-76

§ 12:01.   Revenue Ruling 88–76: Partnership Classification (Wyoming Limited Liability Company) (1988–2 IRB 360).

Section 7701.—Definitions

26 CFR 301.7701–1: Classification of organizations for tax purposes.

Partnership classification. An unincorporated organization operating under the Wyoming Limited Liability Company Act is classified as a partnership for federal tax purposes under section 301.7701–2 of the regulations.

Rev Rul 88–76

ISSUE

Whether a Wyoming limited liability company, none of whose members or designated managers are personally liable for any debts of the company, is classified for federal tax purposes as an association or as a partnership.

FACTS

M was organized as a limited liability company pursuant to the provisions of the Wyoming Limited Liability Company Act (Act). The purpose of M is to acquire, own, and operate improved real property. M has 25 members, including A, B, and C.

The Act provides that a limited liability company may be managed by a designated manager or managers, or by its members. If the limited liability company is managed by its members, management authority is vested in its members in proportion to their capital contributions to the company. M is managed by its designated managers, A, B, and C.

Under the Act, neither the members nor the designated managers of a limited liability company are liable for any debts, obligations, or liabilities of the limited liability company.

The Act also provides that the interest of a member in a limited liability company is part of the personal estate of the member; however, each member can assign or transfer the member's respective interest in the limited liability company only upon the unanimous written consent of all the remaining members. In the event that the remaining members fail to approve the assignment or transfer, the assignee or transferee has no right to participate in the management or become a member of the limited liability company. However, the assignee or transferee is entitled to receive the share of profits or other compensation and the return of contributions to which the transferring member would otherwise be entitled.

A limited liability company formed under the Act is dissolved upon the occurrence of any of the following events: (1) when the period fixed for the duration of the company expires; (2) by the unanimous written consent of all the members; or (3) by the death, retirement, resignation, expulsion, bankruptcy, dissolution of a member or occurrence of any other event that terminates the continued membership of a member, unless the business of the company is continued by the consent of all the remaining members under a right to do so stated in the articles of organization of the company. Under M's articles of organization, the business of M is continued by the consent of all the remaining members.

LAW AND ANALYSIS

Section 7701(a)(2) of the Internal Revenue Code provides that the term "partnership" includes a syndicate, group, pool, venture, or other unincorporated organization, through or by means of which any business, financial operation, or venture is carried on, and which is not a trust or estate or a corporation.

Section 7701(a)(3) of the Code provides that the term "corporation" includes associations, joint-stock companies, and insurance companies.

Section 301.7701-1(b) of the Procedure and Administration Regulations states that the Code prescribes certain categories, or classes, into which various organizations fall for purposes of taxation. These categories, or classes, include associations (which are taxable as corporations), partnerships, and trusts. The tests, or standards, that are to be applied in determining the classification of an organization are set forth in sections 301.7701-2 through 301.7701-4.

Section 301.7701-2(a)(1) of the regulations sets forth the following basic characteristics of a corporation: (1) associates, (2) an objective to carry on business and divide the gains therefrom, (3) continuity of life, (4) centralization of management, (5) liability for corporate debts limited to corporate property, and (6) free transferability of interests. Whether a particular organization is to be classified as an association must be determined by taking into account the presence or absence of each of these corporate characteristics. In addition to the six major characteristics, other factors may be found in some cases which may be significant in classifying an organization as an association, a partnership, or a trust.

Section 301.7701–2(a)(2) of the regulations further provides that characteristics common to partnerships and corporations are not material in attempting to distinguish between an association and a partnership. Since associates and an objective to carry on business and divide the gains therefrom are generally common to corporations and partnerships, the determination of whether an organization which has such characteristics is to be treated for tax purposes as a partnership or as an association depends on whether there exists centralization of management, continuity of life, free transferability of interests, and limited liability.

Section 301.7701–2(a)(3) of the regulations provides that if an unincorporated organization possesses more corporate characteristics than noncorporate characteristics, it constitutes an association taxable as a corporation.

In interpreting section 301.7701–2 of the regulations, the Tax Court, in Larson v. Commissioner, 66 TC 159 (1976), acq., 1979–1 CB 1, concluded that equal weight must be given to each of the four corporate characteristics of continuity of life, centralization of management, limited liability, and free transferability of interests.

In the present situation, M has associates and an objective to carry on business and divide the gains therefrom. Therefore, M must be classified as either an association or a partnership. M is classified as a partnership for federal tax purposes unless the organization has a preponderance of the remaining corporate characteristics of continuity of life, centralization of management, limited liability, and free transferability of interests.

Section 301.7701–2(b)(1) of the regulations provides that if the death, insanity, bankruptcy, retirement, resignation, or expulsion of any member will cause a dissolution of the organization, continuity of life does not exist. Section 301.7701–2(b)(2) provides that an agreement by which an organization is established may provide that the business will be continued by the remaining members in the event of the death or withdrawal of any member, but such agreement does not establish continuity of life if under local law the death or withdrawal of any member causes a dissolution of the organization.

Under the Act, unless the business of M is continued by the consent of all the remaining members, M is dissolved upon the death, retirement, resignation, expulsion, bankruptcy, dissolution of a member or occurrence of any other event that terminates the continued membership of a member in the company. If a member of M ceases to be a member of M for any reason, the continuity of M's not assured, because all remaining members must agree to continue the business. Consequently, M lacks the corporate characteristic of continuity of life.

Under section 301.7701–2(c)(1) of the regulations an organization has the corporate characteristic of centralized management if any person (or group of persons that does not include all the members) has continuing exclusive authority to make management decisions necessary to the conduct of the business for which the organization was formed.

Under the Act, a limited liability company has the discretion to be managed either by a designated manager or managers, or to be managed by its members. Because M is managed by its designated managers, A, B, and C, M possesses the corporate characteristic of centralized management.

Section 301.7701–2(d)(1) of the regulations provides that an organization has the corporate characteristic of limited liability if under local law there is no member who is personally liable for the debts of, or claims against, the organization. Personal liability means that a creditor of an organization may seek personal satisfaction from a member of the organization to the extent that the assets of such organization are insufficient to satisfy the creditor's claim.

Under the Act, neither the managers nor the members of M are personally liable for its debts and obligations. Consequently, M possesses the corporate characteristic of limited liability.

Under section 301.7701–2(e)(1) of the regulations, an organization has the corporate characteristic of free transferability of interests if each of the members or those members owning substantially all of the interests in the organization have the power, without the consent of other members, to substitute for themselves in the same organization a person who is not a member of the organization. In order for this power of substitution to exist in the corporate sense, the member must be able, without the consent of other members, to confer upon the member's substitute all the attributes of the member's interest in the organization. The characteristic of free transferability does not exist if each member can, without the consent of the other members, assign only the right to share in the profits but cannot assign the right to participate in the management of the organization.

Under the Act, neither the managers nor the members of M are personally liable for its debts and obligations. Consequently, M possesses the corporate characteristic of limited liability.

Under section 301.7701–2(e)(1) of the regulations, an organization has the corporate characteristic of free transferability of interests if each of the members or those members owning substantially all of the interests in the organization have the power, without the consent of other members, to substitute for themselves in the same organization a person who is not a member of the organization. In order for this power of substitution to exist in the corporate sense, the member must be able, without the consent of other members, to confer upon the member's substitute all the attributes of the member's interest in the organization. The characteristic of free transferability does not exist if each member can, without the consent of the other members, assign only the right to share in the profits but cannot assign the right to participate in the management of the organization.

Under the terms of the Act, a member of M can assign or transfer that member's interest to another who is not a member of the organization. However, the assignee or transferee does not become a substitute member and does not acquire all the attributes of the member's interest in M unless all the remaining members approve the assignment or transfer. Therefore, M lacks the corporate characteristic of free transferability of interests.

M has associates and an objective to carry on business and divide the gains therefrom. In addition, M possesses the corporate characteristic of centralized management and limited liability. M does not, however, possess the corporate characteristics of continuity of life and free transferability of interests.

HOLDING

M has associates and an objective to carry on business and divide the gains therefrom, but lacks a preponderance of the four remaining corporate characteristics. Accordingly, M is classified as a partnership for federal tax purposes.

IRS "CHECK-THE-BOX" TAX CLASSIFICATION REGULATIONS

[deleted material not applicable to most LLC organizers is marked as " [...]".

26 CFR Sec. 301.7701-1 Classification of organizations for tax purposes.

(a) Organizations for federal tax purposes. (1) In general. The Internal Revenue Code prescribes the classification of various organizations for federal tax purposes. Whether an organization is an entity separate from its owners for federal tax purposes is a matter of federal tax law and does not depend on whether the organization is recognized as an entity under local law.

(2) Certain joint undertakings give rise to entities for federal tax purposes. A joint venture or other contractual arrangement may create a separate entity for federal tax purposes if the participants carry on a trade, business, financial operation, or venture and divide the profits therefrom. For example, a separate entity exists for federal tax purposes if co-owners of an apartment building lease space and in addition provide services to the occupants either directly or through an agent. Nevertheless, a joint undertaking merely to share expenses does not create a separate entity for federal tax purposes. For example, if two or more persons jointly construct a ditch merely to drain surface water from their properties, they have not created a separate entity for federal tax purposes. Similarly, mere co-ownership of property that is maintained, kept in repair, and rented or leased does not constitute a separate entity for federal tax purposes. For example, if an individual owner, or tenants in common, of farm property lease it to a farmer for a cash rental or a share of the crops, they do not necessarily create a separate entity for federal tax purposes.

(3) Certain local law entities not recognized. An entity formed under local law is not always recognized as a separate entity for federal tax purposes. For example, an organization wholly owned by a State is not recognized as a separate entity for federal tax purposes if it is an integral part of the State. Similarly, tribes incorporated under section 17 of the Indian Reorganization Act of 1934, as amended, 25 U.S.C. 477, or under section 3 of the Oklahoma Indian Welfare Act, as amended, 25 U.S.C. 503, are not recognized as separate entities for federal tax purposes.

(4) Single owner organizations. Under §§ 301.7701-2 and 301.7701-3, certain organizations that have a single owner can choose to be recognized or disregarded as entities separate from their owners.

(b) Classification of organizations. The classification of organizations that are recognized as separate entities is determined under §§ 301.7701-2, 301.7701-3, and 301.7701-4 unless a provision of the Internal Revenue Code (such as section 860A addressing Real Estate Mortgage Investment Conduits (REMICs)) provides for special treatment of that organization. For the classification of organizations as trusts, see § 301.7701-4. That section provides that trusts generally do not have associates or an objective to carry on business for profit. Sections 301.7701-2 and 301.7701-3 provide rules for classifying organizations that are not classified as trusts.

(c) Qualified cost sharing arrangements. A qualified cost sharing arrangement that is described in § 1.482-7 of this chapter and any arrangement that is treated by the Commissioner as a qualified cost sharing arrangement under § 1.482-7 of this chapter is not recognized as a separate entity for purposes of the Internal Revenue Code. See § 1.482-7 of this chapter for the proper treatment of qualified cost sharing arrangements.

(d) Domestic and foreign entities. For purposes of this section and §§ 301.7701-2 and 301.7701-3, an entity is a domestic entity if it is created or organized in the United States or under the law of the United States or of any State; an entity is foreign if it is not domestic. See sections 7701(a)(4) and (a)(5).

(e) State. For purposes of this section and § 301.7701-2, the term State includes the District of Columbia.

(f) Effective date. The rules of this section are effective as of January 1,1997.

§ 301.7701-2 Business entities; definitions.

(a) Business entities. For purposes of this section and § 301.7701-3, a business entity is any entity recognized for federal tax purposes (including an entity with a single owner that may be disregarded as an entity separate from its owner under § 301.7701-3) that is not properly classified as a trust under § 301.7701-4 or otherwise subject to special treatment under the Internal Revenue Code. A business entity with two or more members is classified for federal tax purposes as either a corporation or a partnership. A business entity with only one owner is classified as a corporation or is disregarded; if the entity is disregarded, its activities are treated in the same manner as a sole proprietorship, branch, or division of the owner.

(b) Corporations. For federal tax purposes, the term corporation means —

(1) A business entity organized under a Federal or State statute, or under a statute of a federally recognized Indian tribe, if the statute describes or refers to the entity as incorporated or as a corporation, body corporate, or body politic;

(2) An association (as determined under § 301.7701-3);

(3) A business entity organized under a State statute, if the statute describes or refers to the entity as a joint-stock company or joint-stock association;

(4) An insurance company;

(5) A State-chartered business entity conducting banking activities, if any of its deposits are insured under the Federal Deposit Insurance Act, as amended, 12 U.S.C. 1811 et seq., or a similar federal statute;

(6) A business entity wholly owned by a State or any political subdivision thereof;

(7) A business entity that is taxable as a corporation under a provision of the Internal Revenue Code other than section 7701(a)(3); and

(8) Certain foreign entities — (i) In general. Except as provided in paragraphs (b)(8)(ii) and (d) of this section, the following business entities formed in the following jurisdictions:

[...]

(c) Other business entities. For federal tax purposes —

(1) The term partnership means a business entity that is not a corporation under paragraph (b) of this section and that has at least two members.

(2) Wholly owned entities — (i) In general. A business entity that has a single owner and is not a corporation under paragraph (b) of this section is disregarded as an entity separate from its owner.

(ii) Special rule for certain business entities. If the single owner of a business entity is a bank (as defined in section 581), then the special rules applicable to banks will continue to apply to the single owner as if the wholly owned entity were a separate entity.

(d) Special rule for certain foreign business entities — (1) In general. Except as provided in paragraph (d)(3) of this section, a foreign business entity described in paragraph (b)(8)(i) of this section will not be treated as a corporation under paragraph (b)(8)(i) of this section if —

(i) The entity was in existence on May 8, 1996;

(ii) The entity's classification was relevant (as defined in §301.7701-3(d)) on May 8, 1996;

(iii) No person (including the entity) for whom the entity's classification was relevant on May 8, 1996, treats the entity as a corporation for purposes of filing such person's federal income tax returns, information returns, and withholding documents for the taxable year including May 8, 1996;

(iv) Any change in the entity's claimed classification within the sixty months prior to May 8, 1996, occurred solely as a result of a change in the organizational documents of the entity, and the entity and all members of the entity recognized the federal tax consequences of any change in the entity's classification within the sixty months prior to May 8, 1996;

(v) A reasonable basis (within the meaning of section 6662) existed on May 8, 1996, for treating the entity as other than a corporation; and

(vi) Neither the entity nor any member was notified in writing on or before May 8, 1996, that the classification of the entity was under examination (in which case the entity's classification will be determined in the examination).

(2) Binding contract rule. If a foreign business entity described in paragraph (b)(8)(i) of this section is formed after May 8, 1996, pursuant to a written binding contract (including an accepted bid to develop a project) in effect on May 8, 1996, and all times thereafter, in which the parties agreed to engage (directly or indirectly) in an active and substantial business operation in the jurisdiction in which the entity is formed, paragraph (d)(1) of this section will be applied to that entity by substituting the date of the entity's formation for May 8, 1996.

(3) Termination of grandfather status — (i) In general. An entity that is not treated as a corporation under paragraph (b)(8)(i) of this section by reason of paragraph (d)(1) or (d)(2) of this section will be treated permanently as a corporation under paragraph (b)(8)(i) of this section from the earliest of:

(A) The effective date of an election to be treated as an association under § 301.7701-3;

(B) A termination of the partnership under section 708(b)(1)(B) (regarding sale or exchange of 50 percent or more of the total interest in an entity's capital or profits within a twelve month period); or

(C) A division of the partnership under section 708(b)(2)(B).

(ii) Special rule for certain entities. For purposes of paragraph (d)(2) of this section, paragraph (d)(3)(i)(B) of this section shall not apply if the sale or exchange of interests in the entity is to a related person (within the meaning of sections 267(b) and 707(b)) and occurs no later than twelve months after the date of the formation of the entity.

(e) Effective date. The rules of this section are effective as of January 1,1997.

§ 301.7701-3 Classification of certain business entities.

(a) In general. A business entity that is not classified as a corporation under § 301.7701-2(b) (1), (3), (4), (5), (6), (7), or (8) (an eligible entity) can elect its classification for federal tax purposes as provided in this section. An eligible entity with at least two members can elect to be classified as either an association (and thus a corporation under § 301.7701-2(b)(2)) or a partnership, and an eligible entity with a single owner can elect to be classified as an association or to be disregarded as an entity separate from its owner. Paragraph (b) of this section provides a default classification for an eligible entity that does not make an election. Thus, elections are necessary only when an eligible entity chooses to be classified initially as other than the default classification or when an eligible entity chooses to change its classification. An entity whose classification is determined under the default classification retains that classification (regardless of any changes in the members' liability that occurs at any time during the time that the entity's classification is relevant as defined in paragraph (d) of this section) until the entity makes an election to change that classification under paragraph (c)(1) of this section. Paragraph (c) of this section provides rules for making express elections. Paragraph (d) of this section provides special rules for foreign eligible entities. Paragraph (e) of this section provides special rules for classifying entities resulting from partnership terminations and divisions under section 708(b). Paragraph (f) of this section sets forth the effective date of this section and a special rule relating to prior periods.

(b) Classification of eligible entities that do not file an election

(1) Domestic eligible entities. Except as provided in paragraph (b)(3) of this section, unless the entity elects otherwise, a domestic eligible entity is —

(i) A partnership if it has two or more members; or

(ii) Disregarded as an entity separate from its owner if it has a single owner.

(2) Foreign eligible entities — (i) In general. Except as provided in paragraph (b)(3) of this section, unless the entity elects otherwise, a foreign eligible entity is —

(A) A partnership if it has two or more members and at least one member does not have limited liability;

(B) An association if all members have limited liability; or

(C) Disregarded as an entity separate from its owner if it has a single owner that does not have limited liability.

(ii) Definition of limited liability. For purposes of paragraph (b)(2)(i) of this section, a member of a foreign eligible entity has limited liability if the member has no personal liability for the debts of or claims against the entity by reason of being a member. This determination is based solely on the statute or law pursuant to which the entity is organized, except that if the underlying statute or law allows the entity to specify in its organizational documents whether the members will have limited liability, the organizational documents may also be relevant. For purposes of this section, a member has personal liability if the creditors of the entity may seek satisfaction of all or any portion of the debts or claims against the entity from the member as such. A member has personal liability for purposes of this paragraph even if the member makes an agreement under which another person (whether or not a member of the entity) assumes such liability or agrees to indemnify that member for any such liability.

(3) Existing eligible entities — (i) In general. Unless the entity elects otherwise, an eligible entity in existence prior to the effective date of this section will have the same classification that the entity claimed under §§ 301.7701-1 through 301.7701-3 as in effect on the date prior to the effective date of this section; except that if an eligible entity with a single owner claimed to be a partnership under those regulations, the entity will be disregarded as an entity separate from its owner under this paragraph (b)(3)(i). For special rules regarding the classification of such entities

for periods prior to the effective date of this section, see paragraph (f)(2) of this section.

(ii) Special rules. For purposes of paragraph (b)(3)(i) of this section, a foreign eligible entity is treated as being in existence prior to the effective date of this section only if the entity's classification was relevant (as defined in paragraph (d) of this section) at any time during the sixty months prior to the effective date of this section. If an entity claimed different classifications prior to the effective date of this section, the entity's classification for purposes of paragraph (b)(3)(i) of this section is the last classification claimed by the entity. If a foreign eligible entity's classification is relevant prior to the effective date of this section, but no federal tax or information return is filed or the federal tax or information return does not indicate the classification of the entity, the entity's classification for the period prior to the effective date of this section is determined under the regulations in effect on the date prior to the effective date of this section.

(c) Elections — (1) Time and place for filing — (i) In general. Except as provided in paragraphs (c)(1) (iv) and (v) of this section, an eligible entity may elect to be classified other than as provided under paragraph (b) of this section, or to change its classification, by filing Form 8832, Entity Classification Election, with the service center designated on Form 8832. An election will not be accepted unless all of the information required by the form and instructions, including the taxpayer identifying number of the entity, is provided on Form 8832. See § 301.6109-1 for rules on applying for and displaying Employer Identification Numbers.

(ii) Further notification of elections. An eligible entity required to file a federal tax or information return for the taxable year for which an election is made under paragraph (c)(1)(i) of this section must attach a copy of its Form 8832 to its federal tax or information return for that year. If the entity is not required to file a return for that year, a copy of its Form 8832 must be attached to the federal income tax or information return of any direct or indirect owner of the entity for the taxable year of the owner that includes the date on which the election was effective. An indirect owner of the entity does not have to attach a copy of the Form 8832 to its return if an entity in which it has an interest is already filing a copy of the Form 8832 with its return. If an entity, or one of its direct or indirect owners, fails to attach a copy of a Form 8832 to its return as directed in this section, an otherwise valid election under paragraph (c)(1)(i) of this section will not be invalidated, but the non-filing party may be subject to penalties, including any applicable penalties if the federal tax or information returns are inconsistent with the entity's election under paragraph (c)(1)(i) of this section.

(iii) Effective date of election. An election made under paragraph (c)(1)(i) of this section will be effective on the date specified by the entity on Form 8832 or on the date filed if no such date is specified on the election form. The effective date specified on Form 8832 can not be more than 75 days prior to the date on which the election is filed and can not be more than 12 months after the date on which the election is filed. If an election specifies an effective date more than 75 days prior to the date on which the election is filed, it will be effective 75 days prior to the date it was filed. If an election specifies an effective date more than 12 months from the date on which the election is filed, it will be effective 12 months after the date it was filed. If an election specifies an effective date before January 1, 1997, it will be effective as of January 1, 1997.

(iv) Limitation. If an eligible entity makes an election under paragraph (c)(1)(i) of this section to change its classification (other than an election made by an existing entity to change its classification as of the effective date of this section), the entity cannot change its classification by election again during the sixty months succeeding the effective date of the election. However, the Commissioner may permit the entity to change its classification by election within the sixty months if more than fifty percent of the ownership interests in the entity as of the effective date of the subsequent election are owned by persons that did not own any interests in the entity on the filing date or on the effective date of the entity's prior election.

(v) Deemed elections — (A) Exempt organizations. An eligible entity that has been determined to be, or claims to be, exempt from taxation under section 501(a) is treated as having made an election under this section to be classified as an association. Such election will be effective as of the first day for which exemption is claimed or determined to apply, regardless of when the claim or determination is made, and will remain in effect unless an election is made under paragraph (c)(1)(i) of this section after the date the claim for exempt status is withdrawn or rejected or the date the determination of exempt status is revoked.

(B) Real estate investment trusts. An eligible entity that files an election under section 856(c)(1) to be treated as a real estate investment trust is treated as having made an election under this section to be classified as an association. Such election will be effective as of the first day the entity is treated as a real estate investment trust.

(vi) Examples. The following examples illustrate the rules of this paragraph (c)(1):

Example 1. On July 1, 1998, X, a domestic corporation, purchases a 10% interest in Y, an eligible entity formed under Country A law in 1990. The entity's classification was not relevant to any person for federal tax or information purposes prior to X's acquisition of an interest in Y. Thus, Y is not considered to be in existence on the effective date of this section for purposes of paragraph (b)(3) of this section. Under the applicable Country A statute, all members of Y have limited liability as defined in paragraph (b)(2)(ii) of this section. Accordingly, Y is classified as an association under paragraph (b)(2)(i)(B) of this section unless it elects under this paragraph (c) to be classified as a partnership. To be classified as a partnership as of July 1, 1998, Y must file a Form 8832 by September 13, 1998. See paragraph (c)(1)(i) of this section. Because an election cannot be effective more than 75 days prior to the date on which it is filed, if Y files its Form 8832 after September 13, 1998, it will be classified as an association from July 1, 1998, until the effective date of the election. In that case, it could not change its classification by election under this paragraph (c) during the sixty months succeeding the effective date of the election.

Example 2. (i) Z is an eligible entity formed under Country B law and is in existence on the effective date of this section within the meaning of paragraph (b)(3) of this section. Prior to the effective date of this section, Z claimed to be classified as an association. Unless Z files an election under this paragraph (c), it will continue to be classified as an association under paragraph (b)(3) of this section.

(ii) Z files a Form 8832 pursuant to this paragraph (c) to be classified as a partnership, effective as of the effective date of this section. Z can file an election to be classified as an association at any time thereafter, but then would not be permitted to change its classification by election during the sixty months succeeding the effective date of that subsequent election.

(2) Authorized signatures- (i) In general. An election made under paragraph (c)(1)(i) of this section must be signed by —

(A) Each member of the electing entity who is an owner at the time the election is filed; or

(B) Any officer, manager, or member of the electing entity who is authorized (under local law or the entity's organizational documents) to make the election and who represents to having such authorization under penalties of perjury.

(ii) Retroactive elections. For purposes of paragraph (c)(2)(i) of this section, if an election under paragraph (c)(1)(i) of this section is to be effective for any period prior to the time that it is filed, each person who was an owner between the date the election is to be effective and the date the election is filed, and who is not an owner at the time the election is filed, must also sign the election.

(d) Special rules for foreign eligible entities — (1) For purposes of this section, a foreign eligible entity's classification is relevant when its classification affects the liability of any person for federal tax or information purposes. For example, a foreign entity's classification would be relevant if U.S. income was paid to the entity and the determination by the withholding agent of the amount to be withheld under chapter 3 of the Internal Revenue Code (if any) would vary depending upon whether the entity is classified as a partnership or as an association. Thus, the classification might affect the documentation that the withholding agent must receive from the entity, the type of tax or information return to file, or how the return must be prepared. The date that the classification of a foreign eligible entity is relevant is the date an event occurs that creates an obligation to file a federal tax return, information return, or statement for which the classification of the entity must be determined. Thus, the classification of a foreign entity is relevant, for example, on the date that an interest in the entity is acquired which will require a U.S. person to file an information return on Form 5471.

(2) Special rule when classification is no longer relevant. — If the classification of a foreign eligible entity which was previously relevant for federal tax purposes ceases to be relevant for sixty consecutive months, the entity's classification will initially be determined under the default classification when the classification of

the foreign eligible entity again becomes relevant. The date that the classification of a foreign entity ceases to be relevant is the date an event occurs that causes the classification to no longer be relevant, or, if no event occurs in a taxable year that causes the classification to be relevant, then the date is the first day of that taxable year.

(e) Coordination with section 708(b). Except as provided in § 301.7701-2(d)(3) (regarding termination of grandfather status for certain foreign business entities), an entity resulting from a transaction described in section 708(b)(1)(B) (partnership termination due to sales or exchanges) or section 708(b)(2)(B) (partnership division) is a partnership.

(f) Effective date — (1) In general. The rules of this section are effective as of January 1, 1997.

(2) Prior treatment of existing entities. In the case of a business entity that is not described in § 301.7701-2(b) (1), (3), (4), (5), (6), or (7), and that was in existence prior to January 1, 1997, the entity's claimed classification(s) will be respected for all periods prior to January 1, 1997, if

(i) The entity had a reasonable basis (within the meaning of section 6662) for its claimed classification;

(ii) The entity and all members of the entity recognized the federal tax consequences of any change in the entity's classification within the sixty months prior to January 1, 1997; and

(iii) Neither the entity nor any member was notified in writing on or before May 8, 1996, that the classification of the entity was under examination (in which case the entity's classification will be determined in the examination).

How to Use the CD-ROM

The tear-out forms in Appendix D are included on a CD-ROM in the back of the book. This CD-ROM, which can be used with Windows computers, installs files that can be opened, printed and edited using a word processor or other software. It is *not* a stand-alone software program. Please read this Appendix and the README.TXT file included on the CD-ROM for instructions on using the forms CD.

Note to Mac users: This CD-ROM and its files should also work on Macintosh computers. Please note, however, that Nolo cannot provide technical support for non-Windows users.

HOW TO VIEW THE README FILE

If you do not know how to view the file README.TXT, insert the forms CD-ROM into your computer's CD-ROM drive and follow these instructions:

- Windows 9x, 2000, Me and XP: (1) On your PC's desktop, double-click the My Computer icon; (2) double-click the icon for the CD-ROM drive into which the forms CD-ROM was inserted; (3) double-click the file README.TXT.
- Macintosh: (1) On your Mac desktop, double-click the icon for the CD-ROM that you inserted; (2) double-click on the file README.TXT.

While the README file is open, print it out by using the Print command in the File menu.

Two different kinds of forms are contained on the CD-ROM:

- Word processing (RTF) forms that you can open, complete, print and save with your word processing program (see Section B, below), and

- Forms from IRS (PDF) that can be viewed only with Adobe Acrobat Reader 4.0 or higher. You can install Acrobat Reader from the Forms CD (see Section C below). Some of these forms have "fill-in" text fields, and can be completed using your computer. You will not, however, be able to save the completed forms with the filled-in data. PDF forms without fill-in text fields must be printed out and filled in by hand or with a typewriter.

See Appendix D for a list of forms, their file names and file formats.

A. Installing the Form Files Onto Your Computer

Before you can do anything with the files on the CD-ROM, you need to install them onto your hard disk. In accordance with U.S. copyright laws, remember that copies of the CD-ROM and its files are for your personal use only.

Insert the Forms CD and do the following:

1. Windows 9x, 2000, Me and XP Users

Follow the instructions that appear on the screen. (If nothing happens when you insert the forms CD-ROM, then (1) double-click the My Computer icon; (2) double-click the icon for the CD-ROM drive into which the forms CD-ROM was inserted; and (3) double click the file WELCOME.EXE.)

By default, all the files are installed to the \LLC Forms folder in the \Program Files folder of your computer. A folder called "LLC Forms" is added to the "Programs" folder of the Start menu.

2. Macintosh Users

Step 1: If the "LLC Forms CD" window is not open, open it by double-clicking the "LLC Forms CD" icon.

Step 2: Select the "LLC Forms" folder icon.

Step 3: Drag and drop the folder icon onto the icon of your hard disk.

B. Using the Word Processing Files to Create Documents

This section concerns the files for forms that can be opened and edited with your word processing program.

All word processing forms come in rich text format. These files have the extension ".RTF." For example, the LLC Filing Office Contact Letter discussed in Chapter 4 is on the file CONTACT.RTF. All forms, their file names and file formats are listed in Appendix D.

RTF files can be read by most recent word processing programs including all versions of MS Word for Windows and Macintosh, WordPad for Windows, and recent versions of WordPerfect for Windows and Macintosh.

To use a form from the CD to create your documents you must: (1) open a file in your word processor or text editor; (2) edit the form by filling in the required information; (3) print it out; (4) rename and save your revised file.

The following are general instructions on how to do this. However, each word processor uses different commands to open, format, save and print documents. Please read your word processor's manual for specific instructions on performing these tasks.

Do not call Nolo's Technical support if you have questions on how to use your word processor.

Step 1: Opening a File

There are three ways to open the word processing files included on the CD-ROM after you have installed them onto your computer.

- Windows users can open a file by selecting its "shortcut" as follows: (1) Click the Windows "Start" button; (2) open the "Programs" folder; (3) open the "LLC Forms" subfolder; (4) open the "RTF" subfolder; and (5) click on the shortcut to the form you want to work with.
- Both Windows and Macintosh users can open a file directly by double-clicking on it. Use My Computer or Windows Explorer (Windows 9x, 2000, Me or XP) or the Finder (Macintosh) to go to the folder you installed or copied the CD-ROM's files to. Then, double-click on the specific file you want to open.
- You can also open a file from within your word processor. To do this, you must first start your word processor. Then, go to the File menu and choose the Open command. This opens a dialog box where you will tell the program (1) the type of file you want to open (*.RTF); and (2) the location and name of the file (you will need to navigate through the directory tree to get to the folder on your hard disk where the CD's files have been installed). If these directions are unclear you will need to look through the manual for your word processing program—Nolo's technical support department will *not* be able to help you with the use of your word processing program.

WHERE ARE THE FILES INSTALLED?

Windows Users
- RTF files are installed by default to a folder named \LLC Forms in the \Program Files folder of your computer.

Macintosh Users
- RTF files are located in the "RTF" folder within the "LLC Forms" folder.

Step 2: Editing Your Document

Fill in the appropriate information according to the instructions and sample agreements in the book. Underlines are used to indicate where you need to enter your information, frequently followed by instructions in brackets. *Be sure to delete the underlines and instructions from your edited document.* If you do not know how to use your word processor to edit a document, you will need to look through the manual for your word processing program—Nolo's technical support department will *not* be able to help you with the use of your word processing program.

**EDITING FORMS THAT HAVE OPTIONAL
OR ALTERNATIVE TEXT**

Some of the forms have check boxes before text. The check boxes indicate:

- Optional text, where you choose whether to include or exclude the given text.
- Alternative text, where you select one alternative to include and exclude the other alternatives.

If you are using the tear-out forms in Appendix D, you simply mark the appropriate box to make your choice.

If you are using the forms CD, however, we recommend that instead of marking the check boxes, you do the following:

Optional text

If you **don't want** to include optional text, just delete it from your document.

If you **do want** to include optional text, just leave it in your document.

In either case, delete the check box itself as well as the italicized instructions that the text is optional.

Alternative text

First delete all the alternatives that you do not want to include.

Then delete the remaining check boxes, as well as the italicized instructions that you need to select one of the alternatives provided.

Step 3: Printing Out the Document

Use your word processor's or text editor's "Print" command to print out your document. If you do not know how to use your word processor to print a document, you will need to look through the manual for your word processing program—Nolo's technical support department will *not* be able to help you with the use of your word processing program.

Step 4: Saving Your Document

After filling in the form, use the "Save As" command to save and rename the file. Because all the files are "read-only" and you will not be able to use the "Save" command. This is for your protection. *If you save the file without renaming it, the underlines that indicate where you need to enter your information will be lost and you will not be able to create a new document with this file without recopying the original file from the CD-ROM.*

If you do not know how to use your word processor to save a document, you will need to look through the manual for your word processing program—Nolo's technical support department will *not* be able to help you with the use of your word processing program.

C. Using IRS Form 8832

An electronic copy of Form 8832 from the IRS is included on the CD-ROM in Adobe Acrobat PDF format. You must have the Adobe Acrobat Reader installed on your computer (see below) to use this form. All forms, their file names and file formats are listed in Appendix D. This form file was created by the IRS, not by Nolo.

Form 8832 has fill-in text fields. To create your document using this file, you must: (1) open the file; (2) fill in the text fields using either your mouse or the tab key on your keyboard to navigate from field to field; and (3) print it out.

Note: While you can print out your completed form, you will *not* be able to save your completed form to disk.

INSTALLING ACROBAT READER

To install the Adobe Acrobat Reader, insert the CD into your computer's CD-ROM drive and follow these instructions:

- Windows 9x, 2000, Me and XP: Follow the instructions that appear on screen. (If nothing happens when you insert the Forms CD-ROM, then (1) double-click the My Computer icon; (2) double-click the icon for the CD-ROM drive into which the Forms CD-ROM was inserted; and (3) double click the file WELCOME.EXE.)
- Macintosh: (1) If the "LLC Forms CD" window is not open, open it by double-clicking the "LLC Forms CD" icon; and (2) double-click on the "Acrobat Reader Installer" icon.

If you do not know how to use Adobe Acrobat Reader to view and print the files, you will need to consult the online documentation that comes with the Acrobat Reader program.

Do *not* call Nolo technical support if you have questions on how to use Acrobat Reader.

Step 1: Opening the IRS File

PDF files, like the word processing files, can be opened one of three ways.

- Windows users can open a file by selecting its "shortcut" as follows: (1) Click the Windows "Start" button; (2) open the "Programs" folder; (3) open the "LLC Forms" subfolder; and (4) click on the shortcut to the form you want to work with.
- Both Windows and Macintosh users can open a file directly by double-clicking on it. Use My Computer or Windows Explorer (Windows 9x, 2000, Me or XP) or the Finder (Macintosh) to go to the folder you created and copied the CD-ROM's files to. Then, double-click on the specific file you want to open.
- You can also open a PDF file from within Acrobat Reader. To do this, you must first start Reader. Then, go to the File menu and choose the Open command. This opens a dialog box

where you will tell the program the location and name of the file (you will need to navigate through the directory tree to get to the folder on your hard disk where the CD's files have been installed). If these directions are unclear, you will need to look through Acrobat Reader's help—Nolo's technical support department will *not* be able to help you with the use of Acrobat Reader.

Step 2: Filling in the IRS File

Use your mouse or the Tab key on your keyboard to navigate from field to field within this form. Be sure to have all the information you will need to complete the form on hand, because you will not be able to save a copy of the filled-in form to disk. You can, however, print out a completed version.

WHERE IS THE PDF FILE INSTALLED?

- Windows Users: Form 8832 is installed by default to a folder named \LLC Forms in the \Program Files folder of your computer.
- Macintosh Users: Form 8832 is located in the "LLC Forms" folder.

Step 3: Printing the IRS File

Choose Print from the Acrobat Reader File menu. This will open the Print dialog box. In the "Print Range" section of the Print dialog box, select the appropriate print range, then click OK.

GET THE FORM FROM THE NET

This form was current when this book went to press, but the IRS revises them from time to time. You can use the Internet to confirm that you're using the most current form, and you can download and print the form (hardware and software permitting) from www.irs.gov/pub. Check the revision data on the form's upper left and lower right corners.

Tear-Out LLC Forms

IRS FORM 8832, ENTITY CLASSIFICATION ELECTION

LLC CONTACT LETTER

RESERVATION OF LLC NAME LETTER

ARTICLES OF ORGANIZATION

ARTICLES FILING LETTER

OPERATING AGREEMENT FOR MEMBER-MANAGED LLC

LLC MANAGEMENT OPERATING AGREEMENT

MINUTES OF MEETING

CERTIFICATION OF AUTHORITY

Form **8832**
(Rev. September 2002)
Department of the Treasury
Internal Revenue Service

Entity Classification Election

OMB No. 1545-1516

Type or Print

Name of entity

EIN ▶

Number, street, and room or suite no. If a P.O. box, see instructions.

City or town, state, and ZIP code. If a foreign address, enter city, province or state, postal code and country.

1   Type of election (see instructions):

a ☐ Initial classification by a newly-formed entity.

b ☐ Change in current classification.

2   Form of entity (see instructions):

a ☐ A domestic eligible entity electing to be classified as an association taxable as a corporation.

b ☐ A domestic eligible entity electing to be classified as a partnership.

c ☐ A domestic eligible entity with a single owner electing to be disregarded as a separate entity.

d ☐ A foreign eligible entity electing to be classified as an association taxable as a corporation.

e ☐ A foreign eligible entity electing to be classified as a partnership.

f ☐ A foreign eligible entity with a single owner electing to be disregarded as a separate entity.

3   Disregarded entity information (see instructions):
a Name of owner ▶ ....
b Identifying number of owner ▶ ....
c Country of organization of entity electing to be disregarded (if foreign) ▶ ....

4 Election is to be effective beginning (month, day, year) (see instructions) . . . . ▶ ____ / ____ / ____

5 Name and title of person whom the IRS may call for more information

6 That person's telephone number

(   )

Consent Statement and Signature(s) (see instructions)

Under penalties of perjury, I (we) declare that I (we) consent to the election of the above-named entity to be classified as indicated above, and that I (we) have examined this consent statement, and to the best of my (our) knowledge and belief, it is true, correct, and complete. If I am an officer, manager, or member signing for all members of the entity, I further declare that I am authorized to execute this consent statement on their behalf.

Signature(s)	Date	Title

General Instructions

Section references are to the Internal Revenue Code unless otherwise noted.

Purpose of Form

For Federal tax purposes, certain business entities automatically are classified as corporations. See items **1** and **3** through **8** under the definition of **corporation** on this page. Other business entities may choose how they are classified for Federal tax purposes. Except for a business entity automatically classified as a corporation, a business entity with at least two members can choose to be classified as either an association taxable as a corporation or a partnership, and a business entity with a single member can choose to be classified as either an association taxable as a corporation or disregarded as an entity separate from its owner.

Generally, an eligible entity that does not file this form will be classified under the default rules described below. An eligible entity that chooses not to be classified under the default rules or that wishes to change its current classification must file Form 8832 to elect a classification. The IRS will use the information entered on this form to establish the entity's filing and reporting requirements for Federal tax purposes.

60-month limitation rule. Once an eligible entity makes an election to change its classification, the entity generally cannot change its classification by election again during the 60 months after the effective date of the election. However, the IRS may (**by private letter ruling**) permit the entity to change its classification by election within the 60-month period if more than 50% of the ownership interests in the entity as of the effective date of the election are owned by persons that did not own any interests in the entity on the effective date of the entity's prior election. See Regulations section 301.7701-3(c)(1)(iv) for more details.

Note: *The 60-month limitation does not apply if the previous election was made by a newly formed eligible entity and was effective on the date of formation.*

Default Rules

Existing entity default rule. Certain domestic and foreign entities that were in existence before January 1, 1997, and have an established Federal tax classification generally do not need to make an election to continue that classification. If an existing entity decides to change its classification, it may do so subject to the 60-month limitation rule. See Regulations sections 301.7701-3(b)(3) and 301.7701-3(h)(2) for more details.

Domestic default rule. Unless an election is made on Form 8832, a domestic eligible entity is:

1. A partnership if it has two or more members.

2. Disregarded as an entity separate from its owner if it has a single owner.

A change in the number of members of an eligible entity classified as an association does not affect the entity's classification. However, an eligible entity classified as a partnership will become a disregarded entity when the entity's membership is reduced to one member and a disregarded entity will be classified as a partnership when the entity has more than one member.

Foreign default rule. Unless an election is made on Form 8832, a foreign eligible entity is:

1. A partnership if it has two or more members and **at least** one member does not have limited liability.

2. An association taxable as a corporation if all members have limited liability.

3. Disregarded as an entity separate from its owner if it has a single owner that does not have limited liability.

Definitions

Association. For purposes of this form, an association is an eligible entity that is taxable as a corporation by election or, for foreign eligible entities, under the default rules (see Regulations section 301.7701-3).

Business entity. A business entity is any entity recognized for Federal tax purposes that is not properly classified as a trust under Regulations section 301.7701-4 or otherwise subject to special

treatment under the Code. See Regulations section 301.7701-2(a).

Corporation. For Federal tax purposes, a corporation is any of the following:

1. A business entity organized under a Federal or state statute, or under a statute of a federally recognized Indian tribe, if the statute describes or refers to the entity as incorporated or as a corporation, body corporate, or body politic.

2. An association (as determined under Regulations section 301.7701-3).

3. A business entity organized under a state statute, if the statute describes or refers to the entity as a joint-stock company or joint-stock association.

4. An insurance company.

5. A state-chartered business entity conducting banking activities, if any of its deposits are insured under the Federal Deposit Insurance Act, as amended, 12 U.S.C. 1811 et seq., or a similar Federal statute.

6. A business entity wholly owned by a state or any political subdivision thereof, or a business entity wholly owned by a foreign government or any other entity described in Regulations section 1.892-2T.

7. A business entity that is taxable as a corporation under a provision of the Code other than section 7701(a)(3).

8. A foreign business entity listed on page 5. See Regulations section 301.7701-2(b)(8) for any exceptions and inclusions to items on this list and for any revisions made to this list since these instructions were printed.

Disregarded entity. A disregarded entity is an eligible entity that is treated as an entity that is not separate from its single owner. Its separate existence will be ignored for Federal tax purposes unless it elects corporate tax treatment.

Eligible entity. An eligible entity is a business entity that is not included in items **1** or **3** through **8** under the definition of corporation above.

Limited liability. A member of a foreign eligible entity has limited liability if the member has no personal liability for any debts of or claims against the entity by reason of being a member. This determination is based solely on the statute or law under which the entity is organized (and, if relevant, the entity's organizational documents). A member has personal liability if the creditors of the entity may seek satisfaction of all or any part of the debts or claims against the entity from the member as such. A member has personal liability even if the member makes an agreement under which another person (whether or not a member of the entity) assumes that liability or agrees to indemnify that member for that liability.

Partnership. A partnership is a business entity that has **at least** two members and is not a corporation as defined on page 2.

Who Must File

File this form for an **eligible entity** that is one of the following:

● A domestic entity electing to be classified as an association taxable as a corporation.

● A domestic entity electing to change its current classification (even if it is currently classified under the default rule).

● A foreign entity that has more than one owner, all owners having limited liability, electing to be classified as a partnership.

● A foreign entity that has at least one owner that does not have limited liability, electing to be classified as an association taxable as a corporation.

● A foreign entity with a single owner having limited liability, electing to be an entity disregarded as an entity separate from its owner.

● A foreign entity electing to change its current classification (even if it is currently classified under the default rule).

   Do not file this form for an eligible entity that is:

● Tax-exempt under section 501(a) or

● A real estate investment trust (REIT), as defined in section 856.

Effect of Election

The Federal tax treatment of elective changes in classification as described in Regulations section 301.7701-3(g)(1) is summarized as follows:

● If an eligible entity classified as a partnership elects to be classified as an association, it is deemed that the partnership contributes all of its assets and liabilities to the association in exchange for stock in the association, and immediately thereafter, the partnership liquidates by distributing the stock of the association to its partners.

● If an eligible entity classified as an association elects to be classified as a partnership, it is deemed that the association distributes all of its assets and liabilities to its shareholders in liquidation of the association, and immediately thereafter, the shareholders contribute all of the distributed assets and liabilities to a newly formed partnership.

● If an eligible entity classified as an association elects to be disregarded as an entity separate from its owner, it is deemed that the association distributes all of its assets and liabilities to its single owner in liquidation of the association.

● If an eligible entity that is disregarded as an entity separate from its owner elects to be classified as an association, the owner of the eligible entity is deemed to have contributed all of the assets and liabilities of the entity to the association in exchange for the stock of the association.

Note: *For information on the Federal tax treatment of elective changes in classification, see Regulations section 301.7701-3(g).*

When To File

See the instructions for line 4.

A newly formed entity may be eligible for late election relief under Rev. Proc. 2002-59, 2002-39 I.R.B. 615 if:

● The entity failed to obtain its desired classified election solely because Form 8832 was not timely filed,

● The due date for the entity's desired classification tax return (excluding extension) for the tax year beginning with the entity's formation date has not passed, and

● The entity has reasonable cause for its failure to make a timely election.

   To obtain relief, a newly formed entity must file Form 8832 on or before the due date of the first Federal tax return (excluding extensions) of the entity's desired classification. The entity must also write "FILED PURSUANT TO REV. PROC. 2002-59" at the top of the form. The entity must attach a statement to the form explaining why it failed to file a timely election. If Rev. Proc. 2002-59 does not apply, an entity may seek relief for a late entity election by requesting a private letter ruling and paying a user fee in accordance with Rev. Proc. 2002-1, 2002-1 I.R.B. 1 (or its successor).

Where To File

File Form 8832 with the Internal Revenue Service Center, Philadelphia, PA 19255. Also attach a copy of Form 8832 to the entity's Federal income tax or information return for the tax year of the election. If the entity is not required to file a return for that year, a copy of its Form 8832 **must** be attached to the Federal income tax or information returns of **all** direct or indirect owners of the entity for the tax year of the owner that includes the date on which the election took effect. Although failure to attach a copy will not invalidate an otherwise valid election, each member of the entity is required to file returns that are consistent with the entity's election. In addition, penalties may be assessed against persons who are required to, but who do not, attach Form 8832 to their returns. Other penalties may apply for filing Federal income tax or information returns inconsistent with the entity's election.

Specific Instructions

Name. Enter the name of the eligible entity electing to be classified using Form 8832.

Employer identification number (EIN). Show the correct EIN of the eligible entity electing to be classified. Any entity that has an EIN will retain that EIN even if its Federal tax classification changes under Regulations section 301.7701-3.

   If a disregarded entity's classification changes so that it is recognized as a partnership or association for Federal tax purposes, and that entity had an EIN, then the entity must use that EIN and not the identifying number of the single owner. If the entity did not already have its own EIN, then the entity must apply for an EIN and not use the identifying number of the single owner.

A foreign person that makes an election under Regulations section 301.7701-3(c) must also use its own taxpayer identifying number. See sections 6721 through 6724 for penalties that may apply for failure to supply taxpayer identifying numbers.

If the entity electing to be classified using Form 8832 does not have an EIN, it must apply for one on **Form SS-4,** Application for Employer Identification Number. If the filing of Form 8832 is the only reason the entity is applying for an EIN, check the "Other" box on line 9 of Form SS-4 and write "Form 8832" to the right of that box. If the entity has not received an EIN by the time Form 8832 is due, write "Applied for" in the space for the EIN. **Do not** apply for a new EIN for an existing entity that is changing its classification if the entity already has an EIN.

Address. Enter the address of the entity electing a classification. Include the suite, room, or other unit number after the street address. If the Post Office does not deliver mail to the street address and the entity has a P.O. box, show the box number instead of the street address.

Line 1. Check box 1a if the entity is choosing a classification for the first time **and** the entity does not want to be classified under the applicable default classification. **Do not** file this form if the entity wants to be classified under the default rules.

Check box 1b if the entity is changing its current classification.

Line 2. Check the appropriate box if you are changing a current classification (no matter how achieved), or are electing out of a default classification. **Do not** file this form if you fall within a default classification that is the desired classification for the new entity.

Line 3. If an eligible entity has checked box 2c or box 2f and is electing to be disregarded as an entity separate from its owner, it must enter the name of its owner on line 3a and the owner's identifying number (social security number, or individual taxpayer identification number, or EIN) on line 3b. If the owner is a foreign person or entity and does not have a U.S. identifying number, enter "none" on line 3b. If the entity making the election is foreign, enter the name of the country in which it was formed on line 3c.

Line 4. Generally, the election will take effect on the date you enter on line 4 of this form or on the date filed if no date is entered on line 4. However, an election specifying an entity's classification for Federal tax purposes can take effect no more than 75 days prior to the date the election is filed, nor can it take effect later than 12 months after the date on which the election is filed. If line 4 shows a date more than 75 days prior to the date on which the election is filed, the election will take effect 75 days before the date it is filed. If line 4 shows an effective date more than 12 months from the filing date, the election will take effect 12 months after the date the election was filed.

Consent statement and signatures. Form 8832 must be signed by:

1. Each member of the electing entity who is an owner at the time the election is filed; or

2. Any officer, manager, or member of the electing entity who is authorized (under local law or the organizational documents) to make the election and who represents to having such authorization under penalties of perjury.

If an election is to be effective for any period prior to the time it is filed, each person who was an owner between the date the election is to be effective and the date the election is filed, and who is not an owner at the time the election is filed, must also sign.

If you need a continuation sheet or use a separate consent statement, attach it to Form 8832. The separate consent statement must contain the same information as shown on Form 8832.

Paperwork Reduction Act Notice

We ask for the information on this form to carry out the Internal Revenue laws of the United States. You are required to give us the information. We need it to ensure that you are complying with these laws and to allow us to figure and collect the right amount of tax.

You are not required to provide the information requested on a form that is subject to the Paperwork Reduction Act unless the form displays a valid OMB control number. Books or records relating to a form or its instructions must be retained as long as their contents may become material in the administration of any Internal Revenue law. Generally, tax returns and return information are confidential, as required by section 6103.

The time needed to complete and file this form will vary depending on individual circumstances. The estimated average time is:

Recordkeeping . . . 1 hr., 49 min.

Learning about the law or the form . . . 2 hr., 7 min.

Preparing and sending the form to the IRS . . . . 23 min.

If you have comments concerning the accuracy of these time estimates or suggestions for making this form simpler, we would be happy to hear from you. You can write to the Tax Forms Committee, Western Area Distribution Center, Rancho Cordova, CA 95743-0001. **Do not** send the form to this address. Instead, see **Where To File** on page 3.

LLC FILING OFFICE CONTACT LETTER

_____

_____

_____

_____

_____

LLC Filings Office:

I am in the process of forming a domestic limited liability company (LLC). Please note:

- ☐ I am _or_ ☐ I am not converting an existing _____ partnership to an LLC.
- ☐ I am _or_ ☐ I am not forming an LLC to perform the professional services of
_____ , which are licensed by the state.

Please send me the following forms, material and other information:

(1) printed, sample or specimen LLC Articles of Organization, with instructions. If your office reviews Articles of Organization for correctness prior to filing, please advise me of the procedure I should follow to obtain this pre-filing review;

(2) the telephone number or address I can contact to determine if a proposed limited liability company name is available for my use, plus any forms necessary to reserve an LLC name;

(3) a current schedule of fees for LLC filings;

(4) other LLC forms and publications provided by your office (or a list of these) that may be helpful in understanding the requirements for forming, operating and dissolving an LLC in this state; and

(5) the name and price of a publication that contains the limited liability company statutes of this state. Please indicate whether it may be ordered from your office or, if applicable, another office or supplier.

If there is a fee for any of the above materials, please advise. Enclosed is a self-addressed, stamped envelope for your reply.

Thank you for your assistance,

_____

_____

_____

_____

Enclosure: self-addressed, stamped envelope

LLC RESERVATION OF NAME LETTER

_____

_____

_____

_____

_____

LLC Filings Office:

Please reserve the following proposed limited liability company name for my use for the allowable period specified under state law:

_____

☐ If the above name is not available, please reserve the first available name from the following list of alternative names:

Second Choice: _____

Third Choice: _____

I enclose a check in payment of the reservation fee. Please send a certificate, receipt for payment, or other acknowledgment or approval of my reservation request to me at my address shown below.

Thank you for your assistance,

_____

_____

_____

_____

Enclosures: check for reservation fee; stamped, self-addressed envelope

ARTICLES OF ORGANIZATION
OF

_____

The undersigned natural person(s), of the age of eighteen years or more, acting as organizers of a limited liability company under the State of _____ Limited Liability Company Act, adopt(s) the following Articles of Organization for such limited liability company.

Article 1. Name of Limited Liability Company. The name of this limited liability company is

_____ .

Article 2. Registered Office and Registered Agent. The initial registered office of this limited liability company and the name of its initial registered agent at this address are:

_____

_____

_____ .

Article 3. Statement of Purposes. The purposes for which this limited liability company is organized are: _____

_____

_____

_____

_____

_____ .

Article 4. Management and Names and Addresses of Initial _____ .
The management of this limited liability company is reserved to the _____ .
The names and addresses of its initial _____ are:

_____

_____

_____

_____

_____

_____

Article 5. *Principal Place of Business of the Limited Liability Company.* The principal place of business of the limited liability company shall be: _____

_____ .

Article 6. *Period of Duration of the Limited Liability Company.* The period of duration of the limited liability company shall be: _____

_____ .

In Witness Whereof, the undersigned organizer(s) of this limited liability company has(have) signed these Articles of Organization on the date indicated.

Date: _____

Signature(s):

_____   _____
Organizer   Typed or Printed Name

_____   _____
Organizer   Typed or Printed Name

_____   _____
Organizer   Typed or Printed Name

_____   _____
Organizer   Typed or Printed Name

_____   _____
Organizer   Typed or Printed Name

_____   _____
Organizer   Typed or Printed Name

LLC ARTICLES FILING LETTER

_____

_____

_____

_____

_____

LLC Filings Office:

I enclose an original and _____ copies of the proposed Articles of Organization of

_____ ,

a proposed domestic limited liability company. Please file the Articles of Organization and

return a file-stamped copy of the original Articles or other receipt, acknowledgment or proof of

filing to me at the address below.

A check/money order in the amount of $ _____ , made payable to your office,

for total filing and processing fees is enclosed.

☐ The above LLC name was reserved for my use _____

_____ ,

issued on _____ .

Sincerely,

_____

_____ , Organizer

_____

_____

_____

Enclosures: Articles of Organization; check

OPERATING AGREEMENT FOR
MEMBER-MANAGED LIMITED LIABILITY COMPANY

I. PRELIMINARY PROVISIONS

(1) Effective Date: This operating agreement of _____

_____ ,

effective_____ , is adopted by the members
whose signatures appear at the end of this agreement.

(2) Formation: This limited liability company (LLC) was formed by filing Articles of
Organization, a Certificate of Formation or a similar organizational document with the LLC
filing office of the state of _____
on_____ .
A copy of this organizational document has been placed in the LLC's records book.

(3) Name: The formal name of this LLC is as stated above. However, this LLC may do
business under a different name by complying with the state's fictitious or assumed business
name statutes and procedures.

(4) Registered Office and Agent: The registered office of this LLC and the registered agent
at this address are as follows: _____

_____ .

The registered office and agent may be changed from time to time as the members may see fit,
by filing a change of registered agent or office form with the state LLC filing office. It will not
be necessary to amend this provision of the operating agreement if and when such a change
is made.

(5) Business Purposes: The specific business purposes and activities contemplated by the
founders of this LLC at the time of initial signing of this agreement consist of the following:

_____

_____

_____ .

It is understood that the foregoing statement of purposes shall not serve as a limitation on
the powers or abilities of this LLC, which shall be permitted to engage in any and all lawful
business activities. If this LLC intends to engage in business activities outside the state of its
formation that require the qualification of the LLC in other states, it shall obtain such
qualification before engaging in such out-of-state activities.

(6) Duration of LLC: The duration of this LLC shall be _____

_____ .

Further, this LLC shall terminate when a proposal to dissolve the LLC is adopted by the
membership of this LLC or when this LLC is otherwise terminated in accordance with law.

II. MEMBERSHIP PROVISIONS

(1) Nonliability of Members: No member of this LLC shall be personally liable for the
expenses, debts, obligations or liabilities of the LLC, or for claims made against it.

(2) Reimbursement for Organizational Costs: Members shall be reimbursed by the LLC for organizational expenses paid by the members. The LLC shall be authorized to elect to deduct organizational expenses and start-up expenditures ratably over a period of time as permitted by the Internal Revenue Code and as may be advised by the LLC's tax advisor.

(3) Management: This LLC shall be managed exclusively by all of its members.

(4) Members' Percentage Interests: A member's percentage interest in this LLC shall be computed as a fraction, the numerator of which is the total of a member's capital account and the denominator of which is the total of all capital accounts of all members. This fraction shall be expressed in this agreement as a percentage, which shall be called each member's "percentage interest" in this LLC.

(5) Membership Voting: Except as otherwise may be required by the Articles of Organization, Certificate of Formation or a similar organizational document, other provisions of this operating agreement, or under the laws of this state, each member shall vote on any matter submitted to the membership for approval in proportion to the member's percentage interest in this LLC. Further, unless defined otherwise for a particular provision of this operating agreement, the phrase "majority of members" means the vote of members whose combined votes equal more than 50% of the votes of all members in this LLC.

(6) Compensation: Members shall not be paid as members of the LLC for performing any duties associated with such membership, including management of the LLC. Members may be paid, however, for any services rendered in any other capacity for the LLC, whether as officers, employees, independent contractors or otherwise.

(7) Members' Meetings: The LLC shall not provide for regular members' meetings. However, any member may call a meeting by communicating his or her wish to schedule a meeting to all other members. Such notification may be in person or in writing, or by telephone, facsimile machine, or other form of electronic communication reasonably expected to be received by a member, and the other members shall then agree, either personally, in writing, or by telephone, facsimile machine or other form of electronic communication to the member calling the meeting, to meet at a mutually acceptable time and place. Notice of the business to be transacted at the meeting need not be given to members by the member calling the meeting, and any business may be discussed and conducted at the meeting.

If all members cannot attend a meeting, it shall be postponed to a date and time when all members can attend, unless all members who do not attend have agreed in writing to the holding of the meeting without them. If a meeting is postponed, and the postponed meeting cannot be held either because all members do not attend the postponed meeting or the nonattending members have not signed a written consent to allow the postponed meeting to be held without them, a second postponed meeting may be held at a date and time announced at the first postponed meeting. The date and time of the second postponed meeting shall also be communicated to any members not attending the first postponed meeting. The second postponed meeting may be held without the attendance of all members as long as a majority of the percentage interests of the membership of this LLC is in attendance at the second postponed meeting. Written notice of the decisions or approvals made at this second postponed meeting shall be mailed or delivered to each nonattending member promptly after the holding of the second postponed meeting.

Written minutes of the discussions and proposals presented at a members' meeting, and the votes taken and matters approved at such meeting, shall be taken by one of the members or a person designated at the meeting. A copy of the minutes of the meeting shall be placed in the LLC's records book after the meeting.

(8) Membership Certificates: This LLC shall be authorized to obtain and issue certificates representing or certifying membership interests in this LLC. Each certificate shall show the name of the LLC, the name of the member, and state that the person named is a member of the LLC and is entitled to all the rights granted members of the LLC under the Articles of Organization, Certificate of Formation or a similar organizational document, this operating agreement and provisions of law. Each membership certificate shall be consecutively numbered and signed by one or more officers of this LLC. The certificates shall include any additional information considered appropriate for inclusion by the members on membership certificates.

In addition to the above information, all membership certificates shall bear a prominent legend on their face or reverse side stating, summarizing or referring to any transfer restrictions that apply to memberships in this LLC under the Articles of Organization, Certificate of Formation or a similar organizational document and/or this operating agreement, and the address where a member may obtain a copy of these restrictions upon request from this LLC.

The records book of this LLC shall contain a list of the names and addresses of all persons to whom certificates have been issued, show the date of issuance of each certificate, and record the date of all cancellations or transfers of membership certificates.

(9) Other Business by Members: Each member shall agree not to own an interest in, manage or work for another business, enterprise or endeavor, if such ownership or activities would compete with this LLC's business goals, mission, profitability or productivity, or would diminish or impair the member's ability to provide maximum effort and performance in managing the business of this LLC.

III. TAX AND FINANCIAL PROVISIONS

(1) Tax Classification of LLC: The members of this LLC intend that this LLC be initially classified as a _____ for federal and, if applicable, state income tax purposes. It is understood that all members may agree to change the tax treatment of this LLC by signing, or authorizing the signature of, IRS Form 8832, Entity Classification Election, and filing it with the IRS and, if applicable, the state tax department within the prescribed time limits.

(2) Tax Year and Accounting Method: The tax year of this LLC shall be
_____. The LLC shall use the
_____ method of accounting. Both the tax year and the accounting period
of the LLC may be changed with the consent of all members if the LLC qualifies for such
change, and may be effected by the filing of appropriate forms with the IRS and state tax
authorities.

(3) Tax Matters Partner: If this LLC is required under Internal Revenue Code provisions or
regulations, it shall designate from among its members a "tax matters partner" in accordance
with Internal Revenue Code Section 6231(a)(7) and corresponding regulations, who will fulfill
this role by being the spokesperson for the LLC in dealings with the IRS as required under the
Internal Revenue Code and Regulations, and who will report to the members on the progress
and outcome of these dealings.

(4) Annual Income Tax Returns and Reports: Within 60 days after the end of each tax year
of the LLC, a copy of the LLC's state and federal income tax returns for the preceding tax year
shall be mailed or otherwise provided to each member of the LLC, together with any additional
information and forms necessary for each member to complete his or her individual state and
federal income tax returns. If this LLC is classified as a partnership for income tax purposes,
this additional information shall include a federal (and, if applicable, state) Form K-1 (Form
1065—Partner's Share of Income, Credits, Deductions) or equivalent income tax reporting
form. This additional information shall also include a financial report, which shall include a
balance sheet and profit and loss statement for the prior tax year of the LLC.

(5) Bank Accounts: The LLC shall designate one or more banks or other institutions for the
deposit of the funds of the LLC, and shall establish savings, checking, investment and other
such accounts as are reasonable and necessary for its business and investments. One or more
members of the LLC shall be designated with the consent of all members to deposit and
withdraw funds of the LLC, and to direct the investment of funds from, into and among such
accounts. The funds of the LLC, however and wherever deposited or invested, shall not be
commingled with the personal funds of any members of the LLC.

(6) Title to Assets: All personal and real property of this LLC shall be held in the name of
the LLC, not in the names of individual members.

IV. CAPITAL PROVISIONS

(1) Capital Contributions by Members: Members shall make the following contributions of
cash, property or services as shown next to each member's name below. Unless otherwise
noted, cash and property described below shall be paid or delivered to the LLC on or by
_____ . The fair market values
of items of property or services as agreed between the LLC and the contributing member are

also shown below. The percentage interest in the LLC that each member shall receive in return for his or her capital contribution is also indicated for each member.

Name	Contribution	Fair Market Value	Percentage Interest in LLC
_____	_____	$ _____	_____
_____	_____	$ _____	_____
_____	_____	$ _____	_____
_____	_____	$ _____	_____
_____	_____	$ _____	_____
_____	_____	$ _____	_____

(2) Additional Contributions by Members: The members may agree, from time to time by unanimous vote, to require the payment of additional capital contributions by the members, on or by a mutually agreeable date.

(3) Failure to Make Contributions: If a member fails to make a required capital contribution within the time agreed for a member's contribution, the remaining members may, by unanimous vote, agree to reschedule the time for payment of the capital contribution by the late-paying member, setting any additional repayment terms, such as a late payment penalty, rate of interest to be applied to the unpaid balance, or other monetary amount to be paid by the delinquent member, as the remaining members decide. Alternatively, the remaining members may, by unanimous vote, agree to cancel the membership of the delinquent member, provided any prior partial payments of capital made by the delinquent member are refunded promptly by the LLC to the member after the decision is made to terminate the membership of the delinquent member.

(4) No Interest on Capital Contributions: No interest shall be paid on funds or property contributed as capital to this LLC, or on funds reflected in the capital accounts of the members.

(5) Capital Account Bookkeeping: A capital account shall be set up and maintained on the books of the LLC for each member. It shall reflect each member's capital contribution to the LLC, increased by each member's share of profits in the LLC, decreased by each member's share of losses and expenses of the LLC, and adjusted as required in accordance with applicable provisions of the Internal Revenue Code and corresponding income tax regulations.

(6) Consent to Capital Contribution Withdrawals and Distributions: Members shall not be allowed to withdraw any part of their capital contributions or to receive distributions, whether in property or cash, except as otherwise allowed by this agreement and, in any case, only if such withdrawal is made with the written consent of all members.

(7) Allocations of Profits and Losses: No member shall be given priority or preference with respect to other members in obtaining a return of capital contributions, distributions or allocations of the income, gains, losses, deductions, credits or other items of the LLC. The profits and losses of the LLC, and all items of its income, gain, loss, deduction and credit shall be allocated to members according to each member's percentage interest in this LLC.

(8) Allocation and Distribution of Cash to Members: Cash from LLC business operations, as well as cash from a sale or other disposition of LLC capital assets, may be distributed from time to time to members in accordance with each member's percentage interest in the LLC, as may be decided by _____ of the members.

(9) Allocation of Noncash Distributions: If proceeds consist of property other than cash, the members shall decide the value of the property and allocate such value among the members in accordance with each member's percentage interest in the LLC. If such noncash proceeds are later reduced to cash, such cash may be distributed among the members as otherwise provided in this agreement.

(10) Allocation and Distribution of Liquidation Proceeds: Regardless of any other provision in this agreement, if there is a distribution in liquidation of this LLC, or when any member's interest is liquidated, all items of income and loss shall be allocated to the members' capital accounts, and all appropriate credits and deductions shall then be made to these capital accounts before any final distribution is made. A final distribution shall be made to members only to the extent of, and in proportion to, any positive balance in each member's capital account.

V. MEMBERSHIP WITHDRAWAL AND TRANSFER PROVISIONS

(1) Withdrawal of Members: A member may withdraw from this LLC by giving written notice to all other members at least _____ days before the date the withdrawal is to be effective.

(2) Restrictions on the Transfer of Membership: A member shall not transfer his or her membership in the LLC unless all nontransferring members in the LLC first agree to approve the admission of the transferee into this LLC. Further, no member may encumber a part or all of his or her membership in the LLC by mortgage, pledge, granting of a security interest, lien or otherwise, unless the encumbrance has first been approved in writing by all other members of the LLC.

Notwithstanding the above provision, any member shall be allowed to assign an economic interest in his or her membership to another person without the approval of the other members. Such an assignment shall not include a transfer of the member's voting or management rights in this LLC, and the assignee shall not become a member of the LLC.

VI. DISSOLUTION PROVISIONS

(1) Events That Trigger Dissolution of the LLC: The following events shall trigger a dissolution of the LLC, except as provided:

(a) the death, permanent incapacity, bankruptcy, retirement, resignation or expulsion of a member, except that within _____ of the happening of any of these events, all remaining members of the LLC may vote to continue the legal existence of the LLC, in which case the LLC shall not dissolve;

(b) the expiration of the term of existence of the LLC if such term is specified in the Articles of Organization, Certificate of Formation or a similar organizational document, or this operating agreement;

(c) the written agreement of all members to dissolve the LLC;

(d) entry of a decree of dissolution of the LLC under state law.

VII. GENERAL PROVISIONS

(1) Officers: The LLC may designate one or more officers, such as a President, Vice President, Secretary and Treasurer. Persons who fill these positions need not be members of the LLC. Such positions may be compensated or noncompensated according to the nature and extent of the services rendered for the LLC as a part of the duties of each office. Ministerial services only as a part of any officer position will normally not be compensated, such as the performance of officer duties specified in this agreement, but any officer may be reimbursed by the LLC for out-of-pocket expenses paid by the officer in carrying out the duties of his or her office.

(2) Records: The LLC shall keep at its principal business address a copy of all proceedings of membership meetings, as well as books of account of the LLC's financial transactions. A list of the names and addresses of the current membership of the LLC also shall be maintained at this address, with notations on any transfers of members' interests to nonmembers or persons being admitted into membership in the LLC.

Copies of the LLC's Articles of Organization, Certificate of Formation or a similar organizational document, a signed copy of this operating agreement, and the LLC's tax returns for the preceding three tax years shall be kept at the principal business address of the LLC. A statement also shall be kept at this address containing any of the following information that is applicable to this LLC:

- the amount of cash or a description and value of property contributed or agreed to be contributed as capital to the LLC by each member;

- a schedule showing when any additional capital contributions are to be made by members to this LLC;

- a statement or schedule, if appropriate, showing the rights of members to receive distributions representing a return of part or all of members' capital contributions; and
- a description of, or date when, the legal existence of the LLC will terminate under provisions in the LLC's Articles of Organization, Certificate of Formation or a similar organizational document, or this operating agreement.

If one or more of the above items is included or listed in this operating agreement, it will be sufficient to keep a copy of this agreement at the principal business address of the LLC without having to prepare and keep a separate record of such item or items at this address.

Any member may inspect any and all records maintained by the LLC upon reasonable notice to the LLC. Copying of the LLC's records by members is allowed, but copying costs shall be paid for by the requesting member.

(3) All Necessary Acts: The members and officers of this LLC are authorized to perform all acts necessary to perfect the organization of this LLC and to carry out its business operations expeditiously and efficiently. The Secretary of the LLC, or other officers, or all members of the LLC, may certify to other businesses, financial institutions and individuals as to the authority of one or more members or officers of this LLC to transact specific items of business on behalf of the LLC.

(4) Mediation and Arbitration of Disputes Among Members: In any dispute over the provisions of this operating agreement and in other disputes among the members, if the members cannot resolve the dispute to their mutual satisfaction, the matter shall be submitted to mediation. The terms and procedure for mediation shall be arranged by the parties to the dispute.

If good-faith mediation of a dispute proves impossible or if an agreed-upon mediation outcome cannot be obtained by the members who are parties to the dispute, the dispute may be submitted to arbitration in accordance with the rules of the American Arbitration Association. Any party may commence arbitration of the dispute by sending a written request for arbitration to all other parties to the dispute. The request shall state the nature of the dispute to be resolved by arbitration, and, if all parties to the dispute agree to arbitration, arbitration shall be commenced as soon as practical after such parties receive a copy of the written request.

All parties shall initially share the cost of arbitration, but the prevailing party or parties may be awarded attorney fees, costs and other expenses of arbitration. All arbitration decisions shall be final, binding and conclusive on all the parties to arbitration, and legal judgment may be entered based upon such decision in accordance with applicable law in any court having jurisdiction to do so.

(5) Entire Agreement: This operating agreement represents the entire agreement among the members of this LLC, and it shall not be amended, modified or replaced except by a written instrument executed by all the parties to this agreement who are current members of this LLC as well as any and all additional parties who became members of this LLC after the adoption of this agreement. This agreement replaces and supersedes all prior written and oral agreements among any and all members of this LLC.

(6) Severability: If any provision of this agreement is determined by a court or arbitrator to be invalid, unenforceable or otherwise ineffective, that provision shall be severed from the rest of this agreement, and the remaining provisions shall remain in effect and enforceable.

VIII. SIGNATURES OF MEMBERS AND SPOUSES

(1) Execution of Agreement: In witness whereof, the members of this LLC sign and adopt this agreement as the operating agreement of this LLC.

Date: _____

Signature: _____

Printed Name: _____ , Member

Date: _____

Signature: _____

Printed Name: _____ , Member

Date: _____

Signature: _____

Printed Name: _____ , Member

Date: _____

Signature: _____

Printed Name: _____ , Member

Date: _____

Signature: _____

Printed Name: _____ , Member

Date: _____

Signature: _____

Printed Name: _____ , Member

(2) Consent of Spouses: The undersigned are spouses of members of this LLC who have signed this operating agreement in the preceding provision. These spouses have read this agreement and agree to be bound by its terms in any matter in which they have a financial interest, including restrictions on the transfer of memberships and the terms under which memberships in this LLC may be sold or otherwise transferred.

Date: _____

Signature: _____

Printed Name: _____

Spouse of: _____

Date: _____

Signature: _____

Printed Name: _____

Spouse of: _____

Date: _____

Signature: _____

Printed Name: _____

Spouse of: _____

Date: _____

Signature: _____

Printed Name: _____

Spouse of: _____

Date: _____

Signature: _____

Printed Name: _____

Spouse of: _____

Date: _____

Signature: _____

Printed Name: _____

Spouse of: _____

LIMITED LIABILITY COMPANY
MANAGEMENT OPERATING AGREEMENT

(1) Effective Date: This operating agreement of _____

_____ ,

effective_____ is adopted
by the members whose signatures appear at the end of this agreement.

(2) Formation: This limited liability company (LLC) was formed by filing Articles of
Organization, a Certificate of Formation or a similar organizational document with the LLC
filing office of the state of _____
on_____ .
A copy of this organizational document has been placed in the LLC's records book.

(3) Name: The formal name of this LLC is as stated above. However, this LLC may do
business under a different name by complying with the state's fictitious or assumed business
name statutes and procedures.

(4) Registered Office and Agent: The registered office of this LLC and the registered agent
at this address are as follows: _____

_____ .

The registered office and agent may be changed from time to time as the members or
managers may see fit, by filing a change of registered agent or office form with the state LLC
filing office. It will not be necessary to amend this provision of the operating agreement if and
when such a change is made.

(5) Business Purposes: The specific business purposes and activities contemplated by the
founders of this LLC at the time of initial signing of this agreement consist of the following:

_____

_____

_____ .

It is understood that the foregoing statement of purposes shall not serve as a limitation on
the powers or abilities of this LLC, which shall be permitted to engage in any and all lawful
business activities. If this LLC intends to engage in business activities outside the state of its
formation that require the qualification of the LLC in other states, it shall obtain such
qualification before engaging in such out-of-state activities.

(6) Duration of LLC: The duration of this LLC shall be _____

_____ .

Further, this LLC shall terminate when a proposal to dissolve the LLC is adopted by the
membership of this LLC or when this LLC is otherwise terminated in accordance with law.

II. MANAGEMENT PROVISIONS

(1) Management by Managers: This LLC will be managed by the managers listed below. All managers who are also members of this LLC are designated as "members"; nonmember managers are designated as "nonmembers."

Name: _____ ☐ Member ☐ Nonmember
Address: _____

Name: _____ ☐ Member ☐ Nonmember
Address: _____

Name: _____ ☐ Member ☐ Nonmember
Address: _____

Name: _____ ☐ Member ☐ Nonmember
Address: _____

Name: _____ ☐ Member ☐ Nonmember
Address: _____

Name: _____ ☐ Member ☐ Nonmember
Address: _____

(2) Nonliability of Managers: No manager of this LLC shall be personally liable for the expenses, debts, obligations or liabilities of the LLC, or for claims made against it.

(3) Authority and Votes of Managers: Except as otherwise set forth in this agreement, the Articles of Organization, Certificate of Organization or similar organizational document, or as may be provided under state law, all management decisions relating to this LLC's business shall be made by its managers. Management decisions shall be approved by _____ of the current managers of the LLC, with each manager entitled to cast one vote for or against any matter submitted to the managers for a decision.

(4) Term of Managers: Each manager shall serve until the earlier of the following events:

(a) the manager becomes disabled, dies, retires or otherwise withdraws from management;

(b) the manager is removed from office; or

(c) the manager's term expires, if a term has been designated in other provisions of this agreement.

Upon the happening of any of these events, a new manager may be appointed to replace the departing manager by _____ .

(5) Management Meetings: Managers shall be able to discuss and approve LLC business informally, and may, at their discretion, call and hold formal management meetings according to the rules set forth in the following provisions of this operating agreement.

Regularly scheduled formal management meetings need not be held, but any manager may call such a meeting by communicating his or her request for a formal meeting to the other managers, noting the purpose or purposes for which the meeting is called. Only the business stated or summarized in the notice for the meeting shall be discussed and voted upon at the meeting.

The meeting shall be held within a reasonable time after a manager has made the request for a meeting, and in no event, later than _____ days after the request for the meeting. A quorum for such a formal managers' meeting shall consist of _____ managers, and if a quorum is not present, the meeting shall be adjourned to a new place and time with notice of the adjourned meeting given to all managers. An adjournment shall not be necessary, however, and a managers' meeting with less than a quorum may be held if all nonattending managers agreed in writing prior to the meeting to the holding of the meeting. All such written consents to the holding of a formal management meeting shall be kept and filed with the records of the meeting.

The proceedings of all formal managers' meetings shall be noted or summarized with written minutes of the meeting and a copy of the minutes shall be placed and kept in the records book of this LLC.

(6) Managers' Commitment to LLC: Managers shall devote their best efforts and energy working to achieve the business objectives and financial goals of this LLC. By agreeing to serve as a manager for the LLC, each manager shall agree not to work for another business, enterprise or endeavor, owned or operated by himself or herself or others, if such outside work or efforts would compete with the LLC's business goals, mission, products or services, or would diminish or impair the manager's ability to provide maximum effort and performance to managing the business of this LLC.

(7) Compensation of Managers: Managers of this LLC may be paid per-meeting or per-diem amounts for attending management meetings, may be reimbursed actual expenses advanced by them to attend management meetings or attend to management business for the LLC, and may be compensated in other ways for performing their duties as managers. Managers may work in other capacities for this LLC and may be compensated separately for performing these additional services, whether as officers, staff, consultants, independent contractors or in other capacities.

III. MEMBERSHIP PROVISIONS

(1) Nonliability of Members: No member of this LLC shall be personally liable for the expenses, debts, obligations or liabilities of the LLC, or for claims made against it.

(2) Reimbursement for Organizational Costs: Members shall be reimbursed by the LLC for organizational expenses paid by the members. The LLC shall be authorized to elect to deduct organizational expenses and start-up expenditures ratably over a period of time as permitted by the Internal Revenue Code and as may be advised by the LLC's tax advisor.

(3) Members' Percentage Interests: A member's percentage interest in this LLC shall be computed as a fraction, the numerator of which is the total of a member's capital account and the denominator of which is the total of all capital accounts of all members. This fraction shall be expressed in this agreement as a percentage, which shall be called each member's "percentage interest" in this LLC.

(4) Membership Voting: Except as otherwise may be required by the Articles of Organization, Certificate of Formation or a similar organizational document, other provisions of this operating agreement, or under the laws of this state, each member shall vote on any matter submitted to the membership for approval in proportion to the member's percentage interest in this LLC. Further, unless defined otherwise for a particular provision of this operating agreement, the phrase "majority of members" means the vote of members whose combined votes equal more than 50% of the votes of all members in this LLC.

(5) Compensation: Members shall not be paid as members of the LLC for performing any duties associated with such membership. Members may be paid, however, for any services rendered in any other capacity for the LLC, whether as officers, employees, independent contractors or otherwise.

(6) Members' Meetings: The LLC shall not provide for regular members' meetings. However, any member may call a meeting by communicating his or her wish to schedule a meeting to all other members. Such notification may be in person or in writing, or by telephone, facsimile machine, or other form of electronic communication reasonably expected to be received by a member, and the other members shall then agree, either personally, in writing, or by telephone, facsimile machine or other form of electronic communication to the member calling the meeting, to meet at a mutually acceptable time and place. Notice of the business to be transacted at the meeting need not be given to members by the member calling the meeting, and any business may be discussed and conducted at the meeting.

If all members cannot attend a meeting, it shall be postponed to a date and time when all members can attend, unless all members who do not attend have agreed in writing to the holding of the meeting without them. If a meeting is postponed, and the postponed meeting cannot be held either because all members do not attend the postponed meeting or the nonattending members have not signed a written consent to allow the postponed meeting to be held without them, a second postponed meeting may be held at a date and time announced at the first postponed meeting. The date and time of the second postponed meeting shall also be communicated to any members not attending the first postponed meeting. The second postponed meeting may be held without the attendance of all members as long as a majority of the percentage interests of the membership of this LLC is in attendance at the second postponed meeting. Written notice of the decisions or approvals made at this second postponed meeting shall be mailed or delivered to each nonattending member promptly after the holding of the second postponed meeting.

Written minutes of the discussions and proposals presented at a members' meeting, and the votes taken and matters approved at such meeting, shall be taken by one of the members or a person designated at the meeting. A copy of the minutes of the meeting shall be placed in the LLC's records book after the meeting.

(7) Membership Certificates: This LLC shall be authorized to obtain and issue certificates representing or certifying membership interests in this LLC. Each certificate shall show the name of the LLC, the name of the member, and state that the person named is a member of the LLC and is entitled to all the rights granted members of the LLC under the Articles of Organization, Certificate of Formation or a similar organizational document, this operating agreement, and provisions of law. Each membership certificate shall be consecutively numbered and signed by one or more officers of this LLC. The certificates shall include any additional information considered appropriate for inclusion by the members on membership certificates.

In addition to the above information, all membership certificates shall bear a prominent legend on their face or reverse side stating, summarizing or referring to any transfer restrictions that apply to memberships in this LLC under the Articles of Organization, Certificate of Formation or a similar organizational document and/or this operating agreement, and the address where a member may obtain a copy of these restrictions upon request from this LLC.

The records book of this LLC shall contain a list of the names and addresses of all persons to whom certificates have been issued, show the date of issuance of each certificate, and record the date of all cancellations or transfers of membership certificates.

IV. TAX AND FINANCIAL PROVISIONS

(1) Tax Classification of LLC: The members of this LLC intend that this LLC be initially classified as a _____ for federal and, if applicable, state income tax purposes. It is understood that all members may agree to change the tax treatment of this LLC by signing, or authorizing the signature of, IRS Form 8832, Entity Classification Election, and filing it with the IRS and, if applicable, the state tax department within the prescribed time limits.

(2) Tax Year and Accounting Method: The tax year of this LLC shall be _____

_____ . The LLC shall use the

_____ method of accounting. Both the tax year and the accounting period
of the LLC may be changed with the consent of all members or all managers if the LLC qualifies
for such change, and may be effected by the filing of appropriate forms with the IRS and state
tax authorities.

(3) Tax Matters Partner: If this LLC is required under Internal Revenue Code provisions or
regulations, it shall designate from among its members or member-managers a "tax matters
partner" in accordance with Internal Revenue Code Section 6231(a)(7) and corresponding
regulations, who will fulfill this role by being the spokesperson for the LLC in dealings with the
IRS as required under the Internal Revenue Code and Regulations, and who will report to the
members and managers on the progress and outcome of these dealings.

(4) Annual Income Tax Returns and Reports: Within 60 days after the end of each tax year
of the LLC, a copy of the LLC's state and federal income tax returns for the preceding tax year
shall be mailed or otherwise provided to each member of the LLC, together with any additional
information and forms necessary for each member to complete his or her individual state and
federal income tax returns. If this LLC is classified as a partnership for income tax purposes,
this additional information shall include a federal (and, if applicable, state) Form K-1 (Form
1065—Partner's Share of Income, Credits, Deductions) or equivalent income tax reporting
form. This additional information shall also include a financial report, which shall include a
balance sheet and profit and loss statement for the prior tax year of the LLC.

(5) Bank Accounts: The LLC shall designate one or more banks or other institutions for the
deposit of the funds of the LLC, and shall establish savings, checking, investment and other
such accounts as are reasonable and necessary for its business and investments. One or more
employees of the LLC shall be designated with the consent of all managers to deposit and
withdraw funds of the LLC, and to direct the investment of funds from, into and among such
accounts. The funds of the LLC, however and wherever deposited or invested, shall not be
commingled with the personal funds of any members or managers of the LLC.

(6) Title to Assets: All personal and real property of this LLC shall be held in the name of
the LLC, not in the names of individual members or managers.

V. CAPITAL PROVISIONS

(1) Capital Contributions by Members: Members shall make the following contributions of
cash, property or services as shown next to each member's name below. Unless otherwise
noted, cash and property described below shall be paid or delivered to the LLC on or by

_____ . The fair market values of items of property or
services as agreed between the LLC and the contributing member are also shown below. The

percentage interest in the LLC that each member shall receive in return for his or her capital contribution is also indicated for each member.

Name	Contribution	Fair Market Value	Percentage Interest in LLC
_____	_____	$ _____	_____
_____	_____	$ _____	_____
_____	_____	$ _____	_____
_____	_____	$ _____	_____
_____	_____	$ _____	_____
_____	_____	$ _____	_____

(2) Additional Contributions by Members: The members may agree, from time to time by unanimous vote, to require the payment of additional capital contributions by the members, on or by a mutually agreeable date.

(3) Failure to Make Contributions: If a member fails to make a required capital contribution within the time agreed for a member's contribution, the remaining members may, by unanimous vote, agree to reschedule the time for payment of the capital contribution by the late-paying member, setting any additional repayment terms, such as a late payment penalty, rate of interest to be applied to the unpaid balance, or other monetary amount to be paid by the delinquent member, as the remaining members decide. Alternatively, the remaining members may, by unanimous vote, agree to cancel the membership of the delinquent member, provided any prior partial payments of capital made by the delinquent member are refunded promptly by the LLC to the member after the decision is made to terminate the membership of the delinquent member.

(4) No Interest on Capital Contributions: No interest shall be paid on funds or property contributed as capital to this LLC, or on funds reflected in the capital accounts of the members.

(5) Capital Account Bookkeeping: A capital account shall be set up and maintained on the books of the LLC for each member. It shall reflect each member's capital contribution to the LLC, increased by each member's share of profits in the LLC, decreased by each member's share of losses and expenses of the LLC, and adjusted as required in accordance with applicable provisions of the Internal Revenue Code and corresponding income tax regulations.

(6) *Consent to Capital Contribution Withdrawals and Distributions:* Members shall not be allowed to withdraw any part of their capital contributions or to receive distributions, whether in property or cash, except as otherwise allowed by this agreement and, in any case, only if such withdrawal is made with the written consent of all members.

(7) *Allocations of Profits and Losses:* No member shall be given priority or preference with respect to other members in obtaining a return of capital contributions, distributions or allocations of the income, gains, losses, deductions, credits or other items of the LLC. The profits and losses of the LLC, and all items of its income, gain, loss, deduction and credit shall be allocated to members according to each member's percentage interest in this LLC.

(8) *Allocation and Distribution of Cash to Members:* Cash from LLC business operations, as well as cash from a sale or other disposition of LLC capital assets, may be distributed from time to time to members in accordance with each member's percentage interest in the LLC, as may be decided by _____ of the

_____ .

(9) *Allocation of Noncash Distributions:* If proceeds consist of property other than cash, the _____ shall decide the value of the property and allocate such value among the members in accordance with each member's percentage interest in the LLC. If such noncash proceeds are later reduced to cash, such cash may be distributed among the members as otherwise provided in this agreement.

(10) *Allocation and Distribution of Liquidation Proceeds:* Regardless of any other provision in this agreement, if there is a distribution in liquidation of this LLC, or when any member's interest is liquidated, all items of income and loss shall be allocated to the members' capital accounts, and all appropriate credits and deductions shall then be made to these capital accounts before any final distribution is made. A final distribution shall be made to members only to the extent of, and in proportion to, any positive balance in each member's capital account.

VI. MEMBERSHIP WITHDRAWAL AND TRANSFER PROVISIONS

(1) *Withdrawal of Members:* A member may withdraw from this LLC by giving written notice to all other members at least _____ days before the date the withdrawal is to be effective.

(2) *Restrictions on the Transfer of Membership:* A member shall not transfer his or her membership in the LLC unless all nontransferring members in the LLC first agree to approve the admission of the transferee into this LLC. Further, no member may encumber a part or all of his or her membership in the LLC by mortgage, pledge, granting of a security interest, lien or otherwise, unless the encumbrance has first been approved in writing by all other members of the LLC.

Notwithstanding the above provision, any member shall be allowed to assign an economic interest in his or her membership to another person without the approval of the other members. Such an assignment shall not include a transfer of the member's voting or management rights in this LLC, and the assignee shall not become a member of the LLC.

VII. DISSOLUTION PROVISIONS

(1) Events That Trigger Dissolution of the LLC: The following events shall trigger a dissolution of the LLC, except as provided:

    (a) the death, permanent incapacity, bankruptcy, retirement, resignation or expulsion of a member, except that within _____ of the happening of any of these events, all remaining members of the LLC may vote to continue the legal existence of the LLC, in which case the LLC shall not dissolve;

    (b) the expiration of the term of existence of the LLC if such term is specified in the Articles of Organization, Certificate of Formation or a similar organizational document, or this operating agreement;

    (c) the written agreement of all members to dissolve the LLC;

    (d) entry of a decree of dissolution of the LLC under state law.

VIII. GENERAL PROVISIONS

(1) Officers: The managers of this LLC may designate one or more officers, such as a President, Vice President, Secretary and Treasurer. Persons who fill these positions need not be members or managers of the LLC. Such positions may be compensated or noncompensated according to the nature and extent of the services rendered for the LLC as a part of the duties of each office. Ministerial services only as a part of any officer position will normally not be compensated, such as the performance of officer duties specified in this agreement, but any officer may be reimbursed by the LLC for out-of-pocket expenses paid by the officer in carrying out the duties of his or her office.

(2) Records: The LLC shall keep at its principal business address a copy of all proceedings of membership meetings, as well as books of account of the LLC's financial transactions. A list of the names and addresses of the current membership of the LLC also shall be maintained at this address, with notations on any transfers of members' interests to nonmembers or persons being admitted into membership in the LLC. A list of the current managers' names and addresses shall also be kept at this address.

Copies of the LLC's Articles of Organization, Certificate of Formation or a similar organizational document, a signed copy of this operating agreement, and the LLC's tax returns for the preceding three tax years shall be kept at the principal business address of the LLC. A statement also shall be kept at this address containing any of the following information that is applicable to this LLC:

- the amount of cash or a description and value of property contributed or agreed to be contributed as capital to the LLC by each member;
- a schedule showing when any additional capital contributions are to be made by members to this LLC;
- a statement or schedule, if appropriate, showing the rights of members to receive distributions representing a return of part or all of members' capital contributions; and
- a description of, or date when, the legal existence of the LLC will terminate under provisions in the LLC's Articles of Organization, Certificate of Formation or a similar organizational document, or this operating agreement.

If one or more of the above items is included or listed in this operating agreement, it will be sufficient to keep a copy of this agreement at the principal business address of the LLC without having to prepare and keep a separate record of such item or items at this address.

Any member or manager may inspect any and all records maintained by the LLC upon reasonable notice to the LLC. Copying of the LLC's records by members and managers is allowed, but copying costs shall be paid for by the requesting member or manager.

(3) All Necessary Acts: The members, managers and officers of this LLC are authorized to perform all acts necessary to perfect the organization of this LLC and to carry out its business operations expeditiously and efficiently. The Secretary of the LLC, or other officers, or one or more managers or all members of the LLC, may certify to other businesses, financial institutions and individuals as to the authority of one or more members, managers or officers of this LLC to transact specific items of business on behalf of the LLC.

(4) Mediation and Arbitration of Disputes Among Members: In any dispute over the provisions of this operating agreement and in other disputes among the members, if the members cannot resolve the dispute to their mutual satisfaction, the matter shall be submitted to mediation. The terms and procedure for mediation shall be arranged by the parties to the dispute.

If good-faith mediation of a dispute proves impossible or if an agreed-upon mediation outcome cannot be obtained by the members who are parties to the dispute, the dispute may be submitted to arbitration in accordance with the rules of the American Arbitration Association. Any party may commence arbitration of the dispute by sending a written request for arbitration to all other parties to the dispute. The request shall state the nature of the dispute to be resolved by arbitration, and, if all parties to the dispute agree to arbitration, arbitration shall be commenced as soon as practical after such parties receive a copy of the written request.

All parties shall initially share the cost of arbitration, but the prevailing party or parties may be awarded attorney fees, costs and other expenses of arbitration. All arbitration decisions shall be final, binding and conclusive on all the parties to arbitration, and legal judgment may be entered based upon such decision in accordance with applicable law in any court having jurisdiction to do so.

(5) Entire Agreement: This operating agreement represents the entire agreement among the members of this LLC, and it shall not be amended, modified or replaced except by a written instrument executed by all the parties to this agreement who are current members of this LLC as well as any and all additional parties who became members of this LLC after the adoption of this agreement. This agreement replaces and supersedes all prior written and oral agreements among any and all members of this LLC.

(6) Severability: If any provision of this agreement is determined by a court or arbitrator to be invalid, unenforceable or otherwise ineffective, that provision shall be severed from the rest of this agreement, and the remaining provisions shall remain in effect and enforceable.

IX. SIGNATURES OF MEMBERS, MEMBERS' SPOUSES AND MANAGERS

(1) Execution of Agreement: In witness whereof, the members of this LLC sign and adopt this agreement as the operating agreement of this LLC.

Date: _____

Signature: _____

Printed Name: _____ , Member

Date: _____

Signature: _____

Printed Name: _____ , Member

Date: _____

Signature: _____

Printed Name: _____ , Member

Date: _____

Signature: _____

Printed Name: _____ , Member

Date: _____

Signature: _____

Printed Name: _____ , Member

Date: _____

Signature: _____

Printed Name: _____ , Member

(2) *Consent of Spouses:* The undersigned are spouses of members of this LLC who have signed this operating agreement in the preceding provision. These spouses have read this agreement and agree to be bound by its terms in any matter in which they have a financial interest, including restrictions on the transfer of memberships and the terms under which memberships in this LLC may be sold or otherwise transferred.

Date: _____

Signature: _____

Printed Name: _____

Spouse of: _____

Date: _____

Signature: _____

Printed Name: _____

Spouse of: _____

Date: _____

Signature: _____

Printed Name: _____

Spouse of: _____

Date: _____

Signature: _____

Printed Name: _____

Spouse of: _____

Date: _____

Signature: _____

Printed Name: _____

Spouse of: _____

Date: _____

Signature: _____

Printed Name: _____

Spouse of: _____

3) Signatures of Managers: The undersigned managers of this limited liability company have read this agreement and agree to be bound by its terms in discharging their duties as managers.

Date: _____

Signature: _____

Printed Name: _____, Manager

Date: _____

Signature: _____

Printed Name: _____, Manager

Date: _____

Signature: _____

Printed Name: _____, Manager

Date: _____

Signature: _____

Printed Name: _____, Manager

Date: _____

Signature: _____

Printed Name: _____, Manager

MINUTES OF MEETING OF THE

_____

OF

_____

A meeting of the _____ of the above named limited liability company

was held on _____ , at _____ __.M.,

at _____

_____ , State of _____ ,

for the following purpose(s):

_____

_____

_____

_____ .

_____ acted as chairperson,

and _____ acted as secretary of the meeting.

The chairperson called the meeting to order.

The following _____ were present at the meeting:

_____

_____

_____

_____

_____

_____ .

The following persons were also present at the meeting, and any reports given by these

persons are noted next to their names below:

Name and Title   Reports Presented, If Any

_____   _____

_____   _____

_____   _____

_____   _____

_____   _____

_____   _____

After discussion, on motion duly made and carried by the affirmative vote of

_____ of the _____ ,

the following resolution(s) was/were adopted:

_____

_____

_____

_____

_____

_____

_____

_____

_____

_____

_____

_____

_____

_____

There being no further business to come before the meeting, it was adjourned on motion duly made and carried.

Date: _____

Signature(s): _____

_____

Title: _____

CERTIFICATION OF AUTHORITY

    This LLC is managed by its _____ . The names and addresses of each of its current _____ as of _____ are listed below. Each of these persons has managerial authority of the LLC and is empowered to transact business on its behalf.

Name of _____   Address

_____   _____

    _____

_____   _____

    _____

_____   _____

    _____

_____   _____

    _____

_____   _____

    _____

_____   _____

    _____

    Further, each of the following _____ is specifically authorized to transact the following business on behalf of the LLC:

_____

_____

_____

Date: _____

Name of LLC: _____

by _____

Printed Name: _____

Title: _____

Index

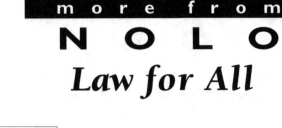
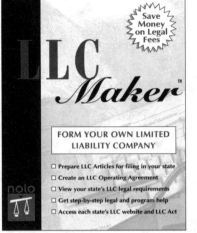

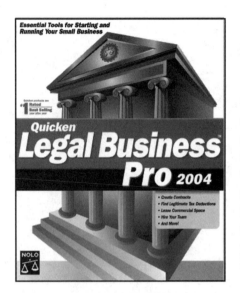

CATALOG

...more from Nolo

	PRICE	CODE

BUSINESS

	PRICE	CODE
Buy-Sell Agreement Handbook: Plan Ahead for Changes in the Ownership of Your Business (Book w/CD-ROM)	$49.99	BSAG
The CA Nonprofit Corporation Kit (Binder w/CD-ROM)	$59.95	CNP
Consultant & Independent Contractor Agreements (Book w/CD-ROM)	$29.99	CICA
The Corporate Minutes Book (Book w/CD-ROM)	$69.99	CORMI
Create Your Own Employee Handbook	$49.99	EMHA
The Employer's Legal Handbook	$39.99	EMPL
Everyday Employment Law	$29.99	ELBA
Dealing With Problem Employees	$44.99	PROBM
Drive a Modest Car & 16 Other Keys to Small Business Success	$24.99	DRIV
Federal Employment Laws	$49.99	FELW
Form Your Own Limited Liability Company (Book w/CD-ROM)	$44.99	LIAB
Hiring Independent Contractors: The Employer's Legal Guide (Book w/CD-ROM)	$34.99	HICI
How to Create a Noncompete Agreement	$44.95	NOCMP
How to Form a California Professional Corporation (Book w/CD-ROM)	$59.95	PROF
How to Form a Nonprofit Corporation (Book w/CD-ROM)—National Edition	$44.99	NNP
How to Form a Nonprofit Corporation in California (Book w/CD-ROM)	$44.99	NON
How to Form Your Own California Corporation (Binder w/CD-ROM)	$59.99	CACI
How to Form Your Own California Corporation (Book w/CD-ROM)	$34.99	CCOR
How to Get Your Business on the Web	$29.99	WEBS
How to Write a Business Plan	$34.99	SBS
Incorporate Your Business	$49.95	NIBS
The Independent Paralegal's Handbook	$29.95	PARA
Leasing Space for Your Small Business	$34.95	LESP
Legal Guide for Starting & Running a Small Business	$34.99	RUNS
Legal Forms for Starting & Running a Small Business (Book w/CD-ROM)	$29.99	RUNS2
Marketing Without Advertising	$24.00	MWAD
Music Law (Book w/CD-ROM)	$34.99	ML
Nolo's Guide to Social Security Disability	$29.99	QSS
Nolo's Quick LLC	$24.95	LLCQ
Nondisclosure Agreements	$39.95	NAG
The Small Business Start-up Kit (Book w/CD-ROM)	$29.99	SMBU
The Small Business Start-up Kit for California (Book w/CD-ROM)	$34.99	OPEN
The Partnership Book: How to Write a Partnership Agreement (Book w/CD-ROM)	$39.99	PART
Sexual Harassment on the Job	$24.95	HARS
Starting & Running a Successful Newsletter or Magazine	$29.99	MAG
Take Charge of Your Workers' Compensation Claim	$34.99	WORK
Tax Savvy for Small Business	$36.99	SAVVY
Working for Yourself: Law & Taxes for the Self-Employed	$39.99	WAGE
Your Crafts Business: A Legal Guide	$26.99	VART
Your Limited Liability Company: An Operating Manual (Book w/CD-ROM)	$49.99	LOP
Your Rights in the Workplace	$29.99	YRW

CONSUMER

	PRICE	CODE
How to Win Your Personal Injury Claim	$29.99	PICL
Nolo's Encyclopedia of Everyday Law	$29.99	EVL
Nolo's Guide to California Law	$24.95	CLAW
Trouble-Free Travel...And What to Do When Things Go Wrong	$14.95	TRAV

Prices subject to change.

	PRICE	CODE

ESTATE PLANNING & PROBATE

8 Ways to Avoid Probate	$19.99	PRO8
9 Ways to Avoid Estate Taxes	$29.95	ESTX
Estate Planning Basics	$21.99	ESPN
How to Probate an Estate in California	$49.99	PAE
Make Your Own Living Trust (Book w/CD-ROM)	$39.99	LITR
Nolo's Simple Will Book (Book w/CD-ROM)	$36.99	SWIL
Plan Your Estate	$44.99	NEST
Quick & Legal Will Book	$16.99	QUIC

FAMILY MATTERS

Child Custody: Building Parenting Agreements That Work	$29.99	CUST
The Complete IEP Guide	$24.99	IEP
Divorce & Money: How to Make the Best Financial Decisions During Divorce	$34.99	DIMO
Do Your Own California Adoption: Nolo's Guide for Stepparents and Domestic Partners (Book w/CD-ROM)	$34.99	ADOP
Get a Life: You Don't Need a Million to Retire Well	$24.99	LIFE
The Guardianship Book for California	$39.99	GB
A Legal Guide for Lesbian and Gay Couples	$29.99	LG
Living Together: A Legal Guide (Book w/CD-ROM)	$34.99	LTK
Medical Directives and Powers of Attorney in California	$19.99	CPOA
Using Divorce Mediation: Save Your Money & Your Sanity	$29.95	UDMD

GOING TO COURT

Beat Your Ticket: Go To Court and Win! (National Edition)	$19.99	BEYT
The Criminal Law Handbook: Know Your Rights, Survive the System	$34.99	KYR
Everybody's Guide to Small Claims Court (National Edition)	$26.99	NSCC
Everybody's Guide to Small Claims Court in California	$26.99	CSCC
Fight Your Ticket ... and Win! (California Edition)	$29.99	FYT
How to Change Your Name in California	$34.95	NAME
How to Collect When You Win a Lawsuit (California Edition)	$29.99	JUDG
How to Seal Your Juvenile & Criminal Records (California Edition)	$34.95	CRIM
The Lawsuit Survival Guide	$29.99	UNCL
Nolo's Deposition Handbook	$29.99	DEP
Represent Yourself in Court: How to Prepare & Try a Winning Case	$34.99	RYC
Sue in California Without a Lawyer	$34.99	SLWY

HOMEOWNERS, LANDLORDS & TENANTS

California Tenants' Rights	$27.99	CTEN
Deeds for California Real Estate	$24.99	DEED
Dog Law	$21.95	DOG
Every Landlord's Legal Guide (National Edition, Book w/CD-ROM)	$44.99	ELLI
Every Tenant's Legal Guide	$29.99	EVTEN
For Sale by Owner in California	$29.99	FSBO
How to Buy a House in California	$34.99	BHCA
The California Landlord's Law Book: Rights & Responsibilities (Book w/CD-ROM)	$44.99	LBRT
The California Landlord's Law Book: Evictions (Book w/CD-ROM)	$44.99	LBEV
Leases & Rental Agreements	$29.99	LEAR
Neighbor Law: Fences, Trees, Boundaries & Noise	$26.99	NEI
The New York Landlord's Law Book (Book w/CD-ROM)	$39.99	NYLL
New York Tenants' Rights	$27.99	NYTEN
Renters' Rights (National Edition)	$24.99	RENT
Stop Foreclosure Now in California	$29.95	CLOS

IMMIGRATION

Becoming a U.S. Citizen: A Guide to the Law, Exam and Interview	$24.99	USCIT
Fiancé & Marriage Visas	$44.95	IMAR
How to Get a Green Card	$29.99	GRN
Student & Tourist Visas	$29.99	ISTU

ORDER 24 HOURS A DAY @ www.nolo.com
Call 800-728-3555 • Mail or fax the order form in this book

	PRICE	CODE
U.S. Immigration Made Easy	$44.99	IMEZ

MONEY MATTERS

	PRICE	CODE
101 Law Forms for Personal Use (Book w/CD-ROM)	$29.99	SPOT
Bankruptcy: Is It the Right Solution to Your Debt Problems?	$19.99	BRS
Chapter 13 Bankruptcy: Repay Your Debts	$34.99	CH13
Creating Your Own Retirement Plan	$29.99	YROP
Credit Repair (Quick & Legal Series, Book w/CD-ROM)	$24.99	CREP
Getting Paid: How to Collect from Bankrupt Debtors	$24.99	CRBNK
How to File for Chapter 7 Bankruptcy	$34.99	HFB
IRAs, 401(k)s & Other Retirement Plans: Taking Your Money Out	$34.99	RET
Money Troubles: Legal Strategies to Cope With Your Debts	$29.99	MT
Stand Up to the IRS	$24.99	SIRS
Surviving an IRS Tax Audit	$24.95	SAUD
Take Control of Your Student Loan Debt	$26.95	SLOAN

PATENTS AND COPYRIGHTS

	PRICE	CODE
The Copyright Handbook: How to Protect and Use Written Works (Book w/CD-ROM)	$39.99	COHA
Copyright Your Software	$34.95	CYS
Domain Names	$26.95	DOM
Getting Permission: How to License and Clear Copyrighted Materials Online and Off (Book w/CD-ROM)	$34.99	RIPER
How to Make Patent Drawings Yourself	$29.99	DRAW
Inventor's Guide to Law, Business and Taxes	$34.99	ILAX
The Inventor's Notebook	$24.99	INOT
Nolo's Patents for Beginners	$29.99	QPAT
License Your Invention (Book w/CD-ROM)	$39.99	LICE
Patent, Copyright & Trademark	$39.99	PCTM
Patent It Yourself	$49.99	PAT
Patent Pending in 24 Hours	$29.99	PEND
Patent Searching Made Easy	$29.95	PATSE
The Public Domain	$34.95	PUBL
Trademark: Legal Care for Your Business and Product Name	$39.95	TRD
Web and Software Development: A Legal Guide (Book w/CD-ROM)	$44.95	SFT

RESEARCH & REFERENCE

	PRICE	CODE
Legal Research: How to Find & Understand the Law	$39.99	LRES

SENIORS

	PRICE	CODE
Choose the Right Long-Term Care: Home Care, Assisted Living & Nursing Homes	$21.99	ELD
The Conservatorship Book for California	$44.99	CNSV
Social Security, Medicare & Goverment Pensions	$29.99	SOA

SOFTWARE
Call or check our website at www.nolo.com for special discounts on Software!

	PRICE	CODE
LeaseWriter CD—Windows	$129.95	LWD1
LLC Maker—Windows	$89.95	LLP1
PatentPro Plus—Windows	$399.99	PAPL
Personal RecordKeeper 5.0 CD—Windows	$59.95	RKD5
Quicken Legal Business Pro 2004—Windows	$79.95	SBQB4
Quicken WilMaker Plus 2004—Windows	$79.95	WQP4

Order Form

Name

Address

City

State, Zip

Daytime Phone

E-mail

Our "No-Hassle" Guarantee

Return anything you buy directly from Nolo for any reason and we'll cheerfully refund your purchase price. No ifs, ands or buts.

☐ Check here if you do not wish to receive mailings from other companies

Item Code	Quantity	Item	Unit Price	Total Price

Method of payment

☐ Check ☐ VISA ☐ MasterCard
☐ Discover Card ☐ American Express

Subtotal	
Add your local sales tax (California only)	
Shipping: RUSH $9, Basic $5 (See below)	
"I bought 3, ship it to me FREE!"(Ground shipping only)	
TOTAL	

Account Number

Expiration Date

Signature

Shipping and Handling

Rush Delivery—Only $9

We'll ship any order to any street address in the U.S. by UPS 2nd Day Air* for only $9!

* Order by noon Pacific Time and get your order in 2 business days. Orders placed after noon Pacific Time will arrive in 3 business days. P.O. boxes and S.F. Bay Area use basic shipping. Alaska and Hawaii use 2nd Day Air or Priority Mail.

Basic Shipping—$5

Use for P.O. Boxes, Northern California and Ground Service.

Allow 1-2 weeks for delivery. U.S. addresses only.

For faster service, use your credit card and our toll-free numbers

**Call our customer service group
Monday thru Friday 7am to 7pm PST**

Phone	1-800-728-3555
Fax	1-800-645-0895
Mail	Nolo
950 Parker St.
Berkeley, CA 94710

Order 24 hours a day @
www.nolo.com

Remember:

Little publishers have big ears.
We really listen to you.

Take 2 Minutes & Give Us Your 2 cents

Your comments make a big difference in the development and revision of Nolo books and software. Please take a few minutes and register your Nolo product—and your comments—with us. Not only will your input make a difference, you'll receive special offers available only to registered owners of Nolo products on our newest books and software. Register now by:

PHONE
1-800-728-3555

FAX
1-800-645-0895

EMAIL
cs@nolo.com

or MAIL us
this registration card

fold here

Registration Card

NAME _____ DATE _____

ADDRESS _____

_____

CITY _____ STATE _____ ZIP _____

PHONE _____ E-MAIL _____

WHERE DID YOU HEAR ABOUT THIS PRODUCT? _____

WHERE DID YOU PURCHASE THIS PRODUCT? _____

DID YOU CONSULT A LAWYER? (PLEASE CIRCLE ONE)   YES   NO   NOT APPLICABLE

DID YOU FIND THIS BOOK HELPFUL?   (VERY)   5   4   3   2   1   (NOT AT ALL)

COMMENTS _____

_____

_____

WAS IT EASY TO USE?   (VERY EASY)   5   4   3   2   1   (VERY DIFFICULT)

We occasionally make our mailing list available to carefully selected companies whose products may be of interest to you.

❑   If you do not wish to receive mailings from these companies, please check this box.

❑   You can quote me in future Nolo promotional materials.
Daytime phone number _____.

LIAB 3.3

Nolo in the NEWS

"Nolo helps lay people perform legal tasks without the aid—or fees—of lawyers."

—USA TODAY

Nolo books are ..."written in plain language, free of legal mumbo jumbo, and spiced with witty personal observations."

—ASSOCIATED PRESS

"...Nolo publications...guide people simply through the how, when, where and why of law."

—WASHINGTON POST

"Increasingly, people who are not lawyers are performing tasks usually regarded as legal work... And consumers, using books like Nolo's, do routine legal work themselves."

—NEW YORK TIMES

"...All of [Nolo's] books are easy-to-understand, are updated regularly, provide pull-out forms...and are often quite moving in their sense of compassion for the struggles of the lay reader."

—SAN FRANCISCO CHRONICLE

fold here

Nolo
950 Parker Street
Berkeley, CA 94710-9867

Attn: LIAB 3.3